CONSTITUTIONAL CHANGE IN THE BRITISH WEST INDIES

1880–1903

CONSTITUTIONAL CHANGE IN THE BRITISH WEST INDIES

1880–1903

With special reference to
Jamaica, British Guiana, and Trinidad

H. A. WILL

CLARENDON PRESS · OXFORD

1970

Oxford University Press, Ely House, London W. 1

GLASGOW NEW YORK TORONTO MELBOURNE WELLINGTON
CAPE TOWN SALISBURY IBADAN NAIROBI DAR ES SALAAM LUSAKA ADDIS ABABA
BOMBAY CALCUTTA MADRAS KARACHI LAHORE DACCA
KUALA LUMPUR SINGAPORE HONG KONG TOKYO

Printed in Great Britain by
Alden & Mowbray Ltd
at the Alden Press, Oxford

TO MARY

whose unselfish scholarship inspired this book

PREFACE

THE emphasis of recent historical studies of the British West Indies has been to study these territories in the wider setting of the Caribbean, to emphasize the economic and social aspects of their history, and to study that history from a local rather than an Imperial viewpoint, British colonial policy being relegated to one among many influences. This book diverges from each of these trends. Its scope is limited mainly to Jamaica, British Guiana, and Trinidad, its subject is constitutional development, and one of its central themes is British colonial policy.

It is appropriate to confine a study of constitutional change to the *British* West Indies, because although their economic and social development was shaped largely by conditions common to the Caribbean, their constitutional and political development was influenced mainly by the mother country. Movements for reform took place within a constitutional framework established or adapted by the British government and which could only be changed by its policy decisions. Other factors also give unity to a study of constitutional change which is confined to the British West Indies. The attitudes of those who led and opposed movements for constitutional reform were influenced to a surprising extent by external events and currents of thought in the Empire, and most notably by developments in Britain, Ireland, India, and in other British West Indian colonies. This was largely due to a mature and outward-looking West Indian press, its role in this respect being reinforced by colonial contacts with Britain through kinship, education, and business. The strength of these influences in the period under review was such that it is difficult to study movements for and against constitutional change in one colony in isolation from events elsewhere in the Empire, and particularly in Britain and the British West Indies.

The impact of these external influences was pervasive and complex. There is, for instance, a striking similarity between the economic and social questions being debated during this period in the United Kingdom and in the West Indian colonies, of which the rights of labour in relation to capital was one of the most pressing. This is not to assert that these questions were debated in the West Indies because they were at the centre of British politics; the relation of labour to capital had been the fundamental problem of the West Indies since the introduction of sugar and the plantation system. But attitudes were influenced by the extent to which colonists followed the course of events in Britain and were aware of the similarity of the questions at issue. The terms in which the debate was conducted were, of course, different, for there was no equivalent either in Britain or Ireland to the conditions which limited the rewards to labour in the West Indies, such as a high level of Indian immigration or restrictive crown lands regulations. But the fundamental question of labour's share of the total wealth was the same, and it was debated in both Britain and the British West Indies against the background of European radical influences, and of apprehension regarding the sanctity of property and contract. Not only were there parallel problems; there were also similar responses. In both Britain and the West Indies the propertied classes were on the defensive. Their opposition to constitutional reform in Trinidad in the late 1880s drew strength from the conservative reaction in England during the same period. Conversely, reformers during the 1880s and early 1890s were heartened by the speeches and policies of such liberal statesmen as Gladstone and Ripon. Small strikes in British Guiana and Jamaica followed closely the London dock strike of 1889. Legislation initiated by the British Guiana government in 1876 and 1878 for compulsory education and improvement of public health was contemporary with similar British legislation and to some extent modelled on it. The instances can be multiplied. It would be wrong to underestimate the localism of West Indian political life, or the influences on the British West Indies of the wider political, economic, and demographic changes which were shaping the Caribbean as a whole. But it is also clear from the evidence in this study that British West Indian politics in the late nineteenth century were influenced to an important degree by the course of events and thought in Britain and the Empire.

But how significant were colonial politics so long as they were confined within the limits of crown colony government or a modification of it? What influence did the formal constitutional changes analysed in this study have on the economic and social development of the colonies concerned? In one sense their impact was small, for those elected under the reformed constitutions in Jamaica and British Guiana were generally no more representative of the mass of the people than their nominated or more narrowly elected predecessors. Yet there is evidence that they were more responsive to their needs, particularly in their advocacy of improved education, and that their pressure in this direction, and for improvement of communications to open up the rural areas, was reflected in the policies of colonial governments. But the constitutional changes analysed in this study have a significance beyond their immediate impact on the economic and social development of the colonies concerned, for they span a formative period in the development of crown colony government. The 1880s were marked by constitutional change and experiment both in the British West Indies and elsewhere in the Empire. During this period the Colonial Office showed a greater readiness than it was to do for nearly forty years to consider ways of modifying crown government to permit more effective local representation and control.[1] The conditions were favourable, for liberal currents were still flowing strongly in England, and a more positive interpretation of trusteeship, necessitating closer official control, had not yet been formulated. The subsequent reversal of these liberal trends in the colonies under review during the 1890s was part of a broader movement towards a more conservative policy on constitutional change in the crown colonies, which receives its clearest definition during Chamberlain's secretaryship. Any analysis which throws light on the general considerations underlying this important shift in colonial policy is therefore significant for the constitutional development of the dependent Empire as a whole.

But the central role of the British government in these policy decisions should not obscure the fact that their origin cannot be studied in isolation from currents of thought in Britain, or influences at work in the colonies. The evidence suggests that in this period a 'colonial policy' on constitutional change is a

[1] See, for instance, footnote 5, p. 299.

figment, if by it is meant the execution of decisions evolved within the Colonial Office and based on long-term considerations, though such a description would perhaps be most applicable to Chamberlain's secretaryship. The evolution of policy was a more complex process in which experience in one colony shaped policy towards another, in which expediency was as important as principle, in which governors subject to many local pressures often played a larger part than colonial office officials, and in which political and social attitudes in Britain and the colonies were important influences. To regard colonial policy as one outside influence in the development of the colonies is to misread the situation as largely as to regard it as the only influence, for the forces which shaped policy were local as well as metropolitan. It is in recognition of this, and of the part which events and thought in Britain and the Empire played in shaping colonial attitudes, that throughout this study the author has attempted to study problems of constitutional change from both the local and Imperial viewpoints.

But the central theme of this study is British colonial policy, and for this reason the book is not intended to be a complete account of political radicalism in the three colonies and in the period under review. Movements for constitutional reform are examined only in so far as they led to significant colonial office policy decisions. The most notable omission is the important phase of Trinidad radicalism commencing in the late 1890s with the establishment of the Trinidad Workingmen's Association in 1897 and *The Mirror* newspaper in 1898. The subsequent agitation for constitutional reform was stimulated by the abolition of the Port of Spain borough council in 1899 and the Port of Spain water riots in 1903. These events are of large significance in the history of political radicalism in Trinidad, but they did not lead to any colonial office reconsideration of policy towards constitutional change and they are therefore not dealt with in this study. Dr. Brinsley Samaroo has been working in this important field of Trinidad radicalism and it is hoped that the results of his research will soon be published.[2]

[2] B. Samaroo, 'Constitutional and Political Development of Trinidad, 1898–1925' (London University Ph.D., 1969). Dr. Samaroo's thesis was finished after the draft of this book had been completed, but I should like to acknowledge the generous assistance which he gave me both in conversation and in commenting on the draft.

The author has encountered certain limitations in the material at his disposal. The accounts of reform movements in the colonies, and of local political attitudes generally, have been based largely on the West Indian press, but the objectivity of its reporting was almost certainly affected by the political views of its proprietors and editors. The writer has regretted not being able to draw on the private papers of leading local figures. There are also serious limitations in the colonial office material, the most important of which is reflected in the reliance placed in this study on printed sources, notably command papers and colonial office confidential prints. This has been made necessary by the colonial office practice between 1874 and 1890 of often destroying despatches and enclosures once they had been printed for parliament or for the use of the Colonial Office. Where a printed paper cannot be compared with the original, there is always the danger that the sense of the latter may have been altered by an omission not indicated in the printed paper by the conventional asterisks. A more unusual example of the unreliability of command papers is the inclusion, in the printed papers concerning the *Florence* crisis, of a paragraph in Kimberley's despatch to Musgrave of 27 January 1882 which was in fact struck out of the original colonial office draft despatch; the error was acknowledged by officials.[3] For much of the period it has been necessary to rely on newspaper reports of legislative council debates which, from the extent to which governors amended press reports of their own speeches when they forwarded them to the Colonial Office, seem to have been far from reliable. The shortage of skilled shorthand writers in the colonies also affected the accuracy of evidence submitted with reports of royal commissions. The royal commission of 1883 on West Indian finances, for instance, apparently had no shorthand reporter to assist it.

The writer has also been conscious of less obvious limitations in the colonial office material. It is clear from references in the minutes that there was a considerable private correspondence between the Colonial Office and officials in the colonies, of which only a small proportion has been preserved with the official colonial office papers. Probably most secretaries of state, like Chamberlain, encouraged governors to write to them

[3] See C.–3453, p. 58. P.P. 1882. Also minute paper 1210. CO 137/504.

privately, and certainly most seem to have personally corresponded with them. Similarly there was an important correspondence between colonial office officials, and governors and officials in the colonies. Such correspondence is often revealing for its insights and frankness. This is understandable so far as governors were concerned since even confidential despatches might be copied or seen by a clerk in the local civil service; for this reason most references by governors to racial distinctions or antagonisms were confined to private correspondence. The author has also felt himself particularly handicapped by his inability to trace the private papers of such leading officials and governors as Wingfield and Norman. In other respects the colonial office papers do not tell the whole story. Important policy decisions were sometimes reached at Office conferences or in personal interviews between governors and secretaries of state, to which reference is sometimes made in the minutes, but of which no detailed record was kept; the grounds for these decisions are therefore often obscure. For instance, there is nothing to be found in the colonial office minutes after August 1883 of the considerations which guided Derby and his officials in formulating the important constitutional proposals contained in Derby's despatch to the governor of Jamaica of 1 December 1883. The practice of officials bracketing part of their minutes, or submitting separate memoranda, indicated that there were conventions regarding what should or should not be included in a minute. Those minutes which the writer has studied closely are generally marked by a narrow field of vision, a lack of speculation regarding, for instance, the direction of long-term constitutional change, and an absence of reference to certain considerations such as Britain's strategic interests. It seems unlikely that they reveal the full mind of officials.

The most pleasant task of authorship is to acknowledge the debt owed to those who made it possible. Like most students of history I owe an inestimable debt to the staff of the Public Record Office from whom I have received nothing but most willing and courteous assistance, given sometimes under extremely trying conditions. Similarly I have received much help from the librarians and staff of the Royal Commonwealth Society Library, the West India Committee Library, the British

Museum Reading Room and Newspaper Library, the Bodleian Library, the Foreign and Commonwealth Office Library, and the Libraries of Birmingham University and Christ Church, Oxford. Transcripts of Crown-copyright records in the Public Record Office are reproduced by permission of the Controller of Her Majesty's Stationery Office. Extracts from Chamberlain's letters are reproduced by courtesy of the University of Birmingham and of Chamberlain's literary trustee; the extract from Salisbury's letter is reproduced by courtesy of Lord Salisbury. I was assisted in the cost of micro-filming by the Central Research Fund of London University.

I am also indebted more personally in a number of other ways. The Royal Military Academy, Sandhurst, originally stimulated my interest in colonial history and permitted me to indulge it by the generous concession of a sabbatical term. The Institute of Commonwealth Studies, by the grant for two years of a Dame Lillian Penson Junior Research Fellowship, enabled me to do the research and most of the writing for the thesis on which this book is closely based, and gave me a very happy home in which to do it. Doreen Howard, amidst many domestic preoccupations, typed the manuscript so accurately and intelligently that not only did she make the checking of it a formality but she also corrected a number of my own errors. Catherine Judson put at my disposal the resources of one of London's leading secretarial colleges; but to her I also owe a more personal debt for her continual assistance, interest, and encouragement, which I cannot repay. I owe a similar debt to my family who have shown patience and understanding during the trials of authorship. I have received advice from several scholars which I have acknowledged individually in the footnotes. Dr. Alan Adamson generously permitted me to quote from his unpublished thesis. The Reverend John Carroll read and helpfully commented on the Jamaica chapters. But my greatest debt is to Mary Cumpston. To refer to her as 'supervisor of my thesis' does not adequately convey the advice and inspiration which she has given me unstintingly. To her this book is dedicated; without her it would probably not have been written.

CONTENTS

SECTION 5

THE EXECUTIVE COUNCILS, 1880–1903

AUTHOR'S NOTE ON THE USE OF TERMS

'CREOLE', from the Spanish 'criollo', originally applied to anyone born and bred in the country. During this period it was, however, commonly used in the West Indies to refer only to Negroes. It is in this sense, of West Indian-born Negro, that I have used it throughout this study unless otherwise stated.

I have used 'coloured' in its narrower sense of mulatto, that is the offspring of European and Negro. I have applied the description with diffidence and caution. The evidence for its use has been mainly drawn from colonial office minutes, governors' private letters, and occasionally from despatches. Such judgements were necessarily subjective and in the case of those of colonial office officials generally second-hand; not too much reliance should be placed on them.

The word 'movement' recurs in the text. In using it I am conscious of exposing myself to the criticism of attributing a greater degree of political organization and purpose to the events described than the evidence warrants. The word should be taken in its more general sense, of describing the aims and actions of a group of persons which were, with varying degrees of enthusiasm and steadfastness, directed towards the same broad end.

INTRODUCTION

A CENTRAL dilemma of British colonial policy in the nineteenth century was the incompatibility in the European-settled tropical dependencies of a favourable policy towards both whites and non-whites. The former, so long as they could control it, sought representative government,[1] but their hostility or indifference to measures for the welfare of the latter often meant that such measures could only be implemented by authoritarian government. These conflicting considerations were prominent in 1810 when Lord Liverpool, the secretary of state for the war and colonial departments, formally recognized and defended in Trinidad what was later to be called crown colony government.[2] Among the reasons which he gave for retaining crown rule was the need to make the abolition of the slave trade effective; so long as this and slave amelioration, and ultimately the abolition of slavery, remained British policy, neither he nor his successors were prepared to surrender the controlling authority of the Crown in Trinidad or, in its modified form, in British Guiana.

After the abolition of slavery in 1834 colonial office opinion was divided on the future constitutional development of these colonies.[3] For instance, Viscount Goderich and his parliamentary under-secretary, Lord Howick, were among those who argued that emancipation had removed the main ground for crown control, and they seem to have favoured the grant of elected assemblies to the two colonies on the lines of those established in Jamaica and most of the British West Indian

[1] Representative government refers in this study to a constitution under which the full number of elected members could under all conditions command a majority in the legislature. It thus excludes the Jamaica constitution of 1884.

[2] For the purpose of this study crown colony government is defined as that system of colonial government in which there was an official majority in the legislature. The Colonial Office also regarded colonies with nominated unofficial majorities in the legislatures as crown colonies, officials sometimes distinguishing the former from the latter by the prefix 'pure'.

[3] The following account of colonial office opinion is based on D. J. Murray, *The West Indies and the Development of Colonial Government*, 1801–1834 (Oxford, 1965), ch. XII.

colonies. Henry Taylor advanced the opposing view. He argued that in a society where property and knowledge were not widely diffused and the mass of society not yet fit to exercise the vote, elected assemblies led to government by an irresponsible oligarchy of either black or white. Taylor's views influenced British colonial policy for nearly half a century. Representative government was not extended to Trinidad or British Guiana, and even the prospect in 1850 of its extension to the Cape Colony did not lead to a change of policy in the West Indies. Writing to the governor of Trinidad in 1850, Lord Grey, the secretary of state for the war and colonial departments, argued that the unfitness of a large part of the population to participate in government precluded a legislative council of nine elected and nine nominated members. He continued:

> I think however it will be highly desirable that such a change should be effected whenever by the diffusion of Education & the advancement of Civilization of the Inhabitants, they are qualified to take such part. . . .[4]

Grey expressed a similar view with regard to the establishment of an elected assembly in British Guiana. The same fear of a narrow representation leading to an oligarchy also influenced his successors against weakening crown control in the British Guiana Court of Policy, or conceding an elected element in the Trinidad legislature. The final triumph of Taylor's views was reflected in the constitutional retrogression from representative to crown colony government which took place in Jamaica and other British West Indian Colonies during the 1860s and 1870s.[5]

The theoretical justification for crown colony government was that the Crown should retain a controlling authority until the mass of the population had become educated for representative institutions and, more generally, 'raised in the scale of society'.[6] But the effective exercise of this controlling authority

[4] Grey to Harris, Conf., 16 May 1850. 3197. CO 295/170. The wording follows a minute by Grey whose policies in southern Africa and New Zealand reflected the same faith in the future progress of the native races.

[5] In most cases the initiative came from the white-dominated assemblies which preferred colonial office rule to possible Negro supremacy.

[6] The phrase is Taylor's. *Autobiography of Henry Taylor 1800–1875* (London, 1885), vol. 1, p. 252.

required positive government based on long-term policies which in practice the Colonial Office was not well placed to conceive or implement. Its knowledge of local conditions was second-hand and necessarily incomplete, although it could partly redress the inadequacy of governors' despatches by reference to local newspapers and petitions,[7] by the reports of local or royal commissions, and by informal contacts with official and unofficial opinion in the colony. Its control over the colonial authorities was imperfect for delay and misunderstanding were inseparable from the exchange of despatches over long distances and intervals of time. Moreover, the secretary of state normally had no sanctions against a governor, except admonition or recall, for to have repudiated his actions would have weakened the authority of the Crown. The press of immediate events and officials' preoccupation with administrative *minutiæ* obscured the need for constructive thought for the future. The organization of colonial office business to provide for the *answering* of despatches emphasized that the Colonial Office was often reacting rather than initiating. The case can be overdrawn. On some issues, notably humanitarian ones such as the treatment of indentured Indian immigrants, prison conditions, or the flogging of females, a clear policy was initiated from London. In reacting to situations presented by governors, Office attitudes developed and administrative principles emerged; but the evolution of a comprehensive long-term policy was difficult so long as the area of decision-making was limited to issues raised by governors who often chose them from personal enthusiasm or pressing necessity. In fact governors were better placed than the Colonial Office to govern constructively in the interests of the unrepresented classes, but their achievement was often limited through lack of continuity, or ability, or of the rare moral courage required to implement a policy in opposition to the planter and merchant interests

[7] Petitions were important for apart from a few newspapers they were the only direct contact which the Colonial Office had with local opinion outside the planting, merchant, and professional classes, whose representatives normally monopolized the unofficial seats in the legislatures. There is evidence in this study that colonial office officials treated petitions seriously although they found their significance often difficult to interpret. For instance, signatories might misunderstand the petition, or support it in order to get rid of the agents who pressed them to sign; the latter were sometimes paid according to the number of signatures they obtained, which practice probably led to fraudulent signatures.

which dominated the narrow social circles in which a governor moved. Both governors and Colonial Office were dependent on the efficiency of the local administrative machinery, the inadequacies of which often stultified the best-conceived policies.[8] Finally, as Henry Taylor recognized, colonial policy was sensitive to the parliamentary and other pressures exerted by the planting interest.

The controlling authority of the Crown was, by 1880, further limited by law and convention in two of the three colonies under discussion, only Jamaica being governed as a 'pure' crown colony.[9] In 1866 the Jamaica Assembly had surrendered its powers and in its place Edward Cardwell, the secretary of state for the colonies, had established a Legislative Council of the governor, six officials, and a maximum of six unofficials. The opposition of some merchants, planters, and others to this form of government was soon expressed in the press and, after 1874, through the Jamaica Association,[10] but their demands for constitutional change were cautious and the support for them limited.[11] In 1876 the Jamaica Association drew up a petition to the secretary of state praying for a constitutional change leading to greater financial control by the inhabitants. In order to gain the support of influential gentlemen for the petition, the Council of the Association withdrew an appendix proposing the introduction of elected members into the Legislative Council,[12] the secretary intimating

[8] Henry Taylor noted that the purpose of legislation in colonies such as Jamaica was 'very commonly defeated . . . by the want of competent executory agency'. Newton (Lt.-Govr.) to Hicks-Beach, No. 365, 15 Dec. 1879. 635. CO 137/491. Minute by H.T., 29 Feb. 1880. The failure to implement the compulsory clauses of the British Guiana education ordinance of 1876 was a good example of this.

[9] See footnote 2, p. 1.

[10] The Jamaica Association was established in Sept. 1874. Although it summarized its aims as the promotion of the 'political, social and religious interests' of Jamaica, it seems mainly at this time to have represented the sugar interest, members of which were prominent among its founders. It was active in conjunction with the West India Committee in 1876 in pressing for an unofficial nominated majority in the Legislative Council and for a larger government contribution to the cost of Indian immigration. Subsequently it seems to have had periods of fitful vigour, notably in years of constitutional crisis such as 1882 and 1899. For the rules of the Association and a list of members see R(oyal) C(ommonwealth) S(ociety) Lib(rary), pamphlet $\frac{73}{4}$.

[11] See also below, pp. 18–19.

[12] The franchise was to be limited to those who paid 20s. annually in direct taxes and who could read and write. It seems that a majority of the Association

that the petitioners would be satisfied with an increase in the number of nominated unofficials. Yet in spite of this concession to conservative opinion Sir William Grey, the governor, estimated that only fifty of the 2,447 signatures were those of men of position and substance. The lack of support probably reflected among other things the weakening influence of the Jamaica planters, which was itself a manifestation of the declining importance of sugar in the Jamaica economy.[13] This trend was not, however, reflected in the Legislative Council where throughout the 1870s the sugar interest dominated the unofficial seats.

Underlying the agitation against crown government were the unfavourable conditions facing the sugar industry during the 1870s. The British Guiana and Trinidad planters had successfully met these by the amalgamation and modernization of estates, and by a high level of Indian immigration which enabled them, particularly in British Guiana, to depress the level of wages in the free labour market. The Jamaica planters lacked the scale of production, the resources, and the confidence to invest as heavily, and they were further handicapped by a shortage of labour caused by the dispersal of the Negro peasantry and the planters' inability to finance an adequate level of Indian immigration. The demands of those agitating against crown government centred on a larger contribution from the general revenue towards the costs of Indian immigration,[14] a reduction in allegedly extravagant public expenditure, particularly in the administration of justice and on public works, and a lessening of the burden of taxation. Expenditure could be reduced, the planters argued, if the unofficial nominated element in the Council was strengthened, and they cited the concession of an unofficial nominated majority to Trinidad in 1862; any more extensive change would, they claimed, 'be

and 'many gentlemen of influence' opposed this. The Second Half-Yearly Report of the Jamaica Association, 17 Dec. 1875 (Kingston, 1876).

13 Average value of exports of home-produced sugar, rum and molasses as a percentage of total value of exports, excluding gold bullion and specie and, for Jamaica, silver specie:

	Jamaica (%)	*Trinidad* (%)	*British Guiana* (%)
1869–70–71	59.2	71.0	93.0
1879–80–81	46.6	47.3	91.9 (1879)

14 After 1873 only the cost of commuting return passages was defrayed from the general revenue. By 1877 Indian immigration had ceased.

earnestly deprecated by the great majority' of those with property interests in Jamaica.[15]

Lord Carnarvon, the secretary of state for the colonies, was unwilling to concede an unofficial nominated majority. Charles Cox, the head of the West India department, summarized the colonial office view. 'This is a question', he wrote, 'that hardly calls for a moment's consideration.' He continued:

> We have succeeded in getting rid of an old Constitution that worked as badly as was possible. And having obtained one that puts full power of legislation in . . . the Governor & Secretary of State it would be folly to surrender that power.[16]

Carnarvon did, however, meet the view of Sir Robert Herbert, the permanent under-secretary, that there was '*much* ground' for the opinion that Jamaica was 'expensively & defectively administered',[17] by appointing Sir Anthony Musgrave as governor, and entrusting him with the task of enquiry, retrenchment, and administrative reform.[18] Musgrave agreed with the Colonial Office on the need to retain an official majority in the Jamaica Legislative Council, but on his advice Sir Michael Hicks-Beach, Carnarvon's successor, agreed in August 1878 to enlarge the Council. It subsequently comprised until 1884 a maximum of nine officials in addition to the governor with an original and casting vote, and nine nominated unofficials.[19]

The authority of the Crown in the three colonies under review was most circumscribed in British Guiana. The central feature of its complex constitution was the division of financial and other business between the Combined Court and the Court of Policy respectively. The latter had an official majority since

[15] See 'Proceedings at a deputation to the Earl of Carnarvon of Proprietors and Merchants interested in the Island of Jamaica'. May 1877. Reprinted as Conf(idential) Print, Misc. No. 31, CO 885/4.

[16] Grey to Carnarvon, No. 220, 9 Dec. 1876. 15437. CO 137/482. Minute by C.C., 21 Feb. 1877.

[17] Grey to Carnarvon, No. 161, 5 Oct. 1876. 13007. CO 384/111. Minute by R.G.W.H., 4 Dec. 1876.

[18] Carnarvon also agreed to a larger contribution from the general revenue towards the cost of Indian immigration, amounting in effect to one third.

[19] Musgrave added two officials and two nominated unofficials to the council in November 1878; he appointed a ninth official in May 1881. His choice of unofficials reflected his policy of widening the representation to include interests other than sugar.

it was presided over by the governor with an original and casting vote, and comprised in addition four officials and five indirectly elected members. Each of the latter was chosen by the members of the Court of Policy from two nominations submitted by the College of Electors, the seven members of which were directly elected for life. The Court had executive as well as legislative functions, the former being similar to those of an executive council in crown colonies.

The Combined Court, which was responsible for financial matters and in which there was an elected majority, comprised the Court of Policy, and six financial representatives directly elected by the same constituency which chose the College of Electors. It was established in the united colony of Demerara and Essequebo in 1796, its powers being initially limited to the raising of taxes and the examination of accounts. Although not specifically sanctioned by the Crown, it was given validity by the terms on which the colony surrendered to the British in September 1803, which guaranteed 'the laws and usages of the Colony' and 'the mode of taxation' then in use. In an important opinion in 1840 the crown law officers stated that these terms were 'binding in good Faith upon the Crown', and, further, that in strict law the Crown's sanction for the two Courts since the cession had given them the same force 'as if they had been established by an Express Grant from the Crown, like the legislatures in Colonies, settled by British Subjects'. It therefore followed that any tax could only be lawfully imposed by the Combined Court or by 'the interposition of the Imperial Parliament'.[20] The Colonial Office interpreted this important opinion to mean that parliamentary legislation was required for any constitutional amendment leading to the abolition of the Combined Court, or a curtailment of its original powers of taxation. It was a consideration which profoundly influenced colonial office policy towards constitutional change in British Guiana. In 1812 the Combined Court acquired further powers. By amalgamating the Colleges

[20] Law Officers to Russell, 21 Oct. 1840. 1931. CO 111/187. In their reference to 'the interposition of the Imperial Parliament' the law officers had in mind a reform of the constitution which would give the power of taxation to a legislature in which the Crown commanded a majority. In the Declaratory Act of 1778 Parliament had renounced the power to tax the North American and West Indian colonies for revenue purposes, so that 'interposition' in this sense was excluded.

of Electors and Financial Representatives, acting governor Carmichael placed the latter in a strong position *vis-à-vis* the elected members of the Court of Policy, whom they now both sat with and chose; the Combined Court was thus able to effect 'a silent and unresisted usurpation' over the control of expenditure, in addition to the powers of raising taxes and examining accounts which it had enjoyed since 1796. In 1831 Goderich ended the Court's unauthorized control over expenditure and separated the Colleges of Electors and Financial Representatives. He confirmed, however, the Court's power over taxation, which the crown law officers were to uphold in their important opinion of 1840.[21] Further constitutional difficulties, including the refusal of the Combined Court to vote supplies, led to a final compromise settlement in 1836, which was subsequently renewed at seven-year intervals between 1842 and 1889, and thereafter at less regular intervals until 1927. In return for the Combined Court voting a civil list the Crown granted to the Court for the currency of the civil list the control of the revenues of the King's chest,[22] and the right 'to discuss in detail, freely and without reserve' the annual estimates. This was interpreted by secretaries of state to include the power to reduce or negate expenditure, but they resisted the attempts of the Combined Court to increase or initiate money votes. The settlement of 1836 left untouched the Combined Court's power of taxation which Goderich had confirmed in 1831.

This constitution was incompatible with the role of the Crown as the guardian of the interests of the unrepresented classes. The planters controlled the five unofficial seats in the Court of Policy through the exclusive property qualification for membership[23] and the system of indirect election. Although the qualifications for membership of the two directly elected Colleges of Electors and Financial Representatives were less

[21] See above.

[22] The main income of the King's chest, known under Dutch rule as the Company's chest, had been the head-tax on slaves; the loss of this independent source of revenue after abolition weakened the Crown's position *vis-à-vis* the Combined Court. The income was not made good until the 1880s and 1890s when the development of the gold industry brought a rising revenue to the King's chest from licences, fees, and royalties.

[23] The possession of eighty acres of land of which forty had to be in *bona fide* cultivation. Ord(inances) 1 and 16, 1864. CO 113/4.

exclusive,[24] both normally comprised planters or merchants associated with them, elections being rarely contested until the 1880s. By their virtual monopoly of the elected seats in the Combined Court the representatives of the planting interest, being in a majority, could withhold supplies and, so long as the civil list compromise existed, veto expenditure, including officials' salaries not secured by the civil list or by legislation. The knowledge of the existence of these powers, and the overwhelming economic and social preponderance of the British Guiana plantocracy, reinforced the tendency which Herbert noted in all sugar colonies for officials 'to take the Planters' view of things'. The local exercise of a trusteeship on behalf of the unrepresented classes therefore depended largely on the governors, none of whom during the late 1860s and 1870s proved equal to the task. Nor did the Colonial Office redress the balance effectively, although Herbert recognized as early as 1872 that the constitution could not 'be left untouched much longer' for 'the poorer classes are insufficiently represented, & there is no guarantee that their requirements or complaints will be attended to . . .'.[25] Herbert favoured crown colony government on other grounds, for he argued that 'much harm might be done in an Indian Immigrant crisis by the Combined Court impeding the action of the Government on some financial ground'.[26] But he did not press his view, and had he done so it is doubtful if it would have prevailed since its implementation was generally held in the Colonial Office to require parliamentary legislation. The most effective remaining weapon against an obdurate Combined Court was the threat to end Indian immigration. Kimberley used it in 1872 to hasten the passage of legislation improving the condition of Indian immigrants, but, in general, the Colonial Office seem to have

[24] The qualifications were as for the elected members of the Court of Policy, or the ownership or minimum twenty-one year leaseholdship of house, or house and land, of 'annual or rental value' of £250, or clear annual income of £300 derived from property not mentioned in the previous qualifications, or from any trade or profession carried on in the colony. Ord. 15, 1849. CO 113/2. For convenience, throughout this study, the dollar, which was the British Guiana unit of account, has been converted to sterling at the official rate of 4s. 2d.

[25] Emigration Board to Colonial Office, 21 Mar. 1872. 3001. CO 318/266. Minute by R.G.W.H., 27 Apr. 1872.

[26] Rushworth to Kimberley, No. 182, 24 Nov. 1873. 13353. CO 111/399. Minute by R.G.W.H., 8 Jan. 1874.

regarded it as an extreme measure, to be used only to press reforms beneficial to Indian immigrants. This threat apart, Taylor summarized accurately the working of the British Guiana constitution during the 1870s:

. . . a merchant & planters' oligarchy, not much tempered, perhaps, by any apprehension that the Crown will really exert the latent power it claims of supreme & absolute legislation.[27]

The controlling authority of the Crown was also limited, though to a much lesser extent, in Trinidad. In this case the Colonial Office had placed informal limits on its control over finance by its deference in matters of expenditure to the view of a majority of the nominated unofficial members of the Legislative Council,[28] who were normally representatives of the planting interest. This self-imposed limitation coincided with the colonial office view of the best guarantee of prudent financial administration, and with their recognition of the political, economic, and social importance of the planting interest in the West Indian colonies and in Britain. In 1862 the Duke of Newcastle strengthened and extended this convention by adding two nominated members to the Legislative Council,[29] thus establishing an unofficial majority of one in a council comprising the governor, six officials, and eight nominated unofficials. He did so on condition that the unofficial majority should not make 'a practice of voting together habitually . . . so as to render the official votes in the Council nugatory . . .'.[30] Herbert, in particular, regretted this concession. In January 1879 he minuted:

We shall none of us live to overcome the mischief done by former Governments in allowing unofficial majorities in Crown Colony

[27] Scott to Kimberley, No. 160, 7 Nov. 1871. 11623. CO 111/387. Minute by H.T., 5 Dec. 1871. In 1842 the crown law officers had modified their opinion of 1840 to the extent of confirming that the Crown had not parted with the supreme legislative authority over the colony vested in it by right of conquest, and that it could therefore legislate by order in council so long as no duty or tax was imposed. It was this rather than parliamentary legislation which Taylor had in mind. Such legislation could be frustrated, if it involved expenditure, by the Combined Court withholding supplies.

[28] See, for instance, Newcastle to Keate, No. 510, 3 Sept. 1862. CO 296/25.

[29] Goderich had established a Council of Government in 1831, comprising the governor, six officials, and six nominated unofficials. In 1862 the Council of Government was renamed the Legislative Council.

[30] Newcastle to Keate, No. 510, 3 Sept. 1862. CO 296/25.

Councils & in the legislatures of other Colonies where the coloured races predominate.[31]

On his advice, Hicks-Beach in July 1878 informed the governor of Trinidad, Sir Henry Irving, that he favoured the re-establishment of an official majority, but in deference to the strong opinion of Irving, endorsed by his successor, Sir Sanford Freeling, he did not press the change.

During the late 1840s and early 1850s Grey had sounded an optimistic note regarding the future development of the non-white races, a development which he hoped would ultimately fit them for participation in representative institutions. This optimism is not reflected in the minutes of colonial office officials in the 1870s. By this period they seem to have come to regard crown colony government on its own merits, as administratively a more workable system, rather than as an intermediate stage before the mass of the people were educated for representative government. Colonial office confidence in crown colony government was reflected in the wide extension of that system in the British West Indies during the 1870s;[32] it was also reflected in the attitude of those officials like Herbert and Cox, who in spite of evidence of administrative failures opposed its modification in Jamaica, and favoured its extension to British Guiana and its rigid application in Trinidad. Neither they nor secretaries of state seem to have regarded these colonies as suited for representative government in the foreseeable future. Yet in 1884 Lord Derby conceded a constitutional change in Jamaica which, although falling short of representative government, substantially modified the existing system of crown colony government, and seemed to offer the promise of further constitutional advance. The new departure of 1884 inaugurated a period of constitutional change in the West Indies, and elsewhere, in the largely uncharted field between pure crown colony government and representative government.[33] The methods of Derby and his successors were pragmatic and uncertain, their aims were sometimes obscure, and

[31] Irving to Hicks-Beach, Conf., 25 Nov. 1878. 16251. CO 295/282. Minute by R.G.W.H., 2 Jan. 1879.

[32] During the late 1870s nominated legislative councils with official majorities were established in St. Kitts, Nevis, Grenada, St. Vincent, and Tobago.

[33] See footnote 5, p. 299.

after 1895 their tentative course was reversed by Chamberlain. Nevertheless their policies represented a further experiment by the British Empire in the art of 'the government of men by themselves'. Such is the theme of this study of constitutional change in three West Indian colonies between 1880 and 1903, and of the influences in the Colonial Office and in Britain, and in colonial government and society, which shaped it.

Section 1

Jamaica

1880–1895

I

THE NEW DEPARTURE

The concession of semi-representative government[1] *to Jamaica, 1880 to 1884*

SIR ANTHONY MUSGRAVE'S governorship fulfilled neither the hope of the Colonial Office that it would lead to administrative reform and retrenchment, nor of the sugar interest, the grievances of which Carnarvon had instructed him to investigate and, if necessary, remedy.[2] Arriving in Jamaica in August 1877, favourably disposed, as he later claimed, towards the planters, he soon concluded that most of their assertions concerning the extravagance of crown government were without foundation. Their purpose was, he claimed, 'to discredit the present form of government' in the hope of securing a constitutional change which would restore to the planters control of legislation and finance. Musgrave's refusal to admit the need for substantial administrative reform or retrenchment alienated the sugar interest, which he further antagonized by pressing what it regarded as an unfavourable interpretation of Carnarvon's scheme for financing Indian immigration.[3] Nor did Musgrave retain the confidence of the Colonial Office which considered him too sanguine regarding the level and cost of establishments and unsound in matters of political economy. This distrust seems to have affected the value which it attached to his judgement in other matters, most notably the issues raised by the *Florence* crisis.

The schooner *Florence*, allegedly bound for St. Thomas with a cargo of arms and ammunition, arrived in distress at Kingston

[1] The phrase is used by H. H. Wrong, *Government of the West Indies* (Oxford, 1923), ch. VII. It is used in this study to describe a constitution in which there was either an unofficial nominated and elected majority in the legislature, or an elected majority, either of which could be reversed by the appointment of the full complement of officials.

[2] See p. 6.

[3] See footnote 18, p. 6.

on 22 July 1877. Musgrave, wrongly advised by his attorney-general, detained the ammunition and refused to allow the schooner to sail with the arms until a bond had been given for their legitimate disposal. The owner of the cargo brought two actions against the governor which were finally concluded in July 1881, damages of £6,700 being awarded against Musgrave. These judgements raised the question whether the governor should be indemnified from Imperial or colonial funds. Herbert argued that Musgrave had acted in Imperial interests and that Imperial funds should be used. Edward Wingfield, the under-secretary responsible for West Indian business, shared this view, but pressed it less strongly. Herbert was, however, overruled by Leonard Courtney, the parliamentary under-secretary, on whose advice Lord Kimberley, the secretary of state for the colonies, instructed Musgrave to apply to the Legislative Council for a vote to cover the damages and costs awarded against him. This decision aroused strong feeling in Jamaica, where it was argued in the press and at public meetings that colonial funds should not be applied in a matter where only Imperial interests were involved, nor should the colonists be made responsible for the mistakes of officials in whose appointment they had no say and for whose actions they were not responsible. The critics of crown government were also quick to seize on the fact that Musgrave, on his own responsibility and before a vote had been taken in the Legislative Council, had ordered the payment of the full amount from the colonial treasury, though in the form of an advance. For them the *Florence* affair exemplified both the powerlessness of the Legislative Council to control expenditure and the incompetence of crown government. Kimberley did not give way to this agitation, or to Musgrave's plea that Imperial funds should be used. His instruction that the officials must support the vote led to the resignation of Samuel Burke, the crown solicitor, and John Mackglashan, the auditor-general, both Jamaican-born. Musgrave was unable to replace them since no official would accept a seat in the Legislative Council on the condition of supporting the vote. With the official side thus weakened, the Council on 11 January 1882 passed a resolution by seven unofficial to five official votes,[4] which

[4] One official abstained and one was absent from the colony.

Musgrave accepted as tantamount to a rejection of the *Florence* vote, and he therefore withdrew it.

Wingfield and Courtney advised a policy of firmness, the latter minuting:

It is well to realize the truth that this is a crucial test of the possibility of maintaining the Crown Colony form of Govt. in the W.I.[5]

Herbert, more sensitive to local and parliamentary opinion, urged the payment of the full amount from Imperial funds. Kimberley finally accepted a compromise proposed by Courtney, whereby the Treasury was to be asked to pay a part of the sum, and the remaining balance was to be voted by the Legislative Council after two officials, pledged to support it, had been appointed to replace the two who had resigned. Musgrave strenuously opposed this course of action which, in his view, would 're-kindle expiring angry feeling' against the constitution, but he was overruled by Kimberley. On the secretary of state's instructions Musgrave carried through the Legislative Council on 9 November 1882 a vote for half the damages and costs incurred in the *Florence* affair. He did so by using the full official vote, having replaced the two officials who resigned in January with two further officials,[6] pledged to support the government not only on the *Florence* question but always when called on. On the following day six unofficial members resigned; Henry Sewell had previously resigned, George Solomon was out of the colony but subsequently resigned, and one unofficial seat was vacant. A more popular governor might have avoided this denouement;[7] a governor more influential with the Colonial Office might have rendered it unnecessary.

The collective resignation of the unofficial members, and the

[5] Musgrave to Kimberley, No. 369, 9 Dec. 1881. 14. CO 137/501. Minute by L.C., 16 Jan. 1882.

[6] T. Capper, the inspector of schools, and A. H. Alexander, the protector of immigrants.

[7] Musgrave had his defenders, for example *The Budget* newspaper which was the organ of the coloured community. Even his critics, many of whom were connected with the sugar interest, acknowledged his achievement in such fields as secondary education, railway extension, and the establishment of an electric telegraph. But they considered him hostile to the planters, and as having failed to effect necessary measures of retrenchment, reform of the administration, establishment of industrial schools, and strict laws against praedial larceny and vagrancy.

events leading up to it, transformed the movement for constitutional reform in Jamaica. To understand this it is necessary briefly to examine Jamaican opinion before 1882. Its diversity makes generalization difficult, but from 1875 there seem to have been two main views among those favouring a reform of the Legislative Council. An influential minority of the Jamaica Association favoured a return in a modified form to representative government, with a majority of elected members chosen on a moderate to narrow franchise. The main weight behind this demand after 1875 came from *The Colonial Standard and Jamaica Despatch*, which was owned by George Levy, a Jewish merchant closely associated with the sugar interest. On the other hand, the majority of the Jamaica Association, including such prominent planters as Henry Westmorland, were unwilling to go beyond the Trinidad precedent of an unofficial nominated majority in the Legislative Council,[8] and they probably spoke for most influential Jamaican opinion which favoured constitutional change. The West India Committee continued to press this limited demand until 1883. It seems that between 1876 and the *Florence* crisis there was a slight shift in Jamaican opinion towards favouring a return to representative government, to which dissatisfaction with Musgrave's governorship and difficult economic conditions contributed. But the overall impression of the period between 1875 and 1882 is one of conservatism and apathy towards constitutional reform. Many Jamaicans continued to favour crown colony government. As late as April 1880 the Jamaica Association, which was revived in 1879, rejected the very moderate proposal that public lectures should be given on 'Constitutional Government', to be followed by debates on the subject in Kingston and the parishes.

Musgrave's first attempt to pass the *Florence* vote through the Legislative Council in January 1882 certainly raised the political temperature in Jamaica, but it gave little impetus to the reform movement. Most of the press concentrated on the narrow issue of the injustice of using colonial funds, at the direction of the secretary of state, for Imperial purposes. It is true that the Jamaica Association was again active in the early months of 1882 and that it now favoured a return in some form

[8] See pp. 4–5.

to representative government.[9] Various schemes for constitutional change were also canvassed in the press. The most radical of these was the proposal of Wellesley Bourke, a coloured solicitor, who favoured representative government with adult manhood suffrage subject only to a literacy test. On the other hand, the unofficial nominated members supported the West India Committee proposal for an increase in their own number, and they probably still represented the majority opinion among Jamaicans favouring constitutional change.[10] Nor was Bourke's attitude representative of the coloured community who, Musgrave reported, had held aloof from the agitation. Its organ, *The Budget*, opposed constitutional change, fearing that it would lead either to a white oligarchy, or to representative government which Negroes would control by weight of numbers.[11] In Musgrave's view, the agitation came from 'the Jews and the dregs (?) of the old plantocracy . . .'.[12] This was a prejudiced judgement, though it is probably true that there was still little public support for constitutional reform in the spring of 1882. A considerable body of influential Jamaicans continued to favour crown government, as they had done since 1875. By May 1882 the Jamaica Association was unable to obtain a quorum.

Jamaican opinion changed sharply after Musgrave, on Kimberley's instructions, forced the *Florence* vote through the Legislative Council in November 1882. The pressure placed on the officials to support the vote seems to have convinced many Jamaicans of what they regarded as the bankruptcy of crown colony government; in particular, they pointed derisively to the pledge given by Alexander and Capper to support

[9] The Association seems to have adopted George Levy's suggestion for parochial meetings to elect delegates to a general conference in Kingston which would frame proposals for constitutional change. Supporters of the scheme hoped that it would lead to demands for an elective franchise.

[10] Various schemes were put forward to associate a limited number of Jamaicans with the governor's choice of nominated members, through the submission of nomination papers. See, for instance, Robert Craig's proposal, *The Colonial Standard and Jamaica Despatch*, 28 Feb. 1882.

[11] For instance, *The Budget*, 27 Mar. 1882 and 12 Oct. 1882.

[12] Musgrave to Wingfield (personal), 9 Mar. 1882. 3440. CO 137/507. The Jews were an influential community in Jamaica, Musgrave describing Kingston as practically a Jewish community so far as the upper classes were concerned; many members of the parochial municipal boards were Jews.

the government on all occasions when called on.[13] Musgrave doubted the genuineness of their resentment over this issue, which he felt was being used to lend weight to agitation for a constitutional change which would transfer power to a local oligarchy. But the evidence suggests that the events of November 1882 had done more than give impetus to a narrowly based and long-standing agitation for an increase in the number of nominated unofficials; it broadened the movement for constitutional change and turned it towards representative government, which previously only a few had advocated. Thus William Morrison[14] wrote in January 1883:

> ... recent events have ... turned the preponderance of public opinion in favour of some form of Government including the principle of direct effective representation.[15]

Other evidence supports this view. Leading colonists such as George Henderson,[16] L. C. Shirley, a sugar planter, J. W. Fisher, *custos* of Trelawney, and Dr. J. C. Phillippo, an eminent Kingston practitioner, who had all previously supported crown government, now advocated a modification of it. A. Lindo, a greatly respected Jamaican, prominent in politics before 1865, emerged from retirement to play a leading part in the agitation for reform. The protest against the *Florence* vote was also backed by white landowners and businessmen such as Robert Craig, W. Kerr, and J. M. Farquharson. But they and other leading white Jamaicans were not, it seems, present at a public meeting in Kingston on 2 November 1882, which approved a draft memorial to the House of Commons praying that the colonists might 'through their Representatives ... control the raising and expenditure of the Revenues ...'.[17] Their absence emphasized the increasing prominence of leading coloured men in the agitation for constitutional change, such as Richard

[13] Feeling against Capper was particularly strong perhaps because he had been appointed from England in preference to three local candidates.

[14] The joint principal of the Church of England and Collegiate High School and editor of *The Jamaica Daily Telegraph*. He was formerly secretary of the Jamaica Association.

[15] Reprinted in C. 3840, p. 193. P.P. 1884 (XLVI).

[16] A printer and bookseller, owner of coffee plantations, and a nominated unofficial member of the Legislative Council. He had been a member of the former House of Assembly.

[17] *The Daily Gleaner*, 3 Nov. 1882.

Jackson, a solicitor, and Wellesley Bourke. Among the newspaper editors at the meeting was C. L. Campbell, a coloured man and editor of *The Budget*, who previously had supported crown government.[18] This broader agitation overshadowed the movement for an unofficial nominated majority, some of the advocates of the latter, such as George Solomon,[19] transferring their support to it. It seems probable that they and the leaders of the coloured community now supported the agitation for representative government in the hope of controlling it, and turning any resulting elective system to their advantage. Yet although most advocates of constitutional change now found common ground on the introduction of an elective element into the Legislative Council, there still remained wide differences regarding the degree of representation to be sought.

Although Kimberley's impolitic decision to instruct Musgrave to force the *Florence* vote through the Legislative Council was the primary reason for this more broadly based agitation, it is probable that it was also influenced by conditions within and outside Jamaica to which attention must now be directed. The 1870s had witnessed a decline in the fortunes of the Jamaica sugar industry, but the latter part of the decade and the early 1880s also saw a fall in the value of other major exports, notably coffee and logwood. Its impact on living standards is difficult to assess, but the general belief that there was a deep commercial depression is as important as its exact measurement. Declining revenue without a corresponding fall in public expenditure[20] necessitated increased taxation, and

[18] The other editors or proprietors present were George Levy, C. J. de Cordova, *The Daily Gleaner*, Morrison, *The Jamaica Daily Telegraph*, and James Gall, *Gall's Newsletter*. de Cordova was a Jew and a member of the former House of Assembly. Both Morrison and Gall were Scots-born.

[19] A leading Jewish merchant and planter, and a nominated unofficial member of the Legislative Council. He had been a member of the former House of Assembly. With his cousin, Michael Solomon, he played a prominent part in the reform movement between 1882 and 1884. Michael was also a leading merchant associated with the sugar interest, and a wealthy landowner, who by 1882 was regarded as the leader of the nominated unofficial members. His views seem to have been more liberal than those of his cousin, but by 1889 C. A. Harris, an official in the West India department, claimed that he had come to regret the change from crown colony government in 1884.

[20] The expenditure on public works already commenced could not be easily cut back; the cost of servicing the increased public debt further contributed to the inelasticity of public expenditure.

lent weight to the attacks on the alleged extravagance of crown colony government.[21] The hurricane of August 1880, and the droughts and floods which preceded and followed it, increased the colony's economic difficulties. Rising literacy[22] enabled the press to exploit this discontent. Musgrave wrote of 'a large semi-educated class who can easily be persuaded that "the Government", is in some way culpable, and has despotically imposed heavier taxation'.[23] Phillippo wrote differently of the impact of education: 'The steam-engine and the telegraph have, with instruction in English history and English books, created English notions of political freedom among our clerks, artisans and peasantry. . . '.[24]

Conditions outside Jamaica also favoured agitation for reform. Jamaicans advocating change drew encouragement from the climate of opinion in England, and from constitutional reform and unrest elsewhere in the Empire. 'The spirit and genius of a free and progressive age', wrote the leader-writer of *The Colonial Standard and Jamaica Despatch*, 'are fighting on our side.'[25] The editor of *The Budget* saw Ireland as 'the great question of the day',[26] no less than twelve of the twenty-six issues of *The Budget* for January 1881 reporting Irish affairs. Jamaicans sympathized with Irish aspirations but condemned violence and agrarian outrage. The leader-writer of *The Daily Gleaner*, pressing in early 1882 for the revival of the Jamaica Association, cited the contribution of the Land League to the passage of the Irish Land Bill of 1881 as an example of successful organized agitation.[27] He was also encouraged by the view that Irish agitation had compelled Gladstone to offer constitutional concessions; '. . . we may surely take heart', he wrote, 'in endeavouring to win back rights which Ireland never

[21] Criticism was not confined to the colony. Herbert minuted: 'The cost of Governing is unquestionably large, in relation to the resources of Jamaica, & presses rather heavily on the population.' Musgrave to Hicks-Beach, No. 215, 9 July 1879. 12084. CO 137/490. Minute by R.G.W.H., 28 Dec. 1879.

[22] The total literate population had risen from 31.3 per cent of the population over five years of age in 1861 to 45.7 per cent in 1881. *Census*, 1881, p. 201. CO 140/184. See also pp. 33–4 below.

[23] Musgrave to Hicks-Beach, Conf., 2 July 1879. 12186. CO 137/490.

[24] J. C. Phillippo, *Jamaica; Its Government and its People* (Kingston, 1883), p. 4.

[25] *The Colonial Standard and Jamaica Despatch*, 9 Dec. 1881.

[26] *The Budget*, 26 Jan. 1881.

[27] *The Daily Gleaner*, 17 Jan. 1882. The same view was put forward by a correspondent of *The Colonial Standard and Jamaica Despatch*, 24 Oct. 1881.

lost . . .'. The time was ripe for 'united, concerted action' in Jamaica. Gladstone's policy was 'a hint to Crown Colonies like Jamaica. . . . The sauce for Ireland will serve Jamaica as well.'[28] He likened the Jamaica Association to the Irish Home Rule Confederation, and after the resignation of the nominated unofficial members in November 1882 he suggested that the boycott might be used to prevent their seats being filled. He also argued that proposed constitutional changes in Natal were a further reason for maintaining constitutional agitation, and he gave a detailed account of Ripon's policy of establishing local self-government in India, of which he wrote: '. . . those efforts have an extreme interest for us in Jamaica . . .'.[29] Nor was the example of other British West Indian colonies forgotten. The leader-writer of *The Colonial Standard* commended the constitution of Barbados as the only one suitable for a free people. '. . . we believe', he wrote, 'that our political emancipation will be all the sooner achieved if we can effect with the people of Trinidad and other Crown Colonies a close, cordial alliance . . .'.[30]

Kimberley's policy in the *Florence* affair had been pressed against the advice of Herbert and Musgrave, who had both foreseen that it would lead to a renewal of the agitation which had died down after the withdrawal of the *Florence* vote in January 1882. Evelyn Ashley, the parliamentary under-secretary, defended it in the House of Commons on 9 March 1883 on the grounds that the colonies should share in the fulfilment of Imperial obligations.[31] Musgrave claimed that this policy had been carefully considered by the Cabinet,[32] and Gladstone had minuted 'I entirely agree' on Kimberley's despatch of 8 September 1882 which instructed Musgrave to bring the reduced vote before the Legislative Council. In fact the decision to press the *Florence* vote had been influenced largely by Courtney, from a wish to assert the authority of the

[28] *The Daily Gleaner*, 21 Feb. 1882. For Froude's view of the impact of the Irish question on the 'keener-witted' Trinidad Negro, see footnote 68, p. 173.

[29] *The Daily Gleaner*, 10 July 1882.

[30] *The Colonial Standard and Jamaica Despatch*, 12 Apr. 1880.

[31] *Hansard('s Parliamentary Debates)*, Third Series (276), 1946.

[32] See report of speech to Legislative Council, 9 Nov. 1882. Reprinted in C. 3453, pp. 94–95. P.P. 1882 (XLVI).

Colonial Office as much as to defend the principle of local responsibility for Imperial interests, which was only precisely defined later to justify a position already adopted. But whatever the aims of Kimberley's policy, the political price paid for it in Jamaica was high. Not only did the reform movement take on a wider and more radical character, but the resignation of the unofficial members created a political deadlock, for Musgrave reported in January 1883 that it was impossible to find anyone qualified and willing to replace them. In the circumstances an order in council was passed authorizing the Council to legislate with only the officials present, Kimberley instructing Musgrave to refrain from all but absolutely necessary legislation.

These events were part of a wider pattern of political unrest in the crown colonies. For instance, in October 1882 F. N. Broome, the lieutenant-governor of Mauritius, forwarded a petition from the colony for a Council of Government of ten officials, ten nominated, and ten elected members.[33] In November 1882 General Sir A. Borton, the governor of Malta, reported the election of two members to the Council of Government who were 'notoriously unfit persons to perform the duties of elected members';[34] this unusual expression by the electorate of long-standing discontent with the constitution had been followed by the resignation of five of the elected members.[35] In December 1882 Lord Derby replaced Kimberley at the Colonial Office.

The political deadlock in Jamaica was the main reason for a reversal of colonial office policy,[36] though there is evidence of a shift in Herbert's thinking before the resignation of the unofficial members. In October 1882 he noted: '. . . we must move in the direction of popularising the administration of

[33] Broome to Kimberley, 31 Oct. 1882. Reprinted in C. 4074, p. 36. P.P. 1884 (LV). The Mauritius Council of Government comprised the governor, eight officials, and eight nominated unofficials.

[34] Borton to Kimberley, 16 Nov. 1882. Reprinted in C. 3524, p. 7. P.P. 1883 (XLVII).

[35] The Malta Council of Government comprised the governor, nine official, and eight elected members. Among the grievances voiced by the elected members was the use of the official majority in matters of local interest. They also pressed for a civil governor.

[36] As late as 7 Apr. 1881, Grant Duff had stated in the House of Commons that it was impossible 'to hold out any hope of the existing Constitution being altered'. *Hansard*, Third Series (260), 877.

affairs as far as we safely can'.[37] Herbert's minute suggests that he saw this as the only alternative to the 'beneficent despotism' of Sir John Grant,[38] and that he could see no present or future prospect of finding so able a governor. The difficulty of finding good governors is a recurring theme in the colonial office minutes of this period. Both Freeling, the governor of Trinidad, and C. H. Kortright, the governor of British Guiana, were regarded in and outside the Office as ineffective. But the first indication in the colonial office papers of a definite change of policy towards Jamaica is a minute by Herbert written in December 1882: 'The official majority cannot be dispensed with', he wrote, 'but we can consent to have part of the unofficial members elected.'[39] He was also inclined to agree with Wingfield that the nomination of 'one or two black men may be good'. Kimberley initialled this minute, and before he left office in December he was considering the possibility that some or all of the unofficial members might be elected. The first public hint of a change of policy was given by Ashley in the House of Commons on 9 March 1883 when, speaking of Jamaica, 'he hoped that before long they would be able to grant some sort of a return in a modified form to elective representation'.[40]

Policy towards Jamaica was also influenced by the appointment of Lord Derby as secretary of state. In his younger days he had shown interest in the West Indies, which he had toured in 1848, revisiting Jamaica in 1849 and 1850. In 1850 and 1851 he had published two pamphlets arguing the case for the maintenance of differential sugar duties.[41] The introduction of elected members into the Legislative Council was under consideration when he took office, but in contrast to Kimberley he showed a strong sympathy for constitutional change in

[37] Musgrave to Kimberley, No. 284, 18 Sept. 1882. 17998. CO 137/506. Minute by R.G.W.H., 24 Oct. 1882.

[38] Sir J. P. Grant was governor of Jamaica from 1866 to 1874 and was highly regarded in the Colonial Office. He had served in the Indian Civil Service from 1828 to 1862, rising to lieutenant-governor of Bengal.

[39] Musgrave to Kimberley, Conf., 14 Nov. 1882. 20967. CO 137/507. Minute by R.G.W.H., Dec. 1882. The minute was written between 4 and 6 Dec.

[40] *Hansard*, Third Series (276), 1947.

[41] Hon. E. Stanley, *Claims and resources of the West Indian Colonies* (London, 1850). Lord Stanley, *Farther facts connected with the West Indies* (London, 1851). (Brit(ish) Mus(eum) Catalogue No. 8155d, 67 and 68.)

Jamaica and other crown colonies which was perhaps not unconnected with his appointment.[42] Speaking in the House of Lords on 9 March 1883, he described proposed changes in the Malta Council of Government as 'evidence of a desire to make local self-government in matters not affecting Imperial interests a reality and not a mere show'.[43] There is no substantial minute by Derby on constitutional reform in the Jamaica papers, but in May 1883 he wrote: 'You cannot long govern a colony like Jamaica without representative institutions in some shape.'[44] This broad conviction was a new factor in colonial office thinking, for the willingness of officials to consider constitutional change in Jamaica was based on the narrower grounds of pressing administrative expediency. Derby gave the reasons for his view in a letter to Gladstone of 30 September 1883:

> The new, or despotic system, has come to a dead lock . . . in any case I do not think that a population of 800,000 now fairly prosperous, and living close to the U. States, can be permanently governed without some admixture of an elective process. On the other hand, responsible government as in Canada and Australia is scarcely suited to a negro population.[45]

He repeated these views, except the last, to a deputation of Jamaica planters and others who saw him on 8 November 1883. He was reported to have told them that the size and intelligence of Jamaica's population and the island's proximity to the United States made 'a despotic or *quasi*-despotic Government' a provisional state of affairs.[46]

Another factor influencing policy was Kimberley's appointment, in December 1882, of a royal commission to enquire into the finances of all the West Indian colonies except Barbados, Trinidad, and British Guiana.[47] Although Kimberley did not specifically instruct this commission to report on constitutional

[42] The writer has not found any evidence on this point in the Gladstone Papers.

[43] *Hansard*, Third Series (276), 1888.

[44] Musgrave to Derby, No. 145, 17 Apr. 1883. 7831. CO 137/509. Minute by D., 13 May 1883.

[45] Derby to Gladstone, 30 Sept. 1883. Gladstone Papers. Brit. Mus. Additional M(anuscript)s 44,141.

[46] *The European Mail*, West Indies edition, 17 Nov. 1883, pp. 37–39.

[47] Royal Commission appointed in Dec. 1882 to inquire into the public revenues, expenditure, debts, and liabilities of the Islands of Jamaica, Grenada, St. Vincent, Tobago, and St. Lucia and the Leeward Islands. C. 3840. P.P. 1884 (XLVI).

questions except indirectly in so far as they affected expenditure, Derby and his officials clearly hoped for guidance on Jamaica's constitutional problems for they postponed consideration of them until they had received the commissioners' report.

Influential parliamentary opinion supported Jamaica reform. Speaking in the House of Commons on 9 March 1883 Gladstone expressed sympathy for the restoration of representative institutions in Jamaica.[48] On 2 October he wrote to Derby: 'I cannot regret that the affair of the Florence has had the effect of a reconsideration of the constitution under which Jamaica is now ruled.'[49] The occasion of Gladstone's speech in the House of Commons was a debate on the *Florence* affair which had revealed the support of the 'Fourth Party' and the Irish members for the Jamaican reformers. Speaking for the Irish members F. H. O'Donnell had expressed their interest in the *Florence* affair 'in view of the transformation of Ireland into a Crown Colony . . .'.[50] In a later debate on the Jamaica constitutional changes W. Redmond explained more fully the Irish members' support: '. . . this question was one that involved the principle of self-government, the principle he and hon. Gentlemen with whom he sat were charged to support, not only in the case of their own country, but in the case of people all over the world who were asking that right'.[51] Other notable friends of Jamaica were Serjeant Simon, born in Jamaica of Jewish parents and Liberal member for Dewsbury, and Captain George Price, member for Devonport and descended from an old-established Jamaican landed family. But parliamentary interest in Jamaica was not great; notice was given of forty members not being present during the *Florence* debate, and in the second debate on the Jamaica constitution in April 1884 the House was counted out.[52] In short, the resignation of the nominated unofficial members and the resulting political deadlock had caused officials to consider and tentatively favour constitutional change; they were pro-

[48] *Hansard*, Third Series (276), 1966.

[49] Gladstone to Derby, 2 Oct. 1883 (copy). Gladstone Papers. Brit. Mus. Additional MSS. 44,546.

[50] *Hansard*, Third Series (276), 1948.

[51] 25 Apr. 1884. *Hansard*, Third Series (287), 723.

[52] This is not conclusive proof of lack of parliamentary interest. It was alleged in *The Colonial Standard* that government members deliberately withdrew in order to bring an embarrassing debate to a close. Ibid., 23 May 1884.

bably also influenced by doubts regarding the administrative competence of the Jamaica government. Their attitude was reinforced by the liberal convictions of Gladstone and Derby, and the small but vocal group of 'friends of Jamaica' in the House of Commons. A decision was, however, postponed until the report of the royal commission was known, and Derby and his officials had consulted personally with Musgrave.

The differing constitutional proposals before the Colonial Office by August 1883 reflected the diversity of Jamaican opinion favouring reform. In February, August, and November 1882 the West India Committee had pressed their request for an unofficial nominated majority on the lines of Trinidad, the need for retrenchment remaining their overriding consideration. In December 1882 they informed Derby of the view they had previously communicated to Kimberley, that a return to representative institutions 'would be strongly opposed by the great majority of those who possessed influence and property in the Island'.[53] On the other hand, in April 1883 Musgrave forwarded a petition signed by 4,677 persons, including in his view 'many very illiterate', which asked for a legislature of twenty-two, comprising eight nominated, and fourteen elected members. The latter were to be elected by those who could sign their names, and were paying poor rates on a floored and shingled dwelling, or direct taxes of not less than 20s. annually, or were in receipt of an annual salary of not less than £50.[54] This petition for representative government, which many reformers probably supported though it does not appear to have been influentially signed, had originated at a public meeting in Falmouth and was based on a pamphlet attributed to Lindo;[55] it embodied the most radical constitutional change advocated in England or Jamaica during this period, and was

53 West India Committee to Derby, 23 Dec. 1882. 22316. CO 137/507.

54 Enclosed with Musgrave to Derby, 17 Apr. 1883. Reprinted in C. 3854, p. 3. P.P. 1884 (LV). Captain Price edited a pamphlet in the introduction to which he vigorously supported these demands for representative government. *Jamaica Papers relating to proposed change in the form of government.* (London, 1884) (F(oreign and) C(ommonwealth) O(ffice) Lib(rary) P. 9446). The pamphlet was sent to members of parliament; *The Colonial Standard* estimated some 1,500 copies were circulated in England and Jamaica, the expenses of printing being met by funds raised in Jamaica.

55 *A Statement of the causes and the object of the present political agitation in Jamaica.* 20 Jan. 1883. A copy is filed with minute paper 3048, CO 137/508.

similar to the proposals of the more liberal minority of the Jamaica Association in 1876. Between the extremes of an unofficial nominated majority and representative government were the moderate proposals of Henderson[56] and Phillippo. Phillippo, for instance, suggested a mixed council of nine officials, nine members nominated for life, and nine members elected for seven years on a franchise somewhat similar to Lindo's.[57] In contrast to these proposals, there was a letter submitted to the royal commissioners by six Negroes of Kingston and allegedly read and explained to hundreds of others in and around Kingston. The writers wished for the continuance of crown government until the improved system of education[58] had borne fruit, but if popular representation was conceded, they asked that it 'should take effect in the British House of Commons by members elected in Jamaica . . . and that an executive council be instructed to carry out the routine business of Jamaica, subject to immediate control from the Imperial Parliament.'[59] William Betton, an educated Jamaican Negro, writing in February 1884 from Barbados, informed Derby that the mass of the Negroes were not opposed to crown government which, he claimed, had benefited them, particularly by expenditure on education.[60] George Baden-Powell, one of the royal commissioners of 1883, also wrote of the Negroes' preference for crown colony government. Musgrave, although recognizing faults in the existing system, at first opposed any change on the grounds that it would be for the worse; he recommended nominating further unofficials after the excitement had died down. He later modified this opinion in the light of the inexpediency of governing with a purely official council and the impossibility of finding suitable persons to accept nomination; in these circumstances he favoured the introduction of elected members, a step which in his view had advantages and disadvantages which he did not specify.[61] The

[56] See letter of 18 Jan. 1883. Reprinted in C. 3840, p. 130.

[57] J. C. Phillippo, op. cit.

[58] See pp. 22, 33–4.

[59] See letter of 17 Feb. 1883. Reprinted in C. 3840, p. 165. For further evidence of Negro opposition to the reform movement see W. P. Livingstone, *Black Jamaica. A study in evolution* (Kingston, 1899), p. 117.

[60] Betton to Derby, 9 Feb. 1884. 3439. CO 137/519.

[61] Musgrave to Herbert, 28 Aug. 1883. Reprinted in Conf(idential) Print, West Indian No. 52 A. CO 884/4.

royal commissioners gave conflicting advice. In their report they stated:

It cannot be denied that improvement and reform in the existing system of government, tending towards more representative institutions and judiciously meeting the legitimate desire of residents in Jamaica to exercise some practical influence on the raising and disposal of the local revenue, is both possible and urgently desirable. . . .[62]

They were, however, unable to agree on detailed measures. Baden-Powell proposed a legislative council of five *ex-officio* members, seven indirectly elected members, and seven nominated for seven years of whom a maximum of four would be officials. Charles Harris, the secretary to the commission and an official in the West India department, reported that Colonel Crossman, the other royal commissioner, favoured an elective franchise, and he himself supported the proposal of the West India Committee for an unofficial nominated majority.[63]

Wingfield and Herbert rejected all these proposals. In their view, to follow Musgrave's initial advice of governing temporarily with an official council would cause the colonists still greater exasperation. They accepted that in the present state of public feeling persons could not be found to accept nomination to the unofficial seats and that therefore a change in the constitution was inevitable. Wingfield rejected out of hand the West India Committee demand for an unofficial nominated majority; it would, in his view, at once inaugurate an oligarchy of planters and 'the reign of jobbery corruption and mismanagement'.[64] Herbert also considered it an 'impossible' proposal. Harris had been of the opinion that the unofficial nominated majority in Trinidad worked well. Wingfield contested this:

. . . fortunately no burning question has arisen there but if any such question should arise—e.g. a question of taking off taxes on food we should soon find the Leg: Council unmanageable.[65]

Finally, Wingfield and Herbert rejected representative

[62] C. 3840, para. 410.

[63] These three proposals are filed with or included in minute paper 11961. C O 137/512.

[64] Ibid. Minute by E.W., 11 Aug. 1883.

[65] Minute paper CO 11961. 137/512. Minute by E.W., 11 Aug. 1883.

government because of the desirability of retaining a power of legislation for the Crown. Wingfield's minute was based on this assumption, though he did not give the reasons for it. Herbert was less sure. He feared that Jamaicans might not accept a constitution in which the Crown held a balance in the legislature, in which case

we may be obliged (though I should apprehend bad consequences) to consent to something like Dr. Phillippo's constitution, reserving a very extensive control over money & administration & power of refusing to carry out votes & resolutions of the majority.[66]

This minute is the first indication in the Jamaica colonial office papers after 1875, of officials considering the possibility of a partial relaxation of crown control. Herbert's minute is particularly significant in the light of his long-held conviction of the benefits of crown colony government. Only eight months earlier he had expressed this conviction in broad terms when minuting a proposal to reform the Mauritius Council of Government on lines very similar to Phillippo's scheme for Jamaica:

In a tropical country, where the agricultural settlement of a European population is impossible, and where there is an overwhelming majority of coloured people, there can be only one safe & workable constitution—that of a 'Crown Colony' with a Government majority in the Legislature.[67]

'Safe' and 'dangerous' recur in Herbert's minutes on the crown colonies. It was the danger of religious or natural combinations which caused him to deplore the settlement of a large Indian population in Mauritius, where, he argued, 'an Elective Chamber would obviously be a very dangerous force . . .'.[68] He regarded the influence exercised by the planters over the civil service in British Guiana as 'practically dangerous', and he foresaw possible harm arising from the Combined Court impeding the colonial government in an Indian immigrant crisis. Herbert seems to have been more conscious than his colleagues of the dangers of a violent upheaval in racially mixed colonial communities with small European populations,

[66] Ibid. Minute by R.G.W.H., 16 Aug. 1883.

[67] Broome to Kimberley, No. 519, 31 Oct. 1882. 20602. CO 167/603. Minute by R.G.W.H., 6 Jan. 1883.

[68] Ibid.

and his fears seem to have centred particularly on the large Indian populations in Mauritius and British Guiana. Although he regarded the Negroes as 'the dangerous combustible material'[69] in Jamaica, the absence of a significant Indian population in that colony[70] possibly lessened his apprehension of the effects of a relaxation of crown control. How did he reconcile such a relaxation with the self-imposed duty of the Colonial Office to protect the interests of the unrepresented majority of the population? The minutes do not speak clearly, though the problem occurred to Herbert for he minuted on the Jamaica petition of April 1883 that it would be interesting to know 'how many of the poorer negroes desire that power should be placed in the hands of the planters & traders'.[71] It is possible that he thought that the Crown could reserve adequate powers of veto and of passing legislation, and that the voting qualification could be so low as to enfranchise a large proportion of the population. This latter safeguard against an oligarchy was the most striking feature of Wingfield's final recommendation, a recommendation which, in spite of his doubts that it might not satisfy Jamaican opinion, Herbert accepted as 'safe', and which became the basis of Derby's policy. Wingfield's advice was based on the assumption that a change was inevitable, and that both an unofficial nominated majority and representative government were undesirable; he therefore advised that

> . . . the not unreasonable aspirations of a certain number of the Colonists for representation in the legislature might be partially satisfied and a more vigorous and efficient though perhaps less manageable Council would be obtained by substituting elected for nominated unofficial members—the franchise being made so wide as to prevent the plantocracy and the Kingston Jews from monopolizing the seats.[72]

He recommended that all who could pay taxes and could

[69] Musgrave to Derby, No. 41, 29 Jan. 1883. 3048. CO 137/508. Minute by R.G.W.H., 21 Feb. 1883.

[70] In 1881 the Indians formed only 1.9 per cent of the total population of Jamaica (*Census* 1881, CO 140/184), compared with 68 per cent in Mauritius (*Annual Report of the Registrar-General*, 1881. CO 170/114), and 31.9 per cent in Trinidad which included those born in the colony of Indian parents. (*Abstract of Census Returns*. Council paper No. 48. 1881. CO 298/36.)

[71] Musgrave to Derby, No. 145, 17 Apr. 1883. 7831. CO 137/509. Minute by R.G.W.H., 12 May 1883.

[72] Minute paper 11961. Minute by E.W., 11 Aug. 1883. CO 137/512.

write their names should be entitled to vote; he noted in the margin that in 1881–82 there were 86,948 taxpayers and, according to the census of 1881, 115,418 persons who could read and write. A paper embodying these proposals,[73] namely a legislative council of the governor, nine official, and nine members elected by all taxpayers who could sign their names, was forwarded to Gladstone by Derby at the end of September 1883 and approved by the Cabinet on 10 November.[74] Gladstone raised only one doubt regarding Derby's proposals, namely a provision for minority representation by cumulative or double vote. Derby indicated that he would not make 'any great fight for it', but in defending it he revealed that he did not regard Grey's condition for constitutional advance in Trinidad, namely 'the diffusion of Education',[75] as having been fulfilled in Jamaica. He argued that the colony 'with its Negro population, and the impossibility of finding any counterpoise to the will of the (very ignorant) majority, in the absence of an educated class, seemed a case where some drag chain (?) of this kind might be useful'.[76] On the other hand, only a month later he was reported to have informed a deputation of Jamaica planters and others of his determination to take 'a new departure' and 'to introduce something of an elective element . . .'.[77] He had been influenced, it was reported, by his belief in the improved relations between the white and coloured populations, and in the advance of the Negro population in wealth, education, and civilization generally, which had lessened the difficulty of admitting them to a share in the government. There was, in fact, some evidence for the view that the Negro population had advanced in education. Between 1861 and 1881 the number of children attending school had risen from 33,521 to 67,402, compared with an increase in the population of school age from 110,518 to 146,934. The royal commission of 1883 estimated that 68,000 coloured, or four in five, and 22,000 adult Negroes, or one in twelve, could read and write;[78] the Jamaica inspector of education put the numbers of literate

[73] Conf. Print, West Indian No. 52. 24 Sept. 1883. CO 884/4.
[74] Gladstone Papers. Brit. Mus. Additional MSS. 44,644, p. 112.
[75] See p. 2.
[76] Derby to Gladstone, 4 Oct. 1883. Brit. Mus. Additional MSS. 44,141.
[77] *The European Mail*, West Indies edition, 17 Nov. 1883, pp. 37–39.
[78] C. 3840, para. 196.

Negroes somewhat higher. Grey and Musgrave both commented on the prosperity of the Negro cultivator and such judgements were generally accepted in the Colonial Office.[79]

Derby's detailed proposals were conveyed to the new governor, Sir Henry Norman, in a despatch of 1 December 1883[80] which was approved by Gladstone. Norman's appointment had caused alarm in Jamaica where it was felt that his military and Indian background[81] presaged an illiberal administration, but his critics did not know that in unrestrained conversation Norman referred to himself as a 'Radical':[82] he was soon to prove it. Derby, while expressing sympathy with Jamaican aspirations, rejected the demand for a representative legislature on the grounds that 'the sudden and complete transfer of control' to such a legislature would not 'secure the various interests which have to be regarded. A moderate step in advance' was preferable, such as would give Jamaicans

> a material share in the decision of those questions which most directly concern them, and more particularly in the control of finance and public expenditure.[83]

His detailed proposals differed in four respects from the scheme which he had submitted to Gladstone in the autumn of 1883. The composition of the Legislative Council was to be as proposed in that paper, namely the governor, nine officials, and nine elected members, but in order that the elected members should have a substantial power over finance, Derby proposed that in the imposition of new taxes or the appropriation of public money, except for the payment of officers then on the fixed establishment, the votes of the official members should not 'as a general rule' be recorded against the votes of

[79] The evidence suggests that the peasantry had benefited during the 1870s and early 1880s from the expansion of output of such products as bananas, coconuts, oranges, and coffee. See, for instance, *Jamaica: Now, and Fifteen Years Since.* A paper read before the Royal Colonial Institute by Sir Anthony Musgrave, 20 Apr. 1880 (F.C.O.Lib., Jamaica pamphlet No. 24).

[80] Derby to Norman, 1 Dec. 1883. Reprinted in C. 3854, p. 6.

[81] Norman had seen extensive military and political service in India. It is a measure of his ability that he was recommended as Viceroy of India in 1893 after Lord Elgin had declined the appointment; Norman also refused the offer. See Ronald Hyam, *Elgin and Churchill at the Colonial Office, 1905–1908* (London, 1968), p. 18.

[82] Lord Olivier, *Jamaica, The Blessed Island* (London, 1936), p. 231.

[83] Derby to Norman, 1 Dec. 1883. Reprinted in C. 3854, p. 7.

six or more of the unofficial members. The Crown was still to retain the sole right of initiating financial proposals. The origin of this qualified veto over financial proposals is not clear. It had been the expressed object of the West India Committee in seeking an interview with Derby in November 1883 to press that the unofficial members should have 'a legitimate control' over public expenditure, and during that interview the secretary of the Committee had suggested that for financial purposes a system similar to the British Guiana Combined Court might with advantage be adopted. Derby may have had this in mind for in his despatch he likened the financial powers which he was conceding, to those enjoyed by the Combined Court. This was misleading since in the latter the elected members outnumbered the officials by eleven to five, including the governor, and exercised complete control over the raising of revenue, and a veto over the appropriation of money subject to the passing of a septennial civil list. In fact Derby's concession was closer to that extended by Cardwell to the Malta Council of Government in 1864, namely that 'no vote of money should be pressed against the majority of the Elected Members, except under very special circumstances in which the public interests or credit were seriously at stake, and never without an immediate Report to the Secretary of State'.[84] The second modification to the original proposals submitted to Gladstone in the autumn of 1883 was Derby's intimation to the governor that there might be other questions of local interest apart from finance, for the determination of which the full number of officials need not be present. Thirdly, he instructed Norman immediately to report the circumstances whenever the united official vote was used. These last two amendments to the original scheme were similar to Derby's instructions nine months earlier to the governor of Malta, namely that not more than eight officials, excluding the governor, should attend the Council of Government; the governor would only use his casting vote against the unanimous vote of the eight elected members when important Imperial interests were involved or the revenue could not bear a proposed increased charge. In either case he was to report his actions to the secretary of state.[85] The fourth departure from

[84] Cardwell to le Marchant, No. 446, 19 Sept. 1864. 8/1070. CO 159/27.
[85] Derby to Borton, 8 Mar. 1883. Reprinted in C. 3524, p. 10.

the original scheme was Derby's instruction to Norman to appoint a royal commission to report on the franchise qualifications; this superseded his earlier proposal that all taxpayers who could sign their names should be enfranchised, with a cumulative vote to protect minority interests. The precedent of a locally appointed franchise commission was followed in Mauritius and, under different circumstances, in Trinidad. Its effect was to weaken colonial office control over the determination of the franchise qualifications. It is true that the terms of reference of the Jamaica commission were based on Derby's despatch and included the principles on which the commission's recommendations should be made.[86] It was nevertheless difficult for officials to advise radical revision of a strongly supported local recommendation, and it seems probable that although they accepted the Jamaica commission's recommendations,[87] they would have preferred a lower franchise.[88]

Herbert's judgement of local opinion had been sound, as it had been in the *Florence* affair, for the publication of Derby's despatch in Jamaica was the occasion for renewed agitation. His proposals were criticized principally on the ground that the elected members could still be outvoted by the officials, the phrase 'as a general rule' being held to be an inadequate safeguard against the use of this power. Other grievances were that the Crown still retained the power to initiate financial proposals, that the governor's presence in the Legislative Council restricted freedom of debate, that Derby's safeguarding of the salaries of officers then on the fixed establishment would protect an unnecessarily large and incompetent body of officials, and that nine members were inadequate to represent the interests of the thirteen country parishes and Kingston. Dissatisfaction on these grounds was forcibly expressed by the white and coloured members of the propertied and professional

[86] See p. 59. [87] See p. 60.

[88] There is little direct evidence in the minutes on this point but Wingfield's proposed franchise (see pp. 32–3) supports this view. In particular, both Wingfield and Herbert inclined against the simple reading and writing test which the commission recommended and which Derby favoured; Herbert minuted that he did not regard ability to read and write as an indication of political capacity. See minute paper 3340. CO 137/513. On Norman's recommendation the education test was not imposed for the first registration (see p. 60). Derby's attitude, taken with his letter to Gladstone of 4 Oct. 1883 (see p. 33), suggests that he was less sanguine than his officials regarding the political capacity of the Jamaican Negro.

community who had been prominent in the agitation after the *Florence* vote. The majority of them continued to demand an elected majority in the Legislative Council. A minority, however, believed that if liberally interpreted Derby's despatch might form the basis of an acceptable constitution. Norman tried to meet these more moderate critics on two points, namely their wish for a definition of the circumstances in which the 'general rule' might be suspended, and their request that the rights and powers of the elected members should be included in the order in council reforming the constitution. Thus he promised to submit to Derby a provision, for inclusion in the order in council amending the constitution, whereby the governor should only overrule six elected members in matters of finance after declaring such matters to be 'of paramount importance to the public interests'.[89] Norman's inability otherwise to meet even the moderate critics of Derby's despatch confirmed many politically active Jamaicans in their view that it effected no material change in the constitution, and that, in particular, the elected members could in the final event be outvoted by the officials. During January 1884 public meetings in favour of a majority of elected members were held at St. Ann's Bay, Kingston, and Mandeville, that at Mandeville numbering, on a police estimate, 300 to 400, and that at Kingston, on the estimate of the chairman of the meeting, over 700. In Norman's view, the movers of this agitation were neither very numerous nor representative; they did not represent the black population and there was, he claimed, 'a very fair proportion' of the white and coloured community who wished to give Derby's scheme a fair trial.[90] Nevertheless the extent of the unrest surprised the Colonial Office and caused Norman to propose important modifications to Derby's proposals of 1 December 1883; its character must therefore be further examined.

The diversity of those who were agitating for reform after

[89] Minute by the Governor of Jamaica, para. 16. Enclosed with Norman to Derby, 8 Jan. 1884. Reprinted in C. 3854, p. 15. The provision was included in the order in council reforming the constitution. See p. 45.

[90] Norman to Derby, No. 15, 8 Jan. 1884. 1589. CO 137/513. Other evidence suggests that some who had supported constitutional change after Nov. 1882 deprecated the renewed agitation. See, for instance, *The Colonial Standard and Jamaica Despatch*, 17 May 1884, for W. Kerr's attitude.

the autumn of 1882 has already been stressed.[91] Increasingly prominent were the solicitors such as Richard Jackson, John Palache, and Arthur Levy, the former two being coloured. But the leaders also included merchants, landed proprietors, and newspaper editors, and they embraced members of the white, coloured, and Jewish communities. Also prominent in the agitation was George Stiebel, a Negro of humble origin who in Norman's view was probably the wealthiest man in Jamaica and 'a gentleman of high respectability'. Their motives are harder to classify. In their attacks on crown government a latent Jamaican nationalism merged with personal interests; they resented colonial office control and they were confident of their ability as Jamaicans to manage their own affairs, but at the same time they were probably not unaware that private interests might be advanced by a local devolution of power, particularly over finance. Musgrave maintained that the attacks on the Public Works Department sprang from disappointment that 'jobbery and favouritism in the expenditure of public money'[92] had been prevented under crown government; the ending of the system of contracts under which planters had undertaken public works such as road repairs was a source of grievance. Similarly in their attacks on officials appointed from England personal disappointment and ambition merged with their consciousness as Jamaicans, and belief in their ability to fill adequately posts held by 'imported officials' without a stake in Jamaica. The royal commission of 1883 estimated that of seven hundred official posts, five hundred and twenty-five were held by Jamaicans by birth or domicile. Of seventeen principal officials excluding the governor, eight were Jamaican-born. The commission regarded the grievance against outside officials as not well-founded, claiming that it arose from the personal disappointment of those who, unable to find openings in trade or agriculture, or to obtain an education for the professions, sought government appointments for which they were unqualified.[93] Norman also reported astonishing pressure to give appointments to men of very mature years who had failed in other walks of life. But not all

[91] See pp. 20–1.
[92] Musgrave to Hicks-Beach, Conf., 23 June 1879. 11373. CO 137/490.
[93] C. 3840, para. 27.

those with an interest in local appointments were failures. Successful Jamaica lawyers coveted district judgeships. Both George Levy and Morrison, in written evidence to the royal commission, referred to the lack of opportunity for the sons of parents who at great sacrifice had educated their children in England, a class not referred to in the commission's report.[94] Although he did not admit so publicly, Norman seems to have regarded the agitation against outside appointments as well-founded, for in February 1886 in a private letter to Edward Fairfield, a colonial office official, he wrote:

Half our troubles in Jamaica have arisen from unjust appointments of Englishmen to the prejudice of perfectly qualified Jamaicans.[95]

Social grievances were also present: the speeches and letters of reformers refer to the *hauteur* and arrogance of officials. But 'Jamaica for the Jamaicans' was not simply the cry of those disappointed professionally or slighted socially. It reflected a consciousness of identity as Jamaicans, and a resentment against the most obvious and tangible sign of colonial office rule, the presence of officials appointed from outside the colony. The shortcomings of some of these officials reinforced the sense of grievance.[96] It is revealing that Norman should have written in July 1884 that the heads of departments available for nomination to the Legislative Council, excluding the four *ex-officio* members and four others, were 'gentlemen whose presence in the Council . . . would . . . add no real strength to the Government'.[97] If the royal commission's estimate of the number of Jamaican-born heads of departments is correct then at least three of those to whom Norman referred must have

[94] S. C. Burke's eldest son, for instance, was educated at Harrow and Jesus College, Cambridge. The grievance was not confined to Jamaica. In Trinidad, *The Port of Spain Gazette* complained of the lack of openings for those who had been educated at the best European schools. Ibid., 27 Nov. 1880.

[95] Norman to Fairfield (personal), 18 Feb. 1886. Attached to minute paper 12934. CO 137/543.

[96] For instance, Norman referred to the failings of some district court judges appointed from England. Norman to Derby, Conf., 1 Oct. 1884. 18117. CO 137/518.

[97] Norman to Derby, Conf., 4 July 1884. 12754. CO 137/516. In December 1887 he informed Knutsford that to appoint more than five officials to the Legislative Council, in addition to the four *ex-officio* members, might mean bringing in men 'not well fitted to cope with the Elected Members in discussion'. Norman to Holland, No. 424, 7 Dec. 1887. 25932. CO 137/532.

been appointed from England. In July 1885 he again commented on the very limited field of selection for nominated officials.

The agitation in Jamaica between 1881 and 1884 in favour of constitutional reform showed greater signs of political maturity than that in Trinidad and British Guiana during the 1880s and early 1890s. Possible reasons lay in Jamaica's long history of representative institutions, its politically articulate and experienced[98] white and coloured community, and the absence of a powerful planting class whose interests were best served, except when challenged, by political apathy. Agitation was facilitated by the well-developed system of parochial government which rendered it easy for a *custos* sympathetic to constitutional reform, such as Michael Solomon of St. Ann, to inspire a political meeting or to organize a petition with at least a formal parochially representative character. The role of the press in stimulating and leading agitation has already been stressed. Nor did the Jamaican reformers confine their agitation to public meetings. In their speeches they often distinguished between the freedom-loving English people and House of Commons to whom they appealed, and a despotic Colonial Office against which they protested. George Solomon, with his close English connections particularly with the West India Committee, showed a knowledge of how such appeals should be made:

> . . . we must send delegates to England, prepare a pamphlet, putting down in it all the wrongs perpetrated on us by Crown Government, send it to every member of the House of Commons, to every member of the House of Lords, to the Colonial Institute; to the West Indian committee and also to every newspaper in London . . .[99]

Their links with the House of Commons were close. It was resolved to forward the resolutions passed at the public meetings held in January 1884 to Serjeant Simon, Captain Price, and Lord Randolph Churchill. The officer administering the government stated in August 1883 that rumours had reached

[98] It is significant that a number of reformers had been members of the former House of Assembly.

[99] Report of political meeting at Kingston on 23 Jan. 1884. Encl. with Norman to Derby, No. 55, 6 Feb. 1884. 3338. CO 137/513.

him that a report of discontent in Trelawney against a rise in poor rates had been 'forwarded to England with the object of its being used in connection with questions in the House of Commons on Jamaica affairs'.[100] In April 1884 Captain Price initiated a debate on the Jamaica constitution, and his close connections with the reformers were indicated in a minute by Ashley, written after he had announced in the House of Commons further constitutional concessions to Jamaica.

There will be a lull in Jamaica for a time. Capt. Price told me yesterday that he was satisfied now there was a considerable concession made and that he should advise cessation from agitation.[101]

Reformers continued to draw encouragement from events outside Jamaica, particularly the agitation for and achievement of franchise reform in England. 'Shall it be said of English Ministers', asked the leader-writer of *The Colonial Standard*, 'that they are anxious to extend the franchise to the utmost possible limit in the Mother Country, while they refuse to give to the people of Jamaica an instalment of real representative power?'[102] Sympathy between Jamaica and Ireland was mutual. A pledge of sympathy and assistance was sent to reformers by the Peckham branch of the 'Irish National League' whose president, W. J. Hurst, wrote: 'The Irish people and the people of Jamaica are struggling for the same identical rights . . .'.[103] Although reformers repudiated Irish methods of violence, the more extreme among them favoured non-violent methods of resistance. As early as December 1882[104] Musgrave had noted that attempts were being made to induce the black

[100] Gamble (O.A.G.) to Derby, No. 273, 23 Aug. 1883. 15659. CO 137/510. The Kingston Standing Committee, formed in the spring of 1884, kept Price and Simon informed of Jamaican affairs through a London intermediary, Alexander Turnbull. The secretary claimed that sixty members of parliament were 'whipped' for an expected debate on Jamaica in March 1884. *The Colonial Standard and Jamaica Despatch*, 16 Apr. 1884.

[101] Norman to Derby, No. 119, 29 Mar. 1884. 6827. CO 137/514. Minute by E.A., 30 Apr. 1884.

[102] *The Colonial Standard and Jamaica Despatch*, 29 Mar. 1884. The same argument was used by Capt. Price, op. cit., pp. v–vi.

[103] Report of secretary of Kingston Standing Committee, *The Colonial Standard and Jamaica Despatch*, 16 Apr. 1884.

[104] Musgrave to Kimberley, Conf., 22 Dec. 1882. 717. CO 137/507. See also *Gall's Country News*, 26 Jan. 1883. Also letter of E. G. Barrett, *The Colonial Standard and Jamaica Despatch*, 7 Feb. 1883.

population to resist the payment of direct parochial taxes. Reformers pleaded for that equality of treatment with the European-settled parts of the Empire which Derby had rejected in his letter to Gladstone.[105] It is hard to judge the representativeness of the Jamaica reformers. There is no doubt, however, of the political sophistication of their argument and agitation. The former is paralleled in this period only, within the writer's knowledge, in Mauritius. The latter was to win for Jamaica further constitutional concessions.

Norman quickly set the tone of his liberal administration by implementing his promise to the moderate critics of Derby's despatch.[106] He wrote privately to the Colonial Office shortly after his arrival, recommending that the concession to the votes of six elected members in financial affairs should be included in the order in council reforming the constitution, the governor's power to override their veto being limited to cases which he declared to be of 'paramount importance to the public interests';[107] in his despatch Derby had merely stated that this power would not be exercised 'as a general rule'. Norman's proposal did not meet the main grievance of Jamaicans, namely the retention of the official majority. He approached this question cautiously, advising against an elected or unofficial majority until he had received the report of the franchise commission.[108] But with this report before him he informed Derby that although he was still opposed to granting 'absolutely' an unofficial or elected majority, he would prefer at first to appoint only six of the full number of nine officials, leaving himself the power in 'real necessity' to call up three more officials, though he hoped this necessity would not arise. Norman thus proposed to place the elected members, at least temporarily, in a majority of two over the combined votes of the governor and six officials. He argued that the concession

[105] See p. 26. [106] See p. 37.

[107] The phrase occurs in minute by the Governor of Jamaica, para. 16, encl. with Norman to Derby, 8 Jan. 1884. Reprinted in C. 3854, p. 15. In Norman's view, with which Derby agreed, such cases might have arisen when legislation of vital importance to the colony or for the maintenance of Imperial interests was under consideration. See minute by E.W., 30 Jan. 1884, on this despatch, for reference to Norman's private letter. Minute paper 1589. CO 137/513.

[108] For Derby's proposal to appoint the commission see p. 36; for its report see pp. 59–61.

would 'gratify those who desire a greater share of Representation' and would discourage 'mere factious opposition'.[109] One of the leading aims of Norman's governorship was to overcome the view of the elected members that it was their duty to consistently oppose the government. He sought at all times to govern with their active assistance and co-operation, and he probably saw this provisional grant to them of legislative power as an essential condition for this. His proposal had other advantages. He informed Derby that it would enable him both to limit membership of the Council to leading officials, and to protect as many Jamaican-born officials as possible from the treatment which they would receive socially and in the press if they voted with the government against the elected members. The effect of Norman's proposals was that the Legislative Council would consist of the governor, four *ex-officio* members, two nominated officials, and nine elected members, thus giving the latter a majority of two over the governor's original vote and the votes of six officials. The secretary of state would retain the power to secure an official majority by appointing three more nominated officials, thus raising them to a maximum of five and the official side, excluding the governor, to a maximum of nine.

These proposals raised two considerations, namely the ability of the governor to administer the colony without an official majority in the Legislative Council, and the ease with which it could if necessary be restored. Norman seemed confident of ordinarily being able to manage the Legislative Council without an official majority, but he recognized 'the possible obloquy' which he would incur if he restored it. Neither issue, on the evidence of the colonial office minutes, was carefully considered by Wingfield or Herbert. Wingfield, it is true, doubted if the arrangement would work, for he minuted that he feared it would 'not be very long' before Norman would have to appoint three more officials, thus incurring 'great personal unpopularity . . .'.[110] Nevertheless he advised acceptance of the proposal out of deference for Norman's opinion. Herbert's primary consideration was also to support Norman. 'He has', he wrote, 'a difficult work before him . . .' and it

[109] Norman to Derby, No. 68, 18 Feb. 1884. 4150. CO 137/513.
[110] Ibid. Minute by E.W., 12 Mar. 1884.

would be 'safest' to adopt his proposals.[111] Norman, Wingfield, and Herbert seem to have gravely underestimated the political difficulty of restoring the official majority. Yet only eighteen months after his proposals were implemented Norman informed Sir Frederick Stanley, the secretary of state, that it would be inexpedient to call up his reserve of nominated members in order to defeat amendments to a pension bill since it 'would lead to a serious collision and possibly to the resignation of the elected members and agitation throughout the Colony'.[112] Similarly Herbert advised Lord Granville, Stanley's successor, in February 1886 that to appoint the full number of officials[113] 'would certainly lead to a serious crisis, perhaps attended with disorder. The Elected members would resign their seats, & others would not be found to replace them. This Constitution therefore requires the most careful handling.'[114] It is probable that in March 1884 administrative expediency obscured these longer-term considerations. Jamaica had been in a state of political turmoil for over two years, and the desire in the Colonial Office to reach a settlement must have been considerable. The strength of the agitation against Derby's original proposals had surprised Harris, the best-informed official on Jamaica affairs in the West India department. The 'friends of Jamaica' were still active in the House of Commons. Nor was administrative expediency the only consideration. Derby's speeches, minutes, and letters, and his despatch of 1 December, reflected a willingness to consider new ways of adapting crown government to meet demands from the colonies for a greater share in the management of local affairs, and it was probably in the light of this policy that Derby and his officials also regarded Norman's proposal. But on the evidence of the minutes the overriding consideration which prompted them to accept Norman's advice was their wish to support the governor in a difficult situation.

The Order in Council of 19 May 1884[115] reforming the consti-

[111] Norman to Derby, No. 68, 18 Feb. 1884. 4150. CO 137/513. Minute by R.G.W.H., 14 Mar. 1884.

[112] Norman to Stanley, Conf., 13 Oct. 1885. 19170. CO 137/523.

[113] Herbert was assuming that the three additional nominated members would be officials. See footnote 9, p. 71.

[114] Minute paper 1817. Minute by R.G.W.H., 15 Feb. 1886. CO 137/529.

[115] P(rivy) C(ouncil) 2/318.

tution is evidence for the view that the Colonial Office was guided not only by immediate administrative expediency but also by a liberal wish to meet Jamaican aspirations, since it contains concessions which, on the evidence of the colonial office papers and the Jamaica press, were not advocated by official or unofficial opinion in the colony. As Norman had requested, the Order in Council defined more precisely than Derby's despatch of 1 December the conditions under which the governor could overrule the votes of any six of the elected members in financial matters, namely by a declaration that the passing of the measure was 'of paramount importance to the public interest'.[116] The same clause also provided more detailed safeguards for the salary and pension rights of officials, and a schedule to the Order in Council specifically secured the salaries of certain principal public officers. Clause 44 of the Order in Council introduced a second important modification to Derby's original proposals of December 1883. The use of the united official majority on other questions of local interest, which Derby had hoped would not always be necessary, was more closely circumscribed, the votes of the *ex-officio* and nominated members only being recorded on any question against the unanimous vote of the nine elected members when the governor declared the decision of it to be 'of paramount importance to the public interest'.[117] It is not clear from the colonial office papers whether this clause originated in the Office or with Norman. It was unimportant so long as the officials were in a minority, but in the event of the full number of nominated members being appointed it strengthened significantly the rights of the elected members. In his despatch of 1 December 1883, Derby had merely instructed that not all officials need attend when questions of local interest other than finance were being determined. Clause 44 applied to all questions including finance and it limited more precisely the use of the full official majority. Derby made a further concession in the composition of the Council, preferring not to specify in the Order in Council whether the nominated members should be officials or unofficials, since he considered it 'advisable not to preclude the appointment of an unofficial person should it hereafter be

[116] Ibid., S. 43. The wording was Norman's. See p. 37.
[117] S. 44, Order in Council, 19 May 1884.

found possible or desirable to relax to that extent the control of the Crown over the Colonial Legislature . . .'.[118] Derby, while giving Norman full authority to appoint provisionally the full number of nominated members 'in case of necessity',[119] expressed the hope that such a situation would not be likely to arise. He also hoped that it would 'be rarely or never necessary' for the governor to override the votes of the elected members by a declaration of paramount importance, though it was his duty to do so 'if in his opinion the public interest absolutely requires it'.[120] In short, the Jamaica Legislative Council was to comprise the governor with an original and casting vote, four *ex-officio* members, two nominated officials, and nine elected members, any six of whom could veto a financial proposal unless the governor made a declaration of paramount public importance. Assuming the governor only used his original vote, the elected majority of two could be reversed by the nomination of three more officials, though the governor could only then override the unanimous vote of the nine elected members in all matters by a similar declaration. He was bound in each case to report to the secretary of state the reasons for a declaration of paramount public importance. He retained the sole power of initiating financial proposals. The Order in Council reserved to the secretary of state the power to alter the balance of the Council by nominating unofficial in place of official members. By conceding the elective principle, a provisional elected majority, and a qualified veto in financial questions to any six, and in all questions to nine, elected members, Derby and his officials showed a willingness born of both principle and expediency to adapt the crown colony system of government to meet local political demands. They did so in a mainly hopeful spirit. Excepting the concession in 1871 of indirectly elected members to the General Council of the Leeward Islands, their proposals represented a 'new departure' in tropical crown colony government.

[118] Derby to Norman, Conf., 28 May 1884. 4431. CO 137/513.

[119] Derby to Norman, No. 161, 28 May 1884. 4431. CO 137/513. Compare the phrases 'real necessity' and 'in case of necessity' in Norman to Derby, No. 68, 18 Feb. 1884. 4150. CO 137/513.

[120] Derby to Norman, No. 161, 28 May 1884. 4431. CO 137/513.

2

THE WORKING OF SEMI-REPRESENTATIVE GOVERNMENT

A shirking of colonial office responsibility?

DERBY had defended his decision not to grant representative government to Jamaica on the grounds that 'the sudden and complete transfer of control' to a legislative council with a majority of elected members would not 'secure the various interests which have to be regarded'.[1] It is probable that in 1884 one of Britain's most important interests in Jamaica was strategic. From the late 1870s the British government had given increasingly close scrutiny to the problems of Imperial defence of which access to secure coaling stations was one of the most pressing. In the view of the Colonial Defence Committee, appointed in 1878,[2] the strategic significance of Jamaica lay primarily in the importance of Port Royal both as a coaling station and, more generally, as 'the principal naval arsenal and depot in the West Indies'.

The Defence Committee, in consideration of the value of the commerce between Great Britain and North America and the West Indies,[3] as well as the position of Jamaica on the direct route to Panama[4] and the Pacific, placed Port Royal fourth in the list of importance of the coaling stations of Her Majesty's ships abroad.[5]

[1] See p. 34.

[2] Not to be confused with the permanent inter-departmental Defence Committee set up in 1885.

[3] The Carnarvon Commission estimated British trade with the West Indies at £21,000,000 annually. Third and Final Report of the Royal Commissioners appointed to inquire into the Defence of British Possessions and Commerce Abroad. 1882. Carnarvon Papers. PRO 30/6. 126.

[4] In January 1881 a French company began construction of the Panama Canal, a project which it finally abandoned at the end of 1888. The Canal was completed in 1914 by United States enterprise; in the intervening years the possibility of its completion remained an important strategic consideration. See, for instance, p. 272.

[5] Fourth Report of a Colonial Defence Committee. Reprinted in Conf. Print, Misc. No. 35c. CO 885/4.

Similarly the Royal Commission on the Defence of British Possessions and Commerce Abroad, more commonly known as the Carnarvon Commission, which reported in 1881 and 1882, included Port Royal among nine first-class indispensable coaling stations. It stressed that Jamaica was the nearest British territory to the Panama Canal, five hundred and sixty miles distant, and that Port Royal was 'the best available station for observing the Panama Canal, Cuba, and the smaller South American Republics . . .'.[6] These considerations were summarized for the Cabinet in 1884 by the inspector-general of fortifications who recommended expenditure of over £100,000 to fortify Port Royal:

Jamaica is the centre of British interests in the West Indies, and will become a place of great importance in the event of the projected canal being made through the Isthmus of Panama. The harbour of Port Royal, where our Naval Establishments have been placed, must be thoroughly protected.[7]

Local opinion was hostile to the fortification of Port Royal, Norman, for instance, reporting in August 1887 that Jamaicans feared it might lead to an attack on the colony. He saw no chance of the Legislative Council agreeing to a colonial contribution towards completing the defensive arrangements. Taken with Herbert's doubts concerning the loyalty of Jamaicans,[8] these considerations were strong reasons for the maintenance of ultimate crown control in Jamaica, and although they are not spelt out in the colonial office minutes, it is a reasonable assumption that they influenced policy. This probability is strengthened by the fact that Sir Henry Holland, later Lord Knutsford,[9] who was secretary of state for the colonies from 1887 to 1892, was a member of the Carnarvon

[6] Third and Final Report of the Carnarvon Commission. See footnote 3 for reference.

[7] Summary of the Recommendations of the Inspector-General of Fortifications. Reprinted in cabinet paper, Defence of Colonial Possessions. No. 13. 1884. Cab. 37/12.

[8] See p. 71. It is probable that as well as the *Florence* affair Herbert had in mind the advocacy in Jamaica in the early 1880s of annexation to the United States, from which country the Carnarvon Commission considered the main threat to the West Indies 'unquestionably' came. For annexationist proposals see, for instance, *The Colonial Standard and Jamaica Despatch*, 15 Dec. 1881, 19 Dec. 1881, and 24 Dec. 1881.

[9] Referred to throughout this study as Knutsford.

Commission. The geographical importance of Jamaica when the Panama Canal was completed was touched on by E. R. Wodehouse, Conservative member for Bath, in the House of Commons debate on Jamaica on 25 April 1884.

The *Florence* affair raised a second Imperial interest, namely the fulfilment by Jamaica of what the British government regarded as the colony's share of the international obligations of the Empire. Musgrave had acted under legislation framed to prevent a possible breach of neutrality by Jamaica through the use of her ports for the shipment of arms. The attitude of the nominated unofficial members, and of Jamaican opinion in general, indicated that a legislature not controlled by the Crown might be unwilling to meet the cost of fulfilling obligations which Jamaicans regarded as Imperial and not colonial. Officials remembered the *Florence* affair when considering proposals for a further relaxation of crown control in Jamaica.[10]

A third Imperial interest, which is touched on most lightly in the colonial office minutes, concerned the public credit of Jamaica, and the safety of British capital in, and its attraction to, the island. In the discussions leading up to the constitutional changes of 1884 the first two points were raised by Baden-Powell, one of the members of the royal commission of 1883, but there is no reference in the official papers to the third point before 1887. Baden-Powell asked whether Jamaica, if she were given as some Jamaicans desired 'the whole of English Self Government on a Representative basis' with only an Imperial veto over legislation, would undertake the consequent 'responsibilities and charges' including the maintenance of public order. If she did so, he asked, 'what would be the effect of [sic] her credit in the money market or on the value of property in the Island?'[11] Phillippo framed his constitutional scheme with this consideration in mind, emphasizing that the rights of British bondholders must be safeguarded by a stable government which would secure the payment of interest and principal on public loans. The writer has seen no evidence of the extent to which Derby and his officials were guided by such

[10] See, for instance, Blake to Ripon, No. 74, 13 Mar. 1894. 5825. CO 137/559. Minute by E.W., 27 Apr. 1894.

[11] Memorandum by G. Baden-Powell, 3 July 1883. Filed with minute paper 11961. CO 137/512.

considerations,[12] but they were brought before the Colonial Office again in 1887 by Edward Noel Walker, the retiring colonial secretary, who wrote privately to Wingfield opposing the possible grant of representative government to Jamaica. He asked whether by irrevocably parting with the official majority in the Legislative Council, Jamaica was not breaking faith with its public creditors who had lent money

> on the understanding and in the guarantee of the Crown's majority and powers to secure the Colony's obligations and liabilities being properly met and its creditors fully protected? I think that they would hardly have invested in the securities of a West Indian Government having to reckon with an Elected majority in its Legislature . . .[13]

Herbert's marginal comment, 'Something in this', does not indicate that he had previously regarded it as a leading consideration. But he minuted that there was force in the argument that the public creditor should be protected by 'securing some control in "matters of paramount public importance" such as repudiation, expenditure causing risk of insolvency, etc. . . .'.[14] The wording and context of Herbert's minute, and the subsequent lack of reference to this point in the colonial office papers, suggest that the safeguarding of Jamaica's public credit from repudiation of debt or bankruptcy did not figure prominently in officials' consideration of constitutional change in Jamaica. There were more immediate though less damaging threats to the public credit of Jamaica. Thus among the positions which the Colonial Office defended most strongly was the security of existing official salaries and pensions.[15] They did so not only to protect the morale and independence of the service, but because they regarded an attack on the salaries or pensions granted or pledged to public officers as an indefensible breach of contract, damaging to the public credit, which it was of

[12] But see p. 52 for Ashley's reference in the House of Commons to the danger of disturbing industrial interests.

[13] Walker to Wingfield (personal), 29 Oct. 1887. Filed with minute paper 22215. CO 137/533.

[14] Norman to Holland, No. 345, 18 Oct. 1887. 22316. CO 137/532. Minute by R.G.W.H., 7 Nov. 1887.

[15] See, for example, Granville to Norman, No. 36, 18 Mar. 1886. N. 1817. CO 137/529.

paramount public importance to check.[16] More generally, Knutsford in December 1891 informed Sir Henry Blake, the governor of Jamaica, that if the rejection of a bill or vote involved a breach of faith by the colonial government 'its passing would under certain circumstances be rightly held to be of paramount importance in the public interest'.[17]

There is no evidence that Derby's decision to retain crown control in Jamaica was influenced by the wish to create conditions favourable to private investment. The point seems to have been raised officially for the first time in connection with Jamaica by Norman in April 1887. He informed the Legislative Council that from all he had heard funds for railway construction were not likely to be forthcoming to any extent 'unless capitalists are pretty well assured that the existing constitution of this Colony is likely to be stable in its principal features'.[18] Norman himself does not seem to have been greatly influenced by this view for only six months later he recommended representative government for Jamaica. Norman's successor, Sir Henry Blake, attached more importance to it, and it was one of the arguments advanced in the Colonial Office against constitutional change in 1894.[19] It seems possible that the Colonial Office might also in certain circumstances have regarded fiscal questions to be of paramount importance. For instance, in December 1893 Ripon and Wingfield agreed that the elected members might be overridden if they insisted on imposing a 20 per cent *ad valorem* tariff, which officials regarded as departing from Gladstonian fiscal canons; the imposition of a tariff might also have been a breach of British treaty obligations though this specific point is not raised on the Jamaica papers.

The evidence is more conclusive regarding the attitude of Derby and his successors to the maintenance of law and order, which was both a local interest and a condition for the protection of Imperial interests. The Colonial Office had historical and more recent reasons for believing that quiet conditions could not be taken for granted in Jamaica. Musgrave referred in January 1883 to the excitable character of the population

16 For instance, Stanley to Norman, Conf., 28 Aug. 1885. 13151. CO 137/522.

17 Knutsford to Blake, Conf., 7 Dec. 1891. 10289. CO 137/545.

18 Address to Legislative Council, 13 Apr. 1887. Encl. with Norman to Holland, No. 100, 18 Apr. 1887. 9369. CO 137/530.

19 See p. 86. For Blake's views see pp. 77, 85, 87, 88.

and, in particular, to the inflammatory effect of the press and public meetings on the Negro population; he regarded the agitation after the *Florence* vote in November 1882 'as likely to be productive of mischief as any "Underhill meetings" in 1865'.[20] Although the Colonial Office was not easily alarmed by reports of racial unrest, they were nevertheless conscious of a possible breakdown of law and order. Herbert regarded the Negroes as 'dangerous combustible material'. Ashley, speaking in the House of Commons on 25 April 1884, referred to the history, and different races and interests of Jamaica, and he defended the retention of crown control on the grounds that there 'was too much risk of collision between classes—too much risk of excitement and agitation . . .'. Similarly he opposed a low franchise on the grounds that it would lead to riot and bloodshed and to 'the disturbance of all social and industrial interests'.[21] Two months later he expressed general agreement with a despatch in which Musgrave stressed the degree of animosity of white and coloured towards the black population in Jamaica, which was unlike anything he had experienced elsewhere in the West Indies. If Norman formed a similar impression of racial tensions in Jamaica he did not communicate it officially to the Colonial Office, but Blake, his successor, shared Musgrave's view. In several despatches and private letters he referred to the possibility of a recurrence 'to some extent' of the events of 1865.[22] Blake was most apprehensive of the relations between the coloured and black population. He argued that the latter hated and distrusted the former; yet paradoxically the coloured man had 'an extraordinary power' over the black man 'of arousing a feeling of vague but dangerous discontent by passionate addresses on the colour question and appeals to consanguinity'.[23] On the whole the Colonial Office discounted Blake's fears. In December 1892 Wingfield minuted: 'I have long noticed from his private letters and from hints in despatches that Sir H. Blake has the fear of black riots on the brain—my own belief is that the slightest display of firm

[20] Musgrave to Derby, No. 41, 29 Jan. 1883. 3048. CO 137/508.

[21] *Hansard*, Third Series (287), 714–15.

[22] For example, private letter to W. A. Baillie Hamilton, 6 Sept. 1892. Filed with minute paper 18749. CO 137/550. Blake to Ripon, Conf., 24 Aug. 1894. 15484. CO 137/563.

[23] Blake to Ripon, Conf., 29 Apr. 1895. 8454. CO 137/565.

determination to resist the bullying of the Kingston lawyers and the scurrilous press which they manipulate would rally the negroes round the Government.'[24]

In short, it is argued that the interests for the preservation of which Derby and his successors believed crown control to be essential and which, apart from the first, they specifically affirmed in despatches,[25] included Britain's strategic interests, the fulfilment of international obligations, the maintenance of law and order, and the safeguarding of Jamaica's public credit from breach of faith, of which the protection of officials' salaries and pensions, and the prevention of repudiation of debt, were aspects. The harmony of Jamaica's fiscal system with well-established British principles, the safety of British capital, and the maintenance of conditions which would attract it to Jamaica, were not publicly or specifically affirmed by officials or secretaries of state as interests of paramount importance, but what evidence there is suggests that these too were regarded by some, both in and outside the Colonial Office, as necessitating crown control. Thus baldly to list British interests is to give the conduct of colonial policy in this period a precision and a logic which it lacked, for it suggests that officials and secretaries of state thought consistently and precisely in these terms. This was far from so, for in the pressure of day-to-day administration expediency often obscured principle. On the other hand, between 1884 and 1895 each of these considerations did at one time or another influence colonial office determination to retain ultimate legislative control in Jamaica. On the evidence of Jamaica's history the maintenance of these interests was, in general, unlikely to conflict with the concession of 'substantial power and substantial responsibility' to a provisional majority of elected members, though the *Florence* affair and Norman's view of Jamaican opinion on the undesirability of naval works at Port Royal suggested possible conflict between Imperial and colonial interests. A further possible clash of interest was raised by Blake in April 1895 when he noted 'a strong movement on the part of the more prominent Coloured people to prevent by any means in their power the introduction of white settlers or

[24] Blake to Ripon, No. 366, 12 Nov. 1892. 23222. CO 137/551. Minute by E.W., 4 Dec. 1892.

[25] See below, pp. 72, 75–6. Also pp. 50–1.

white capitalists'.[26] But two British responsibilities remained which impinged more closely on local interests, namely the responsibility of the Colonial Office for the general conduct of Jamaica's finances, and for the welfare of its unrepresented classes; the former was regarded in the Colonial Office as a condition for the public credit and good government of Jamaica, and the latter had been the grounds for the extension and maintenance of crown control in the decades before 1880. It is improbable that the close exercise by the Colonial Office of either responsibility would have been compatible with the smooth working of semi-representative government, but the matter was not put to the test; the Colonial Office was inactive in the practical discharge of both responsibilities.

Derby's despatches and the Order in Council reforming the constitution did not clearly define the division of financial power between governor, elected members, and Colonial Office; much therefore depended on interpretation and practice. Under Derby's scheme, Norman retained the sole power of initiating financial proposals, though Herbert hoped that the elected members would be a force for economy against the possibly extravagant spending habits of a governor with Indian experience. The power of the elected members in matters of finance depended partly on the degree to which Norman deferred to their views in framing his financial and legislative proposals, and partly on his interpretation of the conditions in which he might overrule the votes of six of them by a declaration of paramount public importance, and, in the event of their being unanimous or nearly so, by the appointment of the full number of nominated members.[27] In both cases Norman's attitude was shaped by his determination to govern with the co-operation of the elected members. Friendly and courteous, he brought to this task not only force of character and intellectual distinction, but the essential qualities of tact, patience, conciliatoriness, fairness, an open mind, and a self-confessed sympathy for representative institutions. Although the elected members had been chosen on a platform of opposition to the government, Norman quickly tried to identify them with it;

[26] Blake to Ripon, Conf., 29 Apr. 1895. 8454. CO 137/565.

[27] The elected members in fact also encountered practical difficulties in the control of expenditure which are analysed on p. 258.

he was careful to consult them closely before measures were drafted or introduced, and his officials freely advised them on the technical details of legislation. Interpreting the elected members' powers most liberally, he correspondingly circumscribed his own. He regarded his power to call up his reserve of nominated members as a measure of last resort. Only once did he obtain the secretary of state's authority to use it, in order to defeat a possible attack on the salaries and pensions of certain officials. But he subsequently concluded that in this case its use was inexpedient since it 'would lead to serious collision and possibly to the resignation of the elected members and agitation throughout the Colony'.[28] He deferred to the views of the elected members in all local matters, financial or otherwise, when they were unanimous or nearly so, and on no occasion did he overrule the votes of six or more of them on a financial question. There were sharp conflicts, particularly on official salaries and pensions; but the weight accorded by Norman to the views of the elected members, who with Norman's encouragement introduced important legislation, and the freedom of voting which he allowed his officials, did much to dispel the tradition, born of representative and crown government, that the role of the unofficial members was to oppose. Norman saw more clearly than his successors that this achievement was an essential condition for the working of semi-representative government.

The Colonial Office under successive secretaries of state fully supported Norman's policy[29] by acting in a liberal spirit towards Jamaica, both in the control which they exercised over the governor and in the respect which they accorded the views of the elected members. They accepted Norman's major recommendations, and on no occasion during his governorship did they advise disallowance of a Jamaica law or the use of the governor's overriding powers. Herbert was particularly insistent in the autumn of 1884 that the secretary of state should not commit himself on such matters as the size of the civil establishment, education, and Indian immigration until

[28] Norman to Stanley, Conf., 13 Oct. 1885. 19170. CO 137/523.

[29] Among officials Harris was noticeably more lukewarm than his colleagues regarding the constitutional changes in Jamaica. By 1888 he was of the view that Norman had gone 'too far and too fast' in Jamaica.

the views of the elected members were known. When these views were clearly and strongly expressed on major issues of local policy, they normally proved as decisive with Derby as with Norman. The same spirit informed the administrations of his successors until 1895. In 1889 Charles Farquharson, an elected member, acknowledged that Knutsford had been 'scrupulously careful to allow the Legislature a free hand when dealing with questions entirely of local interest and importance . . .'.[30] Similarly Knutsford's successor, Lord Ripon, left such questions as free and compulsory education, the reimposition of a literacy test for voting, the postponement of railway extensions, and the possible repurchase of the Jamaica railway from private ownership, to the decision of the colonial legislature and government. Although Jamaica administrative reports revealed what seemed to officials serious defects, they made no attempt to enforce their views. On the sensitive issue of the pensions of public officers, Herbert admitted in December 1890: '. . . it is not possible in Jamaica to enforce such principles & details in regard to pensions as we may think desirable'.[31] The same liberal spirit informed the surrender by Derby of the secretary of state's supervision of the Jamaica estimates. In December 1884 he informed Norman that the formal approval and sanction of the estimates would be discontinued 'in conformity with the spirit in which the Constitution is now being worked . . .'. The estimates would still be sent to the secretary of state so that he could comment on 'points of financial or general policy for the supervision of which H.M. Govt. will continue to be responsible'.[32] No comment was made on the Jamaica estimates until January 1893, when an actual deficit of about £100,000 in 1892–93 and an estimated deficit of £78,000 for 1893–94 prompted Ripon to ask for an explanation for 'a financial policy which prima facie appears unsound and perilous to the financial position of the Colony'.[33] In October 1893 he informed Blake that it would have been more prudent to have financed this deficit from increased taxation,[34] and in

[30] Farquharson to Knutsford, 14 Feb. 1889. 3259. CO 137/541.

[31] Blake to Secretary of State for the Colonies, No. 194, 15 May 1890. 10871. CO 137/543. Minute by R.G.W.H., 26 Dec. 1890.

[32] Derby to Norman, No. 367, 1 Dec. 1884. 19164. CO 137/518.

[33] Ripon to Blake, No. 121, 1 June 1893. 8116. CO 137/555.

[34] Blake had met the deficit by drawing on the accumulated surplus.

June 1894 he enquired how the estimated deficit for the current year was to be met. These comments were not followed up by the Colonial Office, the position up to 1895 being accurately summarized by Robert Meade, a colonial office official, who minuted in July 1890: '. . . we have largely ceased to exercise financial control over Jamaica . . .'.[35]

Further evidence of the transfer of power in financial matters from the Colonial Office and governor to the Legislative Council is provided by the Jamaica railway agreement of 1889; the agreement provided for the sale of the government-owned railway to an American syndicate who undertook to extend it by one hundred and twenty miles. The preliminary agreement, negotiated by Norman in November 1888, was criticized by the Crown Agents as one which the Jamaica government could not entertain 'with the least regard to prudence',[36] though it was supported by Norman, eight of the elected members, and the attorney-general. The agreement raised two issues for the Colonial Office. Firstly, were the elected members representative of Jamaican opinion, and secondly, should that opinion be deferred to on a major financial matter, even if it was thought to be mistaken? On the first point, Wingfield minuted and Knutsford agreed:

> . . . it is out of the question for the S. of State now to assume that the elected members are not really representatives of the public opinion of the Colony.[37]

On the second point, he argued that if the scheme was 'injurious to the interests of the Colony' the law embodying it could be disallowed, but that 'on a question not affecting Imperial interests it would be only in very exceptional circumstances that Her Majesty would be advised to disallow a measure approved by the Colonial Legislature'.[38] Wingfield regarded the scheme unfavourably, and he reconciled this with

[35] Blake to Knutsford, No. 275, 14 July 1890. 14832. CO 137/543. Minute by R.M., 31 July 1890.

[36] Crown Agents to Colonial Office, 22 Dec. 1888. 25302. CO 137/537. In consideration for the Jamaica railway the syndicate offered £100,000 cash and £700,000 of second mortgage bonds secured on the earnings of the whole railway. The bonds ranked after £1,500,000 of first mortgage bonds, in the manipulation of which, the Crown Agents argued, the promoters hoped to make their profit.

[37] C. S. Farquharson to Knutsford, 14 Feb. 1889. 3259. CO 137/541. Minute by E.W., 16 Feb. 1889.

[38] Ibid.

his respect for the Jamaica constitution by advising the imposition of conditions unacceptable to the American syndicate. He was overruled by Herbert who recommended limiting the role of the Colonial Office to that of adviser, 'leaving to the Legislative Council the ultimate responsibility of deciding both on principles and on details'.[39] This was the course followed by Knutsford who declined to press any amendments to the law embodying the final agreement: '. . . we may take it', he minuted, 'that the Legislature has assumed the responsibility of the Law as it stands . . .'.[40] In fact it was not a responsibility which Knutsford could transfer, for as long as Jamaica did not enjoy responsible government he remained ultimately responsible for its finances. What Knutsford had conceded to the elected members was the power to determine a major issue of financial policy for which he alone remained responsible. It was on such insecure foundations that the structure of semi-representative government in Jamaica was raised.

A similar divergence in the theory and practice of colonial policy may be seen in the exercise after 1884 of the secretary of state's responsibility for the welfare of those Jamaicans not directly represented in the Legislative Council. The exercise of this responsibility was compatible with semi-representative government on one of three assumptions. The first was that the secretary of state would if necessary intervene directly in the government of the colony, either by instructing the governor to override the votes of the elected members or by advising the disallowance of colonial legislation. Apart from Ashley's speech in the House of Commons[41] the writer has seen no evidence that such intervention was in the mind of Derby and his advisers when they reserved to the Crown the power to carry necessary legislation. If it was, their purpose soon weakened for it was in conflict with the spirit in which they sought to work the constitution of 1884. Between 1884 and 1895 no secretary of state implemented an important policy decision in opposition to the Legislative Council on the grounds of the welfare of Jamaica's unrepresented classes. Rather the Colonial

[39] Hocking (Jamaica attorney-general) to Herbert, 5 Mar. 1889. 4871A. CO 137/541. Minute by R.G.W.H., 6 Mar. 1889.

[40] Blake to Knutsford, Conf., 13 Aug. 1889. 17334. CO 137/539. Minute by K., 2 Sept. 1889.

[41] See p. 52.

Office seems to have regarded the Legislative Council as representative of Jamaican opinion in the widest sense. Such a view was tenable on one of two further assumptions: either all classes were represented directly in the Council, or its elected members were sensitive to the welfare of those Jamaicans who had no vote. The first of these assumptions raises the question of the franchise.

Initially Wingfield had thought in terms of a wide franchise[42], but the decision to refer the matter to a locally appointed royal commission took the question largely out of the hands of the Colonial Office, although it is true that the commission's terms of reference followed closely the wording of Derby's despatch of 1 December. Norman instructed it to report what franchise would 'constitute a reasonably large Body of Electors, qualified by knowledge and education to form an intelligent judgment on public affairs and so ensure the fair representation of all interests . . .'. He further informed the commission that '. . . a large class of illiterate voters or ignorant Voters' should not be enfranchised, but so long as this was avoided the representation should be 'really popular'.[43] The commission included no officials; five of its seven members were *custodes*, and the large majority of the commission was sympathetic to reform. It recommended enfranchising all males of full age who were either the occupiers of a house assessed for poor rates and who paid on it, with other taxable property which they owned, public and parochial taxes of not less than £1 annually, or who were the owners of taxable property on which they paid not less than £1 10s. annually. Aliens were excluded.[44] A comparison of these qualifications with those for electing members to the House of Assembly before 1865 is difficult, for the latter, although in some respects lower, were restricted by other provisions.[45] On balance, the qualifications recommended by

[42] See pp. 32–3.

[43] *Jamaica Gazette*, 24 Jan. 1884. CO 141/47.

[44] The report of the royal commission is reprinted in C. 4140, p.15. P.P. 1884 (LV).

[45] Until 1859 the franchise qualification of a minimum £6 freehold, commonly estimated at one or two acres of cultivated land and a hut, was subject to a 12s. hereditament tax which had to be paid before the vote could be exercised. In 1857 the tax was abolished, and in 1859 the franchise qualifications were extended to include, for instance, minimum annual payment of taxes of any kind of 20s.; all claims to vote were, however, subject to a 10s. registration tax.

the royal commission were probably more liberal, though they did not enfranchise annual salary earners of £50, and more controversially they imposed a simple reading and writing test from which three members of the commission dissented. Derby accepted Norman's advice that the education test should only be imposed after the first registration of voters, but that otherwise the recommendations of the commission should be implemented, and he did so in spite of Norman's estimate that they would qualify only about 9,000 voters; the commission had estimated that their majority proposals would enfranchise some 15,000 voters. Norman's estimate proved right,[46] a fact which caused the leader-writer of *The Colonial Standard* to attack a franchise which he had earlier regarded as 'broad, liberal and comprehensive'. He argued that for a householder to qualify he must, for instance, occupy a floored and roofed dwelling, and pay tax on a horse and nine acres of cultivated land. He proposed reducing the qualification for the payment of taxes to 10s. 6d. which would have enfranchised a similar householder paying tax on a donkey and one acre.[47] *The Colonial Standard* was the organ of the sugar interest, which apparently did not fear a lower franchise; J. M. Farquharson, a planter, was reported as saying that if the qualification had been lower 'people would have scored for me in thousands'.[48] In the five seats contested in the general election of September 1884, 3,731 voted out of 5,560 entitled to vote.[49] An analysis of voters in April 1886 showed that of 7,443 registered electors, 1,001 were Europeans or natives of Jamaica of European descent, 3,766 were Africans, 2,578 were of mixed races, and 98 were Indians.[50] Thus although the Negro voters formed a majority of the electorate, they were but a small fraction of the total Negro

[46] 9,298 actually qualified at the first registration. *The Handbook of Jamaica* (published by authority, London and Kingston, 1886), p. 87. (See note in bibliography, p. 307.) There were 1,798 registered voters in 1863.

[47] *The Colonial Standard and Jamaica Despatch*, 14 June 1884. See also Arthur E. Burt, 'The First Instalment of Representative Government in Jamaica, 1884'. *Social and Economic Studies*, Vol. 11, 1962.

[48] *The Colonial Standard and Jamaica Despatch*, 14 June 1884.

[49] Norman to Derby, No. 392, 22 Sept. 1884. 17305. CO 137/517. In the general election of 1863 1,031 voted in ten contested elections.

[50] Encl. with Norman to Granville, No. 119, 19 Apr. 1886. 8380. CO 137/525. The practical difficulties of classifying those of mixed race render these figures unreliable.

population which was estimated in 1881 at 444,186; the coloured population at the same date was 109,946, and the Indian population 11,016.

As for membership of the Council, in the discussions leading up to its reform Herbert and Wingfield had contemplated the direct nomination to it of one or two Negroes. Yet they did not dissent from Norman's recommendation that the qualifications for elected membership should be similar to those which existed for the House of Assembly; he suggested the possession of a clear annual income of between £150 and £300 depending on its source, or the payment of direct taxes or export taxes of £10 or more.[51] He considered that possibly these qualifications might 'rightly be somewhat lowered' in the future when the new Council had had time to look into the question.[52]

The elected members of the reformed Legislative Council represented propertied and particularly landed interests, as had the nominated unofficials before 1884. Michael Solomon, Emanuel Levy, and William Malabre had extensive business and agricultural interests, J. M. Farquharson was one of the wealthiest attorneys and proprietors in Jamaica, and George Henderson was the owner of coffee plantations and property in Kingston, though reputed at the time of his election to be in financial difficulties. Charles Farquharson and Robert Craig were businessmen; Harris later alleged that the former had lost all his fortune about 1882, and had entered the Council 'to recoup himself'. Edward Barrett was a radical ex-clergyman and landowner. The only coloured member was John Palache, a Jewish solicitor with agricultural interests, whom Blake described in 1896 as an exponent of the views of Henry George. In short, at least seven of the nine elected members had agricultural interests and at least five were owners of large estates though not all in sugar. Of the nine candidates supported by *The Colonial Standard*, the organ of the sugar interest, six were successful in the general election; the three other members had extensive agricultural interests.[53] Not one of the elected mem-

[51] The higher qualifications did not, of course, exclude all Negroes; for instance, Stiebel was a man of great wealth, and in Norman's view if he had chosen to stand at the general election of September 1884 he would have won Kingston by a very large majority. But the qualifications excluded most Negroes.

[52] Norman to Derby, No. 75, 23 Feb. 1884. 4431. CO 137/513.

[53] For an account of the general election of 1884 see Burt, op. cit., and Ronald V.

bers, Norman wrote in October 1884, 'can be fairly said to be representative of the mass of the population—that is the negroes';[54] in July 1885 he informed Stanley that in some respects the interests of the elected members conflicted with those of the Negroes. At by-elections between 1884 and 1889 Palache, Henderson, Barrett, and Levy were replaced by John Clark, William Espeut, a landowner, Wellesley Bourke, a coloured solicitor, and Thomas Harvey, a solicitor, the last two being associated with the American syndicate which purchased the Jamaica railway. At the general election of March 1889 two further seats changed hands, only one seat out of the nine being contested. These changes did not, in the view of officials in the Colonial Office or the colony, improve the quality of the elective element in the Council, which down to 1894 remained predominantly white.[55] It was alleged in the colonial press and in the Colonial Office, particularly after 1889, that some members were guided too much by personal interest; in 1892 Blake reported that five of the elected members were practically controlled by the American railway syndicate. The general election of 1894 returned more coloured members, but none could be described as genuine advocates of the interests of the rural population and particularly the Negro peasantry. In the writer's view, based on the evidence of legislative council debates, there were only two such members before 1900, Palache and Henry Clarke, a white ex-clergyman elected in 1894; a Negro shopkeeper, Alexander Dixon,[56] was elected in 1899. The absence of advocates of Negro interests is perhaps surprising in view of the reduction in the franchise in 1886.

In October 1885 Norman forwarded a resolution of the Legislative Council favouring a reduction in the franchise qualifications for householders from £1 to 10s. in direct taxes, the enfranchisement of all male adults earning a salary of over

Sires, 'The Jamaica Constitution of 1884', *Social and Economic Studies*, Vol. 3, No. 1, June 1954.

[54] Norman to Derby, Conf., 8 Oct. 1884. 18496. CO 137/518.

[55] For further details of members subsequently elected see pp. 83–4 and 88–9.

[56] Dixon seems to have been an amiable but ineffective member. It was alleged that he was the mouthpiece of Dr. Love (footnote 64, p. 64) to whose support, it seems, he largely owed his election. See W. Adolphe Roberts, *Six Great Jamaicans. Biographical sketches* (Kingston, 1952), p. 79, F. L. Casserly, 'The Hemming–Gideon Correspondence', *The Jamaica Historical Review*, Vol. 3 (1957–1962), pp. 70–71, and Livingstone, op. cit., p. 152, footnote.

£50, and the abolition of the education test.[57] The resolution, which was introduced by Palache, had been carried without a division, a motion to defer its consideration being lost by ten votes to four. Norman recommended its acceptance, observing that although the Royal Franchise Commission had estimated that their proposals would enfranchise about 15,000 voters, there were in fact under 7,000 on the rolls. In a memorandum submitted to the Colonial Office in January 1886,[58] he argued that the maximum of 20,000 voters who would be enfranchised by the lower qualifications would be able to exercise the vote with intelligence; the effect would be to make the legislature more representative and identify more people with government. Norman's advice was welcomed in the Colonial Office, Wingfield proposing that the qualification should be further reduced to payment of 6s. in direct taxes, thus enfranchising all who owned or occupied a roofed house of under £6 in 'annual value', but with an acre or more of land. Granville recommended this lower qualification if in the opinion of the governor and Council it could be safely implemented, but Norman reported in July 1886 that there was insufficient support among the elected members to justify him pressing it. The terms of the resolution of 10 October 1885 were implemented in October 1886, and by August 1887 the number of registered voters had increased to 22,922. In May 1893, however, the Legislative Council passed a bill, introduced by Charles Farquharson, to reimpose the literacy test for voters subsequently registering.[59] None of the elected members present opposed it in principle. A further law[60] ended the facilities for existing illiterate voters to record their votes, thus effectively disenfranchising them. Ripon advised assent to both laws, neither of which provoked significant comment among officials. In 1894 the newly elected Council repealed the second law.[61] In contrast to his earlier support for a wide franchise and his distrust of a literacy test, Wingfield regarded this as 'a step in the wrong direction', but he considered it to be 'a matter in

[57] Resolution of Legislative Council, 8 Oct. 1885. Encl. with Norman to Stanley, No. 374, 10 Oct. 1885. 19162. CO 137/523.

[58] Memorandum by Sir Henry Norman, 16 Jan. 1886. Reprinted in Conf. Print, West Indian No. 56. CO 884/4.

[59] Law 39, 1893. CO 139/106.

[60] Law 40, 1893. CO 139/106.

[61] Law 36, 1894. CO 139/107.

which the local Legislature should be allowed to have their own way'.[62] Ripon did not demur.

The number of registered voters rose to a peak of 42,266 in 1893–94; by 1900–01 it had declined to 16,256. The reimposition of the literacy test was not the only reason. The difficult economic conditions in the late 1890s, leading to non-payment of taxes and receipt of poor relief, both of which disqualified voters, contributed to the decline. Moreover, between 1886 and 1893 registration had automatically followed the payment of taxes; after 1893 a voter wishing to register had to apply in his own hand to the collector of taxes. This affected the numbers subsequently registering, for unlike British Guiana there was no rudimentary registration association to help overcome the prevailing apathy, which seems to have been particularly marked among the Negro population. In Blake's view, they had no political aspirations and took no interest in public affairs. Blake's judgement is confirmed by press and police reports of political meetings in Jamaica, and by the number of registered voters who polled, which was often less than half; in evaluating voting statistics, account must be taken, however, of the lack of canvassing, of the scattered polling stations in the country areas, and of the limited means of transport at the disposal of the Negroes. The absence of Negroes from the Legislative Council also suggests apathy, and is not fully explained by the relatively high qualifications for membership.[63] On the other hand, a notable example of Negro involvement in politics was Dr. J. R. Love,[64] the editor of *The Jamaica Advocate* and a

[62] Blake to Secretary of State, No. 225, 30 May 1894. 10726. CO 137/560. Minute by E.W., 22 June 1894.

[63] For further, though possibly not objective, evidence of political apathy among Negroes during and immediately after the period under review, see Livingstone, op. cit., p. 150, and H. G. de Lisser, *In Jamaica and Cuba* (Kingston, 1910), ch. VII, Livingstone claimed that it was the coloured people who were prominent at elections and who voiced the slogan 'Jamaica for the Jamaicans'. On the other hand, for a striking account by an educated Negro of the political aspirations of his race in Jamaica, see *Jamaica*, described by John Henderson (London, 1906), ch. XIII. Livingstone claimed in 1899 that the circulation of the 'principal newspaper' had recently doubled, the new subscribers being largely Negroes. Op. cit., p. 209. He estimated that there were thirty-three pure Negroes among 218 members of the parochial boards. Ibid., p. 153.

[64] Love was born in the Bahamas, educated in the United States, and spent nine years in Haiti before arriving in Jamaica in 1889. Through the columns of *The Jamaica Advocate* he championed the black man's point of view on social and

strong critic of the government. More generally, there were signs of increasing unrest among the black population after 1895. Blake reported in 1897 that negroes threatened with eviction were combining to keep the land for themselves and to refuse to pay rent. They were acting on the principle, he wrote, 'that God has given the land to the Black Man and they are determined to hold it against all comers'.[65] Wingfield noted that Norman 'was much struck with the bad spirit' of the Jamaican negroes giving evidence before the royal commission of 1897.[66] Stringent economic conditions probably contributed to the unrest, though Blake attributed what he called the new-found 'aggressive insolence' of the negro to such political factors as agitation at elections, the insurrection in Cuba, and the proximity of Haiti.[67]

It is clear from this analysis that a large part of the non-European population, particularly in the rural areas, was not directly represented. The deference of the Colonial Office to the views of the elected members was still compatible with its responsibility to this class, if that small part of the peasantry which was enfranchised spoke for the whole, and if the mainly propertied and professional elected members who represented them were responsive, if not sympathetic, to electoral pressures. There is no way of estimating the representative character of the electorate, but the Colonial Office assumed it, for it attached importance to its verdict on such important issues for the population as a whole as Indian immigration, compulsory education, the sale and possible subsequent repurchase of the Jamaica railway, the fiscal system, and railway extension. Also in certain respects the elected members were responsive to electoral pressures. During the general election of 1884 most candidates had stressed the need to improve and extend the system of elementary education. As early as November 1884 Wingfield noted as 'very remarkable' the 'strong inclination to compulsory education' among the elected members 'which

political questions, and urged Negroes to contest elections for the Legislative Council, to which he himself was elected in 1906. Roberts, op. cit., p. 70. See also p. 271 of this study.

[65] Blake to Chamberlain, Conf., 3 Oct. 1897. 23305. CO 137/583.

[66] Ibid. Minute by E.W., 29 Oct. 1897.

[67] Blake to Maj.-Gen. Hallowes, 29 Apr. 1896 (copy). Encl. with Blake to Chamberlain, Conf., 6 June 1896. 13483. CO 137/574.

evidently reflects the feeling of the constituents . . .'.[68] It probably also reflected the influence in the rural areas of clergymen and schoolmasters, whose literacy and standing made them the natural political leaders in the villages.[69] Between 1883–84 and 1896–97 the annual expenditure on education rose from £25,863 to £68,540, the major part of this increase taking place after the introduction of free education in 1892. In October 1899 Sir A. W. Hemming, the governor of Jamaica, wrote privately to Sydney Olivier, an official in the West India department, of the poorer classes 'being curiously tenacious & sensitive'[70] on the question of education, and Olivier himself noted in 1899 that it was the issue on which the elected members were most afraid of their constituents. There was also pressure from the peasantry for better communications, which probably assisted Blake to carry his policy of road- and bridge-building after 1888. Between 1883–84 and 1896–97 the annual general expenditure on public works and main roads rose from £48,156 to £76,301 with, in the latter year, a further £28,070 appropriated for the maintenance of main roads under Law 17 of 1890; these figures understate the increase in road- and bridge-building, much of which was financed by loans. Thus Herbert's expectation that the elected members would prove a force for economy was not well-founded. A further example of the responsiveness of the Legislative Council to public opinion was in 1886 when it adopted a proposal to end Indian immigration, none of the representatives of the sugar industry dissenting.[71] Norman wrote of the hostility of 'a large part of the population' to Indian immigration as financially burdensome and as reducing the prospects of employment, an attitude which made it inevitable that 'the immigration system could not long survive the introduction of representative legislation into this Island . . .'.[72] In 1888 the Legislative

[68] Norman to Derby, No. 425, 20 Oct. 1884. 19164. CO 137/518. Minute by E.W., 22 Nov. 1884.

[69] See also footnote 40, p. 105.

[70] Hemming to Olivier (personal), 31 Oct. 1899. Filed with minute paper 31803. CO 137/605.

[71] The proposal was included in an amended retrenchment scheme (Appendix XVIII, CO 140/195) which was adopted without dissent by the Legislative Council. Minutes of the Legislative Council, 8 Apr. 1886. CO 140/195. The proposal was implemented by Law 18, 1886, and by proclamation of 23 Oct. 1886. *Jamaica Gazette*, 28 Oct. 1886. CO 141/49.

[72] Norman to Granville, No. 163, 11 May 1886. 9279. CO 384/159. The decision

Council declined to consider a renewal of Indian immigration, except on terms which threw the whole cost on to the planter. Herbert minuted:

This case shows that there are some advantages . . . in the concession of greater power to the Elective members. Under the old system we should have been pressed by the Planters to reverse this decision, & probably should have done so to some extent. Now we can decline to interfere.[73]

In one respect at least, therefore, the elected members could be regarded as more effective trustees than the Colonial Office, which in this case was shielding itself behind them. On the other hand, on the central issue of taxation they declined to shift the burden from customs and excise duties, notably duties on widely consumed imported foods, to property, a course which the Colonial Office had long favoured.[74] One effect of such a change would have been to have increased the number entitled to vote. However, many who knew Jamaica agreed on the strong opposition of the Negroes to higher direct taxes on land, so that to this extent the elected members probably reflected the views of their constituents. The same could not be said for their acceptance of the sharply regressive rates of taxation on land, which bore proportionately far more heavily on the small peasantry and which remained largely unchanged until 1903.[75] Nor did the elected members, with the exception of Henry Clarke and Palache, concern themselves with such pressing social problems as illegitimacy. It is a large question, the detailed examination of which is beyond the scope of this study, but it seems probable that the interests of the non-European population, and particularly the mainly Negro rural peasantry, whether enfranchised or not, were only imperfectly represented by the European and coloured elected members.

of the Legislative Council must also be seen against the background of the sharp fall in sugar prices after 1884.

[73] Norman to Knutsford, No. 380, 26 Oct. 1888. 23037. CO 384/169. Minute by R.G.W.H., 27 Nov. 1888.

[74] See p. 155, and particularly footnote 16, p. 156, which illustrates the conspicuously high duties in Jamaica.

[75] The most extreme example was the education tax. In 1901 the occupier of a house of under £4 annual value on one quarter of an acre planted in vegetables paid 2s. and the occupier of a 1,000 acre estate planted in canes and bananas paid 6s. The total tax paid by each on their properties was 14s. 6d. and £30 5s. 1d. respectively.

The latter were drawn largely from the landed, professional, and small shop-keeping and business classes. On certain issues they were sensitive to their constituents, but divided from many of them by race and interest they were, with one or two exceptions, inadequate guardians of their interests, particularly when those interests conflicted with their own, as in matters of taxation. Yet in practice it was as guardians that the Colonial Office regarded them, for it treated them as representative of Jamaican opinion in general, and it deferred to their views on major issues affecting the welfare of the non-European population, such as franchise qualifications, the level of import duties on widely consumed foods, and the regressive system of land tax. In thus seeking to avoid a collision with the elected members, the Colonial Office, as in the case of finance, was shirking a responsibility which it could not abdicate.

3

CONSTITUTIONAL CHANGE AFTER 1884

An uncertainty of direction

To what extent did the Colonial Office regard the changes of 1884 as a stage in the constitutional development of Jamaica? Derby described his original proposals as 'a moderate step in advance', and Ashley referred to the subsequent concession of semi-representative government as 'a distinct move in the direction of restoring control over their own affairs to the people of Jamaica'.[1] Norman warned Jamaicans in January 1884 of the dangers of 'a too rapid or extensive introduction of Representative Government in Jamaica . . .'.[2] These statements seemed to foreshadow further constitutional advance, and certainly Derby's despatch of 1 December 1883 was thus interpreted in Jamaica.[3] The liberal sentiments underlying these statements seem only to have been shared in this period, among those making or influencing policy, by Gladstone, Derby, Ashley, and Norman. In particular, the latter's subsequent speeches and policy recommendations reflected a strong sympathy for the establishment of representative government in Jamaica. In July 1885 he forwarded a series of resolutions, introduced into the Legislative Council by Henderson, of which the fifth favoured an increase 'as soon as possible' in the number of elected members to fourteen, representing each country parish and Kingston.[4] The elected members, and others, argued that inadequate

1 *Hansard*, Third Series (287), 718.

2 Minute by the Governor of Jamaica (para. 20). Reprinted in C. 3854, p. 16.

3 In March 1894 Blake reported that the coloured elected members of the Legislative Council regarded this despatch 'as a pledge that the change in the constitution . . . was but the first step towards responsible Government'. Blake to Ripon, No. 74, 13 Mar. 1894. 5825. CO 137/559.

4 Norman to Secretary of State for the Colonies, Conf., 21 July 1885. 14022. CO 137/522.

communications and conflicting parochial interests made it impossible for one member adequately to represent combined parishes. The sixth resolution provided for the appointment of four additional nominated members, by implication officials, thus raising the total of nominated officials to six, with power reserved to the Crown to appoint four more, 'thus giving preponderating power in imperial, but not in financial, questions . . .'.[5] Although rejecting this implied limitation to the use of his reserve powers, Norman showed surprising willingness to consider a fundamental change in the Jamaica constitution. In a memorandum submitted to the Colonial Office in January 1886,[6] he recommended representative government for Jamaica. He was probably influenced by the willingness of the elected members to lower the franchise, and by his own conviction, after more than a year's experience of the new constitution, that if the government followed a conciliatory policy it was possible to govern with a permanent majority of elected members. But the main argument of his memorandum, based on his experience of the first two sessions of the Council, was that there was unlikely to be

> any occasion on which the power of the Government to override the vote of a majority of the elected members can usefully or properly be exercised . . .[7]

Underlying this judgement was Norman's view that to override the votes of the elected members would lead to their resignation and to renewed agitation, that practice had shown the elected members were unlikely to be unanimous, and that even if they were it would be unpleasant to override them by nominating three additional officials and using the governor's vote. He therefore concluded that the position of the government would 'be at least as satisfactory, if it is in a permanent minority, as it now is when the Government has the power to call in additional members . . .',[8] a power which he contended it was inexpedient to use. His proposal was for a Legislative Council of the governor, four *ex-officio* and five nominated

[5] Norman to Secretary of State for the Colonies, Conf., 21 July 1885. 14022. CO 137/522. The resolutions were passed on 20 Oct. 1885. See minutes of the Jamaica Legislative Council, CO 140/193. There were, in addition, four *ex-officio* members.

[6] Memorandum by Sir Henry Norman, 16 Jan. 1886. Reprinted in Conf. Print, West Indian No. 56. CO 884/4.

[7] Ibid.

[8] Ibid.

members, by implication officials,[9] and fourteen elected members; it was conditional on the Council passing measures to protect the salaries and pensions of public officers, including the provision of a civil list securing the salaries of the principal public officers.

Norman's recommendation of representative government for Jamaica was a far-reaching one, reflecting his success and confidence in governing with an official minority in the Legislative Council. It is not surprising that Herbert should have hesitated to advise such a radical departure in policy, yet he minuted that he would not have hesitated to do so if Norman could have long remained in Jamaica or if he was certain that his successor would have equal ability and tact. He continued:

It should, however, be very carefully considered whether with a Legislature and people very ignorant of constitutional precedents, and ready to become actively disloyal on insufficient provocation when any unpopular act of State has to be done, it is safe to abandon the ultimate control of the Crown.

I am anxious, and inclined, to think that Sir H. Norman's proposal is expedient & safe, but it involves a considerable departure in policy, & I am not yet convinced.[10]

Frederick Stanley, Derby's brother and successor as secretary of state, minuted shortly before leaving office in February 1886 that he was inclined to consider Norman's proposal favourably, and his successor, Lord Granville, and his parliamentary

[9] The use by governors and Colonial Office of the term 'nominated member' in relation to the Jamaica constitution of 1884 is confusing, for they rarely qualified it by 'official' or 'unofficial'. It is clear from the context, however, that in discussing the possible enlargement of the Council to provide for fourteen elected members both Norman, and the Colonial Office until 1895, had in mind the nomination of further officials. The former wished to establish a compact voting body behind the government, though in a minority; the latter sought to secure, when necessary, a government majority. Similarly when referring to the possibility of appointing the full number of five nominated members under the existing constitution, both Norman and the Colonial Office only visualized the nomination of officials necessary to establish a government majority. Blake, on the other hand, favoured the appointment of unofficials (see pp. 78 and 80), and after the enlargement of the Council in 1896 he nominated, with Chamberlain's approval, two unofficial members on whose support he could rely. Subsequently the Colonial Office sometimes used 'nominated member' in this particular sense; its view of their role remained unchanged, namely to secure, when necessary, a government majority. Where the context clearly indicates it the author has substituted 'nominated official' for 'nominated member'.

[10] Minute paper 1817. Minute by R.G.W.H., 2 Feb. 1886. CO 137/529.

under-secretary, G. Osborne Morgan, also considered Norman's proposals 'desirable & safe'.[11] But Herbert's caution proved decisive. In a despatch of 18 March 1886 Granville accepted Norman's advice, subject to the important provision that the governor in privy council should retain the power to make temporary laws, without the concurrence of the Legislative Council, for the protection of 'Imperial interests or the fulfilment of international or treaty obligations, *or for the maintenance of order and public safety in any grave emergency*'.[12] He suggested that such laws might be in force for six months. Although the provision originated with Herbert, Norman entirely approved it. Herbert explained to Granville that such a power was necessary 'in the event of the unofficial majority being rebellious and declining to legislate in an emergency, or when Imperial or other important interests are at stake . . .'.[13] In his despatch Granville rejected the alternative method, suggested by the elected members, of securing an overriding power for the Crown by the appointment of eleven, or in an emergency fourteen, officials, on the grounds of inconvenience to the public service and the improbability of finding so many officials capable of legislative work.[14] He agreed with Norman that the Legislative Council, as a condition of the change, should pass certain measures safeguarding the salaries and pensions of public officers. Derby had instructed Norman to appoint the full number of nominated members 'in case of necessity'. It could be argued that Granville's precise definition of the circumstances in which the governor in council might legislate, which did not specifically include finance, was a further concession to Jamaicans, in addition to his offer of fourteen elected members. Granville's insistence on the retention for the Crown of an overriding power of legislation was, however, unacceptable to the elected members, and until 1887 the subject seems to have received no further attention in the Legislative Council or the press.

The large increase in the electorate following the lowering of the franchise qualifications in October 1886 led to renewed

[11] Minute Paper 1817. Minute by G.O.M., 17 Mar. 1886. CO 137/529.

[12] Granville to Norman, No. 36, 18 Mar. 1886. N 1817. CO 137/529. The despatch was drafted by Wingfield. The words in italics were underlined by Herbert.

[13] Minute paper 1817. Minute by R.G.W.H., 16 Mar. 1886. CO 137/529.

[14] See footnote 97, p. 39. This consideration weighed heavily with Norman.

demands for the separate representation of each parish. In October 1887 the elected members indicated their willingness to fulfil Granville's conditions for securing the salaries and pensions of public officers, but they were still unwilling to accept the exercise of legislative power by the governor in privy council. Norman advised that it should not be insisted upon as a condition for an increase in the number of elected members to fourteen, although ideally he would have preferred to retain it. Norman's case for representative government remained unchanged. Only 'a most extraordinary state of affairs' would justify him overruling the elected members by calling up his reserve of three nominated members, which would almost inevitably lead to 'the resignation of the Elected members in a body and a practical dead lock in all ordinary legislation'.[15] He argued that in any circumstances in which a temporary power of legislation might be necessary a large majority of the elected members would be with the government, for they were likely to be interested in the maintenance of order and good government; Herbert noted in the margin, 'I fear this is a baseless dream'. Norman also emphasized the powers still available to the governor and Colonial Office, namely the initiation of financial proposals, the withholding of assent to legislation, and the revision of the constitution by order in council. He claimed that a 'compact body' of the governor with an original and casting vote, and four *ex-officio* and five nominated members, would be 'very powerful' against fourteen elected members and 'would generally carry anything . . .'.[16] Herbert noted in the margin, 'Utterly powerless even in a 2nd class crisis'. Norman's judgement was probably influenced by his view of the probable lack of unanimity among the elected members and their less regular attendance.

In a carefully balanced minute Wingfield argued on the one hand, that the present reserve power was not workable since if it was used it would result in a deadlock, but that on the other hand, Norman insufficiently allowed for 'a weaker and less judicious successor . . .'.[17] Wingfield seems also to have been

[15] Norman to Holland, No. 345, 18 Oct. 1887. 22316. CO 137/532.

[16] Norman to Holland, No. 424, 7 Dec. 1887. 25932. CO 137/532.

[17] Norman to Holland, No. 345, 18 Oct. 1887. 22316. CO 137/532. Minute by E.W., 4 Nov. 1887.

influenced by the view of the retiring colonial secretary in Jamaica, Edward Noel Walker, as to the shortage of suitable candidates for election and the lack of public feeling in favour of the change.[18] Wingfield argued that an adherence to a power of temporary legislation would not therefore lead to 'any general agitation . . .'. He made no precise recommendation, but it is probable that he regarded this final point as decisive. Herbert was less ambivalent:

There is hardly any Colony in which the experiment would be less hopeful. There is hardly a gentleman in the Island, & the active politicians are Kingston Jews & lawyers, and coloured men; all with axes to grind. There is no respectable press, & no hope of improving & educating public opinion.

If we rush down this incline in Jamaica, we shall have to do so in Mauritius, Trinidad, Malta, and wherever else the constitution has been or is being weakened; & ultimately there will hardly be a Crown Colony left.[19]

The first paragraph could have been written by almost any member of the West India department. Wingfield wrote of 'the Jew lawyers and newspaper editors who are the curse of Jamaica'.[20] Harris referred to the Jews who would 'not rest content without the substantial power which means unlimited jobbery . . .'.[21] But such hostility towards the politically active class in Jamaica is a new note in Herbert's minutes and it is not easy to account for the different tone of this minute compared with that of 2 February 1886.[22] Norman did not share officials' views regarding the quality of political life in Jamaica. He wrote without animus of the Jewish population. He referred, for instance, to Palache as 'a gentleman' who as a member of the Legislative Council 'has shown himself very independent . . .';[23] Harris described him as 'a coloured Jew and solicitor with a strong bent for jobbery'.[24] After three and a

[18] Walker to Wingfield (personal), 29 Oct. 1887. 22215. CO 137/533.

[19] Norman to Holland, No. 345, 18 Oct. 1887. 22316. CO 137/532. Minute by R.G.W.H., 7 Nov. 1887.

[20] Norman to Derby, No. 469, 8 Nov. 1884. 20262. CO 137/518. Minute by E.W., 1 Dec. 1884.

[21] Norman to Derby, No. 15, 8 Jan. 1884. 1589. CO 137/513. Minute by C.A.H., 29 Jan. 1884.

[22] See p. 71.

[23] Norman to Granville, No. 194, 6 June 1886. 11472. CO 137/526.

[24] Norman to Derby, No. 54, 6 Feb. 1884. 3337. CO 137/513. Minute by C.A.H., 28 Feb. 1884.

half years in Jamaica Norman wrote: '. . . I have always found that I could rely upon the honour of gentlemen engaged in political life even when strenuously opposing the Government'.[25] In April 1888 he described the mass of Jamaicans as at present 'intensely loyal'.

The hostility of officials towards most Jamaican politicians rarely influenced their advice decisively and it is probable that for Herbert the reasons in the second paragraph of his minute weighed more heavily. The Mauritius reform agitation, during which the example of Jamaica had been often cited by agitators, had led to the concession by Stanley in the autumn of 1885 of an unofficial nominated and elected majority. In July 1887 the governor of Trinidad had forwarded a petition, asking for a royal commission to be appointed 'as was recently done in Jamaica'[26] to advise on constitutional change leading to the introduction of elected members into the Legislative Council. In September 1887 Knutsford informed him that 'H.M. Govt. are not indisposed to consider whether the Colony may not now receive a Constitution as nearly resembling that of Jamaica as the circumstances of Trinidad may justify';[27] in the light of this despatch it might have been difficult to have resisted the application to Trinidad of further constitutional change in Jamaica, and it would have been characteristic if Herbert, more far-sighted than his colleagues, had considered this. It is not clear where Herbert saw 'the incline' leading, though Walker, whose private letter to Wingfield he had read, wrote that any further concession would encourage a section of the elected members to agitate for responsible government.

Knutsford agreed with Herbert that '. . . we must . . . keep the reins in our hands in times of emergency or of settlement of important Imperial questions'. He continued: '. . . this is not only important as regards our position in Jamaica, but our position in other colonies, where similar claims will be advanced.'[28] But he informed Norman[29] that, although he preferred to secure the control of legislation in 'Imperial interests

[25] Norman to Holland, Conf., 5 May 1887. 10425. CO 137/530.

[26] See p. 170.

[27] See p. 175.

[28] Norman to Holland, No. 345, 18 Oct. 1887. 22316. CO 137/532. Minute by H.T.H. (undated).

[29] Holland to Norman, No. 285, 16 Nov. 1887. 22316. CO 137/532, and No. 5, 6 Jan. 1888. 25932. CO 137/532.

or Colonial emergencies' by a power of temporary legislation for the governor in privy council, he was willing to accept the terms of the Legislative Council's sixth resolution of 20 October 1885; under this an official majority against fourteen elected members would have been secured by the nomination of four more officials in addition to the two already nominated, with power reserved to the Crown to appoint if necessary four further nominated officials.[30] The latter would not be appointed, Knutsford wrote, 'unless . . . there should be an urgent necessity for doing so, not connected with purely local questions whether financial or otherwise'.[31] The power of controlling legislation was necessary in 'matters of Imperial interest, or in grave emergencies affecting the maintenance of order and public safety . . .'.[32] Knutsford's offer was subject to the Legislative Council implementing Granville's conditions regarding the security of official salaries and pensions. Otherwise he conceded the demands embodied in the legislative council resolution of October 1885, even to the extent of excluding 'purely local questions whether financial or otherwise' from those matters in which the Crown might overrule the votes of the elected members. However, Knutsford's insistence on retaining a reserve power of legislation for the Crown made his offer unacceptable to the elected members, who now seemed to be opposed to it in any form.

Sir Henry Blake, who succeeded Norman as governor in December 1888, was less successful in managing the elected members. During the spring session of 1891 they used their financial veto to defeat five government proposals, prompting Blake to raise the possibility of either enlarging the Council, thereby lessening the chances of unanimity among the elected members, or of resorting more freely than was originally contemplated to his power of declaring a matter of paramount importance. He preferred the former course, but feared 'great difficulty in securing an additional number of desirable representative members . . .';[33] the sense of Blake's despatches sug-

[30] See p. 70. The official side would thus have comprised the governor with an original and casting vote, four *ex-officio* members, and six nominated officials, with four further nominations in reserve.

[31] Holland to Norman, No. 285, 16 Nov. 1887. 22316. CO 137/532.

[32] Holland to Norman, No. 5, 6 Jan. 1888. 25932. CO 137/532.

[33] Blake to Knutsford, No. 106, 4 May 1891. 10289. CO 137/545.

gests that he had in mind Europeans of 'stake and position'. This problem remained at the centre of his thinking on constitutional change in Jamaica, and he attributed the difficulty partly to the unwillingness of many Europeans to contest elections with coloured candidates and to solicit the votes of a Negro electorate.[34] Others were perhaps deterred by the time and expense of attending sittings in Kingston. Any increase in the number of elected members therefore raised the possibility that they would comprise a larger coloured professional element from Kingston, particularly solicitors who had an aptitude for legislative work and public speaking, and who could conveniently combine their professional and legislative council duties. Blake regarded this prospect with more apprehension than Norman, partly because he was more conscious of racial tension and partly because the aims of his governorship were very different. Norman was particularly concerned with the political development of Jamaica, Blake with its economic development. Himself a part-owner of one of the largest groups of property in the island and highly regarded by Jamaican commercial interests in London, Blake believed that the future of Jamaica lay in the attraction of white settlers and capital, to which, he claimed, some prominent coloured men were opposed;[35] in his view, they sought rather the continued decline of the white population whose social and economic position they hoped to inherit. Sir A. Birch, agent of the western branch of the Bank of England, also noted after a visit to Jamaica the jealousy of the coloured population towards 'anyone outside their class who attempts to press forward any enterprise in the Island'.[36] Blake's emphasis on the need for white settlers and capital was influenced by his pessimistic view of the potential of the coloured population. They were a hybrid race and 'Nature has declared against this'.[37] In his view, 'all progress' depended on the white population. He implied that a condition for attracting settlers and capital was 'a strong Government' which would secure that 'local affairs shall go smoothly . . .'.[38]

[34] For example, Blake to Ripon, Conf., 21 Aug. 1893. 15286. CO 137/556; and Blake to Ripon, Conf., 29 Apr. 1895. 8454. CO 137/565. In 1896 he commented on the unwillingness of white parents to allow their sons to compete with black candidates in examinations for the public service.

[35] See pp. 53–4.

[36] Memorandum of Sir A. Birch (copy), 26 Dec. 1893. 2238. CO 137/563.

[37] Blake to Ripon, Conf., 29 Apr. 1895. 8454. CO 137/565.

[38] Ibid.

A favourable condition for such government was the presence of men of 'stake and position' in the Legislative Council. Since such men would not stand for election, Blake favoured the nomination of unofficials, a proposal which recurs in his despatches. Blake's predisposition towards strong government was strengthened by his apprehension of racial conflict and his belief that an elected majority by frustrating government would cause discontent among the Negro population. He thus regarded the system inaugurated by Norman as 'a great mistake',[39] and he was strongly opposed to any further surrender of crown control; 'for the maintenance of public confidence', he wrote, 'it will always be necessary in a mixed community where the negro population enjoys so wide a franchise', for the Crown to retain ultimate legislative control.[40] Blake's emphasis on strong government was also influenced by a paternalist and pessimistic attitude towards the black population, whom he regarded as having only the veneer of civilization, and among whom 'the foundation of a stable Society'[41] was not yet assured. He stressed in particular the absence of family life, a condition that he was not confident that education could improve 'at least for a considerable time'. '. . . the people of Jamaica', he wrote to Meade, 'like all other black colonies require to be "personally conducted" . . .'.[42] Similar considerations led him to the view, expressed in August 1892, that the government of the colony could not be satisfactorily carried on without an official majority in the Legislative Council.

Blake's views conflicted with the growing aspirations of the coloured politicians. 1891 marked the start of a radical agitation led by George Levy, through the columns of *The Colonial Standard*, and by coloured solicitors, who advocated an increase in the number of elected members and who attacked the

[39] Blake to Wingfield (personal), 13 Nov. 1892. Filed with minute paper 24858. CO 137/551.

[40] Blake to Ripon, No. 74, 13 Mar. 1894. 5825. CO 137/559.

[41] Blake to Ripon, Conf., 29 Apr. 1895. 8454. CO 137/565. This important despatch includes many of the assumptions on which Blake's governorship was based. It was influential in the Colonial Office where it strengthened the growing pessimism regarding the moral and social progress of the Negro race. See pp. 242–245. Blake seems to have shown real concern for the Negro peasantry. Olivier regarded him as being 'entirely devoid of race-prejudice', and one of his critics described him as a 'pronounced Negrophilist'. Olivier, op. cit., pp. 252 and 317.

[42] Blake to Meade (personal), 20 Jan. 1896. 2857. CO 137/571.

appointment of non-Jamaicans to official posts. The agitation was carried on by public meeting, in the press, and through petitions from some of the parochial boards for separate representation of each parish. In Blake's view, it aroused no general interest, and even *The Colonial Standard* upbraided the 'apathy', 'indifference', and 'inertness' of Jamaicans. Underlying the demands for separate representation of each parish was strong hostility towards the elected members who had supported the sale of the Jamaica railway from, allegedly, motives of self-interest; a larger Council, Levy argued, would end the 'Happy Family character . . .' of the present one. The attack on outside appointments, summarized in the slogan 'Jamaica for the Jamaicans', partly reflected the resentment of an overcrowded legal profession[43] against the selection of non-Jamaicans for positions such as resident magistracies; but also underlying it was a sense of social inferiority felt by some of the coloured population towards the officials appointed from England, which in Blake's view was none the less real although it was not officially acknowledged. Thus William Andrews, a prominent coloured solicitor and one of the leaders of the movement, referred to the strangers who 'delight in openly insulting us, and turning us into ridicule . . .'.[44] This sense of grievance was heightened by the appointment in April 1892 of H. M. Perry as resident magistrate of St. Thomas. Perry was a competent but quick-tempered Englishman with strong racial prejudices; he replaced a local solicitor who had held the post temporarily, and the Jamaica press waged a bitter vendetta against him. Andrews and Levy sought to link this radical movement with agitation elsewhere in the British West Indies. At a meeting held under police protection in Kingston on 19 May 1892, and attended by twenty-six persons including the editors of *The Budget* and *The Daily Gleaner*, it was resolved that a local branch of the West Indian Civil Rights Defence Union should be formed, the general object being 'that all the West Indian Islands should join themselves together for their

[43] In 1893 the attorney-general estimated the number of solicitors in Jamaica at eighty-one, of whom sixty were in practice and twenty-four of less than seven years' standing. Report encl. with Blake to Ripon, No. 129, 1 May 1893. 8113. CO 137/555. The census returns showed an increase in the number of lawyers from thirty-seven in 1881 to eighty in 1891.

[44] *The Daily Gleaner*, 21 May 1892.

mutual protection . . .'; West Indians were making a stand 'to show they were as good intellectually and in every respect' as Europeans.[45]

Blake opposed the separate representation of each parish on the grounds that suitable candidates, by which he meant men of property, would not be forthcoming, and he strongly recommended that after the next dissolution the full number of five nominated members should be appointed, by implication officials. If, however, the elected members were increased to fourteen then he favoured the nomination of the full number of ten nominated members,[46] since this would provide an opportunity of appointing perhaps five non-officials 'of intelligence and position . . .'. In his view, their presence would strengthen the government, which, he apparently assumed, could rely on their votes; colonial office officials with the *Florence* affair in mind were less sure. Unlike Norman, Blake saw no difficulty in selecting further officials capable of holding their own in debate with the elected members.[47]

Wingfield agreed with Blake in advising against the separate representation of each parish, since there was 'no strong or general wish' for it and he had heard from other quarters of the shortage of competent candidates, but he opposed Blake's advice to appoint the full number of five nominated members. In his view, to establish a Crown majority without 'any special reason would be a breach of the understanding' conveyed in Derby's despatch of 28 May 1884, to the effect that 'the power was only to be exercised when it was required for the decision of a question of paramount importance'.[48] Wingfield was mistaken, for Derby had instructed Norman that the full number of nominated members might be appointed 'in case of necessity'; Wingfield was, however, explicitly acknowledging the more precise limitation on the power of the governor to appoint the full number of nominated members which had been

[45] Speech by W. Andrews. Report of meeting held in Kingston, 19 May 1892. *The Daily Gleaner*, 21 May 1892. For an account of the West Indian Civil Rights Defence Union see pp. 195–200.

[46] See p. 70 and footnote 30, p. 76.

[47] For Blake's views see Blake to Knutsford, No. 275, 8 Aug. 1892. 16949. CO 137/549. Also Blake to Knutsford, Conf., 8 Aug. 1892. 16950. CO 137/549.

[48] Blake to Knutsford, No. 275, 8 Aug. 1892. 16949. CO 137/549. Minute by E.W., 3 Sept. 1892.

implied in the despatches of Granville of 18 March 1886, and of Knutsford of 16 November 1887 and 6 January 1888. Sir Robert Meade, Herbert's successor as permanent under-secretary, expressed the same view in stronger terms:

To call up our reserves of official votes would be such an open breach of the constitutional understanding, as to invite, & even justify, a refusal to vote supplies. There is no pressing emergency of paramount importance to warrant such a step.[49]

Thus advised, Ripon informed Blake that his proposal to appoint the full number of five nominated members was not 'feasible in the face of the understanding conveyed by Lord Derby's despatch . . .',[50] and, further, that he did not contemplate a change in the Jamaica constitution, though he reserved a final opinion on both points until after the next dissolution of the Council. Meade's advice reflected his predecessor's caution. In November 1891 Herbert had minuted: 'There will no doubt be a very serious deadlock, terminating probably in Sir H. Blake's enforced retirement, if he handles injudiciously the delicate engine of the uncalled official votes . . .'.[51] Herbert showed a similar apprehension of the injudicious use of the governor's power to override the votes of six or nine elected members by a declaration of paramount importance. Either course would, in his view, almost certainly have led to a grave crisis in which the power and influence of the governor would have been seriously weakened.

Blake's wish to strengthen his position in relation to the Legislative Council also influenced his proposal in August 1892 that he should no longer preside over it.[52] Since the middle 1870s Jamaican reformers had pressed for the removal of the governor from the Council, but it was not out of deference to local opinion that Blake recommended the change. He seems to have found his position as president an uncomfortable one; the nimble-witted Jamaica lawyers were probably more than his match in debate.[53] Blake argued that the governor's

[49] Blake to Knutsford, Conf., 8 Aug. 1892. 16950. CO 137/549. Minute by R.M., 10 Oct. 1892.

[50] Ripon to Blake, No. 243, 26 Sept. 1892. 16949. CO 137/549.

[51] Blake to Knutsford, No. 106, 4 May 1891. 10289. CO 137/545. Minute by R.G.W.H., 24 Nov. 1891.

[52] Blake to Knutsford, Conf., 8 Aug. 1892. 16950. CO 137/549.

[53] Some of the Jamaica lawyers were extremely able. For instance, Philip Stern,

presence in the Council lessened his dignity, exposed him to pressure when government legislation was under consideration, and removed the independent check of his assent to legislation; the implication of the last point was that if the governor was outmanoeuvred on a particular measure in debate, or otherwise gave way, it was difficult for him to subsequently withhold his formal assent to the bill. Wingfield acknowledged the force of these arguments, but on the whole he did not favour a change. Meade, on the other hand, saw the chance to 'stave off, for the present, any amendment of the Constitution'.[54] Both he and Sydney Buxton, the parliamentary under-secretary, seem at this time to have had in mind the possibility of an amendment necessitated by deteriorating relations between Blake and the elected members, to which, in Meade's view, Blake's 'police manner'[55] contributed; in the light of Meade's attitude a month later to Blake's proposal to restore the official majority, the amendment which he contemplated could hardly have been in the direction of crown colony government. Buxton also favoured Blake's proposal, and thus advised, Ripon informed the governor that a crown nominee should take his place as president of the Council; he would normally be a person not holding office under the Crown, who would have a casting but not an original vote. The Council was to elect its own vice-president. In order to balance the loss of the governor's original vote, the collector-general was to be added to the official side.[56] These proposals were indifferently received by the elected members, who criticized them on the grounds that they had not been consulted, that the collector-general's appointment would strengthen the official vote since the governor had rarely used his original vote, and that the president should have been elected. The death in November 1893 of Phillippo,

who was elected to the Legislative Council in 1895, practised in England from 1878 to 1893 where, a biographer claims, 'he ranked as high as any leading criminal lawyer . . . in England. Those capable of judging put him in the class of . . . Sir Edward Marshall Hall.' Jacob A. P. M. Andrade, *A Record of the Jews in Jamaica from the English Conquest to the Present Time* (Kingston, 1941), p. 172.

[54] Blake to Knutsford, Conf., 8 Aug. 1892. 16950. CO 137/549. Minute by R.M., 10 Oct. 1892.

[55] Blake had served in the Royal Irish Constabulary from 1859 to 1876 before being appointed a resident magistrate in Ireland.

[56] Ripon to Blake, No. 27, 31 Jan. 1893. 765. CO 137/553. The changes were effected by Order in Council, 30 Jan. 1893.

the first president, prompted a colonial office reappraisal of the decision. Wingfield minuted that he had understood that the governor's absence from the Council had 'given dissatisfaction to everyone except himself';[57] this was an uncharacteristic exaggeration, but it seems that some of the elected members had expressed dissatisfaction. Charles Farquharson probably spoke for them when he pointed to the likelihood of friction between governor and Council, if the former instead of, as president, guiding the Council in its decisions, could now only approve or veto them after they had been taken. In December 1893 Ripon informed Blake that he proposed to restore the governor to the Council, though he gave no reasons for the decision.[58] The Order in Council effecting this change provided for the collector-general's continued *ex-officio* membership, the governor in future having a casting vote only.[59] Ripon's unexplained decision was strongly attacked by the coloured members of the Legislative Council which had been newly elected in February 1894,[60] but he refused to reverse it. Blake disapproved of the decision, though paradoxically it was the increasing influence of his view of the need for strong government in Jamaica which influenced the Colonial Office not to reconsider it. W. A. Baillie Hamilton, an official in the West India department, minuted: 'The great thing in dealing with people like the Jamaica negroes is firmness, & anything approaching to vacillation is apt to be dangerous.'[61]

The general election of February 1894 led to an increase in the coloured membership of the Legislative Council. J. H. Levy, a merchant in general business, and Andrews, who had both earlier won by-elections, were re-elected. They were joined in the Council by three newly elected solicitors, Jackson, Palache, and Samuel Burke, the former crown solicitor who had resigned during the *Florence* affair; Blake described these five members as coloured, and the last four as leading solicitors in the colony. The four white members were J. M. Farquhar-

57 Blake to Ripon, Conf., 22 Nov. 1893. 20613. CO 137/557. Minute by E.W., 8 Dec. 1893.

58 Ripon to Blake, tel., 13 Dec. 1893. Secret No. 492. CO 694/18.

59 Order in Council, 29 Jan. 1894. PC 2/354.

60 See below.

61 Blake to Ripon, No. 74, 13 Mar. 1894. 5825. CO 137/559. Minute by W.A.B.H., 17 Apr. 1894.

son, John Kerr, a landowner, Thomas Sharp, managing director of a fruit-growing company, and Henry Clarke, an ex-clergyman and managing director of a building society. Five out of the nine seats were contested, 8,369 voting out of a registered electorate of 24,422.[62] Charles Farquharson, Harvey, and Bourke, all closely associated with the Jamaica railway agreement, were defeated. Blake informed Ripon that the aim of a majority of the Council would 'be in the direction of the establishment of an Executive Committee after the principle adopted in Barbados, as a step towards responsible Government . . .'.[63] The radical tendencies of the coloured members were reflected in their attitude to the representation of each parish, a motion in favour of which was introduced by Burke on 9 March 1894 and carried unanimously by the elected members, the officials abstaining. The four white members, however, only favoured the change if the *ex-officio* and nominated members were increased proportionately, a condition which Andrews, Jackson, and Palache strongly opposed. The coloured members argued, in support of the resolution, that the election had shown that public opinion favoured it and there was a danger of agitation if it was refused. Its concession, they argued, was implicit in Derby's despatches of 1 December 1883 and 28 May 1884, by which they had been led to expect 'a further step in advance'. They also cited the example of the grant of responsible government to Natal. All the elected members stressed the practical difficulties of canvassing combined parishes and representing possibly conflicting parochial interests.

In the Legislative Council and in a despatch to Ripon,[64] Blake supported an increase to fourteen elected members, a

[62] *Jamaica Blue Book for 1894–1895*. CO 142/108.

[63] Blake to Ripon, Conf., 20 Feb. 1894. 4104. CO 137/559. The Barbados Executive Committee was established in 1881, and comprised the governor, the Executive Council, one member of the Legislative Council, and four members of the House of Assembly. It was responsible for the preparation and introduction of the estimates, and the initiation of money votes in the Assembly. More generally it advised the governor on all measures to be brought before the Assembly and acted as a useful link between it and the executive. See Barbados Act 32, 1881, and Act 65, 1891. Wingfield noted in 1898 that though the Committee had worked fairly well in Barbados there was not the same need for it in Jamaica, where there was a large official element in the Council. See minute paper 26978. CO 137/598.

[64] Blake to Ripon, No. 74, 13 Mar. 1894. 5825. CO 137/559.

change which he had opposed in 1892; he later made clear his grounds for this change of view, namely his belief, 'based on the assurance received from many quarters that good local candidates would be forthcoming'.[65] Although Blake insisted that a condition for the change should be a corresponding increase in the number of *ex-officio* and nominated members to fifteen, he was now willing to agree to the initial appointment of only eleven, on the lines of Derby's concession of May 1884. In contrast to Granville in 1886 and Knutsford in 1887, he defined the ultimate power thus reserved to the Crown as not 'of legislation, but of finance'.[66] He remained particularly concerned with the maintenance of conditions favourable to outside capital, for he was reported to have warned the Council to be sure that those elected were such 'that the credit of the country should not be minimised nor destroyed in the markets of the world';[67] every Jamaican debenture holder had, in Blake's view, a *locus standi* with regard to the question of the concession of a permanent elected majority.

In the Colonial Office, Henry Lambert, a second-class clerk in the West India department, summarized the case for extended representation which Blake had put forward in earlier despatches. It would foster parochial feeling and hinder the formation of legislative cliques in the Council, which, on the principle of *divide et impera*, might be easier to handle. The accompanying increase in the number of nominated members would provide an opportunity for introducing into the Council 'some of the more respectable members of the community'. Further, Lambert argued, it was difficult to refuse a concession which Granville and Holland had conditionally offered in 1886 and 1887.[68] For Wingfield the strongest argument in favour of change was the 'real and strong feeling'[69] for it in those parishes sharing a representative, which Blake confirmed in conversations at the Colonial Office. Blake's advice carried weight for he was well regarded by officials, Hamilton noting

[65] Blake to Ripon, No. 109, 29 Apr. 1895. 8443. CO 137/565.

[66] Report of debate in Legislative Council. Encl. with Blake to Ripon, No. 74, 13 Mar. 1894. 5825. CO 137/559.

[67] Ibid. See speech by W. Andrews.

[68] Blake to Ripon, No. 74, 13 Mar. 1894. 5825. CO 137/559. Minute by H.L., 11 Apr. 1894.

[69] Ibid. Minute by E.W., 27 Apr. 1894.

that he was the right man in the right place: 'Noone was more successful than he was in dealing with Irishmen, & there are many points of similarity between Irishmen & negroes . . .'.[70] Blake later claimed that Ripon was 'to a certain extent' influenced by his favourable views regarding the availability of candidates, which he pressed personally in several interviews. It was, in fact, on this point that officials were most apprehensive, Lambert, Hamilton, and Meade all fearing the entry of more Kingston solicitors into the Council. This view was most forcibly expressed by Hamilton:

> . . . any change increasing the number of black or brown men or even of Kingston Jews & lawyers in the council might no doubt seriously affect the public credit & the stability of capital.[71]

This minute reflected closely the views of Blake on the possibly adverse influence which a Council with a large proportion of coloured members might have on the confidence of investors, but there is no evidence that this argument carried weight among officials generally. For instance, against a report of a speech by J. M. Farquharson in the Legislative Council, in which he claimed that Jamaica could raise money on favourable terms because its government was still controlled by the British government, an official noted: 'because money is cheap'.[72] In short, Ripon's decision to enlarge the Legislative Council seems to have rested primarily on Wingfield's judgement of public opinion, confirmed by Blake, and on the latter's assurance that suitable candidates would be forthcoming.

As Blake had suggested, Ripon balanced the concession of fourteen elected members by an increase in the number of *ex-officio* and nominated members from seven to eleven, exclusive of the governor, with four further nominations held in reserve, thus maintaining in case of need 'control over legislation in matters of Imperial interest and paramount impor-

[70] Blake to Ripon, No. 74, 13 Mar. 1894. 5825. CO 137/559. Minute by W.A.B.H., 17 Apr. 1894. There are other references in colonial office papers and in contemporary literature to the similarity of Irishmen and Negroes. For an example, interesting because its author was sympathetic to the Negroes, see Musgrave, op. cit., pp. 16–17. Both Hamilton and Blake had served in Ireland and it is interesting to speculate on the extent to which their views on the desirability of strong government had been shaped by the experience.

[71] Ibid.

[72] Report of debate in Legislative Council. Encl. with Blake to Ripon, No. 74, 13 Mar. 1894. 5825. CO 137/559.

tance . . .'.[73] The Legislative Council thus comprised after 1895 the governor with a casting vote only, five *ex-officio* members, six nominated members with four nominations in reserve, and fourteen elected members. Following the precedent of 1884 the Order in Council effecting these changes did not specify whether the nominated members were to be officials or unofficials.[74] Blake took advantage of this to recommend the appointment of two unofficials to the Legislative Council, Dr. J. Pringle and Lt.-Col. J. C. Ward. He described both as wealthy men, representing 'every interest in the Island', of whose 'loyal support' he was confident. Ripon's successor, Joseph Chamberlain, agreed to this proposal. Ripon extended a financial veto to the votes of any nine of the elected members, in place of six, and a veto to the unanimous vote of the fourteen elected members 'on any question', in each case on the same conditions which Derby had imposed in sections 43 and 44 of the Order in Council of 19 May 1884. Ripon made it a condition for the change that the Legislative Council should secure the vested salary and pension rights of serving and retired public officers, and provide for a civil list.

Blake's attitude towards constitutional change was shaped largely by his conviction that any reform must be compatible with stable conditions for capitalists. J. M. Farquharson, John Kerr, and Sharp, the three wealthy property owners and managers in the Council, shared Blake's concern for safeguarding and enhancing Jamaica's credit, but not his confidence regarding the availability of candidates for election. In April 1895 Kerr moved a resolution in the Legislative Council favouring a parochial residential qualification for elected members, or alternatively the ownership of property of 'annual value' or producing an income of £150 in the parish which a member represented. The resolution was carried by the casting vote of the acting president against the votes of four coloured members, and Clarke. Its supporters expressed apprehension regarding the number and quality of Kingston lawyers who might in future be elected. Blake recommended acceptance of the resolution[75]

[73] Ripon to Blake, No. 318, 12 Oct. 1894. 5825. CO 137/559.

[74] Order in Council, 3 Oct. 1895. P.C. 2/361. See S. 3.

[75] Blake to Ripon, No. 109, 29 Apr. 1895. 8443. CO 137/565. Also Blake to Ripon, Conf., 29 Apr. 1895. 8454. CO 137/565.

on similar grounds. The expense for country members of attending the Council was such that he hoped it would lead to 'men of local position', 'the best men in the island', coming forward for election, in contrast to irresponsible candidates who, he wrote privately to Wingfield, would exploit 'an ignorant and hysterical population saturated "au fond" with race antipathy';[76] moreover, a Council composed of a majority of Kingston solicitors would be 'unreliable and very troublesome'.[77] Blake explained his views more fully in his important confidential despatch of 29 April 1895, to which reference has already been made.[78] He stressed the hostility of the prominent members of the coloured community to the introduction of white settlers and white capitalists, and it is probable that this was his overriding consideration when he informed Ripon that there would be difficulty in carrying 'the necessary legislation' in a legislative council in which the number of coloured solicitors was increased. Wingfield advised acceptance of the resolutions as being 'the only hope of preventing the Council from being swamped by the Kingston brown lawyers who are the curse of the Colony'.[79]

The more stringent qualifications for elected members were included in the Order in Council of 3 October 1895, which provided for the enlargement of the Council, but they only partially fulfilled the hopes of their sponsors. In the general election for the enlarged Council in January 1896, 11,544 voted out of a registered electorate of 34,760, one seat being uncontested.[80] Of the fourteen elected members, seven were coloured and seven were white, one of the former and three of the latter being Jews. Clarke, Palache, Burke, and Philip Stern, a Jewish barrister previously elected in place of Jackson, were re-elected; the last three were the only lawyers in the Council. On the other hand, Blake noted there was only one member, Spencer Heaven, a wealthy cattle farmer, 'who in

[76] Blake to Wingfield (personal), 10 June 1895. Filed with minute paper 11176. CO 137/566. [77] Ibid.

[78] See footnote 41, p. 78.

[79] Blake to Ripon, No. 109, 29 Apr. 1895. 8443. CO 137/565. Minute by E.W., 24 May 1895.

[80] *Jamaica Blue Book for 1895–1896*. CO 142/109. Subsequent Blue Books give different statistics but those quoted are closest to the figures in Blake to Meade (personal), 20 Jan. 1896. 2857. CO 137/571.

England would be considered a gentleman',[81] and whom he expected to support the government; he resigned in August 1897. Of the remaining nine members, Blake described four as shopkeepers, and the others as a good practical agriculturalist, an owner of property, and a Baptist minister: two he considered to be without means. Subsequently there was a decline in the coloured representation, thirteen of the fourteen members returned in the election of January 1901 being white; in the seven contested parishes, 2,310 voted out of a registered electorate of 8,543.[82] In March 1897 Blake informed the Colonial Office that the elected members were 'decidedly inferior' to those of former Councils, and showed a tendency to combine.

Jamaican constitutional change was thus widely discussed by secretaries of state and officials during the ten years after 1884, yet there is little evidence in the colonial office papers of their view of its long-term direction. They were willing after 1885 to modify Derby's scheme without surrendering its fundamental principle of the Crown's overriding power of legislation. Beyond that, Norman, and possibly Gladstone, Derby, and Ashley, looked forward to representative government, and of those shaping policy they alone in this period seemed to have had faith in the benefits of representative institutions for Jamaica. Without sharing their faith Herbert hinted in February 1884 that further constitutional change lay only in that direction, for he noted that if those interested in property in Jamaica joined the opposition against the proposed constitution 'the ultimate result must be a serious collision with the people, followed, perhaps, by the surrender of power to the negroes'.[83] For Herbert the only alternative to giving the constitution a fair trial was an alteration 'in the direction of giving the negroes control over the Legislature . . .',[84] though he noted that it was 'most undesirable' to state this publicly. The silence of the colonial office minutes on the future direction of constitutional change in Jamaica possibly reflects the disinclination or inability of officials to formulate long-term policy.

[81] Blake to Meade (personal), 20 Jan. 1896. Filed with minute paper 2857. CO 137/571.

[82] *Jamaica Blue Book for 1901–1902*. CO 142/115.

[83] Minute paper House of Commons 2907. Minute by R.G.W.H., 20 Feb. 1884. CO 137/519.

[84] Ibid.

Preoccupied with pressing administrative problems, they rarely had the opportunity or wish to look beyond the immediate future; if they did so their minutes did not reflect it. They had supported constitutional change in Jamaica as the least inconvenient course of action; the alternative seemed widespread agitation. Their concern was trouble-free administration and not the long-term constitutional development of Jamaica. But Derby excluded the possibility of responsible government for Jamaica, and there is evidence that neither Knutsford nor his officials saw Jamaica set on this path, for they were careful to distinguish it from Western Australia and Natal which conceivably were, but which in the 1880s had Legislative Councils somewhat similar to Jamaica.[85] In January 1887 Norman asked Stanhope whether Jamaica had the right to withdraw from the recently negotiated International Copyright Union, this right having been reserved to colonies possessing elective legislatures, including Natal and Western Australia.[86] John Bramston, assistant under-secretary of state and Richard Ebden, head of the general department, put forward four reasons for distinguishing Jamaica from Natal and Western Australia. Firstly, Ebden suggested that it was difficult to make a distinction between the latter and their responsibly governed neighbours. Secondly, Bramston argued that the legislatures of Natal and Western Australia were not subject to crown control as two thirds of their members were elected. Thirdly, he minuted: '. . . they might any day acquire responsible Govt. pure & simple—I mean complete'.[87] The implication for Jamaica was clear. Norman also believed that 'responsible Government [in Jamaica] was for various reasons impossible . . .',[88] a view which was shared by Blake. One further reason was suggested by Bramston for distinguishing between Jamaica, and Natal and Western Australia, namely that if 'Jamaica were to be given a separate voice in treaties, Mauri-

[85] In 1887 the Western Australia Legislative Council comprised the speaker, five officials, four nominated members, and seventeen elected members. The Natal Legislative Council comprised the speaker, five officials, two nominated members, and twenty-three elected members.

[86] Norman to Stanhope, No. 13, 13 Jan. 1887. 2394. CO 137/530.

[87] Ibid., Minute by J.B., 19 Feb. 1887. See also minute by R.E., 14 July 1887 on minute paper 13489. CO 137/531.

[88] Norman to Derby, Conf., 19 Feb. 1884. 4155. CO 137/513.

tius & Malta would claim the same—which can hardly be'.[89] Advised by Herbert, Knutsford informed Norman that

> the proportion of elected members in the legislatures of Natal and Western Australia is larger than in the case of Jamaica; and that for Colonies in which the Constitution does not provide that there shall be a majority of unofficial members in the Legislative body H.M. Govt. takes the whole responsibility of international engagements.[90]

Officials regarded the question as a delicate one, Wingfield doubting whether it was 'necessary or desirable' to state the reasons for the distinction in a despatch; similarly Knutsford instructed Norman to discourage discussion of the subject in the legislature, a discussion which 'could not be confined to Jamaica . . .'.[91] In this respect it is interesting that Knutsford's despatch raised the possibility of some responsibility for international engagements for representatively governed colonies such as Barbados.

The lines between semi-representative, representative, and responsible government could be drawn but could they be maintained? Constitutional development in the settled colonies since the 1840s had been based on the development of representative into responsible government. Was Jamaica's constitutional development to halt at semi-representative government? The question does not seem to have been raised in the colonial office minutes on Jamaica, but Arthur Pearson, a first-class clerk in the Eastern department, recognized the problem in relation to Mauritius. He minuted that a Council of Government of nine elected, nine nominated, and nine official members was only suitable as a step towards responsible government, 'which, humanly speaking, can never be introduced into Mauritius'.[92] Moreover, could the elective principle once conceded be limited to a narrow franchise? Ashley, writing of Mauritius, thought not, for it 'must always from its very nature be regarded as merely a preparation for and forerunner of

[89] Norman to Stanhope, No. 13, 13 Jan. 1887. 2394. CO 137/530. Minute by J.B., 19 Feb. 1887.

[90] Holland to Norman, Conf., 19 Oct. 1887. 13489. CO 137/531.

[91] Ibid.

[92] Broome to Kimberley, No. 519, 31 Oct. 1882. 20602. CO 167/603. Minute by A.A.P., 21 Dec. 1882.

further extensions'.[93] The London *Morning Post* made the same point in relation to Jamaica:

> To grant any form of suffrage in such a country is to set a ball rolling which can scarcely be stopped while any one remains without a vote. If, then, the question be opened at all, it will have to be faced to the end, and not treated on merely present considerations.[94]

It was, however, on 'present considerations' that colonial office policy on constitutional reform in Jamaica between 1884 and 1895 was grounded.

[93] Ibid. Minute by E.A., March 1883 (undated).
[94] *The Morning Post*, 21 May 1884.

Section 2

British Guiana

1880–1895

4

A MOVEMENT FOR REFORM

The plantocracy on the defensive

THE central feature of British Guiana politics in 1880 was the dominance of the planting interest, which virtually monopolized the elected seats in the Court of Policy and Combined Court,[1] and which by the concentration of ownership among absentee planters[2] was able to bring strong influence to bear on the Colonial Office, mainly through the West India Committee. Although the local political influence of the plantocracy rested on narrow constitutional provisions, it was also rooted in the economic supremacy of sugar and its products, which in 1879 averaged 91.9 per cent by value of the total exports of British Guiana.[3] Most men of property and education were thus connected directly or indirectly with the sugar industry and dependent on its prosperity, and these were the men who in any small colonial society, under any constitution, would have exercised large political influence. But if the political power of the planters was underpinned by their all-embracing economic interests, it also buttressed them. The planters' control over the raising and spending of the revenue enabled them to block any government measures, such as the development of abandoned coastal estates by improved communications and drainage, which would have lessened the dependence of labour on the plantation economy, and thereby weakened the planters' hold over the labour market. In British Guiana, as in Trinidad, command of the labour market was

[1] See pp. 8–9.

[2] A. H. Adamson estimates that in 1884 83.5 per cent of British Guiana sugar estates, weighted according to the size of their labour force, were controlled by absentees, of which 47.25 per cent were in the hands of eight major firms and individuals. Alan Herbert Adamson, 'Sugar and the Economy of British Guiana 1838–1904' (London University Ph.D., June 1964), p. 332 A.

[3] See footnote 13, p. 5.

the central political purpose of the planting interest, and in both colonies it rested primarily on a high level of Indian immigration. It was further strengthened in British Guiana by crown lands regulations which were virtually prohibitive, since they priced land at over £2 an acre with a minimum holding of 100 acres. These stringent regulations had not prevented the establishment of a Negro peasant proprietary, for after the abolition of slavery, Negroes had squatted, or bought and settled, abandoned sugar estates; the task of poldering and draining these lands had, however, proved beyond their resources. The unwillingness of the government to do so before the 1880s partly accounted for the relative failure of the Negro peasantry to become successful cultivators, a failure which increased their dependence on the estates. It was also possible to cultivate land under licences of occupancy from the Crown, nearly 9,000 acres being so held in 1880, to a considerable extent by Portuguese. There is also some evidence of the growth of an Indian peasantry.[4] Nevertheless both policy and geography enabled the planters largely to confine the labouring population to the narrow coastal strip, within reach of, and in dependence on, the estates, and thus to command the labour market more effectively than in Trinidad. The incidence of taxation was a further example of political power used to further economic interests, for it bore most heavily on the general population through considerable duties on such necessities as rice and flour,[5] and high *ad valorem* duties on dry goods. By contrast, many estate supplies were exempt, and on goods such as tobacco and wine the duties discriminated in favour of higher quality. Although the Colonial Office favoured measures to encourage a peasant proprietary and a more equitable distribution of taxation, they did not insist on either against the views of governors and elected members. For instance, as early as 1871 the Emigration Board had recommended[6] a reduction in the price of crown lands from £2 to £1 an acre and in the minimum size of lots from 100 acres to 20 acres. In fact no change was made in the regulations until 1887 when the price was reduced to £1 an acre except for land ten miles

[4] See p. 97; footnote 52, p. 109; pp. 109–10.
[5] See footnote 16, p. 156.
[6] Emigration Board to Colonial Office, 15 May 1871. 4816. CO 318/261.

from a public road. Herbert summarized the colonial office attitude to the British Guiana constitution in 1872:

The Colony is governed by the planters no doubt with special reference to their own interests . . . we are compelled to put aside . . . proposals for reform which we feel it hopeless to press under the existing form of Government.[7]

During the 1870s there was, as in England, a weakening of the economic foundations on which the political and social pre-eminence of the landed class rested. Higher United States duties in 1872 damaged the American market. In 1874 the removal of the remaining sugar duties ended the last advantage enjoyed by British West Indian vacuum pan and muscovado sugars over the white-clayed and partially refined sugars of Cuba, Brazil, and Mauritius.[8] The accelerating and large-scale entry of raw beet sugar into the United Kingdom after 1876, the temporary closure of the American market in November 1877, unprecedented drought during 1878 and 1879, and the general depression in the United Kingdom and her colonies during the late 1870s further contributed to the difficulties of the British Guiana sugar industry.[9]

With the continued high level of Indian immigration, and the planters' discontinuance after 1874 of re-indenturing Indians who had completed their five-year term, there began a spontaneous and largely unplanned settlement by time-expired coolies on abandoned estates and in villages, particularly in Essequebo and Berbice. There was also evidence of a greater number of Negroes growing ground provisions and plantains as a steady industry. This hesitant growth of a peasantry was limited, however, by conditions which only government intervention could change, namely the restrictive crown lands regulations, poor communications, and the need to maintain defences against the sea in the fertile coastal strip, a task

[7] R. H. Whitfield to Kimberley, 10 June 1872. 6046. CO 111/394. Minute by R.G.W.H., 9 July 1872.

[8] R. W. Beachey, *The British West Indies Sugar Industry in the Late 19th Century* (Oxford, 1957), pp. 44–45.

[9] Amalgamation of estates leading to economies of scale, technical advances in the manufacture of sugar, and lower labour costs through their tight hold on the labour market, enabled the British Guiana planters to weather these conditions relatively better than planters elsewhere in the British West Indies. This did not, however, help the rural population, a reflection of their distress being the easier labour market after the early 1870s.

beyond the resources of the small cultivator. Nor did such unplanned settlement alleviate the rural distress caused by more stringent economic conditions. William Haynes Smith, the attorney-general, claimed that when Sir Henry Irving became governor in May 1882 'there was an angry feeling abroad',[10] due mainly to the pressure on the unrepresented classes of falling wages and a high level of indirect taxation. Irving himself described the villagers as being 'in a wretched and semi mutinous condition'.[11] These unfavourable economic conditions emphasized the dependence of the colony on sugar, and they reacted particularly severely on the Georgetown merchants, notably the importers and wholesalers, many of them Portuguese, who supplied the country shops and who depended on the purchasing power of the rural population.[12] Such dry goods merchants did not benefit from the continued relative prosperity of the sugar industry, in so far as this was maintained by reduction of labour costs and therefore of purchasing power in the rural areas. In these circumstances there was an increased interest among the commercial and professional classes of Georgetown in opening up the colony by improved communications, and in encouraging the establishment of a prosperous peasant proprietary and new industries, which would use the capital as a market both for their output and purchases. Their interest in economic diversification stimulated in turn a broadening political interest,[13] since the belief was widespread that a condition for a more equitable fiscal system and for economic diversification was a weakening of the political power of the planters. Such a view had been expressed as early as 1872 by Richard Whitfield, an Irish barrister practising in British Guiana,[14] and it was shared by Haynes Smith, who was

[10] Haynes Smith to Granville, 26 May 1886 (para. 56). Encl. with Irving to Granville, Sep(arate), 28 May 1886. 10271. CO 111/435.

[11] Irving to Granville, Sep., 12 June 1886. 11309. CO 111/435. One measure of the condition of the villagers was failure to pay rates. Between 1874 and 1882 nearly 38 per cent of the rates assessed were uncollected. Adamson, op. cit., p. 223.

[12] For a good example of their grievance see *A series of Letters on the Labour Question; Proposed Railway to Berbice; Inland Lake; Our Free Grown Sugar; and Great Britain's Support of Slave Grown Sugar* (Georgetown, 1875); in particular letter by 'Truth', 20 Mar. 1875, pp. 7–9. (Pamphlet R.C.S. Lib. $\frac{79}{5}$).

[13] Between January 1880 and January 1890 the number of registered electors for the Colleges of Electors and Financial Representatives rose from 715 to 1,596.

[14] See, for example, *The Present Position & Future Prospects of British Guiana*

both sympathetic to constitutional change and a vigorous supporter of a peasant proprietary. He believed that the future of the colony lay in the establishment of 'an independent middle class between the planter and the labourer . . .';[15] '. . . the future welfare of the Colony', he wrote in 1879, 'is bound up with the welfare of the middle class and the time has gone by for considering the Colony only as a sugar factory'.[16] Similarly the *Demerara Daily Chronicle*,[17] founded in 1881 as the organ of the influential Georgetown merchants, supported both a broadening of the British Guiana economy and moderate constitutional reform;[18] it voiced the view of many merchants in regarding the substantial commercial interests of Georgetown as being under-represented.[19] But the forces of political and economic change received their greatest impetus from the appointment of Sir Henry Irving as governor in May 1882.

Irving was well thought of in the Colonial Office. Herbert wrote of him as 'an excellent Governor, one of the few who are wholly indifferent to local popularity'.[20] Ability and courage characterized Irving's governorship of British Guiana which must rank among the most constructive in the history of the colony. His policy was to encourage the cultivation of other products than sugar by a thriving peasant proprietary, for he argued that it was not in the interests of the colony

considered; being a letter from Richard H. Whitfield, Barrister-at-Law, to the Colonists thereof (London and Liverpool, 1872).

15 Haynes Smith to Longden, 3 May 1876. Encl. with Longden to Carnarvon, No. 97, 5 May 1876. 6544. CO 384/110.

16 Attorney-General to Lieut(enant)-Gov(ernor), 4 Oct. 1879. Encl. with Young to Hicks-Beach, No. 221, 6 Oct. 1879. 17180. CO 111/415.

17 The *Demerara Daily Chronicle* (from 1 Jan. 1885 *The Daily Chronicle*) was priced at only 2*d.* and available for daily purchase as well as annual subscription. It soon claimed the largest circulation in the colony, which it estimated at over 1,000 copies a day in November 1882.

18 From the early 1880s its editorials favoured the abolition of the College of Electors, a reduction in the qualification of members of the Court of Policy, and the introduction of the secret ballot for the election of financial representatives. The paper was equivocal on a reduction of the franchise but by 1889 it was firmly opposing it. For further examples of the view that constitutional reform was a condition for economic diversification, see p. 103.

19 The representation in the Court of Policy was not by districts, the only direct representative of Georgetown being the city's financial representative in the Combined Court. Commercial interests in Port of Spain voiced a similar grievance at this time with regard to representation in the Legislative Council.

20 Irving to Hicks-Beach, Conf., 25 Sept. 1878. 13202. CO 295/281. Minute by R.G.W.H., 31 Oct. 1878.

that the cultivation of sugar should be virtually the only cultivation in the country and that outside the limits of the Sugar Estates there should be little to be found but neglected land and undrained and insanitary villages.[21]

Writing in 1886 he recognized that this state of affairs was bound up with the planters' monopoly of political power, which 'has naturally prejudicially affected all other interests than those of the Sugar Industry, and it has acted with special ill effects as regards the rural population outside the Sugar Estates'.[22] Although Irving held this view before 1886,[23] he nevertheless preferred at first to try to effect his policies of rural improvement by subjecting the existing political system to the pressure of public opinion,[24] rather than by attempting to reform it. The nub of his policy lay in transferring to the government the burdens of ownership, such as maintenance of roads, sea-defences, and drainage systems, which early Dutch law had placed on the estate owner, but which the small Negro cultivators in the villages and on the abandoned estates could not shoulder either singly or corporately. By Ordinance 4 of 1883 he placed the administration of the villages under the direct control of the Central Board of Health, their main drainage systems being taken over and maintained by the Public Works Department; for this purpose he obtained an annual vote of over £5,000 from general revenue. Ordinance 3 of 1884 provided for the maintenance by the government of all public roads through estates other than sugar plantations, thus relieving the small cultivator of an uncertain and at times heavy charge. In July 1886 the Combined Court pledged itself to provide up to £20,833 for the draining by the Public Works Department of 21,000 acres outside the villages, the money to be raised by loan and secured on the lands drained. Irving further benefited the rural population by a revision of customs duties, and by establishing in 1886 a single government medical service under the authority of the surgeon-general, which was to be responsible for the entire rural population both on and off the estates; under this scheme the responsibility for the

[21] Speech to Combined Court, 3 Dec. 1885. Reported in *The Daily Chronicle*, 4 Dec. 1885. The speech made a considerable impact on reforming opinion in the colony.

[22] Irving to Granville, Sep., 12 June 1886. 11309. CO 111/435.

[23] See, for instance, p. 113.

[24] See below pp. 101 et seq.

immigration medical service was transferred from the immigration agent-general to the surgeon-general.

These policies met with strong opposition from the sugar interest. On 19 December 1882 the Combined Court rejected by nine votes to five the expenditure necessary for taking over the roads outside the sugar plantations, only one financial representative voting with the government. Irving did not abandon his measure, but withdrew it temporarily to allow time for public opinion to make itself felt. These tactics were successful, for in June 1883 there was the unusual event of a contested election for the seat of financial representative for Georgetown. The two candidates, I. H. de Jonge, the sitting member, and W. Y. Perot, both represented the mercantile interest, de Jonge being an exporter of sugar to the American market and Perot a dry goods merchant. Both campaigned on a 'reform' platform, but de Jonge had opposed Irving's roads measure in the Combined Court and Perot by large publicity projected himself successfully as 'the Reform candidate'. The election was remarkable both for the interest which it aroused, notably among the Georgetown Negroes, and for the progressive programme which Perot put before the Georgetown electorate. He strongly supported Irving's village policy and his roads measure; and, more generally, he favoured opening up the country, and a moderate reform of the constitution by which the elected members of the Court of Policy would be directly elected by those entitled to vote for the financial representatives. He was critical of the unequal incidence of taxation, and advocated the transfer of the whole cost of Indian immigration to the planters.[25] Although Perot was defeated by 187 votes to 123, the expression of public support for Irving's rural policy had been unmistakable; on 20 June 1883 the governor carried the vote for his roads measure in the Combined Court with the support of five financial representatives, including de Jonge, against the votes of the five elected members of the Court of Policy and one financial representative. In similar circumstances Irving secured in July 1886 the

[25] *Demerara Daily Chronicle*, 14 June and 15 June 1883. Perot's attitude to Indian immigration does not seem to have been widely held among reformers, though it was shared by Woolford (see p. 104); the latter also stressed, however, the importance of Indian immigrants to the colony.

Combined Court's approval, without a division, for a unified medical service and the draining of lands outside the villages; the representatives of the planting interest had previously opposed the latter and had severely amended the former scheme. The elected members of the Court of Policy gave way, however, when faced with the support of the financial representatives for Irving's policy, and the demonstration of public opinion in its favour shown at the contested elections for the seats of financial representatives for Georgetown in February 1886 and for New Amsterdam in April 1886.[26] Irving claimed that his policy was only maintained 'by the growing force of public opinion . . .'.[27] In August 1886 Haynes Smith wrote:

> The truth is that the Colonial Government had laid the measures fairly before the public and the Country had replied that their Representatives must support the Government or they would be driven from their seats.[28]

His language was extravagant for in the Georgetown contested election of February 1886, 326 voted out of a registered electorate in January 1886 of 650; 64 voted in New Amsterdam in April 1886 out of a registered electorate of 91. The comparatively small polls are significant against the background of increasing political controversy, but they are not conclusive evidence for political apathy; for instance, reformers claimed that open voting and inconvenient balloting hours (9.00 a.m. to 4.00 p.m.) discouraged voters. The same factors may also have influenced the numbers registering. Nevertheless in 1885 *The Daily Chronicle* claimed that, in spite of increased registrations, political interest was 'vastly below what it might be if all possessing the qualification would register . . .'.[29] It was constantly urging those qualified, to register, and it proposed an association to organize them for this purpose.

Irving's achievement was two-fold. He won the grudging approval of the representatives of the sugar interest for measures which would weaken their command of the labour market by

[26] See pp. 103, 104–5.

[27] Irving to Granville, Sep., 12 June 1886. 11309. CO 111/435. This despatch is a spirited defence of his administration.

[28] Haynes Smith to Stanhope, 2 Aug. 1886. Encl. with Irving to Stanhope, Conf., 6 Aug. 1886. 15042. CO 111/436.

[29] *The Daily Chronicle*, 25 Feb. 1885.

encouraging the growth of a peasant proprietary. To achieve this he stimulated public opinion, not only in favour of his policies of rural improvement, but also in the belief that constitutional reform was an essential condition if they were to be rigorously implemented. This theme was reiterated by 'progressive' candidates in contested elections for financial representatives. R. J. v. R. de Groot, a barrister and the 'reform' candidate in the New Amsterdam election of April 1886, wrote of the planters' 'insensate' opposition to Irving's drainage scheme as pointing 'more conclusively to necessity for Reform, than any of the political meetings lately held . . .'.[30] In a memorial to the Queen in favour of constitutional reform, forwarded by Irving on 9 December 1887,[31] the signatories argued that a widening of representation was the only guarantee that a policy of encouraging the minor industries would be followed in the future. Similarly the petition to Knutsford in favour of reform, of January 1890,[32] referred to the narrow representation in the Court of Policy as tending 'to stifle every other industry save that of sugar'. The acute depression through which the sugar industry passed after 1884 makes it probable that these views would have been advocated under any governor, but Irving's policies and methods undoubtedly encouraged them.

It would be an over-simplification to suggest that British Guiana opinion was divided between a party of reform supporting Irving's measures of rural improvement and economic diversification, and the opposing sugar interest. The latter was itself divided, some resident proprietors being more sympathetic to Irving's policies than the representatives of the absentee proprietors. Nor were the supporters of reform numerous, or unanimous except in their agreement on the continued importance of sugar. The influential Georgetown merchants were primarily concerned with a moderate reform of the constitution which would admit their representatives to the Court of Policy. They supported Irving's policy because they recognized that the prosperity of the rural areas would benefit their commercial interests. Among them were merchants connected with the rising gold industry, the exports of which had increased

[30] Letter, 18 Apr. 1886, *The Daily Chronicle*, 20 Apr. 1886.
[31] See p. 114. [32] See pp. 129–130.

from 40 oz. in 1882 to 11,906 oz. in 1887. The assertion of British sovereignty within the Schomburgk Line,[33] and the confirmation that mining concessions and grants of land could be made without reservation within this area,[34] enabled the search for and recovery of gold to be extended to the north-west territory bordering Venezuela. The development of the industry continued to be hindered, however, by restrictive regulations and by the absence of communications to the interior, particularly to the north-west, which those with gold interests attributed to the indifference if not the hostility of the Combined Court to a new industry, which threatened to attract resources, particularly Negro labour, from the estates.

A group of mainly coloured lawyers, and certain merchants connected with the gold industry, adopted a more radical attitude to constitutional reform. In January 1884 S. B. Woolford, a coloured solicitor, stood for financial representative for Georgetown against B. V. Abraham, a jeweller with wide commercial interests who was supported by the sugar interest and many of the larger merchants; the seat was vacant through the death of de Jonge. Woolford's programme was more radical than Perot's, the main planks being voting by secret ballot, the transfer of the whole cost of Indian immigration to the planters, the encouragement of education, fewer restrictions on the retail rum trade, and the promotion of local men over outsiders in the public service.[35] In advocating the secret ballot, Woolford hinted at the pressure which employers brought to bear on their clerks in the Georgetown elections; it was later alleged that his defeat by Abraham by 190 votes to 154, like Perot's defeat by de Jonge, had been partly due to the exercise of such influence.[36] The growing political prominence of radical lawyers was reflected in two contested elections for financial representatives in 1886. In February, T. W. Phillips, a barrister whose candidature for Georgetown was supported by several other lawyers, defeated Abraham by over 100 votes

[33] See notice in *The London Gazette*, 22 Oct. 1886, p. 5104.

[34] Holland to Irving, No. 212, 5 Sept. 1887. FO 17632. CO 111/442.

[35] *Demerara Daily Chronicle*, 13 Jan. 1884.

[36] For allegations of employers' influence over employees see, for example, speech by T. W. Bracey, *Demerara Daily Chronicle*, 9 May 1882, speech by Woolford, ibid., 13 Jan. 1884, speech by Phillips, *The Daily Chronicle*, 30 Jan. 1886, and speech by W. Cunningham, ibid., 27 Aug. 1889.

in a total poll of 326. Speaking after his election, he was reported as saying: '. . . the dirty hands have got it'.[37] A self-confessed radical, he advocated mass meetings and agitation for constitutional reform, the abolition of the Court of Policy, free education, the extension of the franchise leading ultimately to universal male suffrage, and the establishment of 'a House of Representatives' as in Barbados. Acknowledging the importance of sugar and the need to encourage Indian immigration, he also vigorously supported the development of other industries including gold, and the opening up of the country by railways and less restrictive crown lands regulations. He opposed the colonial office exercise of patronage, and would have placed local appointments in the hands of the governor and 'House of Representatives'.[38] In April 1886 de Groot unsuccessfully contested New Amsterdam. Prominent in his speeches was his advocacy of the promotion of local men over outsiders in the public service. As in the case of Jamaica lawyers, it is probable that his attitude was partly influenced by personal interest. de Groot had been employed in the public service before becoming a barrister, and he referred to the frustrations which he had then encountered as a public servant. Duncan Hutson and Patrick Dargan, two coloured radical barristers who later played a prominent part in British Guiana politics, also worked as clerks in the public service before reading for the bar in England.[39] A fourth contested election for financial representative for Georgetown took place in May 1887, the 'progressive candidate', J. D. Smith, a dry goods merchant, being defeated by M. Bugle. Of 572 on the roll 395 voted, a larger number than in the three previous contested elections in Georgetown. The British Guiana Political Reform Club, founded in June 1887, was further evidence of increasing political awareness in British Guiana politics. Its chairman was J. D. Fileen,[40] a schoolmaster, and its secretary, D. T. Straghan, a reporter of

[37] Ibid., 3 Feb. 1886.

[38] Ibid., 30 Jan. 1886 and 3 Feb. 1886.

[39] In general, however, the agitation against outside appointments was less in British Guiana than in Jamaica and Trinidad. This is probably because in the former colony only the highest posts were held by expatriates. The frustrations referred to by de Groot possibly related to his exclusion from the close knit British Guianan-born families who monopolized many positions in the civil service. de Groot had been born in Dutch Guiana.

[40] Fileen was reported as stressing the need for 'political associations' among the coloured people; the circumstances and context of his speech suggest that he

The Daily Chronicle. Its members included certain barristers such as J. A. Murdoch, W. E. Lewis, a Negro, and Hutson, but it lacked the support of other lawyers and of the larger merchants. Its membership remained narrow and its appeal limited, though it was responsible in late 1887 for organizing a memorial favouring representative government.[41] In a series of meetings in the Demerara villages during November 1887, the club made the first major attempt by Georgetown politicians during the 1880s to agitate the rural population within reach of the city.

The evidence is scanty regarding the extent of interest in constitutional reform in Georgetown outside the merchant and professional classes, but newspaper evidence suggests that it was increasing to a small extent among the artisan class, who were particularly affected by the prevailing adverse economic conditions. The expansion and cheapening of the press, and the local though not fully effective application of the compulsory clauses of the education ordinance of 1876, probably also contributed to this. The connection between expansion of education and increased political activity is difficult to establish. Time lags, unreliable statistics, and the quality of education must all be taken into account. The registered pupils at Georgetown public elementary schools rose from 3,542 in 1876 to 5,044 in 1880 with an average attendance of 3,140,[42] but this improvement was not maintained during the 1880s, the annual numbers registered for the years 1883 to 1886 being lower than for 1880. Progress was less marked in the districts outside Georgetown; between 1876 and 1880 the number of pupils increased from 13,312 to 14,126 with an average attendance of 6,822. The inspector of schools estimated in 1885 that as many as 96 per cent of Georgetown children between 4 and 15 able

was referring mainly to the Negro population. He regarded a people's newspaper as of 'paramount importance' in developing their political character. *The Daily Chronicle*, 2 July 1886. In Gladstone's fight for Irish Home Rule, he saw the same struggle of 'Classes against masses' which was taking place in British Guiana, the phrase being taken from one of Gladstone's speeches. See also p. 108 for evidence of politically active schoolmasters. Clergymen were also prominent in the reform agitation. In Jamaica, too, clergymen and schoolmasters played a significant part in agitating the Negro population, though in the later part of the period it was the schoolmasters who increasingly took the central role. Many were Negroes and their literacy made them natural leaders in the villages.

[41] See p. 114.

[42] These and the following statistics are taken from the Reports of the Inspector of Schools: CO 116 series before 1880 and CO 114 series after 1880.

to attend were attending public or private schools, compared with 38 per cent in the rural areas, where the first tentative attempt to enforce the compulsory clauses of the education ordinance of 1876 was not made until 1894. On the other hand, irregularity of attendance was high, average attendance in Georgetown in 1885 being 60 per cent; in 1891 the inspector of schools reported that the compulsory clauses were 'a dead letter' even in the capital. Perhaps more significant politically was an increase in the quality of education in Georgetown. The number of children passing one or more exams at standards VII and VIII, which included reading with fluency and expression from a newspaper, rose from 1 in 1876 to 14 in 1880 and to 73 in 1887, the comparable figures for the rural areas being 5, 93, and 88. The relatively better Georgetown results may have reflected not only proportionately more numerous and skilled staff but the fact that the town children were sharper than those in the country, a point noted by the inspector of schools in his report for 1876, and of interest in accounting for the greater political interest in Georgetown.

It is not easy to determine the extent to which this interest was shared by the non-European population of the capital. The black population were reported as being greatly excited by the Perot–de Jonge electoral contest in 1883, and the numbers attending political meetings in Georgetown between 1880 and 1890[43] suggest the presence of some Negroes. Artisans and mechanics were among those agitating, and it is possible that they included some Negroes; as early as 1872 Whitfield had noted that 'the native Creole population, like the Portuguese but not to the same extent, have in many instances . . . risen above the ranks of unskilled labour into the mechanic or the artisan class'.[44] The popular appeal of Phillips' candidature and his demand that 'every mechanic' should have a vote

[43] Nearly 1,000 persons were reported to have attended Perot's adoption meeting in June 1883. *Demerara Daily Chronicle*, 14 June 1883. A 'densely packed and enthusiastic audience' which included 'creoles' attended a political meeting in the Town Hall, Georgetown on 22 July 1890. *The Daily Chronicle*, 24 July 1890.

[44] Whitfield, op. cit., p. 7. There is other evidence of Negroes rising in the economic and social scale. Not only were they becoming mechanics, shopkeepers, schoolmasters, and clerks; a few were also reaching the professions. The first Negro to be elected to either legislature seems to have been W. Smith, a merchant, who was elected financial representative in August 1890. See Sir C. Clementi, *A Constitutional History of British Guiana*, p. 542.

suggests increasing political awareness among this class. The memorial of December 1887 favouring reform was signed by 1,900 Georgetown inhabitants compared with a registered electorate in January 1888 of 762, which also suggests political interest among a small part of the non-white population. Political interest among the Portuguese shopkeepers and merchants[45] was stimulated by the recognition given by candidates to the importance of their vote in the contested elections for financial representative. In the New Amsterdam election of 1886 de Groot stood as '. . . the Champion of the Portuguese and down-trodden creoles'.[46]

It is hard to find evidence of widespread political interest in the rural areas, although conditions were favourable for agitation since, on Irving's estimate, agricultural wages fell by at least one-third between 1882 and 1887. A meeting at Belfield in November 1887 was reported to have been attended by over one hundred and thirty villagers, and during the same month the Reform Club[47] organized at least nine other political meetings in the villages at some of which schoolmasters were prominent. Of the 4,647 signatories to the reform memorial of December 1887, 2,382 lived in Demerara but outside Georgetown. The only contested election for financial representative outside Georgetown and New Amsterdam between 1880 and 1890 was in Demerara in October 1890, when Hutson, who was sponsored by the British Guiana Reform Association,[48] was successful; after the canvassing of villagers by the Reform Association, 145 voted out of a registered electorate in January 1889 of 241. Rural political activity seems to have been confined to Demerara,[49] which probably reflected the distribution of the Negro and Indian population, and the difficulties which poor communications imposed on the Georgetown politicians who sought to foster political interest in the districts more remote from the capital. A report in *The Grenada People* in February 1892 pointed out that distance and expense of travelling made it practically impossible for a Georgetown resident to contest an election in Essequebo, unless he was a man of means and

[45] For instance, de Groot's candidature for financial representative in 1886 was supported by Julio de Freitas, a Portuguese spirit dealer.

[46] *The Daily Chronicle*, 8 Apr. 1886. [47] See p. 106. [48] See p. 129.

[49] See also footnote 17, p. 129, and pp. 144, 148.

leisure.[50] No evidence has been found to suggest political activity among the Indians during the 1880s, although there was unrest on some estates, particularly in 1888, which was probably due to lower wages following amalgamation and the introduction of labour-saving machinery; the planters attributed it to the influence of high caste coolies, particularly Brahmins. The lack of the educational[51] and economic[52] opportunities enjoyed by their fellow-countrymen in Trinidad hindered the growth of an English-speaking and literate Indian middle class, the existence of which in Trinidad had been testified by witnesses before the Royal Franchise Commission of 1888.[53] On the other hand, a speaker at a Georgetown political meeting in January 1890 claimed that there were in British Guiana coolies 'both as regarded property and ability perfectly capable of representing the coolie class',[54] and Lord Gormanston, the governor, wrote in 1890 that there were 'very many coolies and some Chinese who are entitled to the franchise . . .'.[55] These last two views probably reflected the continued growth

[50] *The Grenada People*, 18 Feb. 1892.

[51] The statistics for the education of East Indians on the estates are fragmentary. From the report of the inspector of schools for 1885, about 2,689 were attending estate schools not receiving government aid, and a further 515 were at government assisted estate schools; the immigration agent general's report for 1885 estimated that there were 14,935 children resident on estates. The claims of estate work interfered with education, for though there were absolute restrictions on the employment of children under nine and qualified restrictions between nine and twelve, they were not enforced during the 1880s, both parents and employers conniving, from self-interest, at their breach. Surgeon-Major D. W. D. Comins estimated in 1893 that about 10 per cent of Indian children resident on estates attended school. *Notes on Emigration from India to British Guiana* (Calcutta, 1893), p. 58. Religious and national sentiment may have discouraged attendance at schools where teaching was denominational and in English. Comin's Report does not, however, support this view.

[52] The commutation for land of the right to return passage by time-expired indentured Indians, introduced in Trinidad in 1869, was not implemented in British Guiana until 1896, except for tentative schemes in 1872 and the early 1880s. The stringent regulations for the sale of crown lands prevented their purchase by time-expired Indian immigrants, no grant being recorded before 1890. On the other hand, colony lands, being abandoned plantations escheated to the colony for non-payment of road dues, were sold to Indians from the early 1880s. Others bought and rented land privately or simply squatted. Not only the Portuguese but also the Chinese reduced the opportunities for Indians in the retail trades.

[53] See pp. 159, 172–3.

[54] Speech of D. Gibson, *The Daily Chronicle*, 12 Jan. 1890.

[55] Gormanston to Knutsford, Conf., 20 May 1890. 10825. CO 111/456. Gormanston implied that nearly all these Indians were literate, but only in their own language.

of an Indian peasantry, facilitated after 1882 by a reduction in the expense and delay of conveying land belonging to the colony. In 1884 William Russell, a resident planter with wide knowledge of British Guiana, was reported as stating in the Court of Policy that *The Official Gazette* 'showed that land was being transported by and between East Indians in very large quantities; in fact, the Corentyne District, and the West Coast, Berbice, were fast becoming coolie settlements'.[56] This tendency of coolies to settle in certain localities further increased the social isolation which poor communications imposed on the rural population as a whole, and which was accentuated in the case of the East Indians by the absence of inter-racial marriages. By contrast, attempts by the Trinidad government to settle coolies in defined areas had not been successful.[57]

The increased political interest and activity in British Guiana during the 1880s owed much to Irving's reliance on the pressure of public opinion, particularly on the directly elected financial representatives, to secure the passage of his controversial measures for rural improvement. Such tactics led to deteriorating relations between him and the planters, and carried with them the risk that the representatives of the latter would be goaded into precipitating a constitutional deadlock by withdrawing from the Court of Policy, in which they still controlled the elected seats. Such a deadlock occurred in the autumn of 1887 over the publication of the report of the medical inspector, Dr. Alfred Williams. The issue was not itself important, but underlying it was the mutual suspicion and hostility between Irving and the planters, of which one aspect was the jealousy between the immigration department and the medical service following the administrative changes of 1886. In that year the

[56] *Demerara Daily Chronicle*, 23 May 1884. The reports of the immigration agent general for 1884–1890 show a total of 853 transports of land in favour of East Indians to value of £35,783, the largest single one being for £1,458.

[57] Later evidence confirms the lack of political activity among East Indians in British Guiana. As late as 1911 only 251 Indians were registered voters; not until 1916 was an Indian elected to either legislature. Shortage of educated leaders and ignorance of English, in which language ballot papers were printed after 1896, probably contributed to this. See, in particular, Peter Ruhomon, *Centenary History of East Indians in British Guiana, 1838–1938* (Georgetown, 1947), pp. 191–3. After 1891 the literacy test for voting was not confined to the English language though it is probable that given their educational opportunities a literacy test in any language handicapped the East Indians.

immigration medical service had become part of a single medical service under the surgeon-general, and the duty of inspecting estate hospitals, formerly undertaken by the medical officer to the immigration department, was transferred to the medical inspector who was accountable to the surgeon-general. In August 1887 Williams submitted a report for 1886 in which he uncompromisingly criticized the conditions in Indian immigrant hospitals on certain estates. The planters deeply resented the tone of the report which they regarded as a personal attack on themselves. In the absence on leave of Irving, Charles Bruce, the lieutenant-governor, laid the report before the Court of Policy on 10 August 1887. On 23 August he laid before the Court a letter which he had written to the surgeon-general asking him to obtain from Williams certain information regarding the report, an action which the elected members interpreted as a pledge that this information would be passed on to them. Irving, returning to the colony on 26 August, adopted a less conciliatory approach; he disregarded the elected members' request that Williams should not go on leave until he had substantiated his charges, and he refused to give them the information which they considered Bruce had promised. He adopted a more moderate position in a debate in the Court of Policy on 11 October, offering to give the elected members any information which they wanted, but their temper was such that this concession did not satisfy them. Smarting under what they regarded as Irving's 'high-handed, supercilious style of conduct', and goaded by the press, they demanded the withdrawal of the report or they 'must decline to discuss any other business before the Court';[58] they implemented this threat at a meeting of the Court on 25 October, Irving having refused to withdraw the report although in other respects his attitude remained conciliatory. It is difficult to avoid the conclusion, however, that in his handling of the whole affair Irving was either extraordinarily tactless and autocratic in his manner, or that he deliberately provoked a political deadlock. Certainly he welcomed it, for three days after the withdrawal of the elected members from the Court of Policy he wrote privately to Harris in the Colonial Office: 'Everything is going splendidly here . . . the greater the dead-

[58] Minutes of the Court of Policy, 11 Oct. 1887. CO 114/41.

lock & the mischief thereof the greater the sins of these gentlemen in neither resigning nor doing work and the heavier the penalty they are likely to pay for it.'[59] Irving used the deadlock to place the issue of constitutional reform before the public. At the Court of Policy meeting on 25 October he suggested that the dispute could be resolved if the elected members would co-operate with the government in bringing about a reform of the constitution which would allow an appeal to the electorate. He also took advantage of the political crisis to press the Colonial Office for an immediate grant of power to break the deadlock, to be followed by moderate constitutional reform which he believed would receive a broad measure of local support. His two proposals were related, for he believed that the elected members of the Court of Policy would co-operate in passing a moderate measure of reform so long as the government held in reserve the power to overcome any deadlock precipitated by their withdrawal.

In the first instance, Irving telegraphed that an order in council be passed declaring that the governor and four other members should form a quorum in the Court of Policy, thus enabling business to proceed with only the official members present; by unwritten but long-standing usage a quorum was held to be the governor and five members. Knutsford treated this request cautiously. He supported Irving in his refusal to withdraw the report, but instructed him by telegram immediately to give to the Court of Policy the information obtained from Williams before he went on leave, and to assure them that any objections to the statements in the report would be carefully considered. At the same time he trusted that they would 'not persist in refusing to act necessitating such measures as may be necessary for proceedings of Court of Policy going on without their presence'.[60] It seems that Knutsford was prepared to grant Irving's request for an order in council, but that he shared Wingfield's view that '. . . it would be undesirable to resort to such a measure if the deadlock can be otherwise averted'.[61] Underlying this attitude was Wingfield's belief

[59] Irving to Harris (personal), 28 Oct. 1887. 22786. CO 111/440.

[60] Holland to Irving, Tel., 3 Nov. 1887. 21713. CO 111/440.

[61] Irving to Holland, No. 396, 14 Oct. 1887. 21713. CO 111/440. Minute by E.W., 29 Oct. 1887.

that it was undesirable that laws should be voted by the official members of the Court only, and his reluctance to impose a constitutional change against local opinion. Herbert took a stronger line:

I think it would be unfortunate if this difficulty were allowed to be patched up without having resulted in either the establishment of a quorum . . . or a wider reform of the Constitution on the Jamaica lines.[62]

He advised passing immediately the order in council which Irving asked for, and subsequently considering further reform. He held to this view even after he knew of the elected members' return to work following the publication of Knutsford's telegram, and it reflected his opinion, first expressed in 1871, of the desirability of extending crown control in British Guiana.[63] Knutsford did not dismiss the possibility of an order in council if it could be implemented legally and without breach of faith, but he shelved the question when Irving telegraphed that it was no longer necessary, the elected members having returned to work.

Irving's main purpose was to use the political deadlock to initiate in the colony and carry through 'a very moderate instalment of reform'. He wrote:

It has long been obvious that some change in the existing constitution of the Colony is inevitable . . .

A constitution in which one interest only is represented and in which that interest can, when it may deem proper to do so, bring about a deadlock in public affairs . . . is politically indefensible, and necessarily breaks down the moment the Elective Members come into collision with the Government acting on behalf of the unrepresented classes.[64]

He argued that the likelihood of such deadlocks would increase 'as other interests than those of the Sugar Planter increase in importance'.[65] Like Herbert, Irving had penetrated to the heart of the matter, namely that the British Guiana constitution was incompatible with the theory of crown colony

[62] Irving to Holland, No. 407, 22 Oct. 1887. 22765. CO 111/440. Minute by R.G.W.H., 15 Nov. 1887. [63] See p. 9.

[64] Irving to Holland, No. 407, 22 Oct. 1887. 22765. CO 111/440.

[65] Ibid.

government, under which the Crown, acting through the governor and officials, was the guardian of the interests of the unrepresented classes. It was a measure of the weakness of the colonial office commitment to this principle in British Guiana that the constitution had for so long remained unchanged.

Irving's case for reform rested on timing and expediency as well as principle. He argued that conditions for a change were favourable, for the position of the elected members was indefensible, the majority of public opinion supported the government, and there was no political excitement. Behind this analysis lay the fact that the elected members had chosen their ground badly, for the issue over which they had withdrawn from the Court concerned the sugar interest alone. Harris noted that the West India Committee thought they 'have gone too far & made a gross mistake'.[66] Their attitude seemed to many to emphasize narrow motives of class interest, and strengthened demands for constitutional reform.[67] Irving, in fact, claimed that public opinion was 'unanimous' in favour of some constitutional amendment, an assertion which must be qualified by his own admission of the difficulty of judging it in a colony where the legislature and press were unrepresentative. What evidence there is supports Irving's view. On 9 December 1887 he forwarded a memorial praying for 'a Representative Government similar to that recently granted . . . to . . . other West Indian Colonies . . .'.[68] Of the 4,647 signatories, 1,900 were from Georgetown. Irving estimated that the signatories included 685 registered voters out of a total registered electorate in February 1887 of 1,429, and 1,015 signatories who were taxpayers and village proprietors. The secretary of the Reform Club, which sponsored the memorial, later claimed that it had been largely signed by merchants, ministers of religion, doctors, lawyers, and engineers, and by half the taxpayers of Georgetown. Nor was support for reform confined to the non-planting interest. Haynes Smith wrote privately to Herbert that moderate reform could be carried with the unanimous consent of the planters, for the 'extreme planters' as much as the moderates

[66] Irving to Harris (personal), 28 Oct. 1887. 22783. CO 111/440. Minute by C.A.H., 12 Nov. 1887.

[67] See, for example, letter signed 'A Quiet Observer' in *The Daily Chronicle*, 14 Oct. 1887.

[68] Encl. with Irving to Holland, No. 467, 9 Dec. 1887. 25820. CO 111/441.

looked to the government 'to guard them against the extreme party on the other side'.[69] It is probable that he was referring to the Reform Club which during November organized a series of political meetings in the villages in the neighbourhood of Georgetown. His judgement was confirmed on 22 November when the Court of Policy unanimously resolved, all the elected members being present:

That the members of the Court be requested to co-operate with the Governor in considering the question of an amendment of the Political Constitution of the Colony with a view to secure wider representation of the Inhabitants.[70]

In a speech supporting the motion B. H. Jones, a prominent resident planter of liberal leanings, indicated that the elected members would support a moderate measure of reform.

Irving put forward one further argument for reform, namely that if 'a very moderate instalment' was refused there was the 'risk of a political agitation in the Country against the dominant class . . .'.[71] Wingfield doubted this judgement, but Haynes Smith, writing privately to Herbert, confirmed it; in his view not only would a return to the *status quo* lead to bitter disappointment, but also to probable appeals to the Queen in Parliament 'where the people believe they would receive warm support in struggling against the exclusive power of one class'. He believed that Dr. Williams's Report was 'in the hands of the Exeter Hall party and the Parliamentary influence of that party and of the Medical Organizations at Home are invoked . . .';[72] in June 1888 the case of Dr. Williams was raised in the House of Commons by Dr. R. Farquharson. There were other contacts between colonists sympathetic to reform and members of parliament. On 9 December 1887 *The Daily Chronicle* reported that the aim of the Reform Club was to petition 'three influential members of Parliament soliciting their aid on the other side of the waters in the matter . . .'. On 13 March 1888 H. E. Watt,[73] member of parliament for

[69] Haynes Smith to Herbert (personal), 28 Oct. 1887. 22765. CO 111/440.

[70] Irving to Holland, No. 466, 9 Dec. 1887. 25819. CO 111/441.

[71] Irving to Holland, No. 407, 22 Oct. 1887. 22765. CO 111/440.

[72] Haynes Smith to Herbert (personal), 28 Oct. 1887. 22765. CO 111/440.

[73] Watt had extensive gold interests in the Yurari Valley of Venezuela, being chairman of the New Chile Mining Co. which he estimated had invested £1,000,000 in the area. He was interested in a concession in the North-West Province of

the Camlachie division of Glasgow, questioned the parliamentary under-secretary of state, Baron de Worms, on colonial office policy regarding constitutional reform in British Guiana. Referring to this and subsequent questions by Watt, *The Daily Chronicle* claimed in July 1889 that they had 'invariably been put in response to representations made by reformers in this colony'.[74] Watt himself informed Knutsford that at a public meeting in Georgetown in July 1887 he 'was requested under seal of the Town Clerk, to represent the Colony in Parliament'.[75]

It was thus a strong case for constitutional reform, grounded on both principle, timing, and expediency, which Irving and Haynes Smith presented to Knutsford and his officials; the latter's treatment of it reflected their distrust of Irving's judgement and tact, and their cautious attitude towards a reform of the British Guiana constitution. Herbert agreed with Wingfield that a power of dissolution for the governor, and an extension of the franchise to make the Court of Policy more representative of all interests, were desirable. But Irving's hostility towards the planting interest, his tactless and autocratic manner, and the angry tone of his despatches led both Knutsford and his officials to doubt his ability to carry through such changes peacefully. These considerations influenced Knutsford to resist Irving's pressure to bring forward a measure of reform 'without delay'. Irving's governorship was to end on 24 December, and Knutsford agreed with Wingfield that the matter should be left over for his successor.

The scheme which Irving wished to implement was a moderate compromise whereby he hoped that the sugar interest would retain its influence, but at the same time the unrepresented classes would no longer be 'dependent for their protection on the personal qualities of the Governor for the time being'.[76] In order to achieve an adequate representation of all classes and interests, he proposed to increase the officials in the Court of Policy from four to five, excluding the governor,

British Guiana and, with others, he probably believed that constitutional reform would lead to more generous treatment of the gold industry. He was in close touch with reformers in British Guiana and pressed their case both in the House of Commons and with the Colonial Office.

[74] *The Daily Chronicle*, 2 July 1889.

[75] Watt to Knutsford, August 1890 (undated). 15515. CO 111/458.

[76] Irving to Holland, Conf., 27 Oct. 1887. 22778. CO 111/440.

and the elected members from five to six, of whom two would be directly elected for Georgetown on the qualifications of a financial representative,[77] and four would be directly elected for the county divisions on the existing and more restrictive qualification of an elected member of the Court of Policy.[78] His proposal thus involved the abolition of the College of Electors. Irving suggested that some 'moderate improvement' in the franchise might also be effected, but he proposed no change in the composition or powers of the Combined Court. The governor, he considered, should have the power to dissolve both Courts. Wingfield commented: 'If this not very large Reform Bill can be carried without trouble it will be a decided improvement.'[79] This minute summed up Wingfield's attitude towards the reform of the British Guiana constitution, namely a belief in its expediency tempered by an unwillingness to implement it against local opinion and particularly that of the elected members. Irving had sought to reassure the Colonial Office on the state of public opinion, but Knutsford and his advisers doubted his ability to carry peacefully a measure the need for which they acknowledged, and they were unwilling to commit themselves to it while he remained governor.

Knutsford appointed as Irving's successor a more conciliatory governor in Lord Gormanston, who in May 1888 summarized the policy of his administration as one 'which need not be less firm though prompted and maintained in a spirit of patience and conciliation'.[80] Knutsford took quick advantage of the change of governor. In a numbered despatch of 8 February 1888, which was published in the colony, he informed Gormanston that

> . . . Her Majesty's Government are prepared to advise that some amendment of the Constitution of B. Guiana is desirable. The nature and extent of such amendment will receive careful consideration.[81]

In the House of Commons on 13 March 1888 Baron de

[77] See footnote 24, p. 9. [78] See footnote 23, p. 8.

[79] Irving to Holland, No. 435, 11 Nov. 1887. 24026. CO 111/441. Minute by E.W., 28 Nov. 1887.

[80] Gormanston to Knutsford, No. 176, 26 May 1888. 11462. CO 111/445.

[81] Holland to Gormanston, No. 54, 8 Feb. 1888. 25820. CO 111/441. In an accompanying confidential despatch 'expedient' was substituted for 'desirable'.

Worms reaffirmed that some amendment of the constitution was desirable.[82] In a confidential despatch, also of 8 February, Knutsford asked Gormanston for his views and recommendations. Although the numbered despatch was in reply to the memorial in favour of reform, forwarded by Irving on 9 December 1887, its timing suggests that the grounds for Knutsford's decision lay in renewed intransigence on the part of the Combined Court, as well as in the weight of support for the memorial and Irving's advocacy of reform. The despatch was drafted five days after an exchange of minutes between Wingfield, Herbert, and Knutsford, which had been occasioned by an attack on certain official salaries by the elected members of the Combined Court; on 15 December 1887 they had reduced the salaries of Dr. Williams to 1 cent, and that of the colonial civil engineer, W. H. Hutchens, from £1,000 to £600. Their action raised for Wingfield the important consideration of 'whether any and what change can and should be made in the functions of the Combined Court'[83] when the civil list expired on 31 December 1889. This was a new issue, for the colonial office consideration of the British Guiana constitution, initiated by Irving's despatches of late 1887, had been limited to a reform of the Court of Policy. Herbert's attitude to the larger question of a reform of the Combined Court was characteristically more far-sighted and firmer than that of Wingfield. He suggested that the question of the Combined Court might possibly be dealt with at the same time as the reform of the Court of Policy, and he advocated the abolition of the Combined Court so long as 'the people of Br. Guiana do not attach sentimental or other importance to the existing forms of their constitution . . .'. In so commenting Herbert displayed a deep ignorance of political realities in British Guiana as subsequent events were to show. He continued:

My present view is, having regard to the great additional responsibilities which the Government is undertaking in regard to the territory disputed by Venezuela, and the necessity (for considerations of Foreign Policy) that the Government should have an unimpeded control over all administration and legislation (financial

[82] *Hansard*, Third Series (323), 1064.
[83] Irving to Holland, No. 493, 23 Dec. 1887. 425. CO 111/441. Minute by E.W., 13 Jan. 1888.

included) that if an absolute Crown Majority in a single chamber cannot be obtained there should be a single Legislative Council constituted like that of Jamaica, with similar powers reserved to the Governor to legislate in emergencies.[84]

This minute, with which Knutsford agreed, is evidence for the view already expressed, that Herbert was the most consistent advocate within the Colonial Office of a reform of the British Guiana constitution which would strengthen the power of the Crown, though in this case with the important proviso that such a change should be carried with local support. His attitude was based on broader grounds than those of his colleagues. In the 1870s he had been concerned with the needs and dangers of the Indian immigrant population[85] and this concern was still present,[86] but it was now reinforced by considerations of foreign policy. These were prominent in his mind for only three days earlier he had deprecated the action of the colonial government in issuing a proclamation on 31 December 1887, without reference to the Colonial Office, denying the validity of any claims within British Guiana which might be exercised under a railway concession granted by the President of Venezuela. The increased responsibilities to which Herbert referred were the assertion by Britain of her claim to the territory within the Schomburgk Line, and the confirmation by Knutsford that mining concessions could be made without reservation within the area.[87] Herbert's preference for the pure crown colony system over the constitution conceded to Jamaica in 1884 was held more strongly by Wingfield and Harris, who regarded the Jamaica constitution as a bad model; his concern that any change should be supported by local opinion was shared by his colleagues and is a recurring consideration in colonial office minutes on constitutional reform in Jamaica, Trinidad, and British Guiana. Herbert's minute, favouring the abolition of the Combined Court, and written in the belief that public opinion in British Guiana probably supported the change, represents the most radical proposal made within the Colonial Office during the discussions preceding the constitutional reforms of 1891.

In short, during the spring of 1888 Knutsford publicly

[84] Ibid., Minute by R.G.W.H., 2 Feb. 1888.
[85] See p. 9. [86] See pp. 134, 140. [87] See p. 104.

committed the Colonial Office to the consideration of constitutional reform in British Guiana, though he placed the onus for framing a detailed scheme on Gormanston. Within the Colonial Office, opinion favoured making the Court of Policy more representative, and changing the functions of the Combined Court or even abolishing it. At any time during the previous twenty years colonial office officials would have welcomed these reforms. What now led Herbert and his colleagues to advise them was the belief that they could be effected with a large measure of local support. Irving in his despatches had given no ground for this view so far as a reform of the Combined Court was concerned, but it was one of the notable results of his governorship that by its close there existed considerable support even among the planting class for moderate reform of the Court of Policy. Irving's reliance on the pressure of public opinion to win support among the elected members for his policies of rural improvement had stimulated political interest among the merchant and professional classes, reflected for instance in the five contested elections for financial representatives between 1883 and 1887. By the success of his appeals to public opinion implicit in these elections, Irving had overcome the opposition of the planters' representatives, particularly in the Court of Policy, an opposition which had served to emphasize for many the narrowness of the interests they stood for and therefore the desirability of constitutional reform. Of the necessity for the latter it is probable that Irving was never in doubt, but he skilfully chose his ground. By exploiting the political situation following the publication of Williams's Report, he isolated the elected members of the Court of Policy on an issue which emphasized their narrow class interests. He further used the opportunity to place the question of reform before an already favourably disposed public opinion and before the Colonial Office. Irving's success in mobilizing opinion favourable to reform almost certainly led the elected members of the Court of Policy, and the planting interests they represented, to regard some measure of reform as inevitable. Their formal support for it in the autumn of 1887 may thus be seen as an attempt to moderate and control what they regarded as an unwelcome but inevitable change; probably the same motive informed some supporters of Jamaica reform in 1882 and 1883. Irving's measures of rural improvement also directly strengthened the reform movement in so far as they increased that peasant proprietary of whose restiveness the memorial in favour of reform gave some small evidence.

Yet in examining the roots of reform Irving's contribution should not be over-stated. The less favourable economic conditions which faced the sugar industry during the late 1870s and the 1880s, particularly after 1884, would in any circumstances have stimulated interest in economic diversification and in removing the political and economic obstacles which impeded it; it was, moreover, natural that such interest should have been strong among the commercial and professional classes dependent on the prosperity of the sugar industry. Political activity was also fostered by developments which cannot be directly attributed to Irving's policies such as the cheapening and extension of the press,[88] increasing literacy, and the beginnings of the emergence of a coloured and Negro professional class, particularly of barristers with English experience. Also reformers drew encouragement from outside British Guiana. During the 1880s *The Daily Chronicle* reported movements for constitutional reform from Jamaica, Barbados, Trinidad, Tobago, St. Vincent, St. Lucia, St. Kitts, Nevis, and Antigua. It also reprinted calls for inter-colonial action from the more radical section of the West Indian press. For instance, *The Daily Chronicle* reported that *The Trinidad Review*, commenting on the agitation for constitutional reform throughout the West Indies, proposed that 'the Liberal Press of all the West Indies devise some plan of intercourse, by which accurate accounts of the proceedings of associations formed in the different Islands . . . may be generally disseminated'.[89] *The Daily Chronicle* also drew attention to the view of the editor of the more extreme *Grenada People*[90] who, noting the achievement of, or the trend towards, federation in Canada, and the Australian and Cape Colonies, proposed that the 'West Indies too should seek by combination also to have their rights duly protected. . . . The union of two millions of men for a common purpose would be an argument which no English statesman

[88] The *Demerara Daily Chronicle* was founded six months before Irving commenced his governorship.

[89] Reported in *Demerara Daily Chronicle*, 13 Jan. 1884.

[90] See footnote 44, p. 200.

would despise. . . . There must be a West Indian League . . .', which the editor, however, was careful to distinguish from a federation.[91] These sentiments appear to have evoked no response in British Guiana, but supporters of constitutional reform were undoubtedly heartened by the concession of modified representative government to Jamaica in 1884 and Mauritius in 1885, and by the extension of the franchise in Barbados in 1883. Of the constitutional changes in Jamaica and Barbados, the leader-writer of *The Daily Chronicle* wrote: '. . . a like privilege could not—and we feel assured would not—be denied to the inhabitants of British Guiana . . .'.[92] Interest was not confined to the West Indies and Mauritius. Sympathizers of reform in British Guiana noted with satisfaction the agitation for and achievement of franchise reform in England in 1884. The leader-writer of *The Daily Chronicle* did not regard it as surprising 'that the great extension of the franchise in Great Britain and Ireland should have led to the inquiry, "Why not also increase the number of those in possession of the franchise in British Guiana?" '.[93] Even the meeting of the third National Congress in India was reported. Reformers in other colonies also drew encouragement from developments in British Guiana. A correspondent of the Trinidad *New Era*, referring to the movement for a reform of the Court of Policy, wrote: '. . . let us not be too much behindhand—let us have a meeting called too, so that our petition to the Queen may go at the same time, with that of British Guiana'.[94] Such events gave reformers the feeling that the tide was moving with them, but their influence should not be over-stressed. Inter-colonial news travelled slowly and did not make a large impact. Derby's despatch of 1 December 1883 on constitutional reform in Jamaica was published without comment in *The Daily Chronicle* of 3 February 1884. The roots of reform were indigenous; they were nourished from outside.

[91] Reported in *Demerara Daily Chronicle*, 30 Apr. 1884.

[92] *The Daily Chronicle*, 28 Nov. 1886.

[93] Ibid., 24 Dec. 1885.

[94] Letter dated 11 Oct. 1882. Reprinted in *Demerara Daily Chronicle*, 24 Oct. 1882.

5

THE CONSTITUTION OF 1891
A truncated measure

KNUTSFORD'S decision in principle to reform the British Guiana constitution seems to have been taken on two main grounds, namely the unrepresentative character of the Court of Policy, and the undesirability of the Combined Court being able to bring pressure to bear on officials by reducing or threatening to reduce salaries. A reform of the Court of Policy was the less difficult course open to Knutsford, since the necessity for broadening the representation to include commercial interests was widely acknowledged in the colony, even by the planters. There were differences of opinion regarding the qualifications for elected members and the level of the franchise, but they were not as fundamental as those which divided the Colonial Office and local, particularly planter, opinion on any reform limiting the powers of the Combined Court. The protection of official salaries required such a limitation, but, as well as the strength of local opposition, two important assumptions by Knutsford and his advisers adversely affected their ability to implement it.

Firstly, Knutsford had placed the responsibility for framing reform proposals on a pliant and conciliatory governor who was in bad health and who proved unable to withstand the pressure of planter opinion. By relying on local advice and initiative it is probable that Knutsford hoped to secure a measure commanding wide support. Only Herbert questioned the wisdom of this decision. As early as April 1889 he argued that the colonial authorities, and especially Gormanston, were not strong enough 'for the fight that ought not to be avoided'.[1] He advised the appointment of a royal commission from

[1] Gormanston to Knutsford, No. 127, 9 Apr. 1889. 8517. CO 111/452. Minute by R.G.W.H., 30 Apr. 1889.

England to enquire into the constitution and civil list arrangement, which should include an Indian civil officer 'in order to have the full support of the India Office, as concerned for the good treatment and management of Indian Immigrants'.[2] Knutsford showed no inclination for a fight with the planters, and he did not pursue Herbert's recommendation after Gormanston had not surprisingly informed him that the Combined Court declined to pay the expenses of such a commission. Possibly underlying Knutsford's reluctance to precipitate a conflict with the planters was Wingfield's advice that the abolition of the Combined Court, or a reform depriving it of the control of taxation, could only be effected by parliamentary legislation.[3] Wingfield based this view, which had been less firmly held by Sir Henry Taylor, on the opinion of the crown law officers of 1840 and 1842.[4] The inexpediency of such parliamentary legislation was the second limiting assumption of Knutsford and his advisers with regard to British Guiana constitutional reform. Its significance is not diminished by the fact that it is rarely stated or explained in the colonial office minutes.[5] For Wingfield the danger of parliamentary discussion of the British Guiana constitution lay particularly in an appeal being made to the report of a select committee of the House of Commons of 1849, which had recommended that any change in the constitution of British Guiana should 'proceed upon the basis of extending the elective franchise as far as may be deemed practical and prudent' and should at the same time concede to the legislature 'a greater control over the conduct of public affairs than they have hitherto enjoyed'.[6] Gormanston

[2] Gormanston to Knutsford, No. 127, 9 Apr. 1889. 8517. CO 111/452. Minute by R.G.W.H., 3 May 1889.

[3] For example, Gormanston to Knutsford, No. 173, 22 May 1890. 10792. CO 111/456. Minute by E.W., 10 June 1890. The Colonial Office were careful not to publicly commit themselves to this position.

[4] See p. 7, and footnote 27, p. 10.

[5] For evidence that it was a consideration underlying Knutsford's decisions see pp. 141–2.

[6] First report from the Select Committee of the House of Commons on Ceylon and British Guiana. May 1849. 297. Colonial Papers Parliamentary, 1849, vol. 4 (F.C.O. Lib.). The appointment of a select committee seems to have been inspired by Henry Taylor, his object being to obtain parliamentary sanction for a correct definition of the constitutional powers of the Crown, the Court of Policy, and the Combined Court. He claimed to have written the report himself, with the exception of the final paragraph recommending a liberalizing of the British Guiana constitution. See *Autobiography of Henry Taylor*, vol. 2 (London, 1885), p. 38.

foresaw a similar danger, namely that 'in these very democratic days' Parliament would almost certainly amend a bill depriving the Combined Court of the power of taxation, so as to give the inhabitants of the colony larger powers than they already possessed. Wingfield also advised against the alternative way of protecting official salaries, by abolishing the Combined Court's power to examine the estimates, and to approve, reduce, or veto expenditure not secured by ordinance or by the civil list. This power derived from an order in council and not from the terms of the capitulation of 1803.[7] Wingfield argued that its abolition could therefore be effected without parliamentary legislation, but that this raised the possibility of 'a strong appeal . . . to the House of Commons against the reimposition of pure Crown Colony Govt. in a Colony in which an elected body has for so long controlled expenditure—and no doubt the Report of the Select Committee of the H. of C. in 1849 would be much relied on'.[8]

If the powers of the Combined Court remained unchanged the only other way of protecting the salaries of at least the higher public officers was to remove them from the Court's annual review by enlarging the civil list. This became Wingfield's leading aim, but to achieve it he had to establish a bargaining position in relation to the planters, who largely controlled the Combined Court and could precipitate a deadlock in the Court of Policy. Parliamentary considerations precluded the threat of the abolition of the Combined Court, or a withdrawal of its powers of taxation or control of the estimates. Wingfield considered as possible alternative courses a threat to weaken the hold of the planters in the Combined Court by enlarging its membership, with or without an extension of the franchise, or a wide extension of the franchise for the election of members of the Court of Policy. Herbert raised the possibility of a threat to suspend Indian immigration. None of these proposals seemed workable, and it was this failure to establish a bargaining position which finally prompted Wingfield to advise giving way on important issues regarding the reform of the Court of Policy in order to obtain the assent of

[7] See p. 8.

[8] Gormanston to Knutsford, No. 4, 3 Jan. 1890. 1098. CO 111/455. Minute by E.W., 22 Mar. 1890.

the Combined Court to an enlarged civil list. The strategy of the planting interest was to make very moderate constitutional reform the price of such an enlarged civil list, and in this they were assisted not only by the weakness of Knutsford's bargaining position, but also by his decision that the measure should be framed in the colony by a weak governor, and passed by the Court of Policy. The planters could, therefore, the more easily make the moderate character of the reform measure the condition for the passage of an enlarged civil list. The attitude of Knutsford and his advisers to the possibility of parliamentary legislation or discussion, and to the desirability of leaving the initiative and passage of a measure of reform to the governor and local legislature, thus shaped fundamentally the character of the constitutional reforms of 1891.

Gormanston gave Knutsford no indication of his views on constitutional reform during 1888 beyond commenting adversely on the very conservative proposals of the British Guiana Planters Association.[9] During February 1889, however, while on leave in England, he discussed the question with Wingfield and Herbert. There are two conflicting accounts of this meeting. Wingfield claimed that they agreed that the civil list which expired on 31 December 1889 should be enlarged to include the heads of departments, and that an 'extensive reform' of the constitution might be used as a threat to obtain the Combined Court's assent to it. Gormanston, writing in May 1889, gave a different account, claiming that he was of the opinion then, and was still of the same opinion

> that it would be injudicious to attempt to reform the constitution of this Colony; and that, as long as the planting interest . . . acted moderately and threw no unfair obstacles in the way of the Government, no such measure should be introduced.[10]

He had understood that the representatives of the planting interest were to be so informed and this he had done confidentially before leaving England. On his return to the colony he reiterated this view, arguing that it was undesirable to reform the constitution since it was workable; it would, moreover, be impossible to carry a major measure of reform, and it was

[9] See pp. 131–2.

[10] Gormanston to Knutsford, Conf., 24 May 1889. 11595. CO 111/452.

inexpedient to make minor reforms. He proposed to proceed with the re-enactment of the civil list without the extension desired by the Colonial Office.

Gormanston thus placed Knutsford in the dilemma of being publicly committed to a policy of reform which was opposed by the governor. The extent of the commitment was noted by Wingfield and communicated in a despatch to Gormanston, Knutsford referring to his public despatch of 8 February 1888 and to parliamentary pledges, as well as to the expediency of reform implicit in the Court of Policy resolution of 22 November 1887. In Wingfield's view, these considerations, together with the petition forwarded by Irving on 9 December 1887, made a measure of reform inevitable. Further, Wingfield expressed a view widely held in the Office, that the existing constitution gave 'undue power to the planting interest . . . Some reform in the direction of widening the representation in the Court of Policy—if not in both Courts—is due to the rest of the community other than the planters . . .'.[11] On the question of an enlarged civil list, Wingfield maintained the position which he claimed he had adopted at the meeting with Gormanston in February 1889, namely the absolute necessity for at least securing the salaries of the heads of departments for a term of years. Otherwise the power of the Combined Court could be used 'in such a manner as to submit public officers to the temptation of shaping their conduct . . . to meet the wishes and interests of the planting body . . .'.[12] Thus advised, Knutsford instructed Gormanston to delay the introduction of an ordinance renewing the civil list, on the grounds that it should include the principal heads of departments and was 'clearly connected' with the question of reform; '. . . if an adequate Civil List is secured', he explained, 'a more limited measure of reform might be accepted . . .'.[13] He instructed Gormanston to reconsider the question of reform and to submit the heads of a measure which would in his opinion 'give an adequate representation to the inhabitants other than the planting body . . .', and to advise 'as to the prospect of such a measure being favourably received by the Elective members

[11] Ibid. Minute by E.W., 14 June 1889.
[12] Ibid.
[13] Knutsford to Gormanston, Conf., 27 July 1889. 11595. CO 111/452.

of the Court of Policy'.[14] Knutsford's concern to carry planting opinion was also reflected in his suggestion that Gormanston, before submitting a scheme of reform, should approach the elected members privately in an effort to overcome their objections. In a further despatch he stated the principles which should guide Gormanston. The Crown should continue to retain control of legislation by the governor's casting vote in the Court of Policy. As at present advised, Knutsford wished to retain 'the present system of a Court of Policy for general legislation and a Combined Court for fiscal legislation'. The elected members of the legislature 'should represent not, as at present, exclusively or nearly exclusively, a single class, but all classes who are capable of intelligently exercising the franchise'. The interests of the 'large numerical majority of the inhabitants who will not be directly represented . . . must be guarded by the Government through the Official Members of the Legislature'.[15] This last observation is one of the few restatements of Henry Taylor's justification of crown colony government which is to be found in colonial office despatches on constitutional reform in the three colonies and in the period under review.

In framing his proposals Gormanston had to take into account three main bodies of opinion in the colony, radical opinion favouring an extensive reform of the constitution leading to representative government, more moderate opinion represented by the larger merchants who sought representation in the Court of Policy, and the planting interest who opposed reform except of the most moderate kind. Gormanston's proposals, as it proved, were to bridge the narrow gap between the last two groups, and so prepare the way for a conservative alliance of commerce and land in defence of property in the years immediately after 1891. By August 1889 radical opinion was represented by the British Guiana Constitutional Reform Association, founded and presided over by R. P. Drysdale, financial representative for Demerara and mayor of Georgetown, who had extensive commercial and planting interests. Only one leading planter and a few of the prominent merchants supported the Association, which drew its main strength

[14] Knutsford to Gormanston, Conf., 27 July 1889. 11595. CO 111/452.
[15] Knutsford to Gormanston, No. 266, 27 Sept. 1889. 18529. CO 111/453.

from the commercial and professional classes of Georgetown. The Association resembled a rudimentary political party. It advocated not only constitutional reform but also the opening up of the country and the development of the minor industries, particularly gold. It planned weekly meetings, annual subscriptions, and countrywide branches. It sponsored Duncan Hutson, a coloured barrister, as candidate in the election of 1890 for financial representative for Demerara,[16] and it attempted to overcome political apathy by printing and circulating application forms for the registration of voters: between January 1889 and January 1890, when the Association was most active, the number of registered voters rose from 1,596 to 2,210.[17] Apart from activity in the colony, both the Association and the Reform Club[18] sought support in England, particularly in Parliament. They were successful in enlisting the interest of Watt,[19] who was active on their behalf both in the House of Commons and in correspondence with the Colonial Office; he visited British Guiana in September 1889, meeting several 'reform leaders' and receiving an address of thanks from the Reform Club. Support for reform also came from the Aborigines Protection Society and the Cobden Club.[20] There is no evidence in the colonial office papers of activity by other individuals or organizations in England on behalf of the radical reformers; early in 1890 the Reform Association attempted to form a committee in London, apparently without success, Watt declining the presidency of it. The Association's programme, drawn up during the summer of 1889 and finally

[16] Hutson stood as a special advocate of the interests of the villagers and mercantile community. He defeated his opponent, R. Allen, who was supported by the sugar interest, by 85 votes to 70. See also p. 144.

[17] The figures indicate the success of the Association in the country districts within reach of Georgetown.

	January 1890	*January 1891*
Demerara excluding Georgetown	264	716
Georgetown	740	835
Essequebo	367	390
Berbice	122	152
New Amsterdam	103	117

Official Gazettes for 18 Jan. 1890 and 24 Jan. 1891. CO 115/71 and CO 115/72.

[18] See pp. 105–6.

[19] See footnote 73, p. 115.

[20] The Cobden Club attacked on grounds both of political economy and justice the high import duties levied on food by the planter-dominated legislatures of the West Indies.

embodied in a numerously signed petition to Knutsford in January 1890,[21] was radical, though not, as Drysdale acknowledged, 'as radical as some might desire'. It proposed the abolition of the two Courts and the College of Electors, and the substitution of an Executive Council of the governor, three officials, and three nominated unofficials, and of a Legislative Assembly of five nominated members, and sixteen elected members with a qualification similar to that of a financial representative under the existing constitution.[22] Voting was to be by secret ballot. A proposal that aliens be enfranchised after three years' residence, and if subject to a liability for militia service, had been amended in deference to the Portuguese, the militia liability being abandoned. There was evidence of disagreement within the Association regarding the level of the franchise, that finally adopted being the existing qualification for electing financial representatives,[23] with a reduction in the income qualification from £125 to £62. 10*s.* 0*d.* Gormanston alleged that the reduction had only been carried at a meeting of the Council of the Association in the face of 'great opposition and doubts . . .'.[24] The petition was not supported by the planting interest nor, on the evidence of the only page of signatures preserved, by the leading merchants and barristers; the leader-writer of *The Daily Chronicle* attacked it as too radical and lacking the support of 'the more intelligent classes'.[25] Gormanston's attitude to both the Association and the petition was hostile; he dubbed the former as 'so-called reformers', a 'small section of the Community' whose proposals 'have not excited any general interest . . .'.[26]

The second main body of reform opinion was represented by the leading merchants; it was not formally organized but its

[21] Encl. with Gormanston to Knutsford, No. 23, 17 Jan. 1890. 2137. CO 111/455.

[22] See footnote 24, p. 9. The possibility of the extension of an income qualification of £300 to the elected members of the Court of Policy was to be strongly opposed by the sugar interest. See pp. 137, 142–3.

[23] The qualifications included possession or occupation of a house or house and land, the qualifying values of which differed for the county and town voter. There was also a common qualification of a minimum annual income of £125 or minimum annual payment of £4. 3*s.* 4*d.* in direct taxes. Ord. 15, 1849. CO 113/2. Controversy centred on the level of the income qualification.

[24] Gormanston to Knutsford, Conf., 20 May 1890. 10825. CO 111/456.

[25] *The Daily Chronicle,* 10 Jan. 1890.

[26] Gormanston to Knutsford, No. 292, 15 Aug. 1889. 17290. CO 111/453.

views were probably close to those of *The Daily Chronicle*,[27] and it was certainly consulted by Gormanston. The governor was mainly influenced, however, by the planters, to whose opinions he largely deferred and with whom he was in the closest touch throughout his negotiations with the Colonial Office; indeed he acted largely as their spokesman. In July 1888 the British Guiana Planters' Association had submitted a scheme of reform, and in September 1889 H. K. Davson, an independent proprietor and elected member of the Court of Policy, informed Knutsford of the constitutional amendments which in his view would be acceptable to the Court of Policy and the colony at large. Eight years later he claimed that 'it was only after my interview with Lord Knutsford, who wanted a very much enlarged representation, that I sketched, at his request, the present Constitution as a compromise'.[28] In fact the reformed constitution of 1891 differed in at least one important respect from Davson's proposals, which were similar in principle to those of the Planters' Association. Both schemes retained the indirect election of members of the Court of Policy for a term of years, but provided for an increase in their number to allow for the representation of commercial interests, with a corresponding increase in the number of officials. The Planters' Association recommended the election of two additional members on a less restrictive property qualification than that of the five existing members, who were to continue to fulfil the 1864 qualification of ownership of eighty acres of land of which forty had to be in *bona fide* cultivation. Davson proposed six county members with the latter qualification and four town members with a less exclusive qualification.[29] Both proposals aimed to qualify for membership of the Court of Policy a restricted class of propertied merchants and professional men; by contrast, the Reform Association aimed to include in their proposed legislature a wider class drawn from commerce and the

[27] See footnote 18, p. 99.

[28] Davson to Wingfield (personal), Conf., 11 Nov. 1897. 24682. CO 111/500.

[29] Davson's proposed property qualifications were somewhat higher than those of the Association which had not, however, proposed an income qualification. Davson recommended, in addition to the existing qualification, the possession of a house of minimum value of £2,083. 6*s*. 8*d*., or ownership of freehold or minimum twenty-one-year leasehold of house or house and land of 'annual value' of £250, or a clear annual income of £800.

professions who would have qualified under an income qualification of £300. Neither the Planters' Association nor Davson favoured a reduction in the franchise qualifications for electing members of the two Colleges.

Gormanston forwarded a considered scheme of reform[30] in January 1890,[31] which he believed 'would secure the adhesion of the moderate men . . .'. He had previously submitted it to Nevile Lubbock, the chairman of the West India Committee who was visiting British Guiana, and although he did not inform the Colonial Office in his covering despatch, his scheme had also been considered and approved at a meeting of planters held in Georgetown on 21 December 1890. Gormanston proposed an increase in the elected members of the Court of Policy from five to eight, of whom five would represent the counties, two Georgetown, and one New Amsterdam;[32] the official majority would be retained by a corresponding increase in the number of officials from four to seven, in addition to the governor with an original and casting vote. He advised the adoption of the property qualification which Davson had suggested for his four 'town members' without the income qualification of £800;[33] he proposed to apply it, however, to all the elected members. He also went further than the planters would have wished by recommending the abolition of the College of Electors, and the direct election of members of the Court of Policy by those qualified to elect members of the College of Financial Representatives. Gormanston suggested a reduction in the income qualification for voting from £125 to £100;[34] this was a concession to the planters, who had originally opposed any reduction in the franchise, for in his preliminary scheme Gormanston had suggested an income qualification of £60,[35] or £2. 10*s.* 0*d.* below the figure favoured by the Reform Association. The governor accepted the planters' view that

[30] He had submitted a preliminary scheme in August 1889 which differed in three important respects from his final scheme. In the former he had proposed a reduction in the income qualification for voting from £125 to £60, and he had accepted the property qualifications for elected members of the Court of Policy proposed by the Planters' Association, which were lower than Davson's. He had not recommended an increase in the elected members of the Court of Policy.

[31] Gormanston to Knutsford, No. 4, 3 Jan. 1890. 1098. CO 111/455.

[32] Previously only the financial representatives had represented districts.

[33] See footnote 29, p. 131.

[34] See footnote 23, p. 130.

[35] See footnote 30 above.

aliens should be excluded from both Courts and from the franchise.[36] He recommended no change in the number or qualifications of the financial representatives, and he reaffirmed the Combined Court's opposition to a permanent or enlarged civil list. Gormanston proposed the formal enactment of the powers of the Combined Court. Of these, the right of the Court to discuss the estimates had previously only been conceded by order in council in consideration for a septennial civil list, and for the currency of that civil list. The right to allow, disallow, or reduce the items of the estimates had never been formally enacted, though the right of the Combined Court to exercise it under the authority of successive orders in council had been acknowledged by secretaries of state. In the opinion of the crown law officers, the right of the Combined Court to impose a tax had been established by the terms of the cession of 1803, but although the Colonial Office accepted this view it was careful not to affirm it publicly. Gormanston's proposal formally to confirm these three powers therefore amounted to a considerable constitutional concession to the elected members of the Court of Policy and Combined Court, and to the planters whom they represented. The governor also suggested certain measures to strengthen the position of the executive. The governor should at any time have power to dissolve both Courts in which, subject to certain conditions, a quorum should be eight, thus enabling business to proceed with only the officials present; the executive functions of the Court of Policy should be transferred to an Executive Council 'with the usual powers and functions . . .'.[37]

Wingfield regarded Gormanston's proposals as the '*via media* which should be aimed at',[38] a *via media*, that is, between Davson's proposals and those of the Reform Association. He argued that having promised reform it would have been impossible to have accepted the former, while the latter

[36] Gormanston seems to have had mainly the Portuguese in mind, 'not one of whom'. he claimed, 'has ever been naturalised . . .'. The Reform Association claimed that the procedure was complex and expensive, and it was simplified and cheapened by Ord. 7 of 1891.

[37] See Chapter 9 for a fuller treatment of this aspect of the 1891 constitutional changes.

[38] Gormanston to Knutsford, No. 4, 3 Jan. 1890. 1098. CO 111/455. Minute by E.W., 22 Mar. 1890.

would be too dangerous an experiment in a Colony so situated—our experience in Jamaica Mauritius and Malta of legislative bodies with a considerable elective majority is not altogether encouraging.[39]

But in fact Gormanston's proposals bore no similarity to those of the Reform Association; they were closer to Davson's scheme on which, with the exception of the abolition of the College of Electors and the reduction in the franchise,[40] they were based.

Herbert's reaction to Gormanston's despatch is puzzling for his minute dealt only with the need to retain crown control in the Court of Policy, a policy which Knutsford had already affirmed and which had not been questioned in the Colonial Office, or in the colony except by the Reform Association. His minute is significant, however, in its reference to the threat to end Indian immigration:

. . . it is to be remembered that we have a powerful argument wherewith to enforce the determination to keep control, in the Coolie Immigration; which the Government of India will not allow to continue unless H.M. Govt. can ensure the safety & welfare of the immigrants in all respects.[41]

The threat had been used by Kimberley in 1872 to hasten the passage of an ordinance implementing some of the recommendations of the coolie commission of 1870, but there is no evidence in the colonial office papers, except for Herbert's minute, that Knutsford and his advisers considered the use of such a threat during the constitutional negotiations of 1887 to 1891. It is probable that the easier labour position in the colony would have made it less effective. If Herbert's attitude is puzzling, it is also hard to judge Knutsford's reaction to the issues raised by British Guiana constitutional reform; Davson hinted that it was a liberal one but as there is no substantial minute by Knutsford on the subject in the colonial office papers it is not possible to confirm this. On the evidence of these papers, he leant heavily on the advice of his officials with whom

[39] Gormanston to Knutsford, No. 4, 3 Jan. 1890. 1098. CO 111/455. Minute by E.W., 22 Mar. 1890.

[40] It was only on the question of the franchise that the planters had made a rea concession, for as early as March 1888 the absentee proprietors had decided not to contest the abolition of the College of Electors. Minutes of a meeting of British Guiana Proprietors and Merchants, 22 Mar. 1888. West India Committee minutes.

[41] Gormanston to Knutsford, No. 4, 3 Jan. 1890. 1098. CO 111/455. Minute by R.G.W.H., 17 Apr. 1890.

he did not disagree on any major point. Of these, Wingfield was the most influential and he undertook the detailed examination of Gormanston's scheme of reform.

Wingfield accepted Gormanston's proposals in outline, but differed from him on four points of substance. Firstly, he favoured the same qualification for elected members of the Court of Policy as for financial representatives, a proposal originally put forward by Irving and followed by the Reform Association. Secondly, he was unwilling to accept Gormanston's proposal of an income qualification for the franchise of £100 without more information; he advised that the governor should be asked what class and number of voters would be enfranchised by the lower rate proposed by the Reform Association of £62. 10*s*. 0*d*. Thirdly, Wingfield and Knutsford favoured voting by secret ballot, Wingfield noting that since it has been adopted in Jamaica, Mauritius, and Malta 'the burden seems to lie on the Governor to shew exceptional reasons for retaining open voting in B. Guiana'.[42] Gormanston had defended open voting only by reference to its past use in municipal elections, and those for the Colleges of Electors and Financial Representatives. Fourthly, in the absence of a permanent civil list, Wingfield argued that the power of the Combined Court to control the estimates should not be enacted permanently but only 'granted' for the currency of the civil list. It was, however, an enlarged civil list which Wingfield sought and on this point he was firm. Gormanston reported that the proposal would probably not command a single elective vote in the Combined Court. In these circumstances Wingfield considered two possible courses of action. The first was to transfer the control of the estimates from the Combined Court to the Court of Policy, but he rejected this on the grounds that it might involve an appeal to the House of Commons in which the report of its select committee of 1849 'would be much relied on . . .'.[43] Further, the Court could still enforce its views on expenditure by withholding supplies. This led Wingfield to consider an increase in the number of financial representatives which would lessen the chance of 'unanimous obstruction to the Govt. or oppression of a too zealous officer';[44]

[42] Gormanston to Knutsford, No. 4, 3 Jan. 1890. 1098. CO 111/455. Minute by E.W., 22 Mar. 1890. [43] Ibid. [44] Ibid.

with a larger representation assigned to the towns there would be a non-planting interest, which might act as an 'equipoise' to the sugar interest and allow the officials 'to turn the balance', if necessary, against the planters. Harris noted and rejected a possible third course, namely 'a wide extension of franchise',[45] since it would open the door to jobbery. In January 1889 he had minuted that he was opposed to 'any further move in the direction of representation: that is a dream that I have for the time had to forget'.[46] A month later he wrote a strong minute opposing the introduction of elected members into the Trinidad Legislative Council, in which he approvingly cited Froude's recently published book on the West Indies;[47] it is legitimate to conclude that his views on British Guiana may also have been influenced by it. Wingfield also rejected a low franchise admitting 'a mass of ignorant voters', as 'so injurious to the interests of the Colony that the Govt. would not be justified in establishing it . . .'.[48] Harris favoured the establishment of crown colony government, but this was a course which Wingfield did not consider, since in his view it would have involved Imperial legislation.

Wingfield's views, endorsed by Herbert and Knutsford, were conveyed to Gormanston in numbered and confidential despatches of 30 April 1890.[49] In the latter, Knutsford favoured lowering the qualifications for the elected members of the Court of Policy by assimilating them to those of the financial representatives, 'subject however to any strong reason which you may be able to advance against it', and he proposed voting by secret ballot unless 'exceptional reasons' could be shown to the contrary. He instructed Gormanston to furnish information as to the class and number of voters who would be admitted under an income qualification of £62. 10*s*. 0*d*. He declined permanently to enact the powers of the Combined Court unless the civil list was made permanent. If the Court

[45] Gormanston to Knutsford, No. 4, 3 Jan. 1890. 1098. CO 111/455. Minute by C.A.H., 27 Jan. 1890.

[46] Bruce (Lieut.-Gov.) to Knutsford, No. 385, 4 Dec. 1888. 25567. CO 111/448. Minute by C.A.H., 1 Jan. 1889.

[47] See p. 184.

[48] Gormanston to Knutsford, No. 173, 22 May 1890. 10792. CO 111/456. Minute by E.W., 10 June 1890.

[49] Knutsford to Gormanston, No. 79, 30 Apr. 1890, and Conf., 30 Apr. 1890. 1098. CO 111/455.

refused to enlarge the civil list to include the heads of departments, Knutsford was disposed to think that the financial representatives should be increased, say to twelve, and he argued the advantages of such a course on the lines of Wingfield's minute. He instructed Gormanston, if he thought it advisable, to convey to the elected members the threat of thus being outnumbered in an enlarged Combined Court by an alliance of non-planters and officials. Knutsford indicated in his numbered despatch that the question of the civil list must be disposed of before 'the future constitution and functions of the Combined Court' were decided, and he instructed Gormanston to invite the Court to enlarge the civil list to include the heads of departments. Gormanston declined to communicate this despatch to the elected members, considering that such a veiled threat would jeopardize even the passing of the civil list in its existing form.

In short, advised by Wingfield, Knutsford substantially accepted a scheme of reform which had been previously submitted to and approved by the planting interest, and which fell short in certain important respects of Gormanston's preliminary proposals of the previous August, which both Wingfield and Knutsford had considered inadequate. Of the controversial points in Gormanston's detailed scheme, Knutsford tentatively pressed a lower qualification for elected members of the Court of Policy and voting by secret ballot, and he left for future decision the level of the income qualification for the franchise. He remained firm, however, on the need for an enlarged civil list, which he was prepared to obtain by the threat of an increase in the number of financial representatives, by which the sugar interest might be outvoted in the Combined Court by an alliance of officials with the non-planting interest.

In a confidential despatch of 20 May 1890,[50] Gormanston defended his proposed property qualification for elected members of the Court of Policy on the grounds that £2,083 was a 'very moderate' amount of capital, the second qualification was the same as that for a financial representative, and that an income qualification was inappropriate for legislators, who should have a stake in the country. Wingfield advised giving way on his earlier proposal to assimilate the qualifications of

[50] Gormanston to Knutsford, Conf., 20 May 1890. 10825. CO 111/456.

elected members of the Court of Policy to those of the financial representatives if the former 'strongly opposed' it. Gormanston defended open voting on the grounds that 'it has been always so', it was used in municipal elections, and its abandonment would involve the printing of ballot sheets in at least three different languages.[51] These were not strong reasons, as Wingfield recognized, but he again advised giving way. Gormanston reported difficulty in assessing the number and class of voters who would be admitted under the lower income qualification of £62. 10*s.* 0*d.* The colonial civil engineer was of the opinion that 'so-called' skilled workmen such as carpenters, masons, and smiths would be enfranchised by the lower qualifications, but the few figures which the governor gave of wages paid on three estates did not confirm this and were quite inadequate for reaching an answer to the question raised. Wingfield advised accepting Gormanston's figure of £100 as the income qualification for the franchise, his decision to yield on this and on open voting being influenced by the governor's view that if the measure of reform was so limited, then it would 'very much facilitate an early and satisfactory solution of the Civil List'.[52] In short, the planting interest had turned the tables on the Colonial Office, and instead of the latter using the threat of an extensive reform of the Combined Court to obtain an enlarged civil list, the planters used the threat of withholding it to prevent anything but a very moderate measure of reform of the Court of Policy. Wingfield was further encouraged to advise giving way by the governor's strong attack on the only alternative course under consideration, namely the implementing of the threat to increase the elected representation in the Combined Court. Gormanston claimed that it would be impossible to find gentlemen even from the towns who were not 'more or less' connected with the sugar interest, and that his experience both in British Guiana and the Leeward Islands convinced him that on any matter of importance the elected members would vote together, particularly against a government measure. The effect of an enlargement of the Court would be to increase its prestige at the expense of the Court of Policy. Wingfield considered that the governor underrated 'the efficiency of the

[51] English, Hindustani, and Chinese.

[52] Gormanston to Knutsford, Conf., 23 May 1890. 10827. CO 111/456.

principle "divide et impera" if skilfully applied',[53] but he advised Knutsford, at least temporarily, to withdraw the threat to increase the number of financial representatives. Wingfield also advised a further concession to local opinion. He had originally suggested that the major constitutional changes should be made by order in council, other matters such as the franchise and qualifications for elected members being dealt with by a local ordinance. The governor had suggested that an ordinance drafted in the colony and incorporating all the changes would be more appropriate, the draft being submitted to the secretary of state before being introduced into the Court of Policy. Wingfield now recommended the adoption of this course if it was less likely to cause friction. In short, Knutsford, advised by Wingfield, gave way on each of the points at issue between Gormanston and the Colonial Office in order to obtain an enlarged civil list, and he agreed to the constitutional changes being incorporated in an ordinance which would in the first instance be drafted in the colony. He further informed Gormanston that he might privately state the extent of the reforms proposed, as a result of which the governor was able to assure Knutsford that after consultation with the elected members of the two Courts, and others, he was assured that if a scheme of reform was limited to the proposals which he had put forward in May, an extended civil list, including all heads of departments, would be passed without very great difficulty.

The final opportunity for colonial office reconsideration of Gormanston's scheme of reform was in July 1890 when he submitted the draft ordinance. It was in Herbert's words 'an *omnium gatherum*', containing one hundred and twenty-six clauses covering changes in the constitution, electoral procedure, the standing orders of the two Courts, and, in opposition to Knutsford's view, a recital of their powers. Wingfield was absent from the Office during the late summer and early autumn of 1890, but Harris immediately seized on this last point, minuting that he understood that Wingfield shared his view that only if the Combined Court passed a permanent and comprehensive civil list should the Crown definitely part with the disputed powers over finance. Wingfield's absence was the

[53] Gormanston to Knutsford, Conf., 20 May 1890. 10825. CO 111/456. Minute by E.W., 10 June 1890.

occasion for Herbert's first major intervention in these long-drawn-out negotiations. On the evidence of the colonial office papers, he had taken only a peripheral part in the discussion of Gormanston's original proposals, and apparently no part in the decision to give way on each of the issues which Knutsford had raised as a result of Wingfield's examination of these proposals. He now gave careful consideration to the draft ordinance and reached conclusions different from those of his colleagues. Referring to the clause which enacted that no money should be procurable by the government for the public services except with the consent of the Combined Court, he minuted:

At present we maintain that the supreme power of legislation on all subjects (including money) rests with the Court of Policy, in which the Government has a majority; and I do not think the supremacy of the Combined Court in money matters should now be affirmed—even if a large permanent Civil List were granted. . . .[54]

Herbert's opinion clashed with that of the crown law officers, which Wingfield had accepted. The words 'we maintain' are therefore puzzling: they were not true of opinion within the Office and no public affirmation of Herbert's view had been made by a secretary of state since at least 1870. There were, however, conditions in which Herbert was prepared to admit 'the supremacy' of the Combined Court in money matters, namely if

either, as in Malta, power is reserved to the Crown to (*inter alia*) legislate, in regard to money, by Order in Council, or, as in Jamaica, power is reserved to the Governor to carry any measure by the official votes against the Elected members if he declares that 'it is of paramount importance to the public interest'.[55]

Herbert's minute was misleading for had either of his conditions been fulfilled the supremacy of the Combined Court in money matters would have been nullified. He concluded:

It is especially important that the Government of B. Guiana should not be liable to be overruled by unofficial votes in regard to money, as expenditure may at any time be necessary for the safety & control of the great number of Indian Immigrants for whom we are responsible to the Government of India, and to the Continental position

[54] Gormanston to Knutsford, Conf., 20 June 1890. 12970. CO 111/456. Minute by R.G.W.H., 16 Aug. 1890.

[55] Ibid.

of the Colony which has its Foreign relations with Venezuela, Brazil & the Netherlands. It would surely be better to take this opportunity, if possible, of abolishing the Combined Court & the Financial Representatives & establishing a simple constitution as in Malta or Jamaica.[56]

These were 'cardinal points of policy' for Herbert, and his minute not only reveals a wide difference between himself and Wingfield, but taken with his minute of 17 April 1890, it is also evidence for his lack of understanding of many of the problems raised by the reform of the British Guiana constitution, and his ignorance of the discussions between Gormanston and the Colonial Office on which the draft ordinance had been based. He took no account of the difficulties raised by any change requiring parliamentary legislation, or of Knutsford's previous commitments regarding the limits of the proposed reform measure.

It is not clear from the colonial office papers whether Knutsford realized that the final recommendation of Herbert's minute ran counter to the policy of very moderate reform which he had accepted and committed himself to only two months earlier. But, on Herbert's advice, he postponed further consideration of the draft ordinance until he had Wingfield's opinion. On his return to the Office the latter was quick to point out the difficulty of going back on proposals which Knutsford had substantially approved, and in contrast to Herbert he reaffirmed his disenchantment with semi-representative government. Referring to Jamaica and Malta he wrote:

. . . our experience so far of the working of those Constitutions is not I think encouraging for the propagation of the species.[57]

He agreed, however, with Harris and Herbert that the ordinance should contain no provision as to the powers of the Court of Policy or Combined Court, apart from a clause transferring the executive and administrative functions of the Court of Policy to an Executive Council. Knutsford accepted Wingfield's advice that it was too late to go back on a moderate measure of reform, 'as I almost pledged myself to this course in former despatches—I am, moreover, not sure that we could

[56] Ibid.

[57] Ibid. Minute by E.W., 4 Oct. 1890.

abolish the Constitution without Imperial Legislation'.[58] Knutsford also acknowledged the force of confining the measure to effecting the necessary constitutional changes and not attempting to consolidate existing ordinances and orders in council, or of enacting the functions and powers of the two Courts.

So far as the details of the ordinance were concerned, Wingfield advised three amendments of substance. He revived his earlier recommendation that the qualifications for elected members of the Court of Policy and of financial representatives should be assimilated, by extending to the former an income qualification of £300. He favoured the omission of the literacy test for voting which Gormanston had included in the draft ordinance without comment.[59] Thirdly, he suggested that the tenure of the financial representatives should be the same as that for the elected members of the Court of Policy, their seats being vacated on a dissolution of the Court of Policy which was to take place after a maximum of five years;[60] general elections for the two Courts would then be held simultaneously. The draft ordinance provided for the election of the financial representatives after a two-year tenure, though the governor could dissolve the Court as a body in which case a general election for both Courts would be held; a dissolution of the Court of Policy would not, however, have involved a dissolution of the Combined Court. So many elections seemed to Wingfield 'unnecessary and inconvenient'. Knutsford pressed Wingfield's amendments, and he also re-emphasized his preference for the secret ballot, informing Gormanston that 'if an amendment in that sense should be desired by a majority of the elected members it should be adopted . . .'.[61]

Gormanston opposed each of the three points raised by Wingfield. He reported 'a very strong consensus of opinion'[62]

[58] Gormanston to Knutsford, Conf., 20 June 1890. 12970. CO 111/456. Minute by K., 7 Oct. 1890.

[59] S. 73 (numbering on Gormanston's draft). Gormanston later argued that a literacy test had 'always existed' in the colony. See footnote 64, p. 143.

[60] This modification was included in the ordinance as passed. S. 42. Ord. 1, 1891. CO 113/8. Taken with the exclusion of a recital of the powers of the Court of Policy and Combined Court, it was the only substantial amendment to the ordinance which the Colonial Office secured, although it was one on which Knutsford did not finally insist. See p. 143.

[61] Knutsford to Gormanston, Conf., 14 Oct. 1890. 12970. CO 111/456.

[62] Gormanston to Knutsford, Conf., 3 Nov. 1890. 22522. CO 111/457.

against assimilation of the qualifications of the elected members of the Court of Policy to those of the financial representatives, on account of opposition to the £300 income qualification of the latter; he suggested, however, that there would be no strong objection to a reduction in the immoveable property qualification from £2,083. 6*s.* 8*d.* to £1,562. 10*s.* 0*d.*, and this change was incorporated in the final ordinance. But he warned Knutsford that if an income qualification of £300 was extended to the elected members of the Court of Policy both they and the financial representatives would give the reform ordinance and the enlarged civil list 'uncompromising opposition'.[63] This threat prompted Wingfield to advise yielding on this point. With regard to the literacy test, Gormanston wrote that its omission 'would cause dissatisfaction to all parties'. The test was not to be confined to the English language as hitherto.[64] Although Gormanston did not press his views against those of Knutsford, Wingfield also advised yielding on this point. On the third point, Gormanston stated that there would be great inconvenience in concurrent elections for the two Courts,[65] but Wingfield considered that he had not made out a case for departing from the revised procedure. Knutsford decided to yield on all three points.[66]

By the middle of 1890 the Reform Association began to show impatience with these long-drawn-out negotiations to which in the colony only the planting interest were privy, and in which Gormanston had acted largely as their spokesman. At a public meeting in Georgetown on 22 July 1890 a 'densely packed and enthusiastic' audience had passed a series of resolutions criticizing the governor's lack of consultation with interests other than those of the planters, the closed-door sittings of the Court of Policy, and the select private gatherings outside the legislature. A further indication of the temper of

[63] Gormanston to Knutsford, Conf., 5 Nov. 1890. 22524. CO 111/457.

[64] The point is a puzzling one. S. 21 of Ord. 15, 1849, which provided for a literacy test, did not specifically confine it to the English language, but presumably this was the practice.

[65] The grounds for Gormanston's view are not clear. It is possible that the planters hoped that separate and more frequent elections would lead to lower polls, making it easier for them to control the outcome. A general election for all elective seats, held in an atmosphere of political excitement and agitation, might have proved damaging to the planting interest.

[66] But see footnote 60, p. 142.

non-planting opinion was the success of Hutson, standing against the sugar interest on the programme of the British Guiana Reform Association, in a contested election for financial representative for Demerara in October 1890.[67] These expressions of public opinion did not affect Gormanston's attitude to reform, which continued to favour the interests of the planters and large merchants. On 27 November 1890 he introduced the reform ordinance in the Court of Policy. His speech was misleading. He was reported to have referred to it as 'a certain measure' which 'was drafted at home'.[68] In fact the ordinance was substantially based on Gormanston's scheme of January 1890 and had been drafted in the colony. Yet it was widely believed by those not close to the governor that the measure had been framed at home, an illusion fostered by Gormanston and encouraged by a cable in early May from Watt to Drysdale, presumably based on colonial office intelligence, to the effect that a draft scheme had been sent out to the colony; this was nothing more than the two despatches of 30 April 1890 containing Knutsford's comments on Gormanston's scheme of January 1890. In his speech the governor also referred to the 'circumstances of a most unexpected nature' which had delayed the bill. This may have been a reference to Wingfield's absence from the Colonial Office, but the governor did not disclose that the bill had also been delayed by Knutsford's two unsuccessful attempts to amend it in a more liberal sense. Finally, Gormanston referred to the consultation which he had undertaken 'with men of the various sections of the community'. Yet there is no evidence that he consulted the Reform Association, and his lack of respect for public opinion is evidenced by the publication of the full text of the bill on 1 December 1890, only three days before its second reading in the Court of Policy. The Reform Association sought a postponement of the second reading to allow for public discussion, which Gormanston granted until 11 December. The substantial reason for his action lay, however, in the demand for it by the elected members of the Court of Policy, who informed him that they would vote neither for the ordinance nor for the extended civil list unless sections 25 and 45 were struck out; under these sections

[67] See p. 129.
[68] *The Daily Chronicle*, 28 Nov. 1890.

business in either Court could proceed, under certain conditions, with a quorum of eight or in effect in the absence of the elected members. Gormanston informed Knutsford that the opposition to these clauses was shared by the whole community and he had withdrawn them.[69] He had, however, retained sections 24 and 42 under which business could proceed in either Court with seven members besides the governor, if a member withdrew without the latter's leave. Wingfield recognized that these clauses did not meet a situation in which the elected members absented themselves rather than withdrew from the Court, and he regarded the loss of the quorum clauses as serious. Nevertheless he minuted:

> ... on the whole he seems to have done right in giving up the obnoxious provision rather than lose the extended Civil List.[70]

On 10 December the Reform Association laid on the table of the Court of Policy a petition containing over forty amendments to the proposed measure, including reductions in the property qualifications of members of the Court of Policy and in the qualifications for the franchise.[71] Gormanston did not inform Knutsford of the receipt of this petition, and it seems that only seven of its less important proposals were debated in the committee stage of the ordinance. In the ordinance as passed only one significant concession was made to the Association, the close of polling being extended from 4.00 p.m. to 5.00 p.m.; the Association had asked for 6.00 p.m., and this was supported by two elected members on the grounds that working men seldom got home before that time. Gormanston's substantial and last minute concessions to the planting interest secured the passage of the ordinance through the Court of Policy with one dissentient vote, and of an extended civil list through the Combined Court by nine votes to three, three financial representatives voting against it, two elected members of the Court of Policy declining to vote, and a third being absent. The measure was accepted by the more influential

[69] The clauses were amended, the effect being to make a quorum in the Court of Policy dependent on the presence of at least two elected members, and in the Combined Court, of at least four elected members.

[70] Gormanston to Knutsford, Conf., 17 Dec. 1890. 98. CO 111/457. Minute by E.W., 3 Jan. 1891.

[71] Printed in *The Daily Chronicle*, 11 Dec. 1890.

merchants as a satisfactory compromise, the leader-writer of *The Daily Chronicle* considering that it contained 'all the changes which are immediately necessary and desirable'.[72] On the other hand, the secretary of the Reform Association informed Watt that it left matters '. . . if anything, worse than at present',[73] and a well attended public meeting in Georgetown on 8 December 1890 passed a resolution expressing regret that 'a thorough system of representative government' had not been granted. Herbert also had his doubts:

I fear the Bill is now 'almost a nullity', and I feel very much doubt whether it has been worthwhile to purchase the 7 years Civil List with its extensions at the price.[74]

There was force in this judgement. The main changes effected by the ordinance[75] were: the Court of Policy was enlarged to sixteen by the addition of three elected members and three officials; the College of Electors was abolished, the elected members of the Court of Policy being elected directly to represent five county and three town districts by the same electorate which was qualified to vote for the election of financial representatives; this electorate was enlarged by lowering the income qualification for the franchise from £125 to £100, but the effect was lessened by the exclusion of aliens and by the retention of open voting; the qualification for elected members of the Court of Policy was widened by adding alternative but high property qualifications, but without the financial representatives' annual income qualification of £300. These were the only changes which the ordinance effected which could be said to further Knutsford's acknowledged aim 'that the elected section of the legislature should represent . . . all classes who are capable of intelligently exercising the franchise'.[76] The main changes in the ordinance which strengthened

[72] *The Daily Chronicle*, 2 Dec. 1890.

[73] Quoted in Watt to Knutsford, Dec. 1890 (undated). 24533. CO 111/458.

[74] Gormanston to Knutsford, Conf., 17 Dec. 1890. 98. CO 111/457. Minute by R.G.W.H., 6 Jan. 1891. The enlarged civil list secured the salaries of nine further heads of departments and the stipendiary magistrates, in addition to the previously secured salaries of the governor, attorney-general, government secretary, solicitor-general, and assistant government secretary. Ord. 27, 1890. CO 113/8. The salaries of the chief justice and puisne judges were permanently secured by Ord. 10 of 1883.

[75] Ord. 1, 1891. CO 113/8. It came into effect on 1 Aug. 1891.

[76] See p. 128.

the hands of the governor and colonial government were the establishment of an Executive Council,[77] the power to dissolve the Court of Policy upon which the financial representatives would vacate their seats, and the truncated quorum clauses which guarded against a deadlock caused by the elected members withdrawing from either Court, but which were ineffective if they absented themselves altogether.

The very moderate nature of the 1891 reform is underlined by the numbers registering under the new franchise and by the results of the general election held in January 1892. In spite of the efforts of the Reform Association, which included the distribution of registration forms and the holding of ward meetings in Georgetown, the number of registered voters actually declined, the first registration under the new qualifications being 2,046 compared with 2,210 registered in January 1891. Several factors may have accounted for this. Ordinance 1, 1891, required the registration of all voters including those already qualified; some of the latter through inadvertence or apathy may not have re-registered. The vested rights of previously enfranchised aliens were not preserved. It seems that there was some fear that registration would be used to compel voters to register their liability for militia service under the Volunteer Militia Ordinance passed early in 1891.[78] Other allegations and complaints made in the press concerned the non-availability of registration forms in some country districts, the fact that the income qualification did not allow for board and lodging, and that obstacles had been placed in the way of coloured people[79] wishing to register. Open voting probably discouraged people from registering, as well as voting.

The general election of January 1892, in which only three seats were contested, also underlined the moderate change

[77] See ch. 9.

[78] Under Ord. 19, 1891, registration for militia service was compulsory for all who fulfilled qualifications similar to those for the franchise, with the exception that the income qualification was £72. 18*s.* 4*d.* with allowance for board and lodging. There was provision in certain circumstances for a compulsory ballot for service from those so registered. A compulsory militia ordinance with similar liability had applied to Georgetown since 1872, but the income qualification excluded journeymen mechanics and artisans, a provision not in the 1891 ordinance which superseded it. Thus after 1891 all registering for the franchise would also in effect have declared their liability for militia service.

[79] 'Coloured' is here used in its broader sense of non-white.

effected.[80] The newly elected Court of Policy comprised five white planters or attorneys, two white merchants, and one coloured barrister, compared with the five white representatives of the planting interest in the unreformed Court, of whom Alexander Barr was the sole survivor; he narrowly won West Demerara from J. A. Murdoch, a Negro barrister. The only other contested election for the Court of Policy was in East Demerara where E. C. Luard, a planter, polled 165 votes against 171 votes of his opponent, J. P. Farnum, a coloured storekeeper from Georgetown who was unseated because he was not in the list of voters. In the same contest W. E. Lewis, a Negro barrister, polled 18 votes. In the College of Financial Representatives the barristers lost ground to the merchants and planters. In the newly elected College there were three white merchants, two white representatives of the planting interest, and one coloured barrister.[81] The only contested election for the College was also in Demerara, George Garnett, a merchant, defeating Patrick Dargan, a coloured barrister, by 245 votes to 230; Murdoch, Farnum, and Dargan had all stood with the support of the Reform Association and it is significant that all had contested seats in Demerara. In short, in the new Combined Court, of fourteen elected members, twelve were white and two coloured; in the unreformed Court, of eleven elected members, eight had been white, two coloured, and one of Negro origin. Of the newly elected members, seven were planters and attorneys, five were merchants, and two were barristers; in the unreformed Court there had been six representatives of the planting interest, three barristers, and two merchants. The coloured and Negro representation had proportionately declined, and both barristers and planters had lost ground to the merchant class on whose attitude depended the balance of power in the new Combined Court. The conservative nature of the changes was further emphasized by the fact that seven of the new members had sat in one of the three elective bodies which had existed before 1891.

The very moderate character of the reform measure of 1891

[80] The following paragraph is based on appendix Q of Clementi, op. cit.

[81] The composition of the College before the election had been two merchants, one white and one Negro, one white representative of the planting interest, and three barristers two of whom were coloured.

must be sought firstly in the attitude of the Colonial Office, and particularly of Wingfield, an attitude shaped by an unwillingness to risk a fight with the planters, and the parliamentary legislation which it might involve, and by the overriding importance which Wingfield attached to obtaining an enlarged civil list; secondly in a pliant governor, unsympathetic to reform, who shielded himself behind the Combined Court and used the intransigence of the planters to oppose colonial office policy; and thirdly in the failure of the more radical reformers to press their case vigorously in the colony or London. It is also possible that Knutsford and his advisers were influenced by the crown law officers' reference to considerations of good faith,[82] though on this last point the writer has found no positive evidence.[83]

Yet the planters had won only a tactical victory. The introduction of the secret ballot in 1896 enabled non-white political leadership and organization to exploit the reforms of 1891 and to change the political balance. In the general election of 1897 the radical Negro and coloured 'Progressive Association', mainly represented by lawyers and allegedly appealing to colour prejudice and hostility to the sugar interest, gained ground at the expense of the planting and merchant interest. In the newly elected Combined Court there were five representatives of the planting interest, three merchants, five lawyers, and one store manager; so far as the writer can establish the last six were coloured or Negro and represented the 'Progressive Association'. The significance of these changes should not be over-estimated. Like the elected members in Jamaica, these 'radicals' represented the professional, clerical, and trading classes rather than the rural population or the urban working class. They showed little interest in social legislation and even their hostility to the sugar interest was by no means wholehearted; although by 1901 Dargan's 'party' stood for a reduction of the immigration vote it was not an issue which they pressed vigorously. The general election of that year left the sugar interest in a strong position in the Combined Court; of the fourteen elected members, four were planters and five were merchants closely connected with the planting interest. On the other hand, the reforms of 1891 and 1896 undoubtedly made

[82] See p. 7. [83] But see p. 113.

the two Courts more responsive to public opinion. For instance, in November 1901 the officer administering the government wrote that nearly every candidate at the general election had felt compelled to commit himself to advocating improvement in the education system. The planters had shown strong powers of survival; their political ascendancy had been weakened but not destroyed.

Section 3
Trinidad
1880–1895

6

REFORM AGITATION IN THE 1880s

The failure of 'Liberal Conservatism'

THE Trinidad sugar planters did not enjoy the political, economic, and social supremacy of the British Guiana plantocracy, though they commanded more local influence than the sugar interest in Jamaica. Their political power rested partly on their near monopoly of the nominated seats in the Legislative Council, the governors' provisional appointments to which were normally confirmed by secretaries of state. Governors usually chose large owners of property who were connected directly or indirectly with the sugar industry,[1] although during the 1880s they inclined towards broadening the representation to include cocoa, commercial, and professional interests; in general, however, the representatives of the sugar planters remained throughout the period of this study the dominant unofficial influence in the Council. Their position was strengthened by the existence of an unofficial nominated majority,[2] but their ability to exploit it was limited by the practical difficulties of securing full attendance and unanimity; close social and family ties favoured the latter, personal antipathies, religious differences, and, less often, conflicting commercial interests impeded it. The use of their majority by the unofficial members was further tempered by the knowledge that factious and continued opposition might lead to the re-establishment of an official majority, a change which the Colonial Office could simply effect by an alteration in the governor's instructions or by not appointing the full number of unofficials. The unofficial members could not initiate money votes and their control over expenditure did not extend to that on the fixed establishment. As in other small

[1] In March 1880 the eight nominated unofficials comprised four sugar planters, two owners of sugar and cocoa estates, one merchant associated with the sugar interest, and one barrister.

[2] See p. 10.

colonial communities, preponderant economic and consequently social influence underpinned the planters' political position, and made it improbable that any but the strongest-willed governor would oppose them. It was this relationship between governor and planters which in the final analysis determined the local political influence of the plantocracy in the sugar-producing crown colonies. In Trinidad it was a relationship which during the 1870s and early 1880s was marked by compromise and co-operation. Thus during Irving's governorship[3] the sugar interest received notable fiscal and other advantages, and perhaps because of this their representatives in the Legislative Council did not block his programme of public works, and particularly his development of railway and road communications.[4] Relations were cordial and, in striking contrast to his subsequent governorship of British Guiana, Irving's administration in Trinidad won the approval of the planting interest.

The sugar planters could also exert influence directly on the Colonial Office, particularly through the West India Committee. In this respect they were well placed for in 1887 almost one-half of the sugar production of the colony was in the hands of four absentee owners.[5] In general, colonial office officials were not favourably disposed towards the sugar interest. They regarded its management as inefficient, and its claims for privileged treatment as extravagant and inimical to other interests; it was an attitude shared, though perhaps to a lesser extent until Chamberlain, by secretaries of state. On the other hand, secretaries of state and officials were reluctant to precipitate a conflict with an economically important and well-represented interest. They thus tended to oppose further concessions to the planters but hesitated significantly to weaken their existing privileged fiscal, economic, and political position. For instance, between 1880 and 1895 the Colonial Office

[3] Sir Henry Irving was governor of Trinidad from 1874 to 1880.

[4] There were probably other reasons for the planters' co-operation. Robinson claimed in 1890 that the Port of Spain to San Fernando railway had been built 'entirely' in the interests of the planters; the road system principally benefited the estates. Robinson to Knutsford, No. 217, 21 July 1890. 15978. CO 295/329.

[5] The Colonial Co. Ltd., Gregor Turnbull, C. Tennant Sons and Co., and W. F. Burnley. See statement encl. with Robinson to Holland, No. 286, 21 Oct. 1887. 22838. CO 295/315. Nevile Lubbock was managing director of the Colonial Co. and Chairman of the West India Committee.

resisted the pressure of the West India Committee and the unofficial members of the Trinidad Legislative Council for temporary government loans to planters,[6] or for any lessening of the planters' contribution to Indian immigration expenses below two-thirds of the total cost;[7] they declined to commit themselves to a permanently high level of Indian immigration.[8] On the other hand, the Colonial Office took no active steps to broaden the representation in the Legislative Council to include interests other than sugar, any initiative in this respect coming from the governors, notably Sir William Robinson.[9] Although deprecating high duties on necessary foods, they did not press their views to the point of conflict with the unofficial members. Sydney Buxton, the parliamentary under-secretary, summarized in April 1895 the colonial office attitude to this issue during the previous fifteen years, when he wrote to H. Hamel Smith, a Trinidad merchant, regretting such duties, but pointing out that the views of the legislature could not be ignored, 'and that even in Crown Colonies the Home Government will not force its views irrespective of local feeling, especially in matters of taxation'.[10] Ashley had expressed a similar view in the House of Commons eleven years earlier.[11] In this instance the Colonial Office seemed to be regarding the unofficial members as representative of local opinion, but it did not always do so. In 1886 Stanhope opposed the appointment of a second puisne judge to Trinidad on the grounds that he regarded the unofficial members as representing only a limited class of taxpayers, it being his duty to protect 'the main body of the tax-payers' against unnecessary expenditure.[12] At times the Colonial Office adopted a more positive attitude. Officials advised the appointment of Sir John Gorrie as chief justice in 1885,[13] although recognizing that the choice would not be

[6] Stanley to Havelock, Tel., 4 Aug. 1885. 10352. CO 295/306.

[7] Holland to Robinson, No. 132, 19 July 1887. 4332. CO 295/313.

[8] Wingfield to Chairman, West India Committee, 6 June 1890. 9528. CO 295/331. The West India Committee sought the introduction on a permanent annual basis of 3,500 immigrants.

[9] Sir William Robinson was governor of Trinidad from 1885 to 1891.

[10] Buxton to Hamel Smith, 10 Apr. 1895. 7146. CO 295/368.

[11] 8 Aug. 1884. *Hansard*, Third Series (292), 265.

[12] Stanhope to Robinson, No. 95, 13 Dec. 1886. 21602. CO 295/311.

[13] For Gorrie see below, in particular pp. 177–9 and pp. 190–4. For his appointment see minute paper 12237. CO 295/307.

popular with the West India Committee. Knutsford and his officials fully supported Robinson in his policy of extending communications and encouraging the minor industries,[14] although the sugar interest was strongly opposed to it.[15] In general, between 1880 and 1895 the Trinidad planters successfully defended, without notably extending, the privileged fiscal position which their political influence and economic importance had won by 1880. Three-tenths of the cost of Indian immigration was borne by the general revenue. As in British Guiana and Jamaica, though to a lesser extent, the weight of indirect tax fell on widely consumed foods such as flour and rice;[16] estate supplies were subject to low or nil rates of duty. Imported refined sugar paid a protective duty of 10*s.* 0*d.* for 100 lb. On the other hand, the inability of the planters to secure conditions which would confine the labouring population to the neighbourhood of the estates emphasized both their weaker political position compared with the British Guiana planting interest, and the differing geographic and economic conditions in the two colonies.

The extent and fertility of the unoccupied crown lands of Trinidad afforded wide opportunity for settlement, in contrast to the narrow coastal belt of British Guiana and its practically inaccessible interior. During the middle decades of the century these lands had begun to be settled by squatters, a movement which the political influence of the planters could not prevent

[14] Knutsford to Robinson, No. 192, 29 Sept. 1890. 15978. CO 295/329.

[15] For Robinson's policy and the opposition of the sugar planters to it, see pp. 204–5.

[16] In 1889 the duties on certain widely consumed foods in Jamaica, British Guiana, and Trinidad were:

	Jamaica	*British Guiana*	*Trinidad*	*Barbados tariff of 1899* which Chamberlain adopted in 1899 as a model for the Windward & Leeward Is.
Dried fish	3*s.*—100 lb.	2*s.* 1*d.*—112 lb.	Free	1*s.* 6*d.*—112 lb.
Flour—196 lb.	8*s.*	4*s.* 2*d.*	3*s.* 4*d.*	4*s.* 2*d.*
Rice—100 lb.	3*s.*	1*s.* 0½*d.*	2*s.* 2*d.*	1*s.* 0½*d.*

For the Barbados model tariff see Chamberlain to the Governors of the Windward and Leeward Islands, 5 Sept. 1899. Reprinted in Conf. Print, West Indian No. 111. CO 884/6.

Sir Arthur Gordon[17] from both legalizing and encouraging. The impetus given to the establishment of a peasant proprietary by Gordon, and maintained by Irving, led in the decade after 1869 to the sale of some 40,000 acres of crown land, mostly in small lots;[18] a further 19,000 acres in 2,643 grants had been taken up by time-expired Indian immigrants under regulations established by Gordon, and subsequently amended, for the commutation of return passages.[19] Many of the creole settlers had specialized in cocoa growing, the volume of home-produced cocoa exported between 1870 and 1880 increasing by over one-half. The settlement of the interior accelerated during the 1880s; between 1878 and 1887 the total export of cocoa increased by over one-third to nearly 14,000,000 lb., worth £413,179, compared with exports of sugar of £800,595. The increasing diversification of the Trinidad economy was also reflected in the growth of other industries such as asphalt and coconuts, and in the development of a considerable local and transit trade with Venezuela. The economy was further stimulated during the 1870s by Irving's programme of public works which attracted an extensive immigration of labourers from other West Indian colonies, notably Barbados. In the decade after 1870 the Trinidad revenue rose by nearly one-half to £435,789. These favourable economic conditions provided opportunities outside the plantation economy, the lack of which was one of the main grievances of the British Guiana reformers, and during the late 1870s they enabled the Trinidad economy to weather more easily the economic depression which adversely affected British Guiana and Jamaica. Even after the sharp break in sugar prices in 1884 rural distress was less in Trinidad than in British Guiana, since in the former the competition of the cocoa estates for labour and the oppor-

[17] Governor of Trinidad 1866 to 1870. See J. K. Chapman, *The Career of Arthur Hamilton Gordon, First Lord Stanmore, 1829–1912* (Toronto, 1964).

[18] Memo. enclosed with Irving to Kimberley, No. 126, 26 May 1880. 8814. CO 295/286. In 1868 Gordon fixed the upset price of crown lands at £1 an acre; the cost of survey was about 7s. 6d. an acre and there were restrictive features in the regulations. See footnote 39, p. 164.

[19] See memorandum on Indian immigration, encl. 2, Fowler (O.A.G.) to Holland, No. 332, 19 Sept. 1889. 20234. CO 295/324. The regulations were frequently amended during the 1870s and 1880s. Grants of land to immigrants in lieu of return passages virtually ceased after 1881, time-expired immigrants using their commutation money to buy crown land under the usual conditions.

tunities for settlement both weakened the sugar planters' command of the labour market, and therefore their ability to reduce wages, and lessened the impact of the fall in wages which took place during 1884 and 1885. The subsequent depression in sugar prices affected the diversifying Trinidad economy more slowly and less extensively than the sugar-dependent economy of British Guiana.

In Jamaica, the colonial office handling of the *Florence* affair had united landowing, merchant, and professional classes in opposition to crown government. In British Guiana a reform movement less widely based than in Jamaica had originated against the background of economic difficulties and rural depression, and as a reaction to the all-pervasive influence of the sugar interest. The merchant and professional classes who supported it sought to secure by political representation wider economic opportunities through the opening up of the colony, and the development of a peasant proprietary and of other industries than sugar. The more hesitant development of a reform movement in Trinidad owed something to the lack of a similar stimulus. No *Florence* affair united the educated people of the colony. The influence of the sugar planters, although considerable, was weaker than in British Guiana. Relative prosperity bred political apathy.

The social differences at all levels of Trinidad society also hindered the growth of a reform movement and in the view of Lionel Fraser, the historian of Trinidad, contributed to the political apathy, which he thus described to the Royal Franchise Commission of 1888:

> It is the peculiarity of Trinidad, but it requires an enormous amount of blowing even to get fire to light, and it goes out immediately afterwards.[20]

In the past the great popular stirrings had been on questions of religion and although in the 1880s sectarian feeling still ran high on issues such as education,[21] it was less deep-seated than

[20] Reported in *The Port of Spain Gazette*, 5 May 1888. The evidence given before the Royal Franchise Commission throws interesting light on social conditions in Trinidad. The writer has been unable to find a printed copy of the evidence in England. Where possible quotations have been taken from the account of the commission's hearings in *The Port of Spain Gazette*, the reporter of which was the shorthand writer for the commission.

[21] Referring in 1889 to controversies regarding the relative status of government

formerly, the main divisive influence being language and nationality. In the country districts and among the older generations, Spanish, French, and the *patois*, a creole French, were still spoken. On the other hand, the expansion of education since the early 1870s[22] had reached the younger generation, many of whom by the middle 1880s could speak English, and the influx of immigrants from the English-speaking islands, particularly Barbados, some of whom settled in the rural areas as artisans and small proprietors, also facilitated the spread of a common language.[23] As in British Guiana, the rural Indian population kept largely to itself, retaining its language and its customs, though here also the impact of education was making itself felt. The work of the Canadian Presbyterian Mission had resulted by 1888 in a school attendance among Indians of 1,960 with an average attendance of over 1,300;[24] the total enrolled school attendance of Indians was about 2,400. In 1888 a Canadian Presbyterian missionary estimated that 5,000 Indians around Naparima, Princes Town, and Oropouche could understand and speak English.[25] These trends lessened but did not remove the obstacles which faced reformers in reaching the rural population by newspaper and public meeting. In Port of Spain and San Fernando, English was widely spoken among all classes but religious and, particularly, national differences

and assisted schools, Robinson alleged that the Catholic Church was freely using 'all methods within its reach of gaining influence as a means of supremacy under a free & more or less popular Govt.' Memorandum by Robinson, 19 Aug. 1889, commenting on Fowler (O.A.G.) to Knutsford, No. 254, 18 July 1889. 15378. CO 295/323.

22 Between 1868 and 1887 the number of schools under inspection, excluding Indian village and estate schools, increased from 35 to 126, the enrolled pupils from 2,836 to 14,290, and the average attendance from 1,672 to 9,811; in 1887 the number of children between 7 and 13 was about 23,000. These statistics are difficult to interpret. After Irving's educational reforms of 1875 there was a rapid increase in the number of assisted schools, but it is not clear how many of these were existing denominational schools. It is probable that most were new schools. The comparable figures for Jamaica in 1887 were 146,974 children of school age of whom 61,571 were enrolled; average attendance was 34,825.

23 On the other hand, J. H. Collens, a teacher with ten years' experience in Trinidad, estimated in 1888 that perhaps half a teacher's pupils might never hear English spoken in their homes; this was not so much the case in the larger towns. *A Guide to Trinidad* (London, 1888), p. 245.

24 Protector of Immigrants to Colonial Secretary, 12 June 1889. Encl. 19 with Fowler (O.A.G.) to Knutsford, No. 254, 18 July 1889. 15378. CO 295/323.

25 Evidence of Revd. K. J. Grant at meeting of the Royal Franchise Commission, 16 Apr. 1888. Reported in *The Port of Spain Gazette*, 25 Apr. 1888.

remained; notable, for instance, among the educated and propertied classes were the old French Catholic families,[26] and also the well-to-do Venezuelans of Port of Spain, many of them refugees from the regime of General Guzman Blanco. These differences of religion, language, and nationality contributed to the more hesitant development of a reform movement in Trinidad.

The initial impetus for constitutional reform in this period came from the press; in origin the movement was a reaction against the governorship of Irving, and as in Jamaica it was sustained during the early 1880s by widely felt dissatisfaction with the continued high level of government expenditure, particularly on public works. The main charges levelled in the press against Irving's administration were the extravagance and inefficiency of his public works programme, his deference to the sugar interest, for instance in his fiscal legislation, his preference for centralized administration, and his hostility towards native-born public officers. More generally, the agitation was a reaction against an able but strong-willed administrator who in pursuit of efficiency ignored local feelings. These grievances were reflected in particularly bitter attacks against the Public Works Department created by Irving. As in Jamaica, it was the largest spending department, it lacked adequate technical staff, and its failures were both costly and obvious. For instance, the San Fernando water works, completed in 1881 at a cost of nearly £17,000, were described by Robinson in 1890 as 'a lamentable failure'. The department employed a large proportion of expatriates, and further grievances were the extent to which its supplies were obtained through the Crown Agents to the disadvantage of local merchants, and the curtailing of the practice by which local landowners could tender for public works such as road repairs. Moreover, the centralizing tendencies of both Irving and his Director of Public Works, J. E. Tanner, had created a department which was regarded both in the Colonial Office and in the colony as over-extended. Tanner himself was subject to such bitter attack in the press that Irving likened his position to that of an official in Ireland 'minus risk of assassination'. Although the reaction against

[26] For example, de Verteuil, Borde, Damian, Lange, and Rostant. The last four were associated with the reform movement in the 1880s.

Irving's governorship was also partly a reaction against the influence of the planters, this aspect of the reform movement was overshadowed between 1880 and 1884 by the resentment of planting and non-planting interests alike against the extravagance of public expenditure, particularly on public works,[27] and the consequent high level of taxation. In this respect and in its attack on incompetent and socially arrogant English officials, the movement had much in common with the reform movement in Jamaica during the late 1870s.

These grievances were not only aired in the press. In September 1883 a petition addressed to the governor, Sir Sanford Freeling, and signed by 809 proprietors, merchants and others, called for a judicious reduction in expenditure on public works and on establishments.[28] The West India Committee pressed similar demands. In November 1883 G. Anderson, a Liberal member of parliament for Glasgow, informed Kimberley that the complaints of his Trinidad correspondents[29] lay in the high salaries of officials, and particularly the 'gross mismanagement' of financial affairs, 'principally through the want of knowledge and ability of those who manage the public works Dept. . . .'.[30] By August 1882 four major newspapers advocated constitutional reform as the only way of adequately controlling expenditure and taxation, though their very moderate proposals emphasized the conservative character of the movement. For instance, *The Port of Spain Gazette* favoured *ex-officio* membership of the Legislative Council for the mayors of Port of Spain and San Fernando, and the further addition of six members elected 'by owners of comparatively large properties to represent the wealth and intelligence of the country . . .'.[31] It also proposed the establishment of an Executive Committee,

[27] The Colonial Office recognized, as in Jamaica, the weight of this grievance. Commenting on the need for supplementary estimates in 1880 and in 1881, Kimberley minuted: 'Such mismanagement, if it continues, would be sufficient to justify a change of Governor.' Freeling to Kimberley, No. 154, 27 May 1881. 10272. CO 295/290. Minute by K., 5 July 1881.

[28] Encl. with Freeling to Derby, No. 198, 24 Sept. 1883. 17637. CO 295/298.

[29] Anderson's interest reflected the close ties between Glasgow and Trinidad through such notable sugar proprietors as W. F. Burnley, and dry goods merchants such as James Wilson and Sons.

[30] Anderson to Derby, 24 Nov. 1883. 20012. CO 295/300.

[31] *The Port of Spain Gazette*, 1 Dec. 1883. The writer was almost certainly Philip Rostant (see pp. 163–5) who was editor of *The Port of Spain Gazette* from January 1881 to October 1884.

as in Barbados.[32] Although heartened by events in Jamaica,[33] the leader-writer of *The Port of Spain Gazette* stressed the differences between that colony, and Trinidad with its heterogeneous population. He regarded both the British Guiana franchise of 1849 and that under which the former Jamaica House of Assembly was elected as too low for Trinidad; the latter franchise would in his view have quadrupled the borough electors of Port of Spain and enfranchised the entire rural population off the estates. He opposed an elected majority in the Legislative Council, preferring a mixed Council of officials, nominated unofficials, and elected members. He regarded the constitution finally conceded to Jamaica in 1884 as 'ruinous to Trinidad'. He probably spoke for most Trinidad reformers at this time in advocating a very moderate reform which would give effective control over taxation and expenditure, with safeguards against 'crude and experimental legislation'.

It was a measure of the political apathy in Trinidad that although the issue of reform was widely canvassed in the press, no formal proposals were made in the Legislative Council, at public meetings, or by petition. In his letter of November 1883, Anderson did, however, ask Kimberley to consider the possibility of conceding an elected council which could control expenditure. Derby, Kimberley's successor, replied that:

> having regard to the number of uneducated negroes and Indians in the Colony . . . an elective constitution would not at present be of advantage to the community generally.[34]

This letter, dated a few days after Herbert's minute favouring the introduction of an elective element into the Jamaica Legislative Council, was drafted on a minute by Harris, amended by Wingfield; it was initialled by Derby. It is evidence for the view that the Colonial Office did not at this time regard possible constitutional concessions in Jamaica as a precedent for other crown colonies.

The close of 1884 saw a significant shift in reform opinion.

[32] See footnote 63, p. 84.

[33] In particular, he hailed Gladstone's speech during the *Florence* debate on 9 Mar. 1883 as bringing the question of reform 'within the immediate range of practical politics.' *The Port of Spain Gazette*, 7 Apr. 1883.

[34] Wingfield to Anderson, 11 Dec. 1883. 20012, CO 295/300.

On 2 December 1884 Philip Rostant published the first number of *Public Opinion*,[35] a newspaper which subsequently filled a role analogous to *The Daily Chronicle* in British Guiana. Rostant was a native of Trinidad, of French descent, who had been educated and had lived for many years in Ireland. As a young man he had been 'personally acquainted' with Daniel O'Connell and Tom Sheil, and had attended numerous meetings of the Repeal Association, 'the monster gatherings of Fr. Mathew and the meetings of Conciliation Hall . . .'.[36] Rostant described himself as a 'conservative liberal'. His conservatism was rooted in a respect for property, which probably derived both from his Catholic background and from the fact that his father was a large landowner and he himself was a cocoa proprietor. A further strand in his political and social thinking was the labour theory of value, reflected in his assertion that those who create wealth are entitled to share in it; the 'value of a thing', he wrote, 'lies in the amount of labour that has been expended to produce it . . .'.[37] He was also influenced by Cardinal Manning's liberal views on social questions. Rostant's influence on the Trinidad reform movement after 1884 was profound. Through the columns of *Public Opinion* he preached an increasingly radical reform programme. By 1887 he was supporting a constitutional change on the lines of Jamaica under which as many as twelve or fourteen members of the Legislative Council would have been elected; giving evidence before the Royal Franchise Commission of 1888, he advocated a franchise lower in certain respects than the reformed Jamaica franchise of 1886. Influenced like the British Guiana reformers by the collapse of sugar prices in 1884, Rostant, while continuing to stress the need for control of public expenditure,

[35] It was founded with the financial assistance of a fellow Frenchman, H. Borde. Like *The Daily Chronicle* it was for daily sale and not annual subscription. Rostant was editor and proprietor. Borde intended it to be a cheap paper on popular lines.

[36] See leading articles *The Port of Spain Gazette*, 17 June 1882, and *Public Opinion*, 3 June 1887. Also report of speech by Rostant at San Fernando, 18 Feb. 1885, in *Public Opinion*, 20 Feb. 1885. Rostant's liking for the mass meeting and petition, which characterized his handling of the reform movement of 1887, probably derived from his Irish experience. He regarded the public meeting as 'the greatest and most powerful lever in the hands of a people struggling for political rights'. *Public Opinion*, 27 Feb. 1885. He found a parallel in Trinidad to the evils of absenteeism and the perversity of English officials in Ireland.

[37] Ibid., 3 Mar. 1885.

particularly on public works,[38] also broadened the grounds for reform by emphasizing the dangers of an undue dependence on sugar. He argued that this could only be avoided by measures designed to encourage a peasant proprietary, such as the encouragement of unindentured immigration from Barbados and elsewhere, less onerous crown lands regulations,[39] lower duties on imports of necessary foods, legislation to cheapen and facilitate the transfer of land, and the fostering of other industries. While acknowledging the progress already made in establishing a peasant proprietary he claimed that it had been achieved in spite of the planters, who had used their political influence to hinder it, and inasmuch as the absentee planting interest still opposed the opening up of the crown lands and unindentured immigration a reform of the constitution was necessary.[40] In his attitude to Indian immigration Rostant was more cautious than Robert Guppy,[41] who strongly advocated its abolition and the encouragement of unindentured immigration. But from defending it in the early 1880s Rostant came by 1886 to advocate the gradual substitution of unindentured immigrants for Indian indentured labour. For Guppy the latter was an evil to be abolished, for Rostant a *pis aller* to be ultimately ended. Both regarded it as economically burdensome and socially degrading, and they argued that with unindentured immigration from neighbouring islands and the abolition of duties on necessary foods an adequate supply of efficient and cheap labour could be obtained. Yet there remained in Rostant's political philosophy a strong element of conservatism born both of conviction and expediency, for he believed that an effective reform movement must bridge the gap between the radical reformers such as Guppy, and the wealthy

[38] In his evidence before the Royal Franchise Commission he stated this was at the root of the movement. Meeting, 10 Feb. 1888, reported in *The Port of Spain Gazette*, 15 Feb. 1888.

[39] Although the price of £1 an acre was lower than in British Guiana, there were restrictive features in the regulations including a minimum sale of ten acres and elaborate rules for survey. The regulations provided for public auction at which the price might and did go above the minimum upset price of £1.

[40] For these views see *Public Opinion*, 3 June 1887.

[41] Robert Guppy was an English-born barrister and Mayor of San Fernando. A moderate radical with a keen awareness of social problems, he was an outspoken critic of the political and economic dominance of the sugar industry. See, for example, his statement to the Royal Franchise Commission, printed in *Public Opinion*, 13 July 1888.

landowners with liberal sympathies. He sought to reassure the latter by emphasizing the need to protect 'the great industries' and 'great institutions' of the country from the 'brutal reign of the ignorant masses'.[42] He strove to mobilize a body of reform opinion drawing its strength from the 'mass of unrepresented property and intelligence',[43] sufficiently liberal to attract the radicals yet not so liberal as to alienate the capitalists, the absence of whom in his view had stultified earlier reform movements.

Opposition to the constitutional changes advocated by Rostant manifested itself inside and outside the Legislative Council. On 10 January 1885 the unofficial nominated members unanimously passed a resolution favouring a change in the constitution, which was so moderate as to suggest an attempt on their part to frustrate the demands for the introduction of elected members by securing a more conservative change. In order to ensure economy in public expenditure the resolution favoured an increase in the unofficial members, or the introduction of financial representatives as in British Guiana, or a change 'in such other manner as Her Majesty may deem fit'.[44] J. Scott Bushe, the officer administering the government, informed Derby that one unofficial had told him that six of their number would resign if their views regarding a constitutional change leading to more effective control over public expenditure were not entertained; the difficulty of replacing them would, in his view, 'be well nigh insurmountable'. He advised some change, for unless a concession was made there would be 'considerable popular agitation . . .'.[45] Both Wingfield and Ashley attributed the movement to the example of Jamaica; it was, in Herbert's view, 'much to be regretted'.[46] None of them favoured a concession, and on their advice Derby informed Sir Arthur Havelock, Freeling's successor as governor, that before considering a reform of the constitution he required proof that the unofficial members inadequately represented the interests of the community, and that they could

[42] *Public Opinion*, 10 Nov. 1885.

[43] Ibid., 4 Dec. 1885. In this respect his language was similar to that of the British Guiana reformers; both stressed the large amount of unrepresented property in the capital.

[44] Minutes of the Legislative Council, 10 Jan. 1885. CO 298/41.

[45] J. Scott Bushe (O.A.G.) to Derby, No. 24, 19 Jan. 1885. 2507. CO 295/305.

[46] Ibid. Minute by R.G.W.H., 16 Feb. 1885.

not effectively control public expenditure without an increase in their number. It was a measure of the enthusiasm of the unofficials for reform that this despatch remained unanswered and that they did not resign.

In November 1885 Sir William Robinson, Havelock's successor, informed Stanley that the unofficial members sought a change in the constitution similar to that effected in Mauritius.[47] This view had been expressed by G. T. Fenwick, planting attorney for the Colonial Co., in a legislative council debate on the estimates in September 1885; he referred to the futility of the nominated members' attempts to control expenditure. Robinson did not recommend a change on the Mauritius lines, but he asked Stanley whether he might not safely introduce a proposal, put forward by Louis de Verteuil, for the establishment of a committee of all the unofficial members and certain officials. The role of the committee would be to discuss the estimates in detail before they were proceeded with in the Legislative Council. He cited the precedent of the Straits Settlements; the concession would reduce the irritation caused by falling revenues and 'excessive Establishments'. Wingfield doubted the advantage of the change, but Herbert minuted in favour:

> . . . it may stave off the inconvenient demand for Home Rule which has been springing up.[48]

The phrase 'stave off' reflected both Herbert's belief in the inevitability of, and his hostility towards, constitutional change in Trinidad. Similarly in January 1886 he advised against opposing what he and his colleagues regarded as retrograde tariff changes sanctioned by the Trinidad Legislative Council. 'If we were to do so', he wrote, 'it wd. become impossible to resist the demand for a change in the constitution; and that would be a much greater evil than a retrograde fiscal policy.'[49] With Stanley's approval, Robinson established the Estimates

[47] In 1885 Stanley conceded a provisional unofficial majority, the Mauritius Council of Government comprising the governor, twelve officials, five nominated unofficials, and ten elected members. An official majority could be secured by appointing two officials in place of two nominated unofficials, the Letters Patent specifying a minimum of three nominated unofficials.

[48] Robinson to Stanley, Conf., 27 Nov. 1885. 21559. CO 295/308. Minute by R.G.W.H., 23 Dec. 1885.

[49] Robinson to Stanley, No. 334, 8 Dec. 1885. 22293. CO 295/308. Minute by R.G.W.H., 16 Jan. 1886.

and Finance Committee, more shortly and commonly known as the Finance Committee, comprising all the unofficial members, with the Colonial Secretary, the Auditor-General, and the Director of Public Works, which would examine the estimates in detail, and report on them to the governor before they were proceeded with in the Legislative Council.

de Verteuil's proposal for a Finance Committee could be interpreted as an attempt to forestall more radical reform such as the introduction of elected members, a reform which after July 1885 was also opposed by *The Port of Spain Gazette.* Its editor and correspondents argued that a period of economic depression was not the time for a constitutional experiment which racial and religious differences rendered hazardous. They stressed the progress of the colony under crown government, the lack of demand for change, and the failure of municipal government particularly in Port of Spain.[50] On the other hand, certain factors favoured the reform movement, notably the appointment of Sir William Robinson as governor in 1885. As governor of Barbados he had introduced legislation extending the franchise and establishing voting by secret ballot. His first address to the Trinidad Legislative Council favoured the abolition of school fees, the removal of tariffs on 'Bread of all kinds', and the development of the minor industries. In his encouragement of economic diversification and of a peasant proprietary, Robinson was to stimulate public discussion on issues which Rostant had linked with constitutional reform. Robinson's influence in this respect was similar to Irving's in British Guiana. The continued depression of the sugar industry after 1884 strengthened his case and, for those who accepted Rostant's arguments, the case for constitutional change. Rostant was further heartened by the appointment of Sir John Gorrie[51] as chief justice in 1885. Rostant shared the sympathy of this humane but quick-tempered judge for the creole and

[50] An elected council, in place of the *Cabildo,* had been established in Port of Spain in 1840, and in San Fernando in 1845. Both Port of Spain and San Fernando were constituted boroughs in 1853. Arima was incorporated as a borough in 1888. In the same year 125 voted out of a registered electorate in Port of Spain of 720, and 56 out of a registered electorate in San Fernando of 140. These figures which are not untypical of the previous seven years do not, however, take into account uncontested elections.

[51] See below, in particular pp. 177–9 and pp. 190–4. Gorrie had previously served in a judicial capacity in Mauritius, Fiji, and the Leeward Islands.

Indian peasantry. Gorrie's views were also close to Rostant's on issues such as unindentured immigration from other West Indian colonies, lower tariffs on necessary foods, and the encouragement of a peasant proprietary. The support for reform of the English-born attorney-general, Stephen Gatty, further encouraged Rostant and contrasts with Gatty's later attitude as chairman of the Royal Franchise Commission.

On 10 December 1886 sixty-nine burgesses of Port of Spain requested the mayor, Francis Damian,[52] to call a meeting to consider the question of a reform of the Legislative Council. Robinson later described the requisitioners as 'men of standing in the Community';[53] they included thirty-one merchants, seventeen planters and proprietors, of whom six were also merchants, and thirteen barristers and solicitors. Among the principal merchants were William Howatson, a partner in the firm of A. Cumming and Co., the largest resident sugar producer in the colony, George Goodwille, an important dry goods merchant, Leon Agostini, a leading commercial man until the bankruptcy of A. Ambard and Son in July 1886, with large interests in sugar as a planter and merchant, and H. B. Philipps, a Barbadian merchant. The majority of the planters did not support the movement, but the requisitioners included P. N. Bernard, a resident director of the Colonial Co., the largest sugar producer in Trinidad, Eugène Lange, a proprietor with large interests in cocoa and to a lesser extent sugar, Fritz Zurcher, and B. Devenish. Among the barristers were Guppy, Henry Alcazar, and Vincent Brown, a coloured solicitor and future solicitor-general. The support of Eugène Cipriani, another wealthy capitalist, further emphasized the propertied character of the movement. Damian, Agostini, Lange, and Cipriani were members of prominent Catholic families, with French antecedents.

The keynote of the movement was set by Rostant in *Public Opinion*: '. . . we warn our friends', he wrote, 'that . . . none but moderate views will avail . . .'.[54] He drafted the moderate

[52] A retired solicitor and wealthy landowner.

[53] Robinson to Holland, No. 206, 21 July 1887. 15634. CO 295/314. Opponents of reform later alleged that Lange had used his influence to obtain some of these signatures, which may account for the French element among them, and that only nine of the sixty-nine requisitioners attended the subsequent public meeting.

[54] *Public Opinion*, 30 Nov. 1886.

resolutions proposed at the reform meeting held on 15 January 1887, and he took a prominent part in drawing up the subsequent petition which was printed at and distributed from the offices of *Public Opinion.* He also circulated in the rural districts a poster advertising the reform meeting, which it was later alleged misled the country people into thinking that they were commanded by the governor to attend. The attendance at the meeting was variously estimated, but probably numbered over 5,000. James Froude's description[55] follows broadly that in *The Port of Spain Gazette* which described it as '. . . a complete fiasco'; in Rostant's view it 'fulfilled the most sanguine expectations of its well-wishers'. Most speakers at the meeting emphasized the need for moderate reform which Damian described as the substitution of elected for nominated unofficial members, the constitution of the Council remaining otherwise unchanged. In support of this change one of the speakers, Dr. Siccard, cited the precedents of Jamaica and Mauritius, and he also referred to the example of Ireland and Bulgaria where home rule and reforms were being demanded. But although there was broad unanimity of aim, the differing emphases of the speakers reflected the breadth of a movement which included capitalists like Lange and moderate radicals like Guppy. The former spoke of the 'very moderate' reform required to secure effective control over finance.[56] The latter, although stressing that 'change must be gradual but . . . effective', strongly criticized the political dominance of the sugar planters who had persistently tried to limit the colony's production to one article. Guppy stressed the failures of crown colony government such as inadequate roads, hospitals, prisons, and asylums, and the high rate of illegitimacy which was partly caused by the barrack system of housing on the estates; like Siccard, he deprecated the number of posts held by expatriates. A further discordant note was struck by Goodwille who criticized the

[55] J. A. Froude, *The English in the West Indies or the Bow of Ulysses* (London, 1888), p. 85. Froude arrived in Trinidad on 14 January 1887 at the start of his tour of the West Indies. He was invited to the reform meeting but did not attend. His host in Trinidad was Gatty. Louis Wharton, a barrister, subsequently attributed Gatty's opposition to reform to the influence of Froude. See report of reform meeting, 22 Oct. 1892. *The Port of Spain Gazette*, 25 Oct. 1892.

[56] This and subsequent quotations from speeches at the meeting are taken from the report in *Public Opinion*, 18 Jan. 1887.

Jamaica franchise as inadequate and hinted at his support for universal suffrage as in the United States.[57]

The petition subsequently drawn up was based on the moderate resolutions passed at the meeting. It stressed the material and intellectual[58] progress of the colony since 1850, and prayed that Her Majesty

be graciously pleased to order that a Royal Commission be named by . . . the Governor as was recently done in Jamaica to enquire and report on the advisability of such a change in the Constitution of the Legislative Council as will admit therein elected members, or such other relief in the premises as to your Majesty may seem meet.[59]

The petitioners were mistaken for the Jamaica franchise commission had been appointed after Derby had decided to introduce elected members into the Legislative Council, and his decision was not therefore dependent on the findings of the commission.

Although the petition was signed by over 5,000 people it is not easy to judge the support for the movement. Evidence given before the Royal Franchise Commission supported the allegation that some of the rural population signed the petition without understanding it and under the impression that it concerned roads, the poor condition and lack of which were widely felt outside the towns. The weight of evidence also strongly supports the view that except among the Barbadians there was no interest in reform in the rural districts. It was

[57] His proposals before the Royal Franchise Commission, although liberal in the context of Trinidad, fell far short of this. See *Public Opinion*, 17 Feb. 1888.

[58] See footnote 22, p. 159. The Trinidad government statist estimated in 1890 that the level of elementary education in Trinidad approximated to that in England fifty years earlier. Council Paper No. 45, 1890. CO 298/47. He based his conclusion on statistics derived from ability to sign the marriage register. Out of every 1,000 men and women married, the number unable to sign was:

England	1841	326 men	488 women
England	1887	91 men	106 women
Trinidad	1890	386 men	510 women

The comparable statistic for bridegrooms in Jamaica in 1892 was 457. Blake to Ripon, No. 196, 16 May 1893. 9537. CO 137/555. The figures for Trinidad probably understated the extent of illiteracy. A synopsis of Wardens' Returns in 1887 showed that out of 12,053 taxpayers outside Port of Spain and San Fernando, only 3,043 could sign their names. Encl. with Robinson to Holland, No. 167, 4 July 1888. 14711. CO 295/318.

[59] Petition enclosed with Robinson to Holland, No. 142, 28 May 1887. 11227. CO 295/314.

further alleged that the petition had been touted in San Fernando; Rostant himself admitted that the organizer there had been paid at the rate of $1 for 1,000 signatures.[60] Captain A. W. Baker, the inspector of police, wrote:

The Franchise Petition represents nothing. It was worked entirely by Mr. P. Rostant, in many instances through paid agents. The signatures were obtained for Roads, Schools etc., etc.[61]

Robinson wrote that the movement had 'certainly never aroused general popular feeling'.[62] On the other hand, he regarded the petition as 'on the whole very respectably signed', and there seems little doubt that the movement initially attracted considerable support among the commercial and professional classes, and to a much lesser extent among the planters. The unofficial members of the Legislative Council did not publicly commit themselves, though Rostant claimed that F. Warner strongly supported the movement, and he hinted that Fenwick, George Fitt, a local-born owner of sugar and cocoa plantations, and George Garcia, a barrister and member of a respected Trinidad family, also favoured a change.

It is hard to find evidence of rural interest except among the Barbadians. Rostant claimed in 1888, however, that the circulation of newspapers had 'increased enormously of late', and that newspapers were to be found on the tables of small proprietors in the most distant parts of the country,[63] several proprietors sometimes jointly subscribing for one copy. Such a claim is plausible in view of the spread of education among the younger generation, but it is difficult to substantiate since circulation figures depended on the unsupported testimony of the editor. In 1887 *The Port of Spain Gazette* claimed a circulation of 550 which Rostant alleged was 275; in January 1888 he asserted that the circulation of *Public Opinion* was three times that of the *Gazette* which if true, and if Rostant's estimate of

60 This admission is not as extraordinary as it seems, for it was not unusual to meet the expenses of those who organized petitions. Payment by signature, however, must have been a strong temptation.

61 Letter read by chairman at meeting of Royal Franchise Commission on 11 July 1888. Reported in *Public Opinion*, 2 Nov. 1888.

62 Report on the Blue Book for 1888. C. 5620–9, p. 18.

63 Evidence before the Royal Franchise Commission, at meeting on 10 Feb. 1888. Reported in *Public Opinion*, 17 Feb. 1888. See also *The Port of Spain Gazette*, 15 Feb. 1888.

the *Gazette* circulation was correct, would have given an approximate circulation of *Public Opinion* of over 800 copies. Rostant stated that a special issue containing a portrait and biography of Gorrie sold 1,500 copies. He also claimed that the editor of *The San Fernando Gazette*, who was by no means friendly to Rostant, admitted that *Public Opinion* 'reached a wide circulation' and was 'widely read by the working-classes . . .'.[64] The evidence of two witnesses before the Royal Franchise Commission supported Rostant's general claim regarding the circulation of newspapers. J. L. O'Connor, the warden for Naparima, noted that English was much more widely spoken, and he agreed with Damian that newspapers in English were largely read and the ideas largely disseminated.[65] The Principal of the College of the Immaculate Conception also commented on the great spread of English among the younger generation during the previous five years, and on the large increase of political interest in the villages stimulated by tailors and shopkeepers who could read and write; newspapers were read 'much more' than formerly.[66] On the other hand, several wardens commented on the lack of spoken and written English in their districts and most witnesses agreed that it was not widely spoken among the older generations in the rural areas.

The evidence given before the commission concerning political interest among Indians was conflicting, but it pointed to some awareness among the younger generation, particularly in and around San Fernando. The most striking testimony was that of Revd. K. J. Grant, a Canadian Presbyterian missionary, who considered that the free Indian element in San Fernando, mainly shopkeepers and clerks, were 'very intelligent' and knew 'everything that has transpired' during the sittings of the commission. They had been talking over the question thoroughly and, in Grant's view, they thought the introduction of elected members 'would be a very good thing . . .'. He attributed their political interest to education in Trinidad, or to contact with those who spoke English; some of them were subscribers to the London *Times* and to Indian newspapers.[67]

[64] *Public Opinion*, 12 Aug. 1887.
[65] Evidence reported in *The Port of Spain Gazette*, 12 May 1888.
[66] Reported in *The Port of Spain Gazette*, 10 Mar. 1888.
[67] Meeting, 16 Apr. 1888. Reported ibid., 25 Apr. 1888.

Political interest among Indians outside San Fernando was probably small since most of the free Indians remained on or near the estates where they were less susceptible to political influence. In general, there seems to have been greater political interest among Indians in Trinidad compared with British Guiana, and this is probably accounted for by the fact that they were less isolated from the rest of the community, and their educational and economic opportunities were greater. Witnesses before the Royal Franchise Commission commented on their intelligence and financial acumen, which was reflected in their virtual monopoly of shopkeeping outside Port of Spain and in their growing role as thrifty and capable cultivators.

Apart from their probable attendance at the reform meeting and signature of the petition, there is surprisingly little evidence of political consciousness among the lower classes of Port of Spain, yet most spoke English and they included many Barbadians. W. L. Lewis, English-born stipendiary magistrate of Port of Spain, told the franchise commission that he was 'very much struck' with the intelligence of the Port of Spain artisan whom he compared favourably with the 'ordinary English artisan'.[68] Their apparent political apathy may possibly be accounted for by the fact that the conservative Trinidad reformers of the 1880s preferred to attempt to agitate the small peasant proprietors, in contrast to the radicals who inspired the Port of Spain water riots in 1903.

Robinson seems to have been sympathetic towards reform but unwilling to press it against local opinion. In his despatch of 28 May 1887 he told Knutsford that so long as there was an official majority he would not object to the unofficial members being entirely elected; indeed he seemed to welcome such a change on account of the age and lack of stake in the colony of some of the unofficial members. Two months later, however, he wrote: 'I do not consider that the majority of the population or that the leading inhabitants are in favour of the change advocated, but I think that a majority would view favourably the introduction by election of new blood and new ideas into

[68] Froude wrote that 'the keener-witted Trinidad blacks' were 'watching as eagerly as we do the development of the Irish problem. They see the identity of the situation'. Op. cit., p. 98.

the Unofficial Section of the Council.'[69] Robinson proposed that the mayors of Port of Spain and San Fernando should become *ex-officio* members of the Legislative Council. Robinson's despatch of July was in reply to Knutsford's enquiry, 'by whom the Petition was originated, whether the signatories include the leading inhabitants, and whether it represents the views of a considerable proportion of the community'.[70] Knutsford's officials gave conflicting advice on the issues raised by the reform petition. Both Wedgwood and Wingfield regarded the concession of elected members to Jamaica as having made a similar concession to Trinidad and other West Indian colonies inevitable. Wedgwood favoured a uniform scheme for the West Indies, with a franchise based on household suffrage. Wingfield, although acknowledging that the petition was supported by 'a considerable number of men of standing', doubted if the time had yet come for introducing elected members. In his view they would not rest content with being a minority in the Council, and a low suffrage would allow the lawyers to dominate the legislature as in Jamaica.[71] On the other hand, Herbert minuted:

> ... I am rather inclined to accept what seems to me to be the inevitable without prolonging the fight, and to tell them that H.M. Govt. is not indisposed to consider whether Trinidad may not receive the same constitution as has been granted to Jamaica. . . .[72]

Herbert's advice was based on expediency, but Knutsford reached the same conclusion on broader grounds, his attention having been drawn by Wingfield to Grey's despatch to governor Harris of 16 May 1850.[73] He minuted:

> Upon the whole I am disposed to think that 'by the diffusion of Education & the advancement in civilization', the conditions imposed by Lord Grey have been fulfilled, & that the inhabitants are qualified to take a more direct part in the legislation of the

[69] Robinson to Holland, No. 206, 21 July 1887. 15634. CO 295/314. This despatch probably reflected the increasing hostility of the propertied classes in Trinidad towards reform, caused by Rostant's handling of the movement and particularly his use of the mass meeting and petition.

[70] Holland to Robinson, No. 115, 27 June 1887. 11227. CO 295/314.

[71] Robinson to Holland, No. 206, 21 July 1887. 15634. CO 295/314. Minute by E.W., 19 Aug. 1887.

[72] Ibid. Minute by R.G.W.H., 23 Aug. 1887.

[73] See p. 2.

Colony. It is difficult, moreover, to refuse to Trinidad what has been granted to Jamaica.[74]

In a despatch drafted by Olivier on these minutes, Knutsford informed Robinson that 'H.M. Govt. are not indisposed to consider whether the Colony may not now receive a Constitution as nearly resembling that of Jamaica as the circumstances of Trinidad may justify'. He continued:

> The question whether one half of the Council . . . can properly be made elective must depend upon the result of an enquiry by a Royal Commission, which should be appointed, as in the case of Jamaica, to ascertain the number of persons who would receive votes under a system of qualifications sufficiently liberal to enfranchise all . . . who are capable of exercising the franchise with intelligence. . . .[75]

There is no evidence that Knutsford and his advisers contemplated the concession of the provisional elected majority and the elected members' veto in financial and other matters which Derby had extended to Jamaica in 1884. For them not to have done so would have been consistent with the colonial office attitude towards constitutional reform in the tropical dependencies in the two decades after 1884; with the exception of Mauritius,[76] colonial office officials did not regard these two unusual constitutional provisions conceded in Jamaica as a precedent for other crown colonies.

Knutsford's despatch contained an important ambiguity, since, like the reform petition, it made a decision on the advisability of reform dependent on the findings of a royal commission to be appointed 'as in the case of Jamaica'; yet in Jamaica Derby instructed Norman to appoint the commission after he had decided to introduce elected members, his decision being in no way dependent on the commission's findings which were confined to recommendations for the franchise and similar details. It is improbable that Knutsford intended a locally appointed commission to advise on the desirability of reform; there was no precedent for such a commission and its decision

[74] Robinson to Holland, No. 206, 21 July 1887. 15634. CO 295/314. Minute by H.T.H., 25 Aug. 1887.

[75] Holland to Robinson, No. 165, 3 Sept. 1887. 15634. CO 295/314.

[76] See footnote 47, p. 166.

would depend on whom the governor appointed, but if this was his intention it was misleading to liken the commission to that in Jamaica. Certainly Robinson seems to have interpreted the despatch to mean that the elective principle was accepted by Knutsford, the role of the commission being to determine the franchise qualifications. On 24 September 1887 the acting colonial secretary informed Damian that Her Majesty's Government were not indisposed to consider whether Trinidad might not receive a constitution as nearly resembling that of Jamaica as circumstances justified. He continued: '. . . the Governor will take the necessary steps to enable Her Majesty's Government to decide upon the question of the Franchise and Electoral Districts.'[77] On 24 October 1887 Robinson informed the Legislative Council that a local commission would probably shortly be appointed 'to inquire into the questions of Suffrage and Electoral Districts'.[78] On Knutsford's instructions the terms of reference of the commission followed those issued by Norman in Jamaica,[79] though unlike the Jamaica commission its membership included officials.[80]

The reformers assumed, and reasonably on the facts already noted, that the commission's work was to be confined to recommending a franchise, but at the first meeting of the commission its chairman, Gatty, stated, 'that the whole question of whether the Constitution of Trinidad is to be altered depends upon the result of this enquiry'; unlike Jamaica 'our report is to be the report upon which the Home Government are going to make up their minds as to whether or not any reform should be made at all'.[81] This interpretation of the commission's terms of reference was strongly contested by Guppy, and also by Damian and Maxwell Philip, but was supported by de Verteuil, Garcia, Wilson, and Baker. Its importance lay in the fact that it kept open the question of the principle of reform and so allowed the significant shift in local

[77] *The Port of Spain Gazette*, 28 Sept. 1887.

[78] *The Port of Spain Gazette*, 26 Oct. 1887.

[79] See p. 59 for the terms of reference of the Jamaica commission.

[80] See p. 59. The chairman was S. H. Gatty, the attorney-general. The remaining official members were D. Wilson, sub-inspector of crown lands and commissioner for northern provinces, Capt. A. W. Baker, inspector of police, and M. Maxwell Philip, local-born solicitor-general. The five unofficial members were Louis de Verteuil, Garcia, Guppy, Damian, and Philipps.

[81] Meeting of 2 Feb. 1888. Reported in *The Port of Spain Gazette*, 3 Mar. 1888.

opinion against reform, which had taken place during 1887, to make itself felt in the Colonial Office.

The hardening of local opinion against reform during 1887 was reflected in the differing emphases of Robinson's despatches of May and July 1887, by Gatty's hostility to reform as chairman of the Royal Franchise Commission compared with his earlier support for it, and by the apparent unwillingness of prominent signatories of the reform petition to give evidence before the commission, among them Cipriani, Bernard, William Cunningham, Leon Agostini, and Howatson.[82] The weakening of support for reform among the propertied classes may have been partly due to Rostant's attempts to give the movement a popular character by the 'monster' petition and meeting. But the more substantial reason lay in the actions of the chief justice, Sir John Gorrie.[83] Gorrie was in the tradition of other liberal colonial judges and governors, whose careers were stormy because their social and political views clashed with the prevailing values of narrow societies in which the rights and privileges of property were pre-eminent. Gorrie's liberal views led him to examine not only the form of Trinidad law but also its working, and to strain judicial procedure in order to administer what he considered was even-handed justice. Informing his attitude was a sense of responsibility towards those who, in their recourse to the courts, were at a disadvantage through poverty, and ignorance of language and law. His openly-expressed sympathy for the poorer creoles and Indians, combined with a quick temper and outspoken, and at times violent, language, soon estranged him from important elements in Trinidad society. In particular, he incurred the strong enmity of lawyers, among them Gatty, Garcia, and Aucher Warner, by his attitude to judicial procedure, which he sought to cheapen and expedite. He also antagonized the merchants who as defendants had profited in the past from the expense of, and delays in, the administration of justice which the poorer plaintiff could not withstand.[84] At first the

[82] The commission invited forty persons to give evidence from a list of fifty names submitted by Rostant, but very few came forward. Meeting of 9 Mar. 1888. Reported in *The Port of Spain Gazette*, 14 Mar. 1888.

[83] Sir John Gorrie had been appointed chief justice in 1885.

[84] Gorrie delivered adverse judgements against such prominent merchants as E. Tripp, C. A. Fabien, and W. Gordon Gordon. In his administration of justice

movement against Gorrie took the form of pressure for a second puisne judge, and hostile criticism in the press, but on 31 August 1887 the Chamber of Commerce laid a petition before the Legislative Council asking for a 'full and formal' enquiry into the administration of justice in the Supreme Court.[85] The effect of these developments on the reform movement was considerable. Planters and merchants who had been divided on reform were united in the defence of property. Further, their attack on Gorrie provoked a demonstration in his favour in which Rostant played a leading part; for some owners of property this identified the cause of reform with which they sympathized with a manner of administering justice which they deplored. Finally, Gorrie's administration of justice created a lack of confidence among capitalists, particularly those connected with the cocoa industry, and a more general feeling of unease among employers of labour and owners of property to which *The Port of Spain Gazette* gave expression:

> There is a feeling of apprehension and anxiety, all over the Colony, amongst owners of property . . . labourers, working-people and domestic servants . . . are assuming airs . . . out of keeping with their station . . . the danger of disturbance on a large scale may not be so remote as some might think.[86]

It would, however, be an over-simplification to suggest that every opponent of Gorrie became an opponent of reform. For instance, both Garcia and Fabien, who clashed bitterly with Gorrie, supported reform. The failure of some of the prominent

Gorrie sought particularly to redress the balance in favour of the small cocoa contractor and against their proprietors, who were often large merchants who exploited the frequently unwritten contracts on which the relationship rested. Gorrie also pressed for an amendment to the law of mortgage which would have protected the small cocoa proprietor from their merchant mortgagors to whom they were sometimes heavily indebted.

[85] Encl. with Robinson to Holland, Conf., 12 Sept. 1887. 19809. CO 295/315.

[86] *The Port of Spain Gazette*, 10 Dec. 1887. See also pp. 191 and 192 for the allegation that Gorrie encouraged the spread of socialist ideas. It is interesting to compare the fear for the sanctity of property and contract which informed much of the opposition to Gorrie, with the similar anxiety of the propertied classes in England during the 1880s, an important influence of which was the Irish Land Act of 1881. In the same year H. M. Hyndman's *England for All* and the first English edition of Henry George's *Progress and Poverty* were published. Henry George visited England in 1882 and 1884, and in the latter year Hyndman founded the Social Democratic Federation. In February 1886 the Trafalgar Square rioters showed scant respect for private property.

requisitioners of the reform meeting of January 1887 to give evidence may also have been due to fear of hostile cross-examination by Gatty. It nevertheless seems probable that the opposition of lawyers such as Gatty and A. Warner, and the apparent indifference of large proprietors and merchants such as L. Agostini and Cipriani, all of whom had earlier supported reform, was influenced by Gorrie's administration of justice.

Gatty's hostility to reform was reflected in his handling of the commission's proceedings. His cross-examining of leading reformers such as Rostant and Lennon as to the grounds of their support for reform reflected his belief that the signatories of the reform petition should 'state their case, as if they were plaintiffs in a suit . . .'.[87] Although he regarded the commissioners' role as 'that of Judges', an interpretation Guppy strenuously contested, Gatty's attitude was sometimes closer to that of prosecuting counsel, for he sought to test the political intelligence of less-educated witnesses by difficult questioning, to the extent of one witness complaining: 'We are not in Court.' This prompted Rostant to advise the country people not to appear before the commission in person. Gatty almost certainly shared the view of Capt. A. W. Baker, the inspector of police, that by so conducting the commission it would be shown 'that educated men who signed the original petition are now opposed to any sweeping change . . . and . . . that others whose names appear on the petition know or care nothing whatever about the franchise or reform . . .'.[88] Gatty's hostile questions also reflected his belief, expressed at the first public meeting of the commission, that 'in not many years, the coolie vote . . . would have a very considerable preponderance in the Island.'[89] Witnesses did not share his fears, for most, like Rostant, proposed no other franchise disabilities for Indians than completion of the five-year indenture or the full ten years of industrial service, and the ability to pass an education test in English; no witness confirmed Gatty's fear that Indians might combine politically, using their organization of *panchayets*, or councils. Gatty's questions also reflected anxiety regarding the political activities of Barbadians and the possibility that they might

[87] Meeting, 2 Feb. 1888. Reported in *The Port of Spain Gazette*, 3 Mar. 1888.
[88] Meeting, 22 Mar. 1888. Reported in *The Port of Spain Gazette*, 24 Mar. 1888.
[89] Meeting, 10 Feb. 1888. Reported in *The Port of Spain Gazette*, 15 Feb. 1888.

combine to form a 'party'; there were grounds for Gatty's apprehension, for witnesses favouring reform outside the propertied and professional classes were nearly all English-speaking immigrants from other West Indian islands, notably Barbados. They were particularly numerous in Arima which seems to have been the only rural area where there was much interest in reform. The protector of immigrants remarked on the energy of the Barbadians compared with the Trinidad creole.[90] The most radical franchise proposals suggested to the commission came from Rostant and two barristers, Alcazar and Louis Wharton, the latter estimating that his proposals would enfranchise a little over 15,000; their schemes were based on the reformed Jamaica franchise of 1886, though both Rostant and Alcazar favoured an education test. On the other hand, Lange proposed indirect election and a franchise including the payment of £2 in direct taxes, compared with 10*s.* favoured by Rostant; most of the merchants supported Lange's figure. The evidence of both English and local-born officials was unanimous in the view that the colony was not yet ripe for reform.

The findings of the commission were conveyed to Knutsford in three papers, reflecting its division on the commission's terms of reference and on the advisability of reform. The majority of de Verteuil, Garcia, Guppy, Damian, and Philipps favoured a moderate reform and submitted detailed franchise proposals.[91] Gatty and Wilson, although voting on these proposals, were opposed to reform and submitted their views in separate reports to Knutsford.[92] In Gatty's absence from the colony, the majority report favouring reform was drawn up by de Verteuil, the vice-chairman of the commission. It recommended the election of nine members to the Legislative Council on a franchise based on a scheme submitted by Guppy, but modified by the commission, which increased several of Guppy's qualifications and imposed others. Guppy himself opposed

[90] The radical impact of Barbadians on other British West Indian colonies seems to have been considerable at this time. Bronkhurst regarded them as 'fifty years ahead' of the British Guiana Negro. H. V. P. Bronkhurst, *The Colony of British Guyana and its Labouring Population* (London, 1883), p. 68.

[91] Encl. with Robinson to Holland, No. 16, 10 Jan. 1889. 2437. CO 295/321.

[92] See below pp. 181 et seq. Baker left the colony while the commission was sitting and Maxwell Philip, the solicitor-general, died on 30 June 1888.

only one of these amendments: by four votes to three, Guppy, Philipps, and Wilson voting against, the commission recommended excluding from the franchise those who being under forty 'cannot read and write the English language or understand the same when spoken'.[93] The commission estimated that their proposals would enfranchise about 12,000 or considerably less if the education test was imposed. The majority report did not include any statement of the case for reform. In part, this may have reflected de Verteuil's equivocal attitude towards reform. He had informed his fellow commissioners in July 1888 that he favoured a moderate reform though he was not confident of its success. His reservations were reflected in his preference for a high franchise,[94] his proposal for indirect election which was included in a memorandum to the majority report, and his support for the exclusion of aliens. Although as a young man he had been an ardent reformer, there are grounds for Wingfield's view that de Verteuil's real opinion in 1888 was that Trinidad was not yet fit for elective institutions; the latter's support in March 1889 for Knutsford's decision to make no concession confirms this.[95] The case for reform thus went by default, for Robinson gave Knutsford no further guidance beyond referring him to his despatch of 28 May 1887.

The case against reform was strongly argued by Wilson and Gatty. The former was of the firm opinion that the colony was not fit for elective institutions, since it was impossible to find an electorate capable of reaching an intelligent judgement on public affairs and fairly representing all interests.[96] Gatty, in a paper submitted directly to the Colonial Office, forcefully supported this view. In doing so he restated a dilemma which recurs in the arguments of opponents of constitutional reform in the crown colonies:[97]

[93] The majority of witnesses had favoured an education test. The principle was not regarded favourably in the Colonial Office. See, for instance, footnote 88, p. 36, and p. 142.

[94] He proposed that jurors should vote in the counties and burgesses in the towns. This would have given an electorate of about 2,660. He strongly advocated raising Guppy's franchise proposals.

[95] See p. 187. A comparison of Chapters X in the 1858 and 1884 editions of de Verteuil's *Trinidad* is further evidence for his change of view.

[96] Wilson's views were enclosed with the majority report. Robinson to Holland, No. 16, 10 Jan. 1889. 2437. CO 295/321.

[97] In 1883, for instance, Baden-Powell had opposed the elective principle in

An electorate based upon the qualifications of knowledge and education would not be representative of all interests in the Island while an electorate based upon the representation of all interests would necessarily include a very large number of ignorant and illiterate persons.[98]

Gatty rested his case against reform on five main grounds, none of which had been conclusively demonstrated by the evidence given before the franchise commission; they were the lack of homogeneity of the population and particularly the unfitness of Indians for the franchise, the danger of an uneducated peasantry being exploited by their mortgagors in the towns and by the politically active Barbadians, the lack of support for reform, the extent to which constitutional change would damage the confidence of capitalists, and the backward social condition of the colony. With regard to the first consideration, Gatty conceded that the Indian population represented an increasingly important interest, that they were socially more ambitious than the Negro, and that many were thrifty and naturally intelligent. He argued, however, that they had received 'generally speaking no education in Trinidad' and that their vote would be easily purchased. The evidence taken before the commission did not fully bear out these judgements, and it is significant that Gatty emphasized the reliance he placed on the testimony of McHugh, the chief Indian interpreter in the colony, whose imperfect knowledge of Trinidad was shown up under questioning by Guppy and whose work involved him only with illiterate rural Indians. It is probable that the substantial reason for Gatty's hostility to the Indian vote was his belief in its future preponderance. Gatty had stronger grounds for his second contention, namely that the peasant proprietors showed no political interest and that they were in the hands of their mortgagors in the towns who would influence their votes. He argued that their lack of education would lead them to being 'made dupes' as they were in the case of the reform petition; he contrasted them with the

Jamaica on the same grounds: 'If the *Franchise is high* enough to secure an intelligent exercise of the privilege, political power is at once handed over to a class. If the *Franchise is low* all political power is thrown into the hands of the agitator.' Memorandum, 3 July 1883. Attached to minute paper 11961. CO 137/512. Compare also pp. 184–5, 213, footnote 114, 221, 229–30, 232.

[98] Gatty to Under-Secretary of State, 24 Jan. 1889. 1938. CO 295/326.

politically active English-speaking Barbadians in the towns who were 'accustomed to politics in their own Island and are generally adventurers without any stake in the Colony'. It seems that some cocoa contractors and proprietors, and other small cultivators, were certainly exploited by their mortgagors,[99] but colonial office officials failed to notice the inconsistency of Gatty's position. Only six months earlier he had strenuously opposed Gorrie's proposal for legislation to protect cocoa contractors from exploitation. They were, he wrote, 'men of full age and understanding . . . the most adventurous and hardiest portion of the population . . .'.[100] The evidence before the commission concerning the politically active Barbadians was conflicting. R. J. Lechmere Guppy, the inspector of schools, considered that they constituted no danger. Gatty's third contention was that an elective system was not desired by any 'considerable class', that the wardens reported no public interest, that the petition was 'absolutely misleading', and that there had been no public meetings except the 'notorious' meeting of January 1887 to which, he alleged, Indians flocked, thinking they had been commanded by the governor to attend. He also cited the lack of interest in elections for borough councillors. He claimed that the majority of those with a stake in the country did not favour a change. Fourthly, Gatty argued that non-resident English and French capitalists, on whom the prosperity of the country depended, would not like to see unofficial members chosen by 'an Electorate composed of such elements as it must be in Trinidad if it is to be a representative electorate.' Finally, he referred to the prevailing lack of awareness of family duties and responsibilities reflected in the weakness of family ties.

Gatty recommended that the unofficial members should in future be nominated for districts for a period of five years, and that the mayor and burgesses of each borough should submit, say, three names to the governor for members to represent each borough, or the district in which it was situated. Although Gatty was not highly regarded in the Colonial Office and the

[99] See, for instance, minute by C.A.H., 4 Aug. 1890 on Robinson to Knutsford, No. 140, 24 May 1890. 10848. CO 295/328.

[100] Report of attorney-general, 16 June 1888. Encl. 10. Robinson to Knutsford, No. 20, 14 Jan. 1889. 2441. CO 295/321.

evidence to the commission did not fully bear out his conclusions, his statement against reform strongly influenced Office opinion. It provided the two main grounds on which Knutsford decided against the introduction of elected members, it was cited approvingly by Harris in 1893 as a reason for refusing reform in Trinidad,[101] and it appears to have influenced the thinking of both Chamberlain and his parliamentary under-secretary, Lord Selborne.[102]

The Trinidad reform papers were first considered by Harris, who had never been a strong advocate of the elective principle in the crown colonies and whose opposition to it seems to have strengthened during the late 1880s.[103] He minuted his entire agreement with Gatty's views:

> The agitation is that of a small clique, & is very happily hit off by Mr. Froude in his book.[104]
>
> Even if the Jamaica precedent were a success, which I cannot admit, it is no parallel for Trinidad which, with Hindus and Venezuelans, has many material points of divergence.
>
> I beg to record in the strongest possible terms my vote against any further infraction of the Crown Colony principle in the West Indies at present. I quite expect Jamaica to petition for a return to it within 10 years or so.[105]

The reference to Froude's book, which was published in January 1888, is revealing. During his stay in Trinidad Froude had been the guest of Gatty and it is interesting to compare their views. Froude was an outspoken critic of elective councils in the West Indies, which, in his view, served only to foster discontent and encourage jobbery; he posed the same general political dilemma of government in the West Indies as Gatty, though in racial terms: 'The white minority could not be

[101] See p. 213.

[102] Selborne's minute of 3 Aug. 1895 (see pp. 229–30) reflects Gatty's views. In the case of Chamberlain the evidence is more circumstantial but see footnote 16, p. 232.

[103] See p. 136.

[104] Froude, op. cit. See, for example, pp. 85–7. Froude's book seems to have been well regarded in the Colonial Office. Charles Lucas, responsible for West Indian business between 1897 and 1906, wrote of it that, of recent books on the West Indies, it 'takes, of course, the first place'. C. P. Lucas, *A Historical Geography of the British Colonies*, Vol. II, The West Indies (Oxford, 1890), p. 74.

[105] Robinson to Knutsford, No. 16, 10 Jan. 1889. 2437. CO 295/321. Minute by C.A.H., 4 Feb. 1889.

trusted with the exclusive possession of political power. The blacks could not be trusted, with the equally dangerous supremacy which their numbers would insure them.'[106] It is not clear whether Froude included Indians in the term 'blacks'; for Gatty their possible political preponderance was a matter of much concern. In his book Froude drew many parallels between the West Indies and Ireland. Each constitutional concession to the former, he argued, would as in the case of Ireland make the maintenance of the connection with England harder, and this, in his view, was a further reason for resisting change.

Wingfield, like Harris, accepted Gatty's conclusions though not all the grounds for them. He doubted if the heterogeneity of the population was a strong argument against reform, believing that the Indian would vote more intelligently than the creole though his vote might be more easily purchased, and he ignored the effect of a change on capitalists' confidence. His opposition to reform rested on the conviction, based on a reading of Gatty's paper, that there was no general desire for elected members under any but an oligarchic franchise, that many of those who would probably be enfranchised would be 'an easy prey to mischievous demagogues', and that many of the peasant proprietors would be in the hands of their mortgagors. On the other hand, Wingfield acknowledged that there was a feeling of dissatisfaction arising both from the nominated members holding their seats in effect for life, and from the country districts being neglected. He minuted:

> . . . there is ground for this feeling—Governors have nominated either large planters or the merchants in Port of Spain or leading barristers and so far as the unofficial members are concerned the interests of the lower classes have not received much consideration.[107]

He therefore favoured members holding their seats for a limited period. Herbert summarized the case against reform:

> Trinidad is the most prosperous and progressive West Indian Colony; there have been no grave difficulties or shortcomings in connection with its administration or Legislature; there is no strong or general demand for a constitutional change and we have

[106] Froude, op. cit., p. 208.

[107] Robinson to Knutsford, No. 16, 10 Jan. 1889. 2437. CO 295/321. Minute by E.W., 21 Feb. 1889.

every reason to believe that the proposed change would be injurious to the Island.[108]

Knutsford accepted the unanimous advice of his officials against conceding elected members, giving as his reasons the four grounds expressed in Herbert's minute.[109] The colony had enjoyed 'remarkable prosperity' under the existing constitution. There had been no serious failure in the existing legislative system; a paragraph drafted by Herbert referred to 'judicious legislation' and 'a liberal expenditure on public works', although Wingfield had minuted that there was some truth in Guppy's allegation that the sugar planters in the Legislative Council had legislated in their own interests. These two arguments could have been advanced in 1887 and cannot therefore be considered the substantial reasons for the change of policy. The main grounds for Knutsford's decision seem to have been the third and fourth reasons given in his despatch, namely that there was 'no strong and general expression of public opinion' in favour of constitutional change, and that such a change would not 'be likely to conduce to the public good'. The meaning of the latter phrase is obscure, but on the evidence of the minutes it probably referred to the danger of an ignorant electorate being exploited by a small politically active class, and the possibility of peasant proprietors being controlled politically by their mortgagors; it was perhaps the former consideration which Herbert had in mind when he drafted into the despatch a reference to the difficulty of refusing 'demands fostered by unscrupulous politicians for the extension of the limited franchise which would be established in the first instance . . .'. Knutsford recommended that members should be nominated to represent districts, and that they should hold their seats for a limited period. On the advice of Herbert, he also indicated a willingness to consider further Gatty's suggestion regarding the representation of the boroughs. Both Robinson and Wingfield opposed the scheme, the former on the grounds that it would lead to a collision between the local government and borough councils, the latter because by nominating, say, two undesirable names out of three the

[108] Robinson to Knutsford, No. 16, 10 Jan. 1889. 2437. CO 295/321. Minute by R.G.W.H., 28 Feb. 1889.

[109] See Holland to Robinson, No. 56, 6 Mar. 1889. 2437. CO 295/321.

boroughs could force their nominees on the governor. Knutsford did not press the proposal, the changes finally effected by the despatch being limited to the nomination of members for five years[110] to represent seven districts. Robinson reported that the unofficial members were 'highly gratified'[111] at Knutsford's decision and offered to facilitate the proposed changes by resigning, an offer which proved unnecessary since Robinson simply assigned the existing unofficial members to the seven districts, Port of Spain having two members. The insignificance of the change was reflected in the reference by the officer administering the government, Henry Fowler, to the representation by districts as being 'merely a nominal one'.[112]

The reasons for the failure of the Trinidad reform movement lay mainly in the colony, and particularly in the withdrawal of support by the propertied and professional classes; among the reasons for this withdrawal were dissatisfaction with Rostant's methods and the unease created by Gorrie's administration of justice. The conservatism and apathy of Trinidad politics were further reflected in Rostant's unwillingness or inability to organize any public meetings after that of January 1887, and in the fact that by 1889 only one major newspaper, his own, wholeheartedly supported reform. The opponents of reform had a powerful advocate in Gatty, who, by widening the terms of reference of the commission, used its proceedings authoritatively to demonstrate the lack of support for reform and the dangers of conceding it. During the 1880s the support of colonial office officials for the introduction of elected members had been lukewarm. They recommended the change when the immediate weight of demand was such that they considered it impolitic to refuse it, or when they judged that a change was ultimately inevitable. Gatty's letter removed the first ground and weakened the second. The colonial office minutes do not confirm Knutsford's contemporary reputation as a secretary of state who favoured constitutional advance in the crown colonies.[113] His refusal of reform in Trinidad, taken

[110] Additional Instructions to the Governor, 8 June 1889. The existing nominated members were to vacate their seats on 28 June 1894. CO 380/147/24.

[111] Robinson to Knutsford, No. 100, 29 Mar. 1889. 7419. CO 295/321.

[112] Fowler (O.A.G.) to Knutsford, No. 194, 24 May 1889. 11616. CO 295/322. See also p. 233.

[113] For a statement of this reputation see, for example, *The European Mail*, West

with his acceptance of a truncated measure in British Guiana, suggest either a deference to his officials or a lack of conviction regarding the value of constitutional reform in these colonies. Nor, it seems, would Knutsford have regarded changes in Trinidad as a precedent for other West Indian colonies. Replying on his behalf in July 1888 to a question in the House of Commons, Sir John Gorst stated that any limited changes which might be made in Trinidad would not be applicable to other West Indian colonies, where the 'education and political knowledge of the bulk of the population' was 'not yet sufficiently advanced to enable them to exercise the franchise beneficially to their interests'.[114]

Indies Edition, 28 July 1887. Knutsford, as Sir Henry Holland, had been regarded in 1884 as one of the 'well-known friends of Jamaica'. *The Colonial Standard and Jamaica Despatch*, 3 Apr. 1884.

[114] 17 July 1888. *Hansard*, Third Series (328), 1519.

7

THE RENEWAL OF AGITATION

An appeal to a Liberal Government

THE union of Tobago with Trinidad in 1888[1] was the occasion for the temporary ending of the unofficial nominated majority in the Trinidad Legislative Council. Wingfield took the opportunity of the appointment to the Council of the commissioner for Tobago and an unofficial to represent the island, also to press for the addition of the receiver-general.[2] Since he did not recommend the appointment of a further unofficial to balance the receiver-general's vote, the effect of his advice, which Knutsford implemented,[3] was to restore the official majority; the governor's casting vote was now decisive in a Legislative Council in which his original vote and the votes of eight officials balanced those of nine unofficials. Wingfield probably realized the implications of his proposal, though he did not spell them out in his minute. Yet in December 1889 Herbert was still unaware that the governor had an official majority, which suggests that its re-establishment was not a well-considered policy decision. In December 1889 Robinson reported a very strong feeling among the unofficial members against this change. Knutsford received conflicting advice from his officials. Herbert strongly deprecated restoring the unofficial majority. Wingfield, having given the matter closer attention than he had done in January, argued that since the unofficial members had not obstructed business they had grounds for grievance if the official majority had been re-established without the circumstances having occurred which Newcastle had

[1] Tobago's critical financial position was the main reason for the change which was effected by Order in Council of 17 Nov. 1888. CO 380/147/20.

[2] Robinson to Knutsford, No. 5, 2 Jan. 1889. 1407. CO 295/321. Minute by E.W., 23 Jan. 1889.

[3] Additional Instructions to the Governor, 8 Feb. 1889. CO 380/147/22. Also Knutsford to Robinson, Gen., 13 Feb. 1889. CO 380/147/22.

stated would lead to this outcome.[4] Knutsford decided 'not without doubt' to restore the unofficial majority by the appointment of a further nominated member, though he warned Robinson that it might become necessary to withdraw the concession if the unofficial members voted habitually as a party to negate the official vote.[5] In 1893 Ripon effected a further change by appointing the surgeon-general and an additional unofficial to the Council,[6] which thus comprised after February 1893 the governor with an original and casting vote, nine officials, and eleven nominated unofficials. The representatives of Tobago rarely attended.

As a result of the union of the two islands, Gorrie held the Trinidad Supreme Court's first session in Tobago in January 1889, leaving the labouring population in such an excited state that certain planters and merchants petitioned against his return. They alleged that since Gorrie's visit labourers were seeking higher wages and had become rude and disobedient, being emboldened by the belief that the chief justice was their friend rather than their judge; Gorrie's name had become a by-word among them. Tobago grievances against Gorrie were more specifically defined and more forcibly advanced in a series of petitions and legal actions, which followed his second visit to the island in January and February 1890. The central figure behind these was Dr. R. B. Anderson, a small Tobago planter who had certain well-founded legal grievances against Gorrie concerning his interpretation of the rules of court; he was probably mainly motivated, however, by the adverse judgements which Gorrie had delivered against him. His petitions and legal actions against the judges provoked Gorrie and J. Cook, one of the puisne judges, into what a commission of enquiry later called 'judicial persecution',[7] for instance, by demanding excessive bail. Underlying the struggle between Anderson and the Supreme Court, however, were more substantial issues than the conflict between a litigious planter and

[4] Robinson to Knutsford, No. 435, 31 Dec. 1889. 1208. CO 295/325. Minute by E.W., 23 Jan. 1890. For Newcastle's despatch see p. 10.

[5] Knutsford to Robinson, No. 16, 3 Feb. 1890. 1208. CO 295/325.

[6] Ripon to Broome, No. 2, 3 Jan. 1893. 23903. CO 295/340. Additional Instructions to the Governor, 8 Feb. 1893. CO 380/147/26.

[7] Report of Judicial Enquiry Commission (F.C.O. Lib. 9081), p. vii. For its appointment see p. 194.

headstrong judges. Anderson, and the Tobago planters associated with him, complained of those aspects of Gorrie's administration of justice which were still causing much dissatisfaction in Trinidad, notably his efforts to cheapen and expedite justice for the poorer classes, and to protect the weaker party to a contract from exploitation.[8] In his Trinidad judgements Gorrie had sought to prevent what he considered was the exploitation of cocoa contractor by owner, and mortgagor by mortgagee. In Tobago he gave to the metayer a fixity of tenure and a safeguard against eviction which he had not previously enjoyed. Writing in April 1890 Gatty summarized the reaction of the propertied classes: '. . . the United Colony is suffering from paralysis . . . induced by uncertainty and distrust in the administration of the laws relating to property and contracts'.[9] Gorrie's critics also alleged that he had aroused class antagonism between labourer and employer; there is evidence to support this, and also the view that this antagonism had racial as well as economic roots. Both press and police reports of Gorrie's final departure from Trinidad in July 1892 referred to the anti-white feeling of the large crowd of supporters of 'the lowest class' who escorted 'Papa Gorrie' to the jetty, thirty-six of them pulling his buggy; one was reported as saying: '. . . if we were in Barbados to-day we'd fight the white man'.[10] The leader-writer of *The Port of Spain Gazette* saw in the unrest during Gorrie's administration of justice the disruptive effect of socialist ideas.[11]

The turbulent years of Gorrie's chief justiceship,[12] which formed the background to the reform movements of 1887 and

[8] See p. 177.

[9] Report of attorney-general, 9 Apr. 1890. Encl. with Robinson to Knutsford, No. 180, 24 June 1890. 14066. CO 295/328.

[10] Accounts of Gorrie's final departure from the colony in July 1892, encl. with Broome to Knutsford, No. 200, 9 July 1892. 15120. CO 295/339. In Tobago a Negro was reported as saying: 'White did have the country all the time, but thank God since Sir John Gorrie came black have it.' Encl. 8, Robinson to Knutsford, No. 109, 1 Apr. 1889. CO 295/322. Compare pp. 65 and 252–3 for reports of unrest among Jamaican Negroes.

[11] See, for example, leading article 'The Wedge of Socialism' in *The Port of Spain Gazette*, 20 Mar. 1889. He referred to the 'Socialistic propaganda emanating from Europe'; the disturbed state of affairs in Trinidad and Tobago was one aspect of influences at work which would 'leaven modern society to the point of socialistic disruption . . .'.

[12] 1885–92.

1892, marked the impact of a 'political judge'[13] of radical beliefs and humane social convictions on a society in which the privileges of property were strongly entrenched. Gorrie sought to redress the balance in favour of the poor. Where the law in his view was defective he sought to change it. Similarly he administered it in the light of his social beliefs, treating the rules of court as his aids not his masters. This led him into the 'perverse judicial error' of which a commission of enquiry found him guilty,[14] yet Meade too was right when he wrote that the 'quarrels in which he was frequently involved arose from his routing out abuses . . .'.[15] His chief justiceship raised one of the fundamental issues of Trinidad society and politics, the relation of labour to capital, and the reaction of reformers therefore throws valuable light on their aims and beliefs.

A few reformers such as Guppy, Rostant, Howatson, and Goodwille[16] supported Gorrie because they shared his liberal social convictions; for Rostant, and for others of the radical wing of the 1892 reform movement[17] such as J. S. de Bourg and E. A. Nunes, Gorrie was the greatest of reformers. Other reformers while sympathizing with him politically opposed him as a judge. Alcazar summed up their dilemma:

> He . . . was no admirer of Sir John Gorrie but he would do him the justice to say this—that so far as Sir John Gorrie's career as a politician, not as a Judge, was concerned, he had never noticed any ill effects from his policy, in this colony, for if there was any change the labouring classes had learned that they were entitled to hold

[13] The phrase is Herbert's. See Robinson to Knutsford, No. 1, 1 Jan. 1891. 1083. CO 295/332. Minute by R.G.W.H., 19 Jan. 1891. Gatty stated that the judges during Gorrie's administration of justice were regarded as a 'political force', their judgements being often concerned with what the law should be rather than what it was. The leader-writer of *The Port of Spain Gazette* regarded Gorrie as a 'socialist politician'. Ibid., 1 May 1891. Gorrie hoped after his retirement to enter the House of Commons as, it was rumoured, Gladstonian member for St. Andrews Burghs.

[14] See p. 194.

[15] D. Gorrie to Ripon, 24 Aug. 1892. 17003. CO 295/342. Minute by R.M., 3 Sept. 1892.

[16] In November 1889 Goodwille referred to the London dock strike which he had witnessed on a recent visit to England and to the harsh laws which made it possible. He compared the latter with the laws which Gorrie was endeavouring to change in Trinidad. *The Port of Spain Gazette*, 23 Nov. 1889. There are hints that the influence of labour unrest in England was felt in the West Indies. In July 1890 lightermen and coalwomen in Georgetown successfully struck for higher wages. There was also a strike for higher wages by carpenters and labourers preparing the site for the Jamaica exhibition in June 1890.

[17] See pp. 209–11.

up their heads as well as any body else, entitled to look to the future for a change in their position.[18]

Most prominent reformers opposed Gorrie both as a judge and politician, some playing a leading part in the campaign against him, and a few even modified their support for reform on account of his administration of justice. Thus in 1895 Lange attributed his opposition to reform to the 'reign of terror' of a 'socialist' judge;[19] Edgar Tripp, another leading reformer in 1887 and 1888 but less prominent in 1892, argued that in the earlier years he had not seen 'how much harm one hot-headed wrong-minded Radical'[20] could do. Gorrie had delivered adverse judgements against Lange and Tripp. Conversely, some of his own supporters benefited personally from his administration of justice. Among the nominated unofficial members who supported Gorrie were Eugène Cipriani, Charles Leotaud, and George Fitt, who were merchants, and John Bell-Smyth, an Irish planter, all of whom Gorrie had appointed to receiverships or planting attorneyships of estates. They were Catholics but they were not supporters of the reform movement of 1892.[21] John Cumming, a Catholic and the largest resident sugar producer in Trinidad, was sympathetic to Gorrie; he signed the reform petition of 1893. Cook was a Catholic, and practically all the witnesses who gave evidence before the Judicial Enquiry Commission[22] in favour of Cook were Catholics. On the other hand, de Verteuil, Lange, and E. Agostini, also prominent Catholics, were among Gorrie's strongest opponents. Social convictions, professional and commercial interests, religious loyalties, and personal relations shaped a division of opinion which defies generalization. Reformers, large merchants and owners of property, and Catholics were to be found on both sides. But fundamentally the conflict was between numbers and interests. The planter, merchant, and professional classes were over-

[18] Debate in the Legislative Council, 12 Feb. 1895. Reported in *The Port of Spain Gazette*, 14 Feb. 1895.

[19] Debate in the Legislative Council, 4 Feb. 1895. Reported in *The Port of Spain Gazette*, 6 Feb. 1895.

[20] Letter 26 Dec. 1894. Printed in *The Port of Spain Gazette*, 28 Dec. 1894. Tripp was reported to have said in 1893: '. . . I admired Sir John Gorrie as a man; I did all I could to overthrow him as a politician . . .'. Ibid., 28 Mar. 1893.

[21] Fitt was not a Catholic though his wife and children were. So far as the writer has been able to ascertain Gorrie was not a Catholic.

[22] See p. 194.

whelmingly opposed to Gorrie but as Wingfield justly observed: '. . . if a plebiscite were taken Sir John Gorrie would be acquitted triumphantly'.[23] The moral was not lost on Gorrie's supporters who in the second of two petitions addressed to Knutsford referred to 'the want of popular representation to convey their views . . .'[24] to the secretary of state. The reaction of Trinidad reformers to Gorrie's chief justiceship emphasized the complexity and conservatism of Trinidad politics.

Knutsford and his advisers adopted a cautious attitude to the numerous petitions and representations which they received from Tobago and Trinidad during 1890 and 1891. Knutsford, himself a lawyer, was most reluctant to interfere with the Trinidad judiciary, but he finally yielded to a resolution of the Trinidad Legislative Council of 2 November 1891, passed by six unofficial votes to two, calling for 'a full and independent enquiry' into charges of intemperance against Cook, and into the administration of justice in the colony.[25] The two commissioners concluded that the charges against Cook were well-founded and that Gorrie was guilty of 'perverse judicial error' and intemperate language.[26] On the strength of this report, the governor, Sir Frederick Napier Broome, suspended Gorrie, but the latter died in August 1892 before he could prepare his defence. The failure of Knutsford to act sooner in response to petitions from the colony, the seeming injustice of Anderson's imprisonment in January 1891 following his inability to secure bail for £500, and the frustration of appealing from one judge to the full court of which that judge was the senior member, were among the grievances which prompted Gorrie's opponents in the spring of 1891 to assist Anderson to bring an action for malicious prosecution against the Trinidad judges in the Queen's Bench Division of the High Court.[27] A Civil Rights

[23] Broome to Knutsford, No. 8, 14 Jan. 1892. 1726. CO 295/336. Minute by E.W., 20 Jan. 1892.

[24] Encl. with Broome to Knutsford, No. 37, 28 Jan. 1892. 2784. CO 295/336.

[25] Minutes of the proceedings of the Legislative Council, 2 Nov. 1891. CO 298/47. Cipriani and Leotaud voted against the resolution.

[26] Report of Judicial Enquiry Commission (F.C.O. Lib. 9081).

[27] The subsequent account of the organization and activities of the West Indian Civil Rights Defence Union and of the British and West Indian Alliance is based on correspondence and articles in *The European Mail* (West Indies edition), *The Port of Spain Gazette*, *The Colonial Standard and Jamaica Despatch*, and *The Grenada People*. The leading references are given.

Defence Fund was established[28] to assist Anderson to travel to England both to press his own case and to represent the more general grievances against the judiciary. A similar fund was raised in Barbados which Anderson visited in June 1891, and on the initiative of interested Barbadians a West Indian Civil Rights Defence Union was set up with branches in the two colonies. Barbados was subsequently the headquarters of the movement, a Barbadian, Dr. T. Law Gaskin, being its president, and a *West Indian Civil Rights Defence Guardian* being periodically published from the colony. Anderson reached England in the late summer of 1891 and was soon active on behalf of the Union. At the end of September he established the British and West Indian Alliance, with himself as secretary, the Alliance being in effect the English branch of the Union. On 2 December a public meeting in London under the auspices of the Alliance resolved that a deputation should seek an interview with Lord Salisbury, to whom a report of West Indian grievances and proposed remedies should be forwarded.[29] Anderson seems to have been aware from the first that the aims of any movement if it was to command support outside Trinidad must be wider than the redress of grievances against the judiciary; thus he claimed that his object in founding both the Union and the Alliance was 'the gradual extension of free and representative institutions throughout the West Indies . . .'.[30] More generally, the aims of the Alliance were to arouse public opinion both to the general grievances of West Indians, in particular the lack of representative institutions, and to the resources and commercial opportunities of the area. The organization of the Alliance reflected these aims, with a parliamentary committee to conduct such 'militant business' as the defence of civil rights, petitions to Parliament, and correspondence with the Colonial Office, and a general purposes committee to press 'pacific matters' such as the improvement of communications.[31] It seems that Anderson hoped, in particular, to enlist the support

[28] Letter from R. B. Anderson. *The Port of Spain Gazette*, 17 Mar. 1891.

[29] *The Times*, 3 Dec. 1891.

[30] See leading article, *The Grenada People*, 29 Oct. 1891. The third article of the Union's constitution pledged it to foster 'the development of free institutions' in colonies which desired it.

[31] Anderson's speech at dinner in his honour in London on 26 Apr. 1892, reported in *The Port of Spain Gazette*, 13 May 1892.

of 'the great philanthropic societies', and of those with commercial interests in the West Indies.[32]

Anderson's methods were as ambitious as his aims. Having failed in a direct approach to Knutsford and Salisbury, he sought to appeal to public opinion through the press, through public meetings, and through Parliament.[33] The importance of the English press had been recognized in the constitution of the Union and in Anderson's circular describing the aims and methods of the Alliance,[34] for both attached importance to securing arrangements with an English journal which would afford space to promote the aims of the movement. By February 1892, however, Anderson was conceding the reticence of the English press, though he claimed some success with the Liverpool dailies. *The Times* made no further reference to the Alliance after reporting the meeting of 2 December, and *The Daily News* did not even report this. There was, however, a sympathetic leading article in the London *Daily Chronicle* of 26 September 1891. Nor was Anderson more successful in the organization of public meetings on behalf of the Alliance, which he tried to arrange early in 1892 in Edinburgh, Liverpool, Southport, Manchester, Birmingham, Huddersfield, and Leeds.[35] The only meeting reported in the Trinidad press was held in the schoolroom of a Congregational chapel in Southport on 25 April.

Anderson did, however, succeed in interesting certain members of parliament in the Alliance, who seem to have regarded it as a useful channel for securing information on West Indian grievances. Their aims and strategy are clearly reflected in a report of the 'Parliamentary Committee'[36] of the Alliance, which was published in the West Indian newspapers in the

[32] Anderson attended a special meeting of the West India Committee on 18 January 1894 at which he described the aims of the Alliance. Lubbock stated that although the Committee approved of some of them it could not become identified with the Alliance. West India Committee Circular No. 101, 12 Feb. 1894.

[33] See circular of R. B. Anderson, 28 Sept. 1891, published in the British Guiana *Daily Chronicle*, 21 Oct. 1891.

[34] Ibid.

[35] Letter, R. B. Anderson to Secretaries of Trinidad and Tobago branches of the Civil Rights Defence Union, 5 Jan. 1892. Reprinted in *The Port of Spain Gazette*, 29 Jan. 1892.

[36] The correspondence of the Alliance with the Colonial Office during 1893 was apparently referred to this committee. See, for instance, British and West Indian Alliance to Ripon, 3 May 1893. 7449. CO 295/349.

spring of 1892[37] and which recommended certain remedies for West Indian grievances. They included the establishment of a public parliamentary commission to report on the proceedings of the Colonial Office with reference to the West Indies for the past twenty-five years, including an investigation into 'the transaction of the business of the government of these Colonies with this country through the Crown Agents'; the introduction of elected members into the legislative councils in the proportion of nine, to six crown nominees, the governor relinquishing the presidency; an act of parliament to regulate the office and functions of the secretary of state for the colonies, the vague provisions of which seemed aimed at the officials of the Colonial Office, and, in particular, at the alleged secrecy with which they conducted colonial business and the protection which they afforded incompetent officials in the colonies; and finally, a further act 'in the nature of a treaty', providing for the direct representation of the West Indian colonies in the Imperial Parliament. The demand for a parliamentary enquiry, for which the Alliance were preparing a petition to Parliament during the spring of 1892, the advocacy of constitutional reform, and strong hostility towards the Crown Agents and colonial office officials who allegedly shielded incompetent public officers in the colonies, are recurring themes in the correspondence of the Alliance with the Colonial Office. It is difficult to determine the composition of the parliamentary committee, but the reticence of its sponsors on this point suggests a lack of notable names. Anderson merely admitted making every effort to secure the help of 'eminent Liberals',[38] and among those connected with the Alliance were several Liberal parliamentary candidates. During 1893 the Alliance was in touch with A. E. Pease, Sir J. W. Pease, Sir G. Baden-Powell, T. Gibson Bowles, and the Earl of Stamford.[39] During the parliamentary session of 1893–94 the last four asked questions on the West Indies, those by Pease and Stamford concerning the publication of the Trinidad Judicial Enquiry Commission

[37] *The Colonial Standard and Jamaica Despatch*, 2 Apr. 1892, and *The Grenada People*, 5 May 1892.

[38] Letter, R. B. Anderson, 12 Apr. 1892. Reprinted in *The Colonial Standard and Jamaica Despatch*, 2 May 1892.

[39] Letter, G. F. T. Graham to Secretaries of West Indian Union, 9 May 1893. Reprinted in *The Port of Spain Gazette*, 27 May 1893.

report. In October 1893 *The Grenada People* reported that the Alliance was in touch with the newly-formed 'Colonial Party'[40] in the House of Commons, the secretary of which had offered co-operation in redressing legitimate grievances. During the 1893–94 session five members of the 'Colonial Party' asked thirteen questions on West Indian affairs, mostly directed towards the Dominica disturbances of April 1893 and delays in West Indian mails.

In spite of its parliamentary connections the Alliance exerted no discernible influence on colonial office policy, Wedgwood probably echoing the Office view when he described it as 'a busy-body society'. Nor does its impact seem to have been large outside the Colonial Office. This was probably partly due to the limited public and parliamentary interest in the West Indies and to the suspicion that Anderson was not disinterested. Knutsford's decision to appoint a commission to enquire into the Trinidad judiciary weakened the strongest grounds of his appeal, for Anderson admitted that the granting of representative institutions to the West Indian colonies was regarded in England 'as a mixed, delicate and intricate political question with two sides at least to it . . .'.[41] The activity of the Alliance was stimulated largely by Anderson, its correspondence with the Colonial Office coinciding with his presence in England. Those members of parliament associated with it were probably part of a small but growing number dissatisfied with the administration of the crown colonies,[42] and who probably saw in the Alliance a useful weapon in a wider campaign. The hostility of the Alliance and its parliamentary committee to the Crown Agents and to the Trinidad Public Works Department suggests that some with commercial interests in England and the West Indies may have supported the movement from,

[40] *The Grenada People*, 12 Oct. 1893. The Conference of Colonial Members, popularly called the 'Colonial Party', was formed in mid-1893 on the initiative of J. F. Hogan, Irish Nationalist member of parliament for Tipperary. Initially the group concerned itself with Australian affairs, Hogan being a former resident of Victoria, but by October 1893 its interests extended to all the self-governing colonies. I am indebted to Dr. Luke Trainor for this information.

[41] Letter, R. B. Anderson, 29 Aug. 1892. Reprinted in *The Port of Spain Gazette*, 10 Sept. 1892.

[42] See, for example, Stanley Leighton, 'The Colonial Office and the Colonies', *The National Review*, October 1890, vol. XVI (1890–91), pp. 145–60. Some, like Baden-Powell, had commercial interests in the West Indies.

perhaps, resentment at their exclusion from the considerable public works in progress at this time in some of the West Indian colonies. When these works were undertaken by public works departments not only were private contractors excluded but materials were obtained through the Crown Agents to the disadvantage of local merchants.

Anderson also tried to exploit a more general sense of grievance against the Colonial Office on the part of merchants and planters in the West Indies, stemming, for instance, from the failure to negotiate a reciprocity treaty with the United States, and from such local grievances as outside appointments to the public service and the conduct of public works. There was much criticism at this time in the West Indian press directed particularly against the 'bureaucratic underlings' in the Colonial Office, which was compared unfavourably with the machinery of colonial administration in France and Germany. In short, this was not a politically liberal agitation. It gained no support from the philanthropic societies. It had its origins in the judicial grievances of a litigious planter. He sought to redress them by capitalizing on a more general dissatisfaction in England and the West Indies with the alleged bureaucratic and incompetent administration of the Colonial Office. Anderson failed to exploit the dissatisfaction effectively in England. The same disparity between organization and achievement marked his activities in the West Indies.

With the aid of newspaper editors Anderson succeeded in establishing branches of the Civil Rights Defence Union in Jamaica, St. Vincent, and Dominica, and also apparently in St. Lucia, St. Kitts, Nevis, and British Honduras, but they do not seem to have commanded significant support. Personal and inter-colonial jealousies may have been a factor. The judicial grievances which were the mainspring of the Trinidad movement seemed remote to other colonies, with the exception of the judges' alleged abuse of their power to commit for contempt of court, and this was not an issue in Jamaica.[43] The Union's commitment to constitutional reform possibly alienated con-

[43] But controversy over the use of this power seems to have been widespread in this period, cases being reported from Grenada, British Guiana, the Bahamas, and British Honduras. In part, it reflected the sensitivity of judges to press criticism, and was another manifestation of the increasingly radical influence of the colonial press.

servative elements in Trinidad who on other grounds would have supported the movement. Conversely, radical reformers such as Rostant were strongly critical of the Union, the most outspoken attack on it being made by Gallwey Donovan, the Negro editor of *The Grenada People*.[44] Donovan accused Anderson of acting from purely personal motives of self-interest against a chief justice whom Donovan regarded as a champion of the Negro race. Anderson strongly denied that his movement was based on racial distinctions, but his admiration for the Barbados constitution with a registered electorate in 1891 of 2,164 out of a population of 182,306, and his suggestion that colonies not yet prepared for the introduction of elected members should seek an unofficial nominated majority, were grounds for Donovan's assertion that Anderson sought to re-establish the oligarchic rule of the former Assemblies. Nor did the middle-class reformers of Jamaica and Trinidad support the movement. Politically they stood between the conservatism implied in Anderson's support for an unofficial nominated majority, and the radicalism of Rostant and Donovan who sought the enfranchisement of a significant part of the Negro population. They represented in Trinidad the moderate mainstream of middle-class opinion favourable to constitutional reform, and their motives for reviving the reform movement in Trinidad in October 1892 must now be examined.

Several factors contributed to the renewal of the agitation for constitutional reform, which was formally marked by a public meeting held in Port of Spain on 22 October 1892. As early as March 1891 the conservative *Port of Spain Gazette*,[45] which had opposed reform in 1887, advocated a very moderate constitutional change with elected members in the Legislative Council chosen on a franchise similar to that conceded to

[44] Gallwey Donovan was one of the outstanding radical editors in the West Indies during this period. He claimed that extracts from his paper had been quoted by leading London radical and Liberal journals. He founded *The Grenada People* in November 1883, financial difficulties forcing him to discontinue its publication at the end of 1893. He claimed mixed Irish and slave ancestry.

[45] *The Port of Spain Gazette*, 10 Mar. 1891. The paper reflected the progress of the Trinidad press between 1887 and 1892. In April 1887 it became possible to purchase a single copy rather than by annual subscription. The paper was then published twice weekly at 6*d.* a copy. By December 1892 it sold daily at 1*d.* a copy, and by 1897, if not before, it was printed by electricity. In 1898 its circulation was about 3,000 copies.

British Guiana a few months earlier. The paper was apparently under the same ownership as in 1887. The main grounds for its *volte-face* appear to have been dissatisfaction with the allegedly unrepresentative character of the unofficial members, reflected, in particular, in their unwillingness to act against Gorrie; it was alleged he had secured the support of four of them by appointing them to receiverships or planting attorneyships under the Supreme Court.[46] The paper also expressed a widely felt grievance against the appointment of outsiders to posts in the public service; it linked this issue with that of constitutional reform by arguing that greater financial control would enable the Legislative Council to refuse to vote the salaries for such appointments. Almost certainly, however, the factor immediately determining the timing of the movement was the advent to power of a Liberal government in England, and, in particular, the record of its secretary of state for the colonies, Lord Ripon.[47] Alcazar thus expressed the hopes of reformers:

> They had now a Liberal statesman who as Vice-roy of India dealt justice to the people of India in the face of opposition. In such hands their interests were safe. . . .[48]

Supporters of reform were also encouraged by the appointment as governor of Sir Frederick Napier Broome, who as governor of Western Australia had been associated with the grant of responsible government to that colony. Reformers were also heartened by recent or pending constitutional changes in Malta, British Guiana, and Natal. Speaking at the reform meeting on 22 October 1892, Henry Alcazar compared Trinidad with Barbados, Jamaica, Mauritius, the Leeward Islands, Cyprus, Malta, Tasmania, Newfoundland, the Bahamas, Bermuda, and Western Australia, in all of which colonies the right to vote existed.

The movement of 1892 differed significantly from that of 1887, the leadership having passed from Rostant to the younger

[46] See also Robinson to Knutsford, No. 209, 25 June 1891. 14308. CO 295/333.

[47] Ripon's name stood high not only with middle-class reformers, but also with literate Negroes. Betton (see p. 29) wrote approvingly of rulers like Ripon 'who will see that justice is done to all classes . . . irrespective of class and colour'. Betton to Derby, 9 Feb. 1884. 3439. CO 137/519. Donovan regarded Ripon as 'the Home Ruler of Home Rulers'. See also *The Grenada People*, 25 Aug. 1892.

[48] Report of reform meeting, 22 Oct. 1892. *The Port of Spain Gazette*, 25 Oct. 1892.

Port of Spain barristers, notably Vincent Brown, the coloured solicitor-general, and Alcazar. This probably accounted for its more sophisticated direction. They did not attempt to give it a popular character by the kind of mass meeting which Rostant had organized in Queen's Park in January 1887 and which had alienated conservative support. Their moderate proposals were embodied in a petition less numerously but more influentially signed than that of 1887, and were pressed on Lord Ripon personally by a deputation of which Alcazar was a member. There were notable changes in the composition as well as the organization of the movement. de Verteuil now publicly though cautiously supported it, and with Brown and Damian he was one of several Catholics among the leaders. On the other hand, some of the wealthy owners of property and influential French Trinidadians, who were prominent in the reform movement of 1887, had withdrawn their support, notably Lange, Cipriani, C. Stollmeyer, and Leon Agostini. Similarly the planting interest, a few representatives of which had signed the petition of 1887, now unanimously opposed reform with the notable exception of John Cumming, the largest resident sugar proprietor. Their attitude was influenced by Gorrie's chief justiceship, and by the hostility of some reformers to the sugar interest, reflected in their support for the ending of Indian immigration.

The extent of support among reformers for the ending of Indian immigration is hard to determine. Opponents of the reform movement alleged that it was one of the main planks of its programme, but Alcazar strenuously denied this. In fact in this, as in most matters, reformers were divided. Some with planting interests such as de Verteuil and Howatson naturally advocated its continuance. Others such as Brown, Alcazar, and C. Prudhomme David, a Negro barrister and secretary of the 'Reform Committee',[49] opposed it; in doing so they represented an opinion increasingly held in the early 1890s and reflected in the editorials of *The Port of Spain Gazette*. Earlier opposition to Indian immigration had been confined to a few radicals such as Guppy, who had attacked the heavy burden which it imposed on the public revenue for the benefit of the sugar planters, and the social degradation implied in the living condi-

[49] For David see footnote 58, p. 205. For the Reform Committee see p. 209.

tions of Indians on the estates and in the limitations on their personal freedom. During the early 1890s *The Port of Spain Gazette* sounded a new note, stressing the dangers of a coolie rising and the evils of importing a race of uncivilized aliens, some of whom were 'isolated in the crudeness of their paganism, language, and customs . . .',[50] which as in Mauritius might ultimately swamp the West Indian population. These fears were reinforced by the census returns for 1891 which showed an increase, over ten years, of Indians born in the colony from 12,800 to 24,641, and of Indians born in India from 36,020 to 45,577; due, however, to the high level of West Indian immigration the percentage of the population of Indian origin had only increased from 31.88 to 35.10 per cent.[51] There were signs of political rivalry in San Fernando where it was alleged that qualified Indians had been excluded from the list of burgesses. Opponents of coolie immigration also claimed that the presence of large numbers of indentured immigrants depressed the wages of free estate labour; there is certainly some evidence for the view that the continued high level of Indian immigration after 1886 had had this effect, and that this in turn had depressed the general level of wages.[52] Alcazar expressed this point forcibly and in significant language to the West India Royal Commission of 1897:

> Those who have witnessed the very close struggle between capital and organized labour in Western Europe, must be aware of the irresistible effect which an annual introduction of between 2,000 and 3,000 indentured labourers must have among a population of 240,000 all told; how it must give to employers a complete and uninterrupted command of the labour market. . . .[53]

[50] From a leading article entitled 'The Indian Spectre'. *The Port of Spain Gazette*, 5 Dec. 1890.

[51] Census of the Colony of Trinidad, 1891, p. 21. CO 298/50.

[52] See, for example, minutes by the attorney-general and protector of immigrants to governor, 19 Oct. 1890, encl. with Robinson to Knutsford, No. 339, 22 Oct. 1890. 21651. CO 295/330. Also H. J. Clark to Robinson, 25 July 1890, encl. with Robinson to Knutsford, Conf., 31 July 1890. 15998. CO 295/329.

[53] Memorandum by H. A. Alcazar on Indian Immigration. Reprinted in C. 8657, p. 319. P.P. 1898 (L). H. C. Bourne, a first class clerk in the West India department and formerly a public officer in Trinidad, noted in 1903 that Alcazar was the only advocate among the unofficial members 'of the interests of the labourer as opposed to those of the employer'. Moloney to Secretary of State for the Colonies, Conf., 7 Oct. 1903. 38737. CO 295/419. Minute by H.C.B., 24 Oct. 1903.

The hostility of the reformers was directed particularly towards the large sugar planters who were absentees; the government statist estimated in 1890 that four-fifths of the total export of sugar was in their hands. Merchants complained that they did not contribute their fair share of the revenue nor did they buy their estate supplies in the island. The hostility towards absentee owners was reinforced by the opposition of the West India Committee to Robinson's policies of improving communications and developing the minor industries. In a letter to Knutsford in May 1890,[54] extracts of which were published in the colony, the Committee attacked this policy as 'unwise and wasteful in every respect', leading to a dispersal of the population and a reduction in the labour supply of existing industries. The Committee were writing against the background of discussion in the colony on railway extension, particularly eastwards across the island to Mayaro, and in Robinson's view they laid themselves open to the charge of attempting to force down the wages of free labour by confining the free population to the neighbourhood of the estates. Such an open attack on the policy of the colonial government and Robinson's able defence of it, which was also published,[55] focused public attention on an issue previously agitated by a few, such as Guppy and Rostant, and thus summarized by Lionel Fraser, a magistrate and historian of Trinidad:

> . . . it is not the interest of the large sugar planters to encourage the growth of a free peasant class; it is the interest of the Colony to do so.[56]

The attitude of the West India Committee was attacked in the colony, particularly in the press. In January 1891 'a political meeting' in San Fernando passed resolutions supporting Robinson's policies and favouring railway extension. Speaking at this meeting Guppy claimed that the last twelve months had 'narrowed the issue'.[57] For Guppy the issue was the success or

[54] West India Committee to Knutsford, 19 May 1890. 9528. CO 295/331.

[55] Robinson to Knutsford, No. 217, 21 July 1890. 15978. CO 295/329.

[56] Letter printed in *The Port of Spain Gazette*, 6 Feb. 1891.

[57] Reported in *The Port of Spain Gazette*, 13 Jan. 1891. The resolutions were forwarded with Robinson to Knutsford, No. 38, 3 Feb. 1891. 4155. CO 295/332. The issue was narrowed for the planters also, for these years witnessed a drawing together of cocoa and sugar interests. In October 1892 the absentee Trinidad

failure of the endeavours, extending over fifty years, of 'a small party of narrow-minded landowners' to confine all available labour to the neighbourhood of the estates. In this sense the question was similar to that raised by reformers in British Guiana during the 1880s, and in its effect on public opinion the opposition of the West India Committee may be likened to that of the Court of Policy towards Irving's policies. But the parallel cannot be pressed too far for these questions were not debated with the same urgency in Trinidad. The reason is not far to seek. Between 1885 and 1890, 50,765 acres of crown land were sold in Trinidad of which 12,429 acres were purchased by Indians. Between 1880 and 1890 the reports of the crown surveyor in British Guiana recorded four grants by purchase of crown land totalling 178 acres.

The hostility to Indian immigration and the absentee sugar interest was one aspect of the Trinidadian character of the 1892 reform movement. Another aspect was noted by John Bell-Smyth, who claimed that few white people supported it. By contrast, the movement marked the emergence of Negroes to political prominence in this period, notable among whom was Prudhomme David, a barrister and secretary of the 'Reform Committee',[58] and J. S. de Bourg, the spokesman for the radical minority of the Committee.[59] Another Negro, E.

planters agreed that the 'Cocoa industry was very important, and its interests with regard to labour were identical with those of Sugar. There should be a cordial union between the two industries'. West India Committee Circular, No. 84, 7 Nov. 1892.

[58] For the 'Reform Committee' see p. 209. David was one of the few Negroes prominent in the reform movement. Called in 1888, he subsequently achieved eminence at the Trinidad Bar, acting on one occasion as solicitor-general. He was appointed an unofficial member of the Legislative Council in 1904. He strongly opposed state-aided immigration and was a vigorous supporter of representative government. Another Trinidad Negro to achieve political prominence at this time, though outside Trinidad, was Henry Sylvester Williams. Like David and so many other radical Trinidadians, he was a member of Grays Inn and was called to the Bar in 1902. He founded the African Association in London in 1897, which in 1900 became the Pan-African Association with Williams as general secretary. From 1901 he edited the *Pan-African* which was printed in London. Williams regarded education and political reform as powerful factors in the improvement of the Negro race, to which cause, with that of Pan-Africanism, he devoted his life.

[59] For the radical minority of the Reform Committee see pp. 209–11. de Bourg subsequently played a prominent part in radical Trinidad politics. There is some doubt as to his occupation; in 1906 he was described as a commission agent. He claimed to be a founder member of the Trinidad Workingmen's Association, established in 1897, and in 1906 he was on its management committee. His

Marresse-Smith, a young solicitor, was to play a leading role in the Port of Spain water riots; although not prominent in the reform movement, he was one of the most active supporters of Gorrie. Other signs of the Trinidadian character of the movement were the support among reformers for the exclusion of aliens from the franchise, and the use of the slogan 'Trinidad for the Trinidadians'. The most important alien group were the Venezuelans, who in 1891 numbered 2,955 or 1.48 per cent of the total population. They comprised two main groups, a propertied and educated element in Port of Spain, and the small cultivators, mainly cocoa contractors living in the rural districts, particularly Arima and Montserrat. The former were not prominent in the reform movement, but a strong contingent of the latter attended the reform meeting of 22 October 1892 to support Rostant and the radical wing of the reform movement.[60] The motive of reformers with such differing views as Guppy and de Verteuil for excluding aliens is difficult to determine. The latter may have wished to exclude a radical element from the electorate and both may have been influenced by the growing colonial consciousness reflected in the slogan 'Trinidad for the Trinidadians'.

Agitation against the appointment of officials from England was common to the reform movements of Trinidad, Jamaica, and British Guiana, and it was particularly marked after the late 1880s in the first two colonies. In Trinidad, as in Jamaica, it stemmed both from the lack of opportunity for the better educated, particularly in the legal and medical professions, and from a more general resentment against English officials on account of their non-Trinidadian origin, and their alleged incompetence and social arrogance. The legal profession in Trinidad, like that of Jamaica, was particularly overcrowded; in a petition presented to the governor in May 1894 asking for measures to restrict the number of solicitors, the signatories claimed that there were twenty-seven practising barristers,

involvement in the Association reflected both his interest in constitutional reform, which was one of the aims of the Association, and his militant attitude to labour questions. It was the latter which led to his being refused permission to return to Trinidad in 1920 after having attended the British Guiana Labour Union Conference as the official delegate of the Workingmen's Association. I am indebted to Dr. Brinsley Samaroo for help both with this and the previous footnote.

[60] See pp. 209–11.

thirty-eight practising solicitors, and eighteen articled clerks.[61] Among the barristers and solicitors supporting reform were several who were unsuccessful applicants for official posts in the colony or elsewhere in the Empire.[62] The most moderate interpretation of 'Trinidad for the Trinidadians' was that preference should be given to local candidates over English candidates where they were of equal merit, Trinidadians being held to be all who had made their home in Trinidad and had no thought of permanently leaving it. Alcazar appeared to be adopting a more extreme view when he asserted that 'the principal posts in the Civil Service should be held by natives of the soil'.[63] It is not easy to judge the strength of the grounds for this grievance but its existence is as important as its validity. Certainly Ripon had made a notable concession to Trinidad opinion when in 1892 he had appointed two local lawyers, George Garcia and the coloured Vincent Brown, to the attorney-generalship and the solicitor-generalship. But, in general, both he and his predecessors, advised by their officials, favoured outside appointments to the headships of Trinidad departments, as providing for promotion within the service and as injecting new blood into the colonial administration, which otherwise in their view suffered from the close social ties characteristic of a small colonial community. In this respect, and in the number of stipendiary magistracies and wardenships still held by outsiders, there were grounds for the attacks on outside appointments; maladministration on the part of some 'imported officials' lent weight to the grievance.

There is much evidence of administrative failure and dishonesty in the Trinidad public service during this period. H. Hamel-Smith, a prominent Trinidad merchant, claimed in 1895 that all hinged 'on bad Government—legislative and administrative . . . until the present mode of Crown Colony Government is done away with in Trinidad and a large proportion of the . . . inhabitants are enfranchised . . . and allowed to

[61] Encl. 3, Broome to Secretary of State for the Colonies, No. 205, 30 May 1894. 10339. CO 295/353. See also attorney-general's report. Ibid., Encl. 2.

[62] For instance, J. A. Lamy and L. Wharton had unsuccessfully applied for the registrar-generalship, J. Joseph for the stipendiary magistracy of San Fernando, and E. S. Pollard for a legal appointment elsewhere in the colonies.

[63] Report of reform meeting, 22 Oct. 1892. *The Port of Spain Gazette*, 25 Oct. 1892.

take a practical interest in their Government and taxation, things will never go right'.[64] The most notable failures were in the Public Works Department, to which pressure of work resulting from over-centralization and shortage of technically trained staff contributed. The San Fernando water works, completed in 1881 at a cost of over £16,000, supplied in Robinson's view only one-third of the water estimated and required. There had been a delay of over ten years in constructing a much-needed lunatic asylum. A commission appointed to enquire into the administration of the roads reported in 1894 that taken as a whole supervision had not been effective, nor had there been fair or efficient expenditure in labour or materials.[65] In the same year a further commission appointed to enquire into the railways, which were also under the director of public works, referred to the 'enormous extent of the corruption pervading every branch of the traffic department', and concluded that it had been administered 'in a most unsatisfactory, inefficient, and corrupt manner'.[66] Captain S. Buckle, Tanner's successor as director of public works, wrote privately to the Colonial Office that it was probably true that there had been 'enormous waste of money and fraud' in the sub-department responsible for roads, and 'the gravest informalities & irregularities' in that responsible for works and buildings.[67] An enquiry in 1892 into the registrar-general's department revealed deficiencies of nearly £2,000. In an outspoken despatch, subsequently withdrawn and redrafted at the request of Ripon, Broome referred to the 'official Augean stable'[68] which he had found on his appointment in August 1891. In so far as this state of affairs reflected on the honesty and efficiency of local-born officials, it weakened one of the reformers' main planks of 'Trinidad for the Trinidadians', and perhaps for this reason the corruptness and inefficiency of the local administration figured less prominently in their speeches than attacks on outside appointments, and hostility to the sugar interest. Hamel-Smith summarized the latter view when

[64] Hamel-Smith to Barrow, 23 Feb. 1895 (copy). Encl. with R. T. Barrow to S. Buxton, 24 Apr. 1895. 7146. CO 295/368.

[65] Council paper No. 123. 1894. CO 298/53.

[66] Council paper No. 122. 1894. CO 298/53.

[67] Buckle to Baillie Hamilton (personal), 8 Mar. 1894. 4992. CO 295/351.

[68] Broome to Ripon, Conf., 24 May 1894. 10341. CO 295/353.

he argued that the government was 'too much influenced by the Sugar Interest and do not do their duty to the bulk of the population . . .'.[69] Sugar, he wrote, held first place in the eyes of the Legislative Council 'but I am sure would not do so if the members were chosen by ballot . . .'.[70]

Broome summarized the reform agitation as

> . . . a movement against the planting interest and coolie immigration—a middle class upheaval, promoted by some lawyers and business men who desire a form of government more open to *themselves* . . .[71]

But the hostility of reformers to the sugar interest should not be over-stated, for among their leaders were several closely connected with it. Sugar still dominated the Trinidad economy and many other reformers must have been dependent directly or indirectly on its prosperity, as they were to a much greater extent in British Guiana.

The reform movement of 1892, like that of 1887, was weakened by differences of opinion. A radical minority, led by Rostant, was prominent at the reform meeting held on 22 October 1892. Its views emerged more clearly in the 'Reform Committee', which as a result of this meeting was appointed to draw up a petition. The radical minority divided from the majority of the committee on three main issues.[72] It opposed the exclusion of aliens from the franchise, a proposal which was only carried by the casting vote of the chairman, de Verteuil; J. S. de Bourg,[73] the minority's most prominent spokesman, described the resolution as 'a very gross injustice'. On the other hand, the committee by eleven votes to seven deleted the reading and writing test in English which the franchise commission of 1888 had recommended for those under forty. Secondly, the radical minority advocated a lower franchise than the majority, who favoured a moderate reduction in the

[69] Hamel-Smith to Barrow, 23 Feb. 1895 (copy). Encl. with Barrow to Buxton 24 Apr. 1895. 7146. CO 295/368.

[70] Hamel-Smith to Buxton, 16 Apr. 1895. 7146. CO 295/368.

[71] Observation on Petition for amendment of the Trinidad Constitution. Filed with minute paper 13969. CO 295/350.

[72] A copy of the minutes of the 'Reform Committee' and the press accounts of its meetings were enclosed with Fowler (O.A.G.) to Ripon, No. 190, 12 June 1893. 10826. CO 295/345.

[73] See footnote 59, p. 205.

proposals of the franchise commission to take account of the fall in rental values since 1888.[74] Finally, de Bourg opposed the high qualifications for the elected members of the Legislative Council, which the majority fixed at ownership of real estate of £1,500 or a clear annual income of £400. The majority proposals of the committee in fact followed the middle course advocated by Alcazar, for more conservative suggestions had been canvassed; for instance, *The Port of Spain Gazette* favoured the 1891 British Guiana franchise and de Verteuil the unamended proposals of the franchise commission of 1888. de Bourg spoke for the small peasant proprietors, particularly the Negro and Venezuelan cocoa planters. He argued, in particular, that the high qualifications for membership of the Legislative Council would entrench in power the class represented by the nominated members, who had 'proved themselves to be the real enemies of the negro race',[75] and against whom the reform movement should in his view be directed. Similarly Rostant claimed that he had entrusted the reform movement to younger hands on the understanding that there should be a low franchise and no property qualification for members, conditions which the majority of the 'Reform Committee' had abandoned in order to secure the support of 'the plutocrats'.[76]

The radical wing drew its main support from San Fernando where there was an important Barbadian and Venezuelan element,[77] but the writer has seen no evidence that this support was linked with the large numbers of free Indians in the district. Gatty described the town in 1888 as a 'stronghold of reform'. Several factors contributed to this. There was a strong feeling in San Fernando that its interests were neglected in favour of Port of Spain due to the capital's overwhelming representation in the Legislative Council. There was rivalry between them as ports and markets for the interior, reflected in competing plans for railway development. The partial failure of the San Fer-

[74] Estimated by W. S. Clark, the mayor of San Fernando, at 30 per cent. In general, the franchise reductions favoured by the majority seemed to benefit the urban voter, those favoured by the minority the rural voter.

[75] Letter read at meeting of 'Reform Committee' on 17 Dec. 1892. *The Port of Spain Gazette*, 19 Dec. 1892.

[76] Rostant to Ripon, 31 Mar. 1894. Encl. with Broome to Ripon, No. 95, 3 Apr. 1894. 6687. CO 295/352.

[77] Goodwille, in his evidence before the franchise commission, had pointed out that Venezuelans were used to manhood suffrage.

nando water-works was a further cause of dissatisfaction. Gorrie was reported to have been 'not only respected but revered' in the town; his memory seems to have inspired the radical minority, for its leaders, Rostant, de Bourg, and E. A. Nunes, were among his warmest admirers.[78] They dominated a public meeting held in San Fernando on 28 January 1893,[79] at which the majority franchise proposals of the 'Reform Committee' were rejected in favour of a lower franchise put forward by Rostant and later submitted, slightly amended, to Ripon in a minority report.[80] The final proposals were lower at every point than those of the majority and included, for instance, the enfranchising of the owner and occupier of five acres of land compared with the majority proposals of eight acres and a house of value of £20. Following the resolutions adopted at the San Fernando meeting, the minority report also proposed giving aliens the vote and making all qualified voters eligible for election to the Legislative Council. The aim of the minority was to enfranchise the more substantial peasant proprietors regardless of race.[81] If the colonial office attitude to Jamaica constitutional reform between 1883 and 1885 is a guide, their proposals would have been sympathetically entertained during the early 1880s, and it is therefore significant of the trend of colonial office opinion that on the evidence of the minutes the minority report of the 'Reform Committee' received no consideration from officials.

The detailed proposals of the majority of the 'Reform Committee' were forwarded to Ripon by Henry Fowler, the officer administering the government, with a memorial praying for 'a liberal system of elective franchise'.[82] The memorialists, who numbered 3,716,[83] claimed that 'a strong feeling of dissatisfac-

[78] For instance, Nunes was secretary of The Trinidad Loyal and Defence Association, formed to support Gorrie. A Catholic influence may also have informed the radical minority, but the evidence is hard to find.

[79] Reported in *The Port of Spain Gazette*, 31 Jan. 1893.

[80] Encl. with Broome to Ripon, No. 364, 1 Nov. 1893. 19430. CO 295/348.

[81] The writer has seen no evidence of hostility towards free Indians on the part of the leaders of the radical minority; such hostility would have been surprising in warm admirers of Gorrie. On the other hand, David stated that the majority proposals would practically exclude the Asian population.

[82] Fowler (O.A.G.) to Ripon, No. 190, 12 June 1893. 10826. CO 295/345.

[83] The government statist rejected 978 of their signatures as valueless or of doubtful genuineness. See footnote 107, p. 219.

tion' existed among the inhabitants at their virtual exclusion from the management of their local affairs, and they urged that the elective franchise which had been conceded to Jamaica, Mauritius, and British Guiana, and 'other sister colonies' should not be withheld from Trinidad, an argument which Alcazar later described as 'the broad basis of the movement'. The resolutions of the majority of the Reform Committee favoured a legislative council of the governor, four *ex-officio* and three nominated officials, and twelve members elected every three years, the votes of eight of whom were to prevail 'on any matter of finance or of purely local concern'. The last provision, which Alcazar intimated was based on the precedent of Jamaica and was not intended to deprive the governor of an overriding power in emergency, was not supported by Howatson, who also wanted a smaller elected majority. Leading reformers also differed on other questions. For instance, Alcazar intimated personally to Ripon that he favoured a lower franchise, and de Verteuil preferred a legislative council on the lines of the Mauritius Council of Government with the governor, five officials, five nominated unofficials, and ten elected members. Prudhomme David estimated that their proposals would enfranchise between 12,000 and 15,000, the Asian population being 'practically outside the scope of the reform that is contemplated'.[84] Alcazar, however, foresaw an electorate of about 11,000, of whom he estimated 5,000 would be natives of Trinidad, 3,500 natives of the West Indies, 1,200 natives of India, 200 Indians born in Trinidad, 400 born in the United Kingdom, and 1,120 of alien origin though presumably naturalized.[85] In written evidence before the West India Royal Commission in 1897, Alcazar stated that 'it had not been proposed to place power in the hands of the working classes, but only in those of the wealthier middle class'.[86]

Harris, Lambert, and Wingfield unanimously advised Ripon

[84] David to Ripon, 3 June 1893. Encl. No. 3, Fowler to Ripon, No. 190, 12 June 1893. 10826. CO 295/345.

[85] Speech to Legislative Council, 12 Feb. 1895. Reported in *The Port of Spain Gazette*, 14 Feb. 1895.

[86] Memorandum by H. A. Alcazar on Indian Immigration, 28 Feb. 1897. Reprinted in C. 8657, p. 320. P.P. 1898 (L). In his oral evidence before the commission, Alcazar said that he would not give the franchise to the working classes at first on account of their lack of education, but he thought that 'shortly' they would be entitled to a vote.

against constitutional change in Trinidad. Harris referred approvingly to Gatty's 'able report'. He argued that the 'natural idea' that representative institutions were suitable for all communities was 'considerably modified by experience of small Colonies'; the constitutional changes in Jamaica and Mauritius were, he believed, 'admitted . . . to have been mistaken . . .'. Moreover, the leaders of the movement were 'coloured men or aliens . . . who are not to be trusted to use power wisely'. He doubted the strength of opinion behind the movement, and attributed the successful career of Trinidad as being 'largely due to the stability of Crown Government'.[87] Wingfield agreed with Harris:

> The experience of Jamaica does not encourage the extension of the system of partially elective legislatures in the W. Indies. . . .[88]

But he also recognized that if there was 'a very strong and general desire' for reform 'it may be difficult to refuse'. Like Harris, he did not regard the petition as evidence for this, being influenced by the alleged abuses in connection with the securing of signatures for the 1887 petition, and by the prominence of Venezuelans in the movement. Lambert argued that neither Indian nor Creole had shown 'the slightest capacity for self government', yet to exclude them would lead to a narrowly based representation in which jobbery would flourish as in Jamaica, where, he claimed, it was generally said that most of the elected members were corrupt; such a change would 'shake the credit of the island . . .'.[89] These views reflected a dis-

[87] Fowler to Ripon, No. 190, 12 June 1893. 10826. CO 295/345. Minute by C.A.H., 5 July 1893.

[88] Ibid. Minute by E.W., 5 July 1893.

[89] Minute paper 13969, CO 295/350. Minute by H.L., 17 Aug. 1893. Blake's view of the political situation in Jamaica and its possible financial repercussions almost certainly influenced this minute. More generally, the minutes of Harris and Lambert should be seen against the background of a wider questioning of the appropriateness of representative institutions for non-British or non-white peoples. Writing in 1888 Froude condemned in the West Indies and Ireland 'the persistence in applying to conquered countries and colonies a form of self-government which can only succeed among men of our own race . . .'. Unpublished extract from his journal, quoted by Waldo Hilary Dunn, *James Anthony Froude. A Biography. 1857–1894* (Oxford, 1963), p. 549. Speaking with Ireland in mind in May 1886, Lord Salisbury argued that 'self-government' 'works admirably when it is confided to people who are of Teutonic race . . . it does not work so well when people of other races are called upon to join in it.' Lady Gwendolen Cecil, *Life of Robert, Marquis of Salisbury*, Vol. III (London, 1931), p. 302. In 1888 Sir John Gorst wrote of

enchantment among officials with representative institutions in the West Indies, particularly noticeable after 1888; it can be seen in their ready acceptance of Gatty's minority report in 1889 and the very moderate constitutional changes finally effected in British Guiana in 1891. Their attitude was influenced by their belief in the failure of Derby's and Stanley's constitutional experiments in Jamaica and Mauritius, a belief much strengthened in the case of Jamaica by Blake's pessimistic despatches. Harris's suspicion of the coloured and alien population, and Lambert's hostile reference to the creoles and Asians, the former of whom he designated 'niggers', hint at a racialism and nationalism which was to be more clearly expressed in Chamberlain's minute of 3 November 1895,[90] but which it is hard to detect in colonial office minutes of the early 1880s. In this connection it is interesting that Harris should have contrasted the failure of representative institutions in Jamaica and Mauritius with 'the great Eastern colonies which are proud examples of the opposite system of government',[91] a clear echo of Froude and other conservatives who were impressed by what they regarded as the favourable results of firm British rule in India.[92]

Broome rarely gave a forthright recommendation on a major issue, but it seems that his sympathies inclined towards constitutional reform for he was to inform Ripon in June 1894 that the chief object of his governorship had been not only to develop the economy of Trinidad

but also to raise the community in the political scale, and, if possible,

India: 'Nothing could be more mischievous than the crude application of British democratic maxims to India . . .'. S. Gopal, *British Policy in India, 1858–1905* (Cambridge, 1965), p. 181. Similarly Lord Dufferin, the retiring Viceroy of India, stressed the unsuitability of 'democratic methods of government' and 'the Parliamentary system' to India. Speech at Calcutta, 30 Nov. 1888, reported in *The Times*, 3 Dec. 1888. The speech was reported, and commented on favourably, in *The Port of Spain Gazette*.

[90] See pp. 231–2.

[91] Fowler to Ripon, No. 190, 12 June 1893. 10826. CO 295/345. Minute by C.A.H., 5 July 1893.

[92] The classic statement of late nineteenth-century conservatism was James Fitzjames Stephen's *Liberty, Equality, Fraternity*, published in 1873. He described his book as 'little more than the turning of an Indian lantern on European problems'. He regarded India as 'the best corrective in existence to the fundamental fallacies of Liberalism'. There, he wrote, 'you see real government . . .'. Quoted by R. J. White in his Introduction to the 1967 edition of *Liberty, Equality, Fraternity* (Cambridge, 1967), pp. 1 and 11.

to be instrumental in giving it, during my term of office, some of the elements of Representative institutions. . . .[93]

In March 1893 he had introduced into the Trinidad Legislative Council an ordinance providing for the establishment of elective local road boards with power to construct, repair, and manage local roads, and to levy rates. One of his motives for initiating this legislation was to demonstrate whether Trinidad had or had not 'stuff in it for any system of representative government'.[94] Yet although sympathetic to reform, Broome also regarded the existing Legislative Council as a very good legislature. Perhaps these conflicting considerations accounted for his recommendation,[95] forwarded to Ripon while he was on leave in England, that the issue of constitutional reform should be referred to the Legislative Council. Such a course, he believed, would have the advantage of allowing the opponents of reform to state their case, and in order that both sides of the question should be heard he advised that two or three of the reform leaders should be appointed to the Council in place of those members who were to resign in June 1894 after five years' service.[96] He argued that from a full discussion a 'more reasonable and safer' compromise might emerge, and time would be allowed for the success or failure of elective local road boards to be established.

Buxton and Ripon did not find 'the very important question' of Trinidad reform an easy one, Buxton finally advising acceptance of Broome's proposals as 'a possible solution of the difficulty . . .'.[97] In a despatch of 29 August 1893 Ripon instructed Broome to use the opportunity afforded by five unofficial members resigning their seats in June 1894 'to afford to the promoters of the present movement a share of representation . . .', and then to refer the whole question to the Legislative Council which was 'the proper arena for the discussion of such questions . . .'.[98] This decision was an unusual one, for

[93] Broome to Ripon, No. 236, 13 June 1894. 11235. CO 295/354.

[94] Observation on Petition for amendment of the Trinidad constitution. Filed with minute paper 13969. CO 295/350. See also Broome's speech in Legislative Council, 20 Mar. 1894. The measure was passed in March 1894 (Ord. 10) and amended by Ord. 23 of 1894.

[95] Filed with minute paper 13969. CO 295/350. [96] See footnote 110, p. 187.

[97] Minute paper 13969. CO 295/350. Minute by S.B., 22 Aug. 1893.

[98] Ripon to Broome, No. 235, 29 Aug. 1893. 13969. CO 295/350. This was a paraphrase of the wording of Broome's recommendation.

although there had been a debate in the Mauritius Council of Government in December 1883 on the question of whether an elective element should be introduced into the Council, it had taken place on the unauthorized initiative of the governor, Sir John Pope Hennessy; Derby had merely instructed him to consult the Council of Government on a very limited change in the method of nominating the unofficial members. It is hard to see what additional information Ripon hoped to gain, for he had received 'a full verbal explanation' of the memorialists' views, and the case against reform had been cogently summarized in Gatty's minority report. He may have wished to gauge the views of the planting and merchant interests not represented in the reform movement, although the West India Committee spoke for many of them; a debate in the Legislative Council would also afford an opportunity for officials to state their views. To Nevile Lubbock, the chairman of the West India Committee, he was reported to have said that it would 'probably be far safer to have the promoters of the movement for "reform" airing their views in Council rather than agitating outside'.[99] He may have simply wished to postpone a difficult decision. It is revealing that not only did Ripon, by keeping the question of reform open, reject the advice of his officials, but that in one important respect he amended the draft despatch in a liberal direction. He deleted a reference to the success or otherwise of local road boards as having an important bearing on the question, noting that such a view would look like 'indefinite postponement'. The West India Committee criticized Ripon's despatch as likely to increase a gradually 'intensifying . . . class-feeling' in the colony, which was 'already deplorably acute',[100] but their view carried little weight in the Colonial Office.

Broome had appointed Guppy to the Legislative Council in

[99] Chairman, West India Committee to Ripon, 14 Nov. 1893. 19310. CO 295/349. Minute by C.A.H., 20 Nov. 1893.

[100] Chairman, West India Committeee to Ripon, 14 Nov. 1893. 19310. CO 295/349. On the evidence of the colonial office papers and the West India Committee papers, this seems to have been the first intervention by the Committee on the issue of Trinidad reform in the period under review. In May 1889 the Committee stated that it had taken no part for or against a change of constitution in Trinidad: the Committee was referring to the period between 1887 and 1889 when the question of reform was being actively debated in the colony and London. West India Committee Circular, No. 39, 13 May 1889.

April 1893, and acting on Ripon's despatch of 29 August 1893, he nominated Howatson in January 1894 and Alcazar in June 1894. With the re-appointment of de Verteuil there were thus four prominent reformers among the unofficials, who were supported from the official side by Vincent Brown, the solicitor-general and in Bell-Smyth's view the leader of the movement. On 3 December 1894 de Verteuil introduced a motion favouring an amendment of the constitution by 'providing that a fair proportion of the Members of the Legislative Council shall be elected by the people . . .'.[101] The reformers had been weakened by the death of Guppy in November 1894, and were further depleted by the absence of his successor, W. S. Robertson, and Garcia, the local-born attorney-general, both sympathetic to reform. Their places were taken by Conrad Stollmeyer, a diffident supporter of reform, and E. Agostini who spoke against de Verteuil's motion; the temporary absence of Brown also enabled Aucher Warner, the acting solicitor-general, to speak against reform although he had supported it in 1887. The main burden of arguing the reformers' case was to fall on Brown and Alcazar.

The debate on constitutional reform, which occupied six sittings of the Legislative Council, was longer and more heated but less skilful than that in the Mauritius Council of Government in 1883.[102] The case against reform was strongly argued by the representatives of the sugar interest though most of them were opposed to the timing rather than the principle. They argued that its concession in other colonies, such as Mauritius, was not a precedent for Trinidad since conditions differed widely.[103] They pointed to the achievements of crown government reflected in the prosperity of the colony, and recent or pending reforms in the judiciary, education, and the administration of local roads. The speakers against reform also contrasted the existing Legislative Council, the unofficial members of which were able and representative, with the dangers

[101] Minutes of the Legislative Council, 1894. CO 298/53.

[102] A report of the debate in various issues of *The Port of Spain Gazette* was enclosed with Broome to Ripon, No. 56, 16 Feb. 1895. 4101. CO 295/362.

[103] This point was strongly made by Fenwick who had lived in Mauritius for some years. On the other hand, Broome regarded Mauritius, where he had served as Lieutenant-Governor, as 'similar in many respects to Trinidad'. de Verteuil considered the circumstances of Mauritius especially similar to Trinidad.

of a franchise which it would be difficult to limit and which would probably include aliens and Indians. They emphasized the heterogeneity of the population, the low level of education, and the lack of popular demand and agitation for reform, as reasons for the unsuitability of representative institutions for Trinidad; as evidence of this they pointed to the failure of, and lack of interest in, the elective municipal councils[104] and local road boards,[105] and to the divisions in the 'Reform Committee' itself. They accused the reformers of appealing from a Conservative to a Liberal government, and they asked what had occurred since 1889 to weaken Knutsford's case against reform. The stability of crown colony government was necessary both for the raising of money on the London money market and for the inflow of private capital into Trinidad.

Each of these arguments except the last was countered by the spokesmen for reform, who based their case on what they claimed were the widely acknowledged benefits of representative institutions, and on the precedent of other colonies in which they had been conceded, notably Jamaica and Mauritius. They stressed the failure of crown government, citing the lack of roads and public works, particularly hospitals, asylums, schools, prisons, and water supplies. Prosperity was not widely based nor was it commensurate with Trinidad's resources. They alleged that the unofficial members were selected from a narrow class of large property owners, and that they acted in their own interests,[106] being responsible neither to governor nor people. They contended that Canada, Mauritius, and

[104] See footnote 50, p. 167. In 1893 Fowler stated that at the last elections 110 had voted out of 724 registered voters in Port of Spain, 67 out of 113 in San Fernando, and 96 out of 138 in Arima. The latter borough council had not worked well, and in August 1894 Broome transmitted a petition for the revocation of its charter. On the other hand, during the debate both the receiver-general and the assistant director of public works defended the record of the San Fernando borough council.

[105] Three wards had applied for elective road boards under Ord. 10 of 1894, Chaguanas, Arima, and Tacarigua. In the last two wards 72 had voted out of a registered electorate of 1,648 and 102 out of 1,649. In May 1895 Broome reported that five road boards had been established and were working well; a sixth was in course of election. Governor's despatch reporting on Blue Book for 1894, 30 May 1895. Printed as C. 7847b.

[106] Compare Wingfield's view on p. 185. Lambert noted that Broome had told him that although the nominated members comprised the best men in Trinidad 'they all merely looked after their own interests . . .'.

British Guiana showed that representative institutions were compatible with a heterogeneous population. If there was a lack of popular support for reform, this was due to a paternal government which afforded no opportunity for political education; the lack of responsibility between government and governed made agitation useless since it was ignored. The relative failure of existing representative institutions derived from their paltry functions. The supporters of reform admitted the divisions within the 'Reform Committee', but argued that these were not on the principle of reform but on the extent of the franchise. In their view, the earlier reform movement had not been fairly treated, for they argued that Knutsford had conceded the elective principle in 1887, only to withdraw it in 1889 on the evidence of Gatty's minority report which the reformers had had no opportunity of rebutting. de Verteuil's motion was defeated by twelve votes to six; Brown, Alcazar, Howatson, de Verteuil, Stollmeyer, and David Horsford, the receiver-general and a native of Trinidad, voting in favour. An amendment, proposed by Brown, favouring a change in the constitution on the lines of that granted to Mauritius, attracted the additional vote of the surgeon-general, who had served in Mauritius, and of the protector of immigrants, but lost that of Stollmeyer, who thought it too extreme.

It is not easy to assess the support for reform outside the Legislative Council. The three leading newspapers, *The Port of Spain Gazette*, *The Daily News*, and *Public Opinion*, favoured it, but they also stressed 'the dull, leaden apathy' and the 'conspicuous indifference' of Trinidad public opinion towards political affairs. His reading of contemporary British politics prompted the leader-writer of the *Daily News* to advocate a 'Reform Association' to arouse interest, effect greater unity among reformers, and to agitate for reform. After a close examination of the reform petition of 1893 the government statist,[107] who as superintendent of government printing had seen every petition of the previous twenty-two years, considered that it compared favourably in 'the respectability and intelligence' of its signatories with earlier petitions having an equal number of signatures, including 'the most noted of local peti-

[107] H. J. Clark, a Trinidadian sympathetic to reform.

tions', that against the marriage ordinance of 1863.[108] His analysis showed that of 2,738 signatures which he regarded as probably genuine, 1,751 were of people residing in Port of Spain. Of 226 official and professional signatories, 87 were barristers, solicitors, and law clerks.[109] Of 84 self-styled merchants, the government statist considered about half were *bona fide* merchants of whom the majority were 'property-holders'. Prominent among 916 signatories classified as industrial were 170 carpenters, joiners, and cabinet-makers, and 169 tailors; tailors in Trinidad seem to have played a radical role analogous to that of shoemakers in late eighteenth-century and early nineteenth-century England.[110] Of 772 estate-owners, planters, and agricultural labourers, 262 resided in Port of Spain, to which the petitioners seem to have been mainly confined. It was influentially but not enthusiastically supported by the relatively small professional and merchant class, but these statistics, and the absence of public meetings and agitation, suggest a lack of widespread interest particularly in the rural areas. Only 111 signed the petition in San Fernando, but this probably reflected the divisions within the 'Reform Committee'.

Broome did not regard the vote in the Legislative Council or the petition as an accurate reflection of public opinion, for he recommended to Ripon that the opinion of the politically intelligent should be ascertained by 'a kind of referendum' based on the Mauritius franchise, it being 'absurd to consult the mass of the Indian population, or the illiterate and ignorant of the lower class of Creoles . . .'.[111] Ripon rejected this advice as prejudging the question of the existence and size of a constituency capable of exercising the franchise, and he pressed the governor for a more decided opinion. This Broome finally gave, though in a despatch so carefully worded as to afford the Colonial Office little lead.[112] His caution was characteristic, but it also reflected the knowledge that in 1882 as lieutenant-governor of Mauritius he had opposed the introduction of elected members into the Council of Government, a reform

[108] Encls. 2 and 3, Broome to Ripon, No. 186, 15 May 1895. 9411. CO 295/363.
[109] The census of 1891 showed a total of 129. See pp. 206–7 of this study.
[110] See also p. 172.
[111] Broome to Ripon, No. 56, 16 Feb. 1895. 4101. CO 295/362.
[112] Broome to Ripon, No. 186, 15 May 1895. 9411. CO 295/363. The quotations in this and the following paragraph are taken from this despatch.

which Derby and Stanley had subsequently conceded. In Broome's view, the demand for constitutional reform in Mauritius in 1882 was 'undoubtedly a good deal stronger' than the 'present demand' in Trinidad; Broome had estimated in 1882 that 79 out of 300 resident sugar planters in Mauritius had signed a petition for reform. The analogy of Mauritius was uppermost in his mind for he referred Ripon to his despatch to Kimberley of 31 October 1882,[113] 'a good many' of his observations, particularly those concerning the Indian population in Mauritius, being in his view relevant to Trinidad. It is unfortunately not clear to which precise points in the Mauritius despatch he referred.[114] Broome doubted whether the demand for reform in Trinidad was 'quite of the required strength'. He also argued that the colony was prospering under its existing constitution, that relations between executive and legislature were good, and that the presence of reformers in the latter was in itself a notable advance. These considerations seem to have led him to the view that there was no 'present *necessity*' for an immediate change, and that it 'may be the wiser and safer course . . . to wait awhile . . .'. On the other hand, he stressed his personal sympathy for reform, the expediency of giving with grace 'what most thinking people here admit must come about before very long', and the advantages of proceeding 'a little with the political education of the community', which Broome favoured. He concluded:

. . . I should myself feel a greater pleasure and interest in Governing this Colony, or any other, by the help of a Legislative Council composed of, say, 7 Official, 7 nominated, and 7 elected members, than with an exclusively official and nominated Body.

He was strongly of the opinion that of the seven nominated members four should be officials, thus securing an official majority; '. . . there would', he wrote, 'be no difficulty in providing the material for an intelligent choice of 7 elected members . . .'.

[113] Reprinted in C. 4074. P.P. 1884 (LV).

[114] Possibly he had in mind his argument that the franchise proposed by the Mauritius reformers would, in the first instance, place political power in the hands of an oligarchy of planters and merchants; but that gradually Indians would qualify for the vote, though few observers believed that they were 'in any way qualified to exercise political power'. In short 'one evil would thus in time give place to another'.

Broome's despatch was first considered by Hartmann Just, a second-class clerk temporarily serving in the West India department, who interpreted it as leaning to leaving things as they were. Just opposed this course for he was adversely impressed by the unrepresentative character of the Legislative Council. He favoured the introduction of the elective principle so long as there was strong local feeling in favour, the various elements in the population were represented, and an official majority was secured. He suggested a legislative council of nine official, nine elected, and five nominated members, of whom three would be officials and one might represent the Indian population. His advice was influenced not only by his conviction of the Council's unrepresentative character but also by the fear that to make no concession would increase 'a widespread agitation'. He further argued:

By admitting 12,000 or 15,000 to the franchise, the Trinidad Government will be in a far better position to respond to the wishes of the inhabitants, *who are bound to work out their own destiny sooner or later.* [Author's italics][115]

This statement of the advantages of the elective principle has no parallel in the minutes of colonial office officials on constitutional reform in Jamaica, Trinidad, or British Guiana between 1880 and 1895. In general, officials had supported the elective principle in Jamaica and Trinidad not because they believed in the change on its own merits and as advantageous to the colony, but on the grounds of the inexpediency of refusing a concession which was influentially demanded. Of the secretaries of state, only Derby hinted at a view similar to Just's, and it is significant that the latter had acted as his assistant private secretary. Just's reference to the inevitability of what was, by implication, internal self-government is also striking. The conviction that constitutional reform in Trinidad was ultimately inevitable had been shared by other officials, but there is no evidence that they had in mind a change other than the introduction of elected members in a Legislative Council in which there would be an official majority. Exceptionally, Wedgwood, writing in 1890 of a proposal to extend the Trinidad Pitch Lake concession until 1909, minuted:

[115] Broome to Ripon, No. 186, 15 May 1895. 9411. CO 295/363. Minute by H.W.J., 8 June 1895.

In 1909 in all probability the Colony will have a constitution at least as liberal as the present Jamaican one, and probably much more so, and the inhabitants ought to be free at that date to make their own bargain . . . .[116]

Wingfield's advice, like Just's, was influenced by his conviction of the need for a more representative council, a view which he had held at least since 1889.[117] In April 1895 he minuted:

. . . Governors have not . . . been always sufficiently careful to provide for the representation of the views and interests of all classes . . .

unless the Governor is very careful in his selection a majority of nominated unofficials is apt to become a mischievous oligarchy.[118]

Wingfield was confirmed in this view by the Council's approval in December 1894 of relief to the sugar and cocoa industries of over £30,000, to be met by an increase of customs duties of over £43,000 on widely consumed foods such as flour. Only Alcazar had dissented. Such striking evidence of the planters' dominance in the Council inclined Wingfield towards the introduction of elected members. On the other hand, he was influenced against this course, as he had been in 1889 and 1893, by the conviction that the constitutional changes in Jamaica had failed. He minuted:

. . . the experience of Jamaica makes it possible that an elective Council may be chiefly filled with Port of Spain lawyers a class not likely to represent the general interests of the Community and should that be the case capitalists may be expected to fight shy of the Colony.[119]

This minute reflected Blake's influence. Meade shared Wingfield's apprehension of the election of 'Whitey brown lawyers as in Jamaica'.[120] For Wingfield these conflicting considerations

[116] Robinson to Knutsford, No. 428, 23 Dec. 1889. 1201. CO 295/325. Minute by E.H.W., 22 Jan. 1890. [117] See p. 185.

[118] Broome to Ripon, No. 56, 16 Feb. 1895. 4101. CO 295/362. Minute by E.W., 1 Apr. 1895. [119] Ibid.

[120] Broome to Ripon, No. 186, 15 May 1895. CO 295/363. Minute by R.M., 21 June 1895. He stated, however, that he was 'all for a popular representation . . .'. There is no substantial minute by Meade on the desirability of constitutional reform in the colonies under review (though see p. 82), but on this evidence his influence probably was a liberal one and may have guided Ripon's decision to keep open the question of Trinidad reform in 1893.

were resolved by other factors which seemed to him to favour the introduction of elected members. In the first place, the danger of the country districts 'being captured by Port of Spain lawyers or other carpet baggers'[121] might, in his opinion, be met by a residential qualification for election such as Blake had recently proposed in Jamaica.[122] A second consideration was that the introduction of elected members would afford an opportunity for ending the unofficial nominated majority, which Knutsford had restored in 1890 on the reluctant recommendation of Wingfield and against the advice of Herbert.[123] Wingfield's dislike of it seems to have been strengthened by the refusal of the unofficial members on several occasions during 1894 to vote items of expenditure put forward by Broome on the instructions of Ripon. Their control over expenditure was strengthened by the existence of the Finance Committee and by the informal extension of its powers which had taken place since 1886.[124] Wingfield regarded the Committee with hostility for reasons similar to those which underlay his attitude to the unofficial majority, and in October 1894 he had recommended its reform.[125] Although in his analysis of the case for introducing elected members into the Trinidad Legislative Council, Wingfield did not refer to the opportunity which it would afford of abolishing the Finance Committee, the point was made by Pearson; Lord Selborne, Chamberlain's parliamentary under-secretary, later minuted that Wingfield had opposed a change on its own merits but had favoured it as an opportunity for ending both the unofficial majority and the Finance Committee.[126] Two other considerations influenced Wingfield's advice in favour of reform. He believed the demand for it was 'substantial' especially in the towns, though it was not over-

[121] Broome to Ripon, No. 186, 15 May 1895. CO 295/363. Minute by E.W., 20 June 1895.

[122] See p. 87.

[123] See pp. 189–90.

[124] See pp. 166–7 for its establishment. The practice had crept in of submitting supplementary votes to the Committee as well as the annual estimates, and of officials abstaining from voting thus permitting a bare majority of unofficials present to carry a resolution. There had been an increasing tendency for governors to treat these resolutions as binding.

[125] Broome to Ripon, No. 419, 31 Aug. 1894. 16634. CO 295/356. Minute by E.W., 1 Oct. 1894.

[126] Broome to Ripon, No. 186, 15 May 1895. 9411. CO 295/363. Minute by S., 3 Aug. 1895.

whelming. He also regarded its concession as ultimately inevitable:

Sooner or later an elective element . . . must be conceded . . . I think it would be better to take the plunge now.[127]

In short, Wingfield favoured reform on account of the strength of the demand for it, the inevitability of conceding elected members, the unrepresentative character of the nominated unofficial members, and the opportunity which a constitutional change would afford for ending the unofficial nominated majority and the Finance Committee. These considerations outweighed in Wingfield's mind his deep-seated suspicion, based on his reading of Jamaica politics which was largely influenced by Blake, of the kind of men who might be elected under a reformed constitution and the damaging effects of their election on the colony, and particularly on its financial stability. Wingfield and Meade accepted Just's proposal regarding the composition of the Legislative Council, though the former noted that the nominated members proposed by Broome and Just were not very important except as a means of quietly securing a government majority. They did not advise the concession of a veto to the elected members on financial or other questions on the lines of that in Jamaica, and nor, on the evidence of the minutes, did they consider a provisional elected majority as in Jamaica, or a provisional elected and nominated unofficial majority as in Mauritius. Of the latter Wingfield minuted: 'In Mauritius we threw away our Govt. majority and we have found the inconvenience in the matter of the Military Contribution.'[128]

The unanimous advice of the West India department and Meade in favour of reform did not represent a new departure in colonial office policy. The strength of the demand for reform and the inevitability of ultimately conceding it had influenced Herbert to advise Knutsford to accept the elective principle in 1887. Gatty in 1889 had raised doubts as to the first consideration sufficiently strong to overbear the second, but the government statist's report on the petition of 1893 must have partly dispelled these doubts. Colonial office officials, excepting Just

127 Ibid. Minute by E.W., 20 June 1895.

128 Ibid.

and Wedgwood, continued to regard constitutional reform in Trinidad with a scepticism reinforced by their reading of Jamaica politics. They advised it not because they regarded it as beneficial in itself but because from the narrow ground of administrative expediency it appeared the least inconvenient course, especially when combined with the securing of an official majority and the ending of the Finance Committee. Although Meade sounded a cautionary note regarding the attitude of the West India Committee, there can be little doubt that Buxton and Ripon would have accepted this advice. It was Trinidad's misfortune that they left office in June 1895, leaving the final decision on reform to their Conservative successors.

Section 4

The British West Indies

1895–1903

8

CHAMBERLAIN AND CONSTITUTIONAL CHANGE

A policy of retrogression

JOSEPH CHAMBERLAIN took over the Colonial Office in June 1895. On 4 September Salisbury wrote to him: 'Our predecessors have left us a curious set of blunders to get right—Armenia, the Upper Nile, Trinidad, Siam.'[1] The comment reflected a shift in external policy, of which in the colonial sphere Chamberlain's refusal to concede the elective principle in Trinidad is a good example. The Trinidad papers were first seen by Lord Selborne, Chamberlain's parliamentary under-secretary, his minute of nine pages reflecting his careful reading of them. During the previous twenty years there is no minute of more than a few lines by a parliamentary under-secretary on constitutional reform in Jamaica, British Guiana, or Trinidad. Similarly Chamberlain's minute[2] covered one and a half closely written pages. The writer has seen no minute of comparable length or decisiveness by any secretary of state after 1870 on any matter connected with these three colonies. While allowance must be made for the different ways in which secretaries of state conveyed their decisions, it seems that Chamberlain's secretaryship was marked not only by policy changes in the field under review, but also by a shift in the initiative for decisions from officials to the secretary of state.[3] Selborne examined the proposed changes in Trinidad from two points of view, the one internal to Trinidad, the other external. Taking the first, he argued that if Trinidad had been a pure crown colony he would have advised against the elective

[1] Salisbury to Chamberlain, 4 Sept. 1895. *Chamberlain Papers*, JC 11/6.

[2] See pp. 231–2.

[3] This view is borne out by Olivier. See Margaret Olivier, ed., *Sydney Olivier. Letters and Selected Writings* (London, 1948), pp. 32–33.

principle on the grounds that either the franchise and the qualification for candidates must be high in which case an oligarchy would be established, or if the change was made on democratic lines 'we should hand over the government of the island to a population fitted for such a responsibility neither by education nor by political training nor by race'.[4] He was impressed, however, by Wingfield's argument that the concession of elected members would offer an opportunity for securing an official majority and abolishing the Finance Committee; on these grounds, and looking at the matter from the Trinidad point of view, he favoured the change, so long as those with knowledge of the West Indies could assure him that it would not be the starting point for further agitation. Looking at the matter from the point of view 'of the Empire at large', Selborne wrote that he had been told 'that the mutterings of a similar agitation have already been heard from Hong Kong and Ceylon', and he asked what would be the effect on these 'great crown colonies' of a change in Trinidad.

I need not dilate on the very grave objections to any divergence from the pure Crown Colony principle in the case of Hong Kong, a vast depot of trade a great naval station & a fortress, now more than ever to be regarded from the naval & military point of view since the emergence of Japan into the position of a great naval power, nor in the case of . . . Ceylon, which must be considered in exactly the same category as India.[5]

He asked for reassurance on this point, as well as on the improbability of further agitation in Trinidad; unless he received it in both cases he could not recommend the change.

It is probable that officials might have reassured Selborne on the second point, for both Broome and Just had considered that the concession of a legislative council of official, elected, and nominated members, with an official majority, would have satisfied the reformers. But even had they been able to reassure Selborne on the first point, it is unlikely that Chamberlain, on the evidence of his minute of 3 November,[6] would have agreed to a change. On 3 September Meade asked Wingfield if he was aware that 'Mr. Chamberlain has decided that he will not

[4] Broome to Ripon, No. 186, 15 May 1895. 9411. CO 295/363. Minute by S., 3 Aug. 1895.
[5] Ibid.
[6] See pp. 231–2.

move in the direction suggested? Will you tell the Dept. to prepare a draft shunting the matter.'[7] The task fell to Just, whose draft despatch gave three reasons for Chamberlain's refusal to concede constitutional reform, namely the apathy shown in the elections for local road boards and municipal councils, the fact that a moderate concession would not satisfy the 'Reform Party', and the divisions within the 'Reform Committee' itself. These were weak arguments. Selborne himself had minuted that the lack of interest in elections for municipal councils had not been established; moreover, voting figures did not take into account uncontested elections. Broome had written in May 1895 that the five elected road boards already established were working well. Both he and Just had argued that a moderate concession would satisfy the reformers. The 'Reform Committee' had been divided, but not on the principle of reform. The substantial reason for Chamberlain's refusal of elected members lay in the Imperial considerations raised by Selborne, and in Chamberlain's own conviction of the unsuitability of representative institutions for non-white and non-British communities. He expressed this conviction in a long minute[8] which was incorporated, with verbal amendments by Meade,[9] in the Trinidad despatch refusing constitutional reform,[10] as a statement of 'the general principle' by which Chamberlain would be guided in dealing with such matters. Chamberlain argued that demands for representative government from the crown colonies, the populations of many of which were largely composed of 'native or non British races', could not be discussed as if they came from 'a wholly white & British population . . .'. In the former case it was a misuse of terms to talk of representative government.

There is no pretence of giving full representation of the alien or black population & the full concession of the demands of the Reformers would only result in transferring the responsibility of administration from the Rep^e^ of H. Majesty to a small oligarchy of

[7] Ibid. Minute by R.M., 3 Sept. 1895.

[8] Broome to Ripon, No. 186, 15 May 1895. 9411. CO 295/363. Minute by J.C., 3 Nov. 1895.

[9] Meade softened the emphasis of such phrases of Chamberlain's as 'native and non British races', 'a wholly white and British population', and 'the alien or black population'.

[10] Chamberlain to Broome, No. 323, 14 Nov. 1895. 9411. CO 295/363.

white settlers constituting only a fractional percentage of the population. Such a system affords no sufficient guarantee for the interests of the majority which are now safeguarded by H.M. Govt. . . .[11]

Chamberlain did not exclude reform, but argued that each case must 'be considered as a matter of practical expediency & not as affecting the general principle of Representative institutions', in each case due regard being paid 'to the security of the Colony—the efficiency of the administration & the interests of all classes of the population'. The order in which Chamberlain placed these requirements is striking. He concluded his minute by characteristically commending the development of municipal institutions, since the experience and education which they afforded would 'pave the way for a further development of the local government . . .'.[12] Since Chamberlain expressed his views after so short an experience of administering colonial affairs, it is probable that they were already formed when he took office. They bear a striking resemblance to Froude's opinion of internal self-government in the West Indies. The latter wrote: 'The whites cannot be trusted to rule the blacks, but for the blacks to rule the whites is a yet grosser anomaly.'[13] Froude knew and admired Chamberlain and was dining with him as early as 1882.[14] Experience of office did not weaken Chamberlain's conviction that 'liberal Constitutions', like that of Jamaica, were 'not really suited to a black population . . .'.[15] In April 1896 he wrote to Charles Dilke:

Local Government (falsely so-called) is the curse of the West Indies. In many islands it means only the rule of a local oligarchy of whites and half-breeds—always incapable and frequently corrupt. In other cases it is the rule of the Negroes—totally unfit for representative institutions and the dupes of unscrupulous adventurers.[16]

[11] Broome to Ripon, No. 186, 15 May 1895. 9411. CO 295/363. Minute by J.C., 3 Nov. 1895.

[12] Ibid.

[13] Froude, op. cit., p. 262.

[14] Waldo Hilary Dunn, *James Anthony Froude. A Biography. 1857–1894* (Oxford, 1963), p. 492.

[15] Blake to Chamberlain, Conf., 29 Mar. 1897. 7956. CO 137/580. Minute by J.C., 15 June 1897.

[16] Chamberlain to Dilke, 15 Apr. 1896 (copy). *Chamberlain Papers* JC5/24/563. Gatty, in his case against constitutional change in Trinidad (see pp. 181–3), had referred to the Barbadians as 'adventurers' and the creole peasantry as 'dupes'.

It was the first of these alternatives which, in Chamberlain's view, was most common. In October 1896 he noted: 'It is the rule all over the W.I. islands that Rep^{e} Govt. means Govt. by & in the interest of a few planters.'[17] Speaking in the House of Commons on 2 August 1899, Chamberlain stated, '. . . we have already gone too far' in the extension of, what another member had called, constitutional rights in the West Indies:

> . . . these so-called liberal constitutions are really nothing more nor less than oligarchies . . . I am convinced that a Crown Government which pays attention to such public opinion as exists in the colony is the best form of government possible.[18]

Chamberlain made only one minor modification to the Trinidad constitution, by tightening Knutsford's instructions regarding the representation of districts in the Legislative Council; he instructed Broome to choose members who resided or owned property in the district they represented. Local opinion, both official and unofficial, had not regarded the representation of districts as significant, and Chamberlain's instruction did nothing to improve an arrangement which in practice was meaningless, and which he himself ended in November 1898. Broome reported that Chamberlain's decision against constitutional reform in Trinidad had been 'quietly received'; there did not appear 'to be much public interest in the subject at present'.[19] In the light of Chamberlain's conviction of the unsuitability of representative institutions in the West Indies, his decision to maintain the *status quo* in Trinidad was consistent. How far was he prepared to effect a constitutional retrogression in those colonies enjoying the liberal constitutions which he so strongly criticized?

The need for a decision on constitutional reform in Trinidad was not the only reason for Chamberlain's early involvement in West Indian affairs. On 6 July 1895 Malcolm Kearton[20] wrote to him pressing for official recognition of the claims of the West Indies for consideration. Kearton was primarily interested in the possibilities of gold reef mining in the north-west province of British Guiana. In the second of two interviews

17 Rev. H. Clarke to Chamberlain, 19 Oct. 1896. 21944. CO 137/578. Note by J.C., 21 Oct. 1896.

18 *Hansard,* Fourth Series (LXXV), 1190.

19 Broome to Chamberlain, No. 10, 14 Jan. 1896. 2786. CO 295/369.

20 The representative of a group of leading London capitalists.

with Chamberlain he asked for a concession of 40,000 square miles in return for an investment by his syndicate of £250,000.[21] On the same day that Chamberlain saw Kearton for the second time, he wrote to Lord Salisbury:

It appears that there is a very rich auriferous territory close to—& probably over the Schomburgk boundary. I am trying to get it developed & am in communication with firms in the City . . . it may turn out to be another Transvaal or West Australia.[22]

Only a full reading of Chamberlain's minutes and despatches can communicate the personal interest, the energy, and the impatience with which he handled British Guiana affairs during the autumn of 1895. It is clear from his minutes and despatches that his overriding concern was with the development of the colony and particularly 'the possibility of the early and rapid expansion of the gold industry'.[23] By the end of the year South African affairs had distracted his attention from British Guiana. The long-drawn-out negotiations which followed American intervention in the Venezuelan frontier dispute made the granting of concessions close to the frontier impossible; by 1897 it was apparent that the prospects for gold reef mining had been greatly exaggerated. Nevertheless Chamberlain retained his interest in British Guiana development and after the settlement of the frontier dispute in 1899 he took active steps to encourage private capitalists. It was a less feverish interest than he had shown in the autumn of 1895.

The view that a weakening of crown control, or that a majority of coloured persons among the elected members of the Legislative Council, might damage investors' confidence had been expressed in and outside the Colonial Office in connection with constitutional reform in Jamaica and Trinidad; the origin of this view seems to have lain with Blake. For Chamberlain, the attraction of private capital was an essential condition both for the development of British Guiana, particularly its gold, and more generally for the economic development of the crown colonies, to which he was publicly pledged. Thus he considered that 'the future of the West Indies mainly

[21] The correspondence and notes of interviews are filed with minute paper 541. CO 537/3.

[22] Chamberlain to Salisbury, 4 Sept. 1895. *Salisbury Papers*.

[23] Chamberlain to Lees, No. 218, 7 Sept. 1895. 15380. CO 111/479.

depends upon interesting in them men of large capital and commercial experience . . .'.[24] Chamberlain's personal efforts to involve Sir Thomas Lipton and Alfred Jones in the West Indies afford ample evidence that he acted on this view. His business experience enabled him to negotiate personally with capitalists and he was thus well placed to judge their requirements; had their investment decisions been influenced by the degree of crown control in the colonial legislatures or by the racial composition of the elected members this would certainly have been known to him. It is therefore significant that there is no evidence in the colonial office papers that Chamberlain took into account the need to retain or secure investors' confidence when considering questions of constitutional change in Jamaica, British Guiana,[25] or Trinidad. The absence of constitutional issues from his minutes on British Guiana development in the autumn of 1895 is particularly revealing, for Chamberlain's interest in gold was intense and he regarded its development in British Guiana as impossible without private capital. The colony enjoyed a modified form of representative government and had Kearton's syndicate been adversely influenced by this, Chamberlain would almost certainly have been aware of it and considered steps to remedy it. There is no evidence that he did so. In short, it is argued that Chamberlain's policy towards constitutional change in the colonies under consideration was not influenced by one of his cardinal points of policy, namely the need to secure the confidence of private capitalists, and that this reflected the attitudes of investors themselves, with whom Chamberlain was on closer terms than any of his predecessors or indeed his officials.

The direct evidence relating to the attitudes of capitalists towards the West Indies is scanty, but it suggests that given sufficient economic inducement they did not regard absolute crown control in the legislature as an essential condition for investment in West Indian colonies. It is true that J. H. H. Berkeley, the vice-president of the General Legislative Council of the Leeward Islands, informed Knutsford in 1891 that he was assured by capitalists that they would not invest in the Leewards 'if there is to be the slightest semblance of popular

[24] Colonial Office to Treasury, 17 Mar. 1899. 6006. CO 318/296.

[25] But see footnote 49, p. 241.

control';[26] in his view popular representation would 'depreciate largely the value of property'. On the other hand, during the autumn of 1895 at least five groups of London capitalists, besides Kearton's syndicate and including one of which Berkeley himself was a director, were in touch with the Colonial Office with a view to investing in British Guiana. In August 1898 Sir Thomas Lipton informed Selborne that he knew of no political conditions in Barbados, a colony still enjoying representative government, which would affect his decision as to whether or not to invest in a central sugar factory.[27] He may, however, have considered the narrow electorate and the political dominance of the white planters as sufficient safeguards; similar considerations may have favourably influenced potential investors in British Guiana, at least until the general election of 1897. In 1901 Henry Walker, who had lately toured the West Indies preparatory to entering the House of Commons, wrote that 'the investor is likely to look askance at the West Indies if he believes that the inferior race has any considerable measure of power'.[28] In 1891 Harris had commented more bluntly on Berkeley's fears: '. . . it does seem to be the fact that an elective Council of the stamp he fears will stink in the nostrils of Capitalists.'[29]

If Chamberlain had been seeking opportunities to raise the issue of constitutional reform in British Guiana on broader political grounds, the action of the Combined Court, and the advice which he received from his officials and from the colony, would have provided them. During the autumn of 1895 the Combined Court refused, at first, to vote the increases in the police force and its armament which Chamberlain considered essential for the security of the frontier. In March 1897 it struck out the militia vote and reduced that of the police. Chamberlain was much concerned with the security of the colonies. It is therefore revealing that although the Colonial Defence Committee strongly condemned the action of the Combined Court, he took no firmer course than to threaten to

[26] Memo. encl. with Berkeley to Knutsford, 12 Oct. 1891. 457. CO 537/5. Wingfield regarded Berkeley as a ' "regular" promoter and a man of straw'.

[27] Lipton to Selborne, 30 Aug. 1898. 21749. CO 318/299.

[28] H. de R. Walker, *The West Indies and the Empire* (London, 1901), p. 226.

[29] Berkeley to Knutsford, 12 Oct. 1891. 457. CO 537/5. Minute by C.A.H., 29 Oct. 1891.

withhold the Imperial forces which might in the future be necessary to maintain internal order. By contrast, H. K. Davson, a leading planter, argued that the Combined Court's action afforded 'good grounds'[30] for considering the introduction of crown colony government. He pressed this on broad grounds of Imperial co-operation and defence, and he noted with particular anxiety the number of 'native' barristers in the legislature. For Davson, the introduction of crown colony government was second in importance only to the abolition of the sugar bounties. Sir A. W. L. Hemming, the governor, considered that Davson's preference for crown government was shared by 'all the ablest & most thinking (?) men' in the colony. He himself regarded the constitution as 'a farce & unworkable',[31] and he suggested privately to Wingfield that an attempt should be made to induce the Combined Court to surrender its powers in return for the Imperial government taking over the civil list. Both Davson and Hemming were writing after the election of 1897 at which several representatives of the sugar interest had been defeated by coloured and Negro candidates. Nicholas Darnell Davis,[32] the comptroller of customs, writing to Pearson before the elections, pressed for the establishment of pure crown colony government on different grounds, namely as a condition for a policy of development; in his view the co-operation of the planters could be won by a threat to reduce the franchise.[33]

Chamberlain's officials also favoured a reform of the British Guiana constitution. In September 1897 the Combined Court refused to renew the civil list for more than one year, the elected members justifying their action by referring to the pending reports of the West India Royal Commission and a locally appointed civil service commission. Charles Lucas, Wingfield's successor as under-secretary responsible for West Indian business, advised a firm but courteous despatch indicating that 'if the

[30] Davson to Wingfield, Conf., 11 Nov. 1897. 24682. CO 111/500.

[31] Hemming to Wingfield (personal), 28 June 1897. Filed with minute paper 14016. CO 111/500.

[32] Davis seems to have been one among the few officials in the colonies under review who took seriously their role as trustees for the unrepresented classes. He was an expatriate and a prolific writer who vigorously pressed a policy of development in the face of government apathy and planter opposition.

[33] Davis to Pearson (personal), 10 Nov. 1896. Filed with minute paper 1621. CO 111/492.

present constitition is to stand'[34] such a civil list must be voted during 1898. Wingfield, Meade's successor as permanent under-secretary, deprecated the threat of constitutional reform, but acknowledged its possibility if the court refused to vote a civil list, which he considered should be enlarged to include all the civil service; if the Combined Court declined '. . . we may take the opportunity of abolishing it and introducing Crown Colony Government'.[35]

Chamberlain was more cautious than his officials, insisting that he must have 'a very good case' for abolishing the Combined Court; it was necessary, he wrote, to consider most carefully before making 'a definite & positive threat of abolishing an ancient constitution'.[36] Chamberlain did, however, consider the possibility of bringing the Combined Court 'face to face' with the grave financial difficulties, which Hemming attributed to their reluctance to vote increased taxes in spite of the large current deficit. Chamberlain minuted: 'If they will not pass the Taxes we think right—what is their alternative? We might possibly let them try . . . it . . . & if it is a failure it might be an argument for an alteration in the Constitution.'[37] Two main considerations probably underlay Chamberlain's cautious attitude. A leading principle in his later policy towards Jamaica constitutional reform was his need for 'a good Parliamentary case'.[38] This must have seemed to him an even more important consideration in the case of British Guiana since the abolition of the Combined Court raised the possibility of parliamentary legislation.[39] Chamberlain also showed an awareness of the possible sentimental attachment of colonists to long-established constitutional rights, which is revealed most clearly in his reluctance in 1897 and 1898 to consider a reform

[34] Hemming to Lucas (personal), 14 Oct. 1897. Filed with minute paper 23207. CO 111/496. Minute by C.P.L., 8 Nov. 1897. For an analysis of Lucas's attitude to constitutional reform in British Guiana see p. 241.

[35] Ibid. Minute by E.W., 9 Nov. 1897.

[36] Ibid. Minute by J.C., 10 Nov. 1897.

[37] Hemming to Wingfield (personal), 4 Feb. 1897. 4031. CO 111/492. Minute by J.C., 19 Feb. 1897.

[38] See, for instance, p. 253.

[39] See pp. 7 and 124. Such legislation might, in Lucas's view, have been avoided if the Combined Court had voluntarily surrendered its powers by passing the necessary legislation. See his Memorandum, Constitutions of West Indies. 14 Feb. 1898. Filed with minute paper 3845. CO 318/293. It is subsequently referred to as Lucas's Memorandum, Constitutions of West Indies.

of the Barbados constitution. His reference to British Guiana's 'ancient constitution' suggests that this consideration may also have influenced his attitude towards that colony. It was only when the depressed condition of the British West Indian sugar industry seemed likely to provide him with 'the very good case' which he required, that Chamberlain seriously considered the reform of the British Guiana and Jamaica constitutions.

In the autumn of 1896 Chamberlain secured the appointment of a royal commission, under the chairmanship of Sir Henry Norman, to enquire into the condition and prospects of the West Indian colonies. Reporting in September 1897, the commission concluded that the sugar industry in the British West Indies was suffering from severe decline which might lead to its possible extinction.[40] Chamberlain accepted the commission's conclusion but not its majority recommendation against the imposition of countervailing duties on imported bounty-fed beet sugar, for which policy he argued strongly but unsuccessfully in the Cabinet.[41] He succeeded, however, in winning Cabinet approval for placing before Parliament a vote for £500,000, for the benefit of the British West Indian colonies, subject to certain conditions including that where Imperial assistance was given there should be Imperial control. The colonial office papers suggest, though not conclusively, that the decision to impose this condition was reached independently in the Colonial Office and in the Treasury. It was strongly advocated by Lucas in October 1897:

> . . . where Imperial money is given there should be Imperial control. In other words there should be Crown Colonies; and to payment of loans and annual subsidies should be attached, as an indispensable condition, abolition, as far as possible, of the elective element and of unofficial majorities. . . .[42]

On 11 January 1898 the Treasury informed the Colonial Office that as the secretary of state was aware they were willing

[40] Report of the West India Royal Commission. C. –8655. P.P. 1898 (L).

[41] See his cabinet paper, 'The Condition of the West Indian Colonies', 8 Nov. 1897. Cab. 37/45. No. 44. The Cabinet view is summarized in paras. 2–5 of Colonial Office to Treasury, 24 Jan. 1898. 761. CO 318/291.

[42] Memorandum on the Report of the West India Royal Commission, by C.P.L. October 1897. Reprinted in Conf. Print, West Indian No. 79. CO 884/5. Subsequently referred to as Lucas's Memorandum, West India Royal Commission.

to assent to Imperial assistance to those West Indian colonies in need of it, and which were 'subject to the absolute financial control of Her Majesty's Government in regard to both taxation and expenditure',[43] a condition which they restated in the case of Antigua as 'full and positive control of legislation' by the executive. By 'Imperial assistance' the Treasury meant 'free grants'; they did not, as Lucas had done, include loans, nor did they object like Lucas to the elective principle as such. On 24 January Wingfield replied that 'Mr. Chamberlain fully concurs in the view that Imperial assistance to any Colony should as a rule, involve Imperial control . . .'.[44] There is no doubt of the strength of the Treasury's adherence to this principle, for they declined to sanction any aid for Antigua on the strength of Chamberlain's assurance that he was *contemplating* taking steps to secure full Imperial control. The rigidity of the Treasury position was probably influenced by the attitude of the chancellor of the exchequer, Sir Michael Hicks-Beach. In November 1898 Lucas noted that it was his personal decision that a free grant for hurricane relief could only be made to Barbados if its constitution was changed;[45] in a personal letter to Hicks-Beach, Chamberlain described the demand as 'impolitic and ungracious' and the chancellor withdrew it.

The ready acceptance by the Colonial Office of the Treasury view rested on several grounds. In the first place, Chamberlain and his officials were influenced by the recommendation of the West India Royal Commission that a condition for annual subsidies and payments by the Imperial government to the West Indian colonies should be such constitutional changes as were necessary 'to ensure economy and efficient administration'.[46] More fundamental to the colonial office attitude was the hostility of Chamberlain, Wingfield, and Lucas to those West Indian constitutions which were not those of pure crown colonies. Lucas's attitude was notably uncompromising:

There ought to be no semi-self-governing Colonies in the tropical West Indies. I should like to see five Crown Colonies. 1. Jamaica

[43] Treasury to Colonial Office, 11 Jan. 1898. 761. CO 318/291.
[44] Colonial Office to Treasury, 24 Jan. 1898. 761. CO 318/291.
[45] See minute paper 26209. CO 318/291.
[46] C. 8655, para. 541.

and dependencies including the Bahamas. 2. British Honduras. 3. British Guiana. 4. Trinidad and Tobago. 5. The lesser Antilles.[47]

Lucas had particular grounds for his hostility towards the British Guiana constitution. He argued that it led to constant friction and was 'ill adapted to efficient administration'.[48] It was inappropriate to a colony no longer peopled mainly by Dutch, and was likely to become more unsuitable as the colony was 'opened up'.[49] Lucas also argued that British Guiana was 'face to face with Imperial questions',[50] such as the boundary dispute, which made it desirable to retain full control at home. But Lucas's proposal for five crown colonies in the West Indies reflected a general attitude towards constitutional questions for which general grounds must be sought. Lucas was an able administrator, and it was his zeal for efficient and financially prudent administration which strongly influenced his attitude towards those West Indian colonies which were not pure crown colonies. He regarded them as financially irresponsible, borrowing in times of difficulty rather than raising taxes or reducing expenditure. His belief in administrative efficiency and uniformity was reflected in three of the reasons which he advised might be given to Parliament to justify constitutional change in West Indian colonies receiving Imperial aid, namely that such constitutions implied representation without responsibility, that in certain cases they had not worked well, and that the co-existence of crown colony government and representative government, for instance in the Leewards Federation, was anomalous.[51] Each of these reasons was included in an unsigned, undated, typewritten paper, 'Case against the West Indian Constitutions', which other circumstantial evidence strongly suggests, and which the writer assumes, was written by Lucas.[52] Although Lucas in this paper clearly regarded

[47] Lucas's Memorandum, West India Royal Commission.

[48] Lucas's Memorandum, Constitutions of West Indies.

[49] Ibid. In January 1902 Lucas minuted, and Chamberlain agreed, that if the ' "hinterland" ' was opened up 'it will probably become time to consider whether the constitution should be altered or be confined only to a part of the present colony, the rest being constituted a kind of High Com'ship'. Ashmore (O.A.G.) to Chamberlain, No. 453, 17 Dec. 1901. 601. CO 111/529. Minute by C.P.L., 9 Jan. 1902.

[50] Lucas's Memorandum, Constitutions of West Indies. [51] Ibid.

[52] Filed with minute paper 3845. CO 318/293. The paper was addressed to Chamberlain and registered with Lucas's memorandum on the West Indian

crown colony government as a more workable form of government, he did not feel confident of a public case based on particular examples of the ill-working of representative government. '. . . the legislatures', he admitted, 'might possibly make a fair countercase against the Colonial Office and the local Executive'. 'The West Indies', he conceded in a different context, 'have suffered from the want of capable governors and other officers.' Lucas preferred to base his case against the West Indian constitutions on more general grounds. He argued that the 'main or only defence' of representative assemblies without responsible government was as a 'preliminary to complete self government', but 'no one suggests that these Colonies are suited for complete self government'. In Lucas's view, elective assemblies shielded weak governors and hampered strong ones. Such constitutions were oligarchies, in most cases the electorate being 'absurdly small'. Although suitable for communities with a considerable proportion of English settlers, they were unsuitable for what were becoming 'more and more negro colonies', into which the main flow of immigration had been East Indian. In Lucas's view, which was shared by Blake and Hemming, the Negro race of all races probably benefited most from a strong executive.[53]

Underlying this last view was a most important shift in colonial office thinking regarding the suitability of representative institutions in the West Indies, the beginning of which can be traced to the late 1880s and which became more marked during Chamberlain's secretaryship. It was characterized by a growing pessimism in official and unofficial circles regarding the capacity and progress of the Negro race in the West Indies, and a developing sense of trusteeship for its welfare. Both considerations pointed to the maintenance of crown colony government. The present and future capacity of the Negro race

constitutions. The style and content are characteristic of Lucas, it is amended at one point in his handwriting, and its authoritative tone suggests his authorship. The subsequent quotations in this paragraph are taken from it, and it is subsequently referred to as Lucas's Case against the West Indian Constitutions.

[53] In 1890 he wrote: 'Again and again the history of colonisation has shown that the safeguard of coloured races consists in a strong Home government outside and beyond local influences . . .'. C. P. Lucas, *A Historical Geography of the British Colonies*, vol. 2, The West Indies (Oxford, 1890), p. 71. Compare his Introduction to the 1891 edition of Sir George Cornewall Lewis's *An Essay on the Government of Dependencies*, pp. xxxii–xxxiii.

had been widely debated since the abolition of slavery. Colonial office opinion in the early 1880s had inclined towards an optimistic view, Derby's policy towards the Jamaica constitution being based on the past achievement and future promise of the Jamaican Negro.[54] This confidence seems to have weakened during the 1890s, opinion in the Colonial Office reflecting an increasingly widely held view outside, that representative institutions were inappropriate for non-white tropical dependencies.[55] The colonial office attitude was influenced by pessimistic reports from governors regarding social conditions in the West Indies, notably practically stationary Negro populations, high child mortality, a large proportion of illegitimate births, the consequent absence of family life, and the increasing incidence of praedial larceny.[56] The protagonists of the Negro could in each case point to mitigating circumstances, but the overall effect on officials was one of pessimism. Pearson noted on the British Guiana papers in February 1903 that the problem which such evidence revealed was 'very serious', not only from the religious point of view, 'but from the social & political point of view, as the sense of personal responsibility & the family life are the basis of sound & healthy national life'.[57] The earlier influence of these views is reflected in the importance which Chamberlain and Lucas attached to the presence of the

[54] Derby himself seems to have had reservations on this point. See footnote 88, p. 36.

[55] For early examples of colonial office thinking see Harris's minutes of February 1889 (p. 184) and July 1893 (p. 213), and Lucas's views, footnote 53, p. 242. Froude had given strong expression to the same view in 1888 (op. cit.) and it is significant that Lucas quotes him with approval in his introduction to Lewis's book. Benjamin Kidd argued in Ch. X of *Social Evolution* (London, 1894) that if the tropics were to be developed and their peoples to progress they must be administered from the temperate regions by the races of higher social efficiency. First published in January 1894, *Social Evolution* was reprinted nine times in the following twelve months. Kidd developed his argument in *The Control of the Tropics* (New York, 1898). Henry Walker, who toured the West Indies in the winter of 1900–01 preparatory to entering the House of Commons, argued for the increased supervision of the tropical colonies. *The West Indies and the Empire* (London, 1901), pp. 213–14. Compare also the views of Sir C. Quilter on pp. 271–2.

[56] For an influential example see Swettenham to Chamberlain, No. 4, 5 Jan. 1903. 3798. CO 111/536. The Colonial Office had received similar reports about this time from Barbados and Jamaica. For an earlier example see Blake's despatch of 29 Apr. 1895, p. 78.

[57] Swettenham to Chamberlain, No. 4, 5 Jan. 1903. 3798. CO 111/536. Minute by A.A.P., 8 Feb. 1903.

East Indian population in the West Indies; in 1897 Chamberlain informed Hicks-Beach that such a presence would prevent the West Indies 'from sinking to the level to which other negro communities have sunk . . .'.[58]

Pessimism regarding the progress of the Negro race led officials to a more positive view of the responsibility of the Colonial Office. In May 1903 Pearson minuted that '. . . the British Government were in a special way responsible for the well-being of the black population of the West Indies'. '. . . this Office', he wrote, 'could do a great deal directly or indirectly to influence public opinion & the standard of social & political morals'.[59] At least as early as 1899 Olivier seems to have been thinking on similar lines. For instance, he contrasted the West Indies with Ceylon, where Britain had imposed a machinery of administration on 'established organic societies' and where 'the peoples really look after themselves'. In the West Indies, however, there was an artificial population at a very critical stage of development, 'a much more childish people . . . with which you can do more for good and evil than you can with the people of Ceylon or the Malay peninsula'.[60] Colonial office opinion was again reflecting currents of thought outside. Pearson referred approvingly to Kidd's *The Control of the Tropics*; his advice reflected Kidd's belief that the progress of the tropics depended on exposing them to the influence of the higher civilization of the temperate zones. Kidd himself cited with approval the British administration in India and Egypt; he regarded the government of the tropics from the temperate zones 'as a trust for civilization'.[61] Livingstone argued on similar lines to Kidd;[62] Lucas, and probably Chamberlain, had read Livingstone's book,[63] and Olivier's reference to a

[58] Chamberlain to Hicks-Beach, 26 Nov. 1897 (copy). Chamberlain Papers JC/14/3/10. The letter was drafted by Lucas. In October 1897 he advised increasing the East Indian element in the West Indies 'with the distinct object of not leaving any of these Islands entirely to the negro race'. Lucas's Memorandum on the West India Royal Commission. The example of Haiti was most influential at this time. Sir Spenser St. John's book, *Hayti; or the Black Republic* was published in 1884 and a second edition in 1889.

[59] Minute paper 16057. CO 318/309. Minute by A.A.P., 24 May 1903.

[60] Minute paper 4072A. CO 318/298. Minute by S.O., 13 Mar. 1899.

[61] Kidd, *The Control of the Tropics*, p. 53. See footnote 55 above.

[62] W. P. Livingstone, *Black Jamaica. A Study in Evolution* (London, 1899).

[63] See minute paper 35877. CO 137/607.

'childish people'[64] suggests that he too was influenced by it. Such broad currents of opinion are hard to date precisely, but no assessment of Chamberlain's policy towards the West Indian constitutions can ignore them. It is not easy to judge, however, the extent to which Chamberlain was personally influenced by them. His fairness prevented him from adopting the most pessimistic view of the moral condition of the West Indies, and his non-conformist background probably strengthened his doubts as to the wisdom of state interference in such matters. The views outlined above were held more strongly by Lucas, but since he played a large part in shaping West Indian policy they must be regarded as influential.

Among the detailed constitutional reforms in the West Indies which Lucas wished to see were the following changes: in Trinidad the restoration of the official majority; in Jamaica the substitution in the Legislative Council of fifteen officials for five *ex-officio* and ten nominated members (of whom six had actually been appointed), and the ending of the veto of the elected members on financial and other questions; and in British Guiana the abolition of the Combined Court, its functions being transferred to the Court of Policy to which a further official was to be added.[65] Chamberlain's strategy was to make these changes the minimum condition for Imperial aid, and in more general terms by this means to implement where possible throughout the British West Indies, with the exception of Barbados, '. . . the general rule of Crown Colony Government for Tropical Colonies'.[66] By using the occasion for Imperial aid to effect this policy, Lucas and Chamberlain believed that local opposition might be disarmed, the arrangement being in the nature of a friendly bargain. Yet Chamberlain showed characteristic caution in implementing this policy. Although agreeing generally with Lucas's proposals for Trinidad, Jamaica, and British Guiana, he was unwilling to pledge himself to details. Underlying his attitude was a greater concern

[64] Compare Livingstone, op. cit., pp. 227, 242, and 286. Olivier's copy is in the West India Committee Library.

[65] Lucas's Memorandum on Constitutions of West Indies. In short, the principle underlying Lucas's advice was the establishment of an absolute official majority not dependent on the votes of nominated unofficial members. In contrast to his earlier view (see p. 239) his proposals left the elective element undisturbed.

[66] Lucas's Memorandum on Constitutions of West Indies.

for local and parliamentary opinion. He agreed with Wingfield that the governor of British Guiana should be asked confidentially of the prospects of the Combined Court being induced to pass the necessary legislation to abolish itself, but he seems to have been unwilling to raise in a more precise form the question of constitutional retrogression in the three colonies under review until he was able to state exactly what assistance was to be given from Imperial funds. He reminded the Treasury that the political privileges of the West Indian colonies 'have at least some traditional and historical interest, they appeal to local public spirit and they should . . . be dealt with gently . . .'.[67] He personally declined to pledge himself to parliamentary action should the Dominica Legislative Assembly decline to concede the necessary financial control. Lucas favoured overriding possible local opposition by parliamentary legislation. Chamberlain noted: 'I do not want to suggest Imperial legislation. If the local bodies do not agree to our terms they will get no assistance. This will be sufficient in most cases to secure their assent.'[68]

Chamberlain first applied his policy in Antigua and Dominica, the only beneficiaries of the royal commission's recommendations which were not crown colonies.[69] He informed Sir Francis Fleming, the governor of the Leeward Islands, that the condition for Imperial aid for these colonies was the establishment of crown colony government, though so long as official control was secured he would not insist on the abolition of the

[67] Colonial Office to Treasury, 24 Jan. 1898. 761. CO 318/291.

[68] Marginal note by J.C. on draft of Colonial Office to Treasury, 24 Jan. 1898. 761. CO 318/291.

[69] With the exception that provision was made on the supplementary estimates for 1898 for £10,000 for central sugar factories in certain colonies including Barbados. Barbados also benefited from the Imperial Department of Agriculture, but Jamaica, British Guiana, and Trinidad hardly at all.

Both Antigua and Dominica had mixed councils in which the Crown was dependent for control on the votes of nominated unofficial members. The Antigua Legislative Council comprised four *ex-officio* members, eight nominated members, and twelve elected members. The Dominica Legislative Assembly comprised one *ex-officio* member, three nominated officials, four nominated unofficials, and seven elected members. The Dominica nominated unofficials were in a particularly strong position since they could not be removed for merely opposing a government measure. They were, of course, removeable when the Assembly was dissolved. See Act 4/1895. CO 78/22. The difficulty in Antigua was to find sufficient officials to fill the nominated seats. In each case crown colony government could only be established by a local act or by Imperial legislation.

elective system.[70] In Antigua eight out of eleven elected members accepted Chamberlain's bargain, but they favoured a purely nominated council with an official majority; the legislation establishing it was carried in March 1898 against the votes of three elected members.[71] Chamberlain encountered greater difficulty in Dominica where the franchise was somewhat wider. In spite of a dissolution and general election, only one elected member was willing to accept the change to an official majority. Both he and the administrator favoured a nominated council, the legislation effecting it being finally passed in July 1898 by one elected and seven nominated votes against the votes of the remaining six elected members.[72]

Chamberlain faced graver problems in implementing his policy in the three colonies under consideration. In the case of British Guiana, assuming that he did not wish to resort to parliamentary legislation, he had to obtain the assent of the Combined Court to its own abolition. Further, none of the three colonies benefited directly from the royal commission's recommendations. Chamberlain was dissatisfied with the commission's proposals on this account and, more generally, because they offered little assistance to the sugar industry. He suggested to the Treasury that in addition to the total of £160,000 necessary to implement the recommendations of the royal commission up to 31 March 1899, a further £340,000 should be set aside for the direct relief and maintenance of the sugar industry. Of this, he proposed that British Guiana, Trinidad, and Jamaica should receive grants spread over three to five years totalling respectively an estimated £105,000, £45,000, and £25,000, which would enable them to remit duties on certain imports from the United States, thus creating the conditions for a reciprocal agreement with that country under section 14 of the Dingley Tariff.[73] Chamberlain also

70 Chamberlain to Fleming, Conf., 25 Jan. 1898. T 761. CO 318/291, and Chamberlain to Fleming, Conf., 22 Mar. 1898. MO 3845. CO 318/293.

71 Fleming to Chamberlain, No. 194, 30 Mar. 1898. 8305. CO 152/230. The Antigua Legislative Council subsequently comprised the governor, eight official, and eight nominated unofficial members.

72 Fleming to Chamberlain, No. 378, 20 July 1898. 17531. CO 152/234. The Dominica Legislative Council subsequently comprised the administrator, five official, and five nominated unofficial members.

73 For Chamberlain's proposal see Colonial Office to Treasury, 24 Jan. 1898. 761. CO 318/291.

proposed that further grants of £12,000 and £24,000 should be made to Trinidad and British Guiana in order to relieve the planters for one year of the cost of the return passage of time-expired Indian immigrants. The Treasury objected to this last proposal, but agreed to the principle of relief to enable these and other West Indian colonies to enter into reciprocal tariff agreements with the United States. The proposal was finally to lapse with the failure of the United States Senate to ratify the negotiated agreements, but of more immediate significance for Chamberlain's policy were the long-drawn-out reciprocity negotiations which now took place with the United States. Since the Treasury declined to pledge itself in advance of these negotiations, Chamberlain was unable to make a definite offer of aid to British Guiana, Trinidad, or Jamaica. It is true that in June 1898 the Colonial Office was considering proposals to subsidize steamship services between British Guiana and Canada, and Jamaica and England, but both schemes depended on Treasury assent to a departure from the recommendations of the royal commission and on acceptable tenders being forthcoming. The proposed Imperial Department of Agriculture would directly benefit British Guiana, Trinidad, and Jamaica to only a very limited extent. In short, the failure to reach immediately a reciprocity agreement with the United States without which the Treasury would not pledge itself to financial aid to remit import duties, the uncertainty attending the projects for subsidized steamship lines benefiting British Guiana and Jamaica, and the very small extent to which the larger colonies gained from the other recommendations of the royal commission, meant that Chamberlain could make no definite offer of large-scale aid to the three colonies under consideration. The question thus facing the Colonial Office in the summer of 1898 was whether to shelve the policy of constitutional retrogression in British Guiana, Trinidad, and Jamaica, or to proceed without the counter-offer of Imperial aid. The course followed in each colony was dictated partly by the different character of the three constitutions and partly by events in the colonies themselves.

The abolition of the unofficial nominated majority in the Trinidad Legislative Council raised the least difficulties, since it could be simply effected either by Royal Instructions or by not nominating an unofficial in the place of one who retired or died. Since neither the elective principle nor ancient political rights were at stake, the chance of significant opposition in the colony or in England was lessened. In these circumstances, and given the strength of opinion in the Colonial Office favouring pure crown colony government, it is not surprising that Chamberlain seized the first opportunity to restore the official majority in Trinidad. In June 1898 the officer administering the government, C. C. Knollys, reported 'a growing tendency' on the part of some unofficial nominated members to form an organized opposition.[74] He gave little evidence for this view,[75] which was uncritically accepted by Wingfield and Lucas who both advised securing an official majority by adding one more official to the Legislative Council. It reflects the changed climate of opinion in the Colonial Office that Wingfield was now prepared 'to take the bull by the horns'[76] and readily depart from Newcastle's concession of 1862, a concession which in 1890 he had advised restoring.[77] As he himself admitted, '... I was then more scrupulous about departing from the Duke of Newcastle's arrangement ...'. Chamberlain accepted his officials' advice, which was implemented by Royal Instructions,[78] the collector of customs taking the place of the commissioner for Tobago, and the commandant of local forces being added to the council, thus raising the number of officials to eleven including the governor. The number of unofficials was not formally fixed in the Instructions, but in an accompanying despatch Chamberlain limited their number to eleven,[79] thus establishing an official majority dependent on the governor's casting vote.

Chamberlain's cautious attitude to the reform of the British Guiana constitution has been noted; it almost certainly rested on the possible need for parliamentary legislation and his understanding of local attachment to long-enjoyed constitu-

[74] Knollys (OAG) to Chamberlain, No. 226, 14 June 1898. 15180. CO 295/386.

[75] Sir H. E. H. Jerningham, the governor, described his allegations as 'based on the flimsiest of pretexts'. In his view the unofficial members had not systematically opposed the government. Jerningham to Chamberlain, No. 380, 4 Oct. 1898. 24120. CO 295/387.

[76] Knollys (OAG) to Chamberlain, No. 226, 14 June 1898. 15180. CO 295/386. Minute by E.W., 13 Aug. 1898.

[77] See pp. 189–90.

[78] Royal Instructions, 31 Oct. 1898. CO 380/147/29.

[79] Chamberlain to Jerningham, No. 370, 1 Nov. 1898. 15180. CO 295/386.

tional rights. Taken with his inability to offer the colony substantial Imperial aid, it probably accounts for his apparent decision during the summer of 1898[80] to shelve the question of introducing crown government into British Guiana. Imperial considerations subsequently confirmed his caution. Renewed difficulties over the civil list in November 1901 prompted Lucas, after personally learning Chamberlain's views, to write privately to the officer administering the government:

> . . . whatever may be the vagaries of the colonial legislature and however much some of us would like to substitute a more workable machine—there must at present be no attempt to override them and anything like a constitutional crisis must as far as possible be avoided. This is for wider & Imperial reasons. . . .[81]

The Jamaica constitution raised different issues. Lucas argued in February 1898 that there was 'no such reason . . . for being tender' with Jamaica as with Barbados,[82] and he mentioned the period of crown colony government before 1884. He was probably also influenced by the political and financial crisis of the previous spring, precipitated by the opposition of the elected members to increased taxation.[83] On the other hand, the colony had experienced two centuries of representative government before 1866, and since 1884 had enjoyed a modified form of crown colony government. These last considerations may have influenced the sensitivity to local, and particularly parliamentary, opinion which characterized Chamberlain's approach to constitutional change in Jamaica. His caution suggests that, although generally predisposed towards crown colony government, he would not have modified the Jamaica constitution in this direction had not the near bankruptcy of the colony in 1898–99 presented him with a favourable opportunity for doing so. The constitutional history of Jamaica in this period is thus intimately bound up with the economic and financial crisis which the colony experienced in the late 1890s.

[80] There is no evidence of the exact date of this decision, but the acceptance by the Colonial Office in October 1899 of the Combined Court's renewal of the civil list for three years seemed to indicate no immediate intention to reform the constitution.

[81] Lucas to Ashmore (O.A.G.), 26 Nov. 1901. Private. Draft filed with 41462. CO 111/528.

[82] Lucas's Memorandum on Constitutions of West Indies.

[83] See pp. 251–2.

Complex causes underlay Jamaica's economic difficulties. In the first place the elected members of the Legislative Council, to whom Derby had transferred the colonial office responsibility for controlling expenditure, had not proved, after the first few sessions of the Council, the force for economy which Herbert had hoped. Being apparently sensitive to their Negro constituents, they had shown themselves increasingly willing to sanction large expenditure in such fields as education and communications,[84] while opposing increased taxation so long as an accumulated surplus remained. In these circumstances much responsibility rested on the governor, who retained the financial initiative. Blake lacked the political skill and financial acumen of Norman. Moreover, his belief in economic development inclined him to large government expenditure, particularly on communications, and to the avoidance of any action which would damage the confidence of outside investors. Thus it was not until January 1897 that he informed the Colonial Office of the gravity of an economic and financial position which had been deteriorating since 1892.[85] Rising public expenditure unmatched by a similar increase in revenue lay at the root of the crisis, but two factors outside Blake's control contributed to it. The first was the failure of the Jamaica railway under private ownership; in 1893–94 the interest on the second mortgage bonds held by the government was £3,000, compared with a profit on the railway of £28,497 in the final year of government ownership. The second was the fall in the prices of Jamaica's main exports, which began in 1893–94, and accelerated in 1896–97 and 1897–98; in the four years after 1893–94 the value of Jamaica's total home-produced exports fell by nearly one-third, with secondary effects on wages and revenue. In January 1897 Blake estimated a deficit at 31 March 1898 of £75,691 which he proposed to meet by increased taxation of £80,700. By mainly avoiding direct taxation, particularly on land, he hoped to gain the support of the elected members, but the majority refused to consider any increase in taxation until they had examined the estimates; their attitude, which they consistently maintained for the next two years, reflected both their determination, if possible, to

[84] See pp. 65–6.

[85] Blake to Chamberlain, Conf., 30 Jan. 1897. 3687. CO 137/579.

avoid increased taxation, and their hostility towards official salaries, particularly those of outsiders. The elected members reduced the estimates by over £38,000 and pressed for a loan to cover the balance. In these circumstances Blake considered the possibility of declaring his tariff bill of paramount importance and if necessary calling up his reserve of four nominated members,[86] but he decided against this course after apparently consulting with Sir Henry Norman, then in Jamaica with the West India Royal Commission. Blake finally secured the passage of a law raising the excise duty on cigars and cigarettes which, with the economies effected, left an estimated deficit on the financial year of about £16,000.

Blake's difficulties in the spring of 1897 prompted him to raise the question of the withdrawal of the financial veto of nine elected members, there being in his view no popular opinion on the subject. He was influenced less by his immediate difficulties than by the effect on the black population of the spectacle of a powerless government; he argued that the successful opposition of the elected members to the government was engendering a dangerous spirit of insubordination. The need if Jamaica was to progress was for strong government. In these circumstances the possession by the elected members of a financial veto was 'fraught with danger', a view shared by 'every leading official' and those with a large stake in the colony.[87] Blake was writing against the background of increasing unrest among the Negro population.[88] He wrote: 'An assertion is not now uncommon that the white man is going and that the turn of the black man is coming.'[89] He attributed this unrest, in particular, to the attitude of the elected members, some of whom, he informed Meade in January 1896, meant by 'Jamaica for the Jamaicans' that there should only

[86] See pp. 86–7. In using the phrase 'nominated members' in this particular Jamaica context, governors and Colonial Office primarily had in mind the nomination of members who would secure a government majority; they might therefore be officials, or unofficials on whose support the government could rely. Two such unofficials had sat in the Legislative Council since 1896 (see p. 87). See also footnote 9, p. 71, and footnote 118, p. 261.

[87] Blake's views were conveyed by Blake to Chamberlain, Conf., 29 Mar. 1897. 7956. CO 137/580.

[88] See p. 65.

[89] Blake to Chamberlain, Conf., 29 Mar. 1897. 7956. CO 137/580.

be land and employment for Jamaicans and particularly those who were black.[90]

Blake's despatch of 29 March 1897, and the events preceding it, raised two issues for Chamberlain: the expediency of Blake's overriding the votes of nine elected members by a declaration of paramount importance and if necessary calling up his reserve of four nominated members, and the reform of the Jamaica constitution by the abolition of the financial veto of nine elected members. These were to remain the two leading issues for Chamberlain's decision. On the first, it seems possible, though the evidence is not conclusive, that Chamberlain would have agreed in the spring of 1897 to the use of the governor's overriding powers if Blake had not decided against this course. On the second, Wingfield regretted the concession of the financial veto but advised that it would be difficult to abrogate it without 'some very strong instances of the power having been seriously abused',[91] which, in his opinion, were not afforded by the recent session; this view was communicated to Blake. Chamberlain agreed with Wingfield but on broader grounds:

> These liberal Constitutions are not really suited to a black population & some day they will have to be altered. But we must have a strong & an easily understood reason before we propose the abrogation of a Rep^{e} Gov^{t} or the limitation of its powers.[92]

The conviction of the unsuitability of representative institutions for non-white communities, and the insistence on a good case before abrogating them, subsequently governed Chamberlain's policy towards constitutional change in Jamaica. The first consideration he had stated within four months of taking office.[93] The second reflected his strong political sense both of the possible reaction of the House of Commons and to a lesser extent of local opinion. Thus in July 1899 he minuted: '. . . I must have a good Parliamentary case.'[94] Three months later he noted: 'These Jamaica agitators are up to all the dodges of their trade & we may have to defend ourselves in the H of C

[90] Blake to Meade (personal), 20 Jan. 1896. 2857. CO 137/571.

[91] Blake to Chamberlain, Conf., 29 Mar. 1897. 7956. CO 137/580. Minute by E.W., 12 June 1897.

[92] Ibid. Minute by J.C., 15 June 1897.

[93] See pp. 231–3.

[94] Hemming to Chamberlain, No. 323, 22 June 1899. 18825. CO 137/602. Minute by J.C., 20 July 1899.

against attacks by people instructed by them.'[95] He was also sensitive to the reaction of local opinion, declining in 1899 to demand a reform of the Jamaica constitution as a condition for an Imperial subsidy of £10,000 towards steamship communications: 'The local patriots would reject the mess of pottage.'[96]

Jamaica's economic and financial crisis deepened during the summer and autumn of 1897. In the second quarter of 1897 the revenue yielded £27,000 less than Blake had estimated. In July the Jamaica Railway defaulted on its first mortgage bonds, raising the possibility that the trustees of the bondholders, under the terms of the Jamaica railway agreement of 1889, would call on the colonial government to take over the railway.[97] Olivier's thorough investigation of the colony's finances in the autumn of 1897 revealed that the colonial authorities, whether intentionally or not, had disguised the gravity of the position by the inclusion of fictitious assets in the colony's balance sheet and by diverting loan moneys to current expenditure. On figures supplied by Blake, Olivier estimated in February 1898 that Jamaica would face an excess of liabilities over assets on 31 March 1899 of £165,000, which on less favourable assumptions might be as high as £400,000. He further estimated an immediate cash deficit at 31 March 1898 of about £70,000 and a further deficit for the subsequent financial year of nearly £100,000. The need for increased taxation and further retrenchment was clear to both Blake and the Colonial Office, but Chamberlain still displayed

[95] Hemming to Chamberlain, Conf., 11 Sept. 1899. 26146. CO 137/603. Minute by J.C., 20 Oct. 1899.

[96] Crown Agents to Colonial Office, 1 June 1899. 13921. CO 318/296. Minute by J.C., 2 June 1899. The phrase was actually later used by an elected member in a legislative council debate to describe the Imperial aid finally extended to Jamaica.

[97] S. 49, Law 12. 1889. For the circumstances in which the law was passed see pp. 57–8. In this event the Jamaica government was liable for arrears of interest to the bondholders (the ultimate liability was to be about £88,000), and the issue in exchange for their mortgage bonds of £1,500,000 Jamaica 3½ per cent stock, with liability in interest and sinking fund charges of £67,500. This generous provision was described by Hemming as practically amounting 'to a State guarantee of the total expenditure on the extensions with interest at the rate of 3½% . . .'. Both the Colonial Office and the colonial government had been badly outmanœuvred in the negotiation of the railway agreement. Olivier rightly described it as 'a most ill-advised and insecure arrangement'.

caution, declining to give Blake or his successor, Sir A. W. L. Hemming, the *carte blanche* as to the exercise of the governor's reserve powers, which the former considered necessary if measures for increased taxation were to be carried. Chamberlain minuted:

If we are to make any change in the constitution[98] we must have a very strong case & I should give the elected members plenty of rope.

... (he asked) whether we should let them get further into difficulties—say leave salaries unpaid—delay public works etc. and so get a real object lesson in West Indian Rep^e Gov^t. In any case we must move slowly.[99]

The accelerating decline of the Jamaica economy was reflected in the position which Hemming inherited in February 1898. He estimated a deficit at 31 March 1899 of £161,969. His leading proposals to meet this *damnosa hereditas* were a loan of £100,000 and an increase in customs duties to yield £60,000. Chamberlain's initial consent to a loan of only £50,000 to be repaid in three years[100] severely hampered Hemming's attempt to carry increased taxation, to which some of the elected members remained 'bitterly and uncompromisingly hostile'. His financial programme and the estimates for 1898–99 were introduced into the Legislative Council on 20 April. The elected members attacked the loan of £50,000 as inadequate, and sought to avoid increased taxation by substantially reducing the estimates and covering the remaining deficit by a larger loan. Frustrated in a detailed attack on the estimates by lack of unanimity, they finally succeeded in adjourning their consideration for three months to allow time for enquiry into the possibility of further retrenchment. Faced with a total lack of supply, Hemming sought Chamberlain's authority to carry both a vote of credit for £200,000 and the tariff bill, if necessary

98 The context suggests that Chamberlain had in mind the abolition of the veto of the elected members. He seems to have regarded the nomination of four additional members as a politically easier step since no amending order in council was required. He indicated in 1899, however, that he required a good parliamentary case for even this change. See p. 261.

99 Blake to Chamberlain, Conf., 22 Nov. 1897. 26485. CO 137/584. Minute by J.C., 16 Dec. 1897.

100 Chamberlain finally agreed in July to a loan of £100,000 to be raised by debentures repayable over ten years.

by declaring them of paramount importance and nominating the four additional members to the Council. But although Chamberlain approved this course and pledged his support, and although Hemming regarded the elected members as ignorant, obstinate, and unreasonable, the latter still sought an agreement with them, being unwilling to inaugurate his administration by overruling their votes. On 18 May he reported a compromise whereby he had secured the passage of the vote of credit and the tariff bill in return for certain concessions, including limiting the bill to one year and establishing a special committee with a majority of elected members to examine the estimates.[101] His action was generally approved in the Colonial Office, though Lucas admitted to having 'hoped the elected members would remain recalcitrant so that we might have an excuse for changing the constitution . . .'.[102] He was, and remained, the foremost advocate in the Colonial Office of constitutional retrogression in Jamaica.

Further evidence of the extent of Jamaica's financial crisis contributed after mid-1898 to a hardening of Chamberlain's policy. In July Hemming reported that it seemed clear that the government must take over the Jamaica railway, which, allowing for capital improvements, would increase Jamaica's debt by an estimated £1,650,000 and her liability for annual sinking fund and interest charges by £73,500.[103] In August the Crown Agents notified that Jamaica's account was overdrawn by over £66,000, the colony being unable to remit funds. Chamberlain regarded this position as 'very serious', and determined on 'a complete investigation into & overhauling of Jamaica finance',[104] a task which in November 1898 he entrusted to Sir David Barbour. Chamberlain's decision marked the practical resumption by the Colonial Office of the financial control which Derby had surrendered in 1884.[105] It also raised the larger issue of the Jamaica constitution, for among the

[101] Hemming to Chamberlain, Conf., 18 May 1898. 12922. CO 137/590.

[102] Hemming to Chamberlain, Conf., 6 May 1898. 11864. CO 137/589. Minute by C.P.L., 28 May 1898.

[103] See footnote 97, p. 254.

[104] Hemming to Chamberlain, Tel., 13 Aug. 1898. 18170. CO 137/592. Minute by J.C., 23 Aug. 1898.

[105] See p. 56. In August 1899 Chamberlain informed Hemming of the formal resumption by the Colonial Office of responsibility for the Jamaica estimates. Chamberlain to Hemming, No. 291, 9 Aug. 1899. 17429. CO 137/601.

matters which Chamberlain instructed Barbour to enquire into were the general causes of Jamaica's financial difficulties. In a more particular sense the financial crisis shaped Chamberlain's policy towards the Jamaica constitution, for it increased the importance of renewing and possibly enlarging the temporary tariff act to which the elected members were strongly opposed. Since they were unanimous, or nearly so, it seemed likely that its renewal could only be secured by a declaration of paramount importance and the appointment of the full number of nominated members, a course which Hemming recommended and which Chamberlain for the first time specifically authorized. It seems probable that Chamberlain intended the appointments to be permanent, for he did not dissent from Hemming's view that the four members should be appointed before the Council met as part of the general policy of the government, and not for the particular purpose of passing a bill renewing the tariff;[106] Hemming did not, however, follow this course. The governor also raised the larger question of a reform of the Jamaica constitution by the abolition of the financial veto of nine elected members. In his view, the existing arrangement denied the government the power to secure measures necessary for the administration of the colony, for which it alone was responsible.[107] Underlying this judgement was his reluctance to resort to his reserve powers, the effect of which would be to make him 'unpopular, to undermine his position, & make him an object of vilification and abuse'.[108] Chamberlain declined, however, to raise at this stage the issue of the more extensive constitutional change implied in the abolition of the veto of the elected members.[109]

Further evidence of Chamberlain's hardening attitude was a long despatch of 30 November 1898, skilfully drafted by Olivier, in which Chamberlain sought to place a large share of the responsibility for Jamaica's financial difficulties on the

[106] Chamberlain to Hemming, Tel., 9 Jan. 1899. 394. CO 137/595.

[107] For Hemming's views see Hemming to Chamberlain, Conf., 24 May 1898. 12924. CO 137/590. Hemming to Chamberlain, Conf., 27 July 1898. 18510. CO 137/592. Hemming to Chamberlain, No. 598, 31 Dec. 1898. 1525. CO 137/595.

[108] Hemming to Barbour, 23 Feb. 1899. Filed with minute paper 14992. CO 137/607.

[109] See footnote 98, p. 255.

elected members.[110] Chamberlain claimed that during the period in which any nine elected members could veto expenditure, total public expenditure had risen from £545,036 to £844,577; further, the elected members had refused to increase taxation while an accumulated revenue surplus existed, and had subsequently shown a great reluctance to do so. In fact Chamberlain's case against the elected members was a weak one, as he and his officials recognized. The initiative for expenditure lay with Blake and his advisers, who by misleading financial statements and imprudent methods had disguised the true position both from the elected members and the Colonial Office.[111] Moreover, a significant part of the expenditure was secured by law and therefore outside the annual review of the elected members. The latter when faced with the facts in 1897 had reduced the estimates by nearly £40,000, and in the following year by nearly £30,000. In their criticism of expenditure they were handicapped like any legislative assembly by their lack of detailed administrative knowledge and responsibility, and by the fact that the governor, and sometimes the Colonial Office, tended to regard attacks on the estimates, and particularly those concerning the establishment, as invariably ill-judged, which was by no means always the case.[112] With his intimate knowledge of Jamaica, Olivier considered that '. . . the instinct of the Elected Members to attack establishments is not altogether ill-directed'.[113] The economies effected during Hemming's governorship are evidence for this.

Jamaica's third political crisis since 1897 was inevitable and complex. On 15 March 1899 the Legislative Council passed an amendment, moved by Burke and assented to by Hemming,

[110] Chamberlain to Hemming, No. 377, 30 Nov. 1898. 23497. CO 137/594.

[111] Hemming reported that he had understood from Barbour that the latter considered Blake 'almost wholly responsible' for Jamaica's difficulties, though he had not thought it desirable to say so in his report. Hemming to Chamberlain, Conf., 11 Sept. 1899. 26151. CO 137/603. Barbour intimated verbally to Lucas that he felt that he had let off Blake too easily in his report. See minute by C.P.L., 16 Jan. 1900 on minute paper 35877. CO 137/607. Chamberlain and Lucas regarded Blake as largely responsible for Jamaica's financial difficulties (see p. 264). Olivier referred to the 'dense and obstinate blindness' of Blake and his advisers.

[112] For example, Hemming to Chamberlain, No. 547, 22 Sept. 1899. 27748. CO 137/604. Minute by S.O., 14 Oct. 1899.

[113] Hemming to Chamberlain, No. 309, 14 June 1899. 17429. CO 137/601. Minute by S.O., 18 July 1899.

postponing the first reading of a permanent tariff bill until Barbour's report and the estimates had been considered. The move reflected the consistent determination of the elected members to consider expenditure before taxation. The attorney-general subsequently advised Hemming that the amendment might amount to an adjournment *sine die*, which would both prevent the bill being reintroduced during the same session and prevent the collection of duties by order in council under the Revenue Protection Act. Reporting this doubt to Chamberlain, Hemming asked whether he should prorogue the Council, re-assemble it, and pass the bill, if necessary by appointing the full number of nominated members. The wording of his telegram led the Colonial Office to believe that the amendment had been carried *against* the government whereas Hemming had, in fact, assented to it. Thus Chamberlain minuted: 'The fight has fairly begun',[114] and he agreed to any action necessary to secure the first reading of the bill. On 4 April Hemming carried the first reading of the tariff bill by adding four officials to the Council and declaring the matter of paramount importance. His action aroused strong protests in the Legislative Council, in the press, and at public meetings. The subsequent obstruction of business by the elected members and the considerable excitement in the colony influenced Hemming to permit the four recently appointed officials to resign from the Council, in return for a pledge by the elected members that they would co-operate with the government and provide the funds necessary for efficient administration.

Although Chamberlain and his advisers had assented to the nomination of the four officials under a misconception, they regretted Hemming's decision to withdraw them. They regarded his action as a weak one which had given a new lease of life to the constitution. Chamberlain did not, however, repudiate Hemming, although he informed him that the nominated members should not have been withdrawn without his consent. Hemming's action should not have come as a surprise to the Colonial Office for during the crisis, and throughout his governorship, he had sought to conciliate and co-operate with the elected members. Although disapproving

[114] Hemming to Chamberlain, Tel., 16 Mar. 1899. 6532. CO 137/599. Minute by J.C., 16 Mar. 1899.

of the constitution, he was aware that it could only thus be worked. But he was also influenced in his decision to withdraw the nominated members by the intense political and social pressures to which a governor was subject in a small colonial community like Kingston, and which he thus described to Barbour:

The Sec: of State is 5000 miles away—the clamour & anger of the elected members & the press cannot affect him, & his authority is supreme. The Governor is on the spot, has to live amongst & in frequent meeting with the elected members & others & must suffer in prestige & influence from local abuse & slander.[115]

It was a fatal flaw in Derby's constitution that governors such as Norman, Blake, and Hemming should have felt inhibited from using the overriding powers which alone could give it flexibility. In contrast to Norman, however, Hemming's difficulties were increased by his social antipathy towards Jamaican politicians. Olivier noted that Barbour and others thought 'that the social attitude of Govt. House is one of the present causes of trouble, and that distinctions and exclusions are made which react on the political attitude of the "Jamaica Association" '.[116] Hemming referred to Jamaicans in general as 'a beastly lot'.[117]

Three courses were open to Chamberlain during the summer of 1899. He could wait for another political deadlock to provide the opportunity for constitutional change; he could immediately seek grounds for re-nominating the official members withdrawn by Hemming; or he could adopt the most extreme course of re-establishing crown colony government by appointing the full number of nominated members and abolishing the financial and ordinary veto of the elected members. In principle Chamberlain and his officials favoured the last course, which involved an amendment of the Order in Council of May 1884, but Chamberlain, in particular, was aware of the need to justify his policy in the colony and possibly in the House of Commons. This consideration, and his inability to find strong

[115] Hemming to Barbour, 23 Feb. 1899. 14992. CO 137/607.

[116] Hemming to Chamberlain, Conf., 27 Sept. 1899. 27760. CO 137/604. Undated minute (red ink) by S.O. For the Jamaica Association see pp. 4–5, 18.

[117] Hemming to Ommaney (personal), 11 May 1903. Filed with minute paper 19748. CO 137/634.

grounds, politically speaking, for a change, led him to adopt the middle course of appointing the full number of nominated members,[118] though he hesitated until he had what seemed to him the strongest case. One possible ground was provided by the elected members themselves, who in the debates on the estimates during the summer of 1899 strongly attacked the Jamaica establishment, abolishing certain posts and reducing the salaries attached to others. Lucas had no doubt that if Jamaica was to be governed well there must be crown control in the Legislative Council, and he advised that the action of the elected members afforded sufficient grounds for at least appointing the full number of nominated members. Wingfield was more cautious, though he inclined to the view that crown colony government would have to be restored 'very soon', and he tentatively agreed with Lucas that Hemming should be instructed under certain circumstances to fill up the nominated seats in order to protect the salary of the clerk of the Legislative Council.[119] Chamberlain rejected this advice on the grounds that he 'must have a good Parliamentary case'[120] before re-appointing the nominated members, though he instructed Hemming that he must use his reserve powers to prevent injustice to officials. Chamberlain's caution may have been influenced by the sympathy shown by Olivier for the elected members' efforts to reduce the cost of the establishment; on 18 July, after a careful examination of the estimates and reports of the debates, Olivier advised that their action did 'not at all strengthen the case for any *alteration*[121] of the Constitution . . .'.[122] The point was not lost on Chamberlain, who had earlier noted that it would be difficult by a constitutional change to overrule the elected members' proposals for economy. 'They will have',

[118] See footnote 86, pp. 252. The minutes of Chamberlain, Wingfield, and Lucas during the summer of 1899 suggest that they had in mind the nomination of four officials, though Chamberlain finally agreed to the nomination of some unofficials on whose support the government could rely (see pp. 269–70).

[119] Hemming to Chamberlain, No. 323, 22 June 1899. 18825. CO 137/602. Minute by E.W., 20 July 1899.

[120] Ibid. Minute by J.C., 20 July 1899.

[121] See p. 255. Like Chamberlain, Olivier distinguished between a reform of the constitution by the abolition of the elected members' veto, and action under the constitution to establish an official majority.

[122] Hemming to Chamberlain, No. 309, 14 June 1899. 17429. CO 137/601. Minute by S.O., 18 July 1899.

he wrote, 'popular support here & in Jamaica. We ought therefore to be very clear of our ground. . . .' '. . . we must be careful', he argued, 'to have a good case.'[123]

Barbour submitted his report on the finances of Jamaica in June 1899.[124] Among his recommendations, with which Hemming 'heartily and entirely' agreed, was the permanent appointment of the full number of nominated members, on the grounds that only thus could the governor enforce a policy for which he alone was responsible. Olivier at first advised that Barbour's analysis of the extent to which constitutional defects had contributed to Jamaica's financial difficulties afforded 'ample ground'[125] for constitutional changes. He proposed immediately filling up the four nominated seats, and subsequently reducing the number of official and elected members, on account of the strain on the former and the quality of the latter. It is not clear from Olivier's minute whether he favoured the abolition of the veto of the elected members. On 11 August, however, he minuted[126] that his view of what was expedient had changed on account of Chamberlain's inability to offer substantial Imperial aid to assist Jamaica with her railway debt.[127] He now doubted whether Barbour's case regarding the unworkability of the constitution, taken with the small amount of aid which Chamberlain was able to offer, justified either an alteration in the Order in Council or the filling up of the four nominated seats. The former course, leading to crown colony government and undertaken to force through increased taxation, would not in his view be justified either on grounds of expediency or principle. There would be the danger of an agitation against the payment of taxes; moreover the opposition of the elected members to the government had been 'on very popular lines' for the reduction of expenditure on establishments, and against increases of taxes which were, in Olivier's view, already heavy. Nor did he now advise filling up the

[123] Hemming to Chamberlain, No. 247, 13 May 1899. 13838. CO 137/601. Minute by J.C., 14 June 1899.

[124] Filed with minute paper 14927. CO 137/607.

[125] Minute paper 14927. CO 137/607. Minute by S.O., 20 June 1899.

[126] Ibid. Minute by S.O., 11 Aug. 1899.

[127] For the extent of the Imperial aid which Chamberlain could offer Jamaica see p. 263. Olivier had also had time to examine the reports of the legislative council debates on the estimates and to reach the conclusion quoted on p. 261.

nominated seats in advance of implementing Barbour's financial proposals, for to do so would, as he later put it, anticipate and provoke a conflict. He argued that the position both of the Colonial Office and of the Jamaica government would be strengthened by first placing a complete financial programme before the Legislative Council; only if the latter rejected it and no acceptable alternatives emerged should the four nominated seats be permanently filled.

In his minute Olivier raised and dismissed a further ground for constitutional change, namely that it should be a condition for Jamaica receiving Imperial aid. Chamberlain had imposed a similar condition on Antigua and Dominica in the spring of 1898,[128] but then he could point to substantial Imperial grants and to Treasury insistence on the principle. In the case of Jamaica his position was weaker on both points. By August 1899 he had obtained Treasury consent to a loan under the Colonial Loans Act[129] of £348,000 at 2¾ per cent, to which was subsequently added a further loan of £105,000 for Kingston improvements. It is true that the Crown Agents considered that under existing circumstances Jamaica could not borrow in the market, but had she been able to do so at, say, 3½ per cent, the annual saving to the colony in interest would have amounted to only £2,621, and the total amount of annual aid, with the proposed steamship subsidy, to £7,621.[130] Nor could Chamberlain support his case by reference to the Treasury attitude, for the Colonial Loans Act contained no clause providing for financial control over the colonies borrowing under it; in the debate on the bill Chamberlain resisted an amendment to include such a clause on the grounds that it was an emergency bill, and that in the case of Jamaica he already exercised adequate control through his power to appoint a majority of members to the Legislative Council. This was also the Treasury view, for they made it a condition of the proposed

128 See p. 246.

129 The Colonial Loans Act became law in August 1899. It empowered the Treasury to lend specified amounts to certain colonies listed in the schedule of the Act. The loans were to be made from the Local Loans Fund at a minimum rate of interest of 2¾ per cent.

130 See footnote 143, p. 266. The steamship contract then under consideration was for a fruit and modified passenger service between Jamaica and the United Kingdom. The cost of the proposed subsidy was to be shared equally between the Imperial government and Jamaica.

loans to Jamaica that the secretary of state should exercise this control *if* the legislature diminished revenue or increased expenditure beyond what was 'necessary for the proper administration of the Colony . . .';[131] they thus clearly implied that the nomination of the four additional members was not a prior condition for Jamaica borrowing under the Colonial Loans Act.[132] Chamberlain's decision to restore the official majority appears, however, to have influenced the Treasury decision to lend at the minimum rate under the Colonial Loans Act of $2\frac{3}{4}$ per cent.

One final ground for constitutional change was discussed in the Colonial Office, namely the failure of the elected members to control public expenditure. Chamberlain in his despatch of 30 November 1898 had held them 'fully responsible' for the increases which had taken place since 1884. It was, however, widely recognized in the Office that the main responsibility for Jamaica's financial position lay with Blake and his advisers.[133] Thus Chamberlain minuted:

> We say to the elected members 'See how badly you have managed your Finances. We must come in & do them for you'.
>
> They will reply 'You are as bad as we are. What have *your* Governor *your* Treasurer & *your* Col. Secretary done for us?'
>
> The fact is we have been very badly served.[134]

The same point was later made by Olivier, who argued that to contend that the elected members were financially incompetent was a weak ground for constitutional change for they could reply 'very damagingly as to the competency of the advisers of the Govt. . . .'.[135] In Olivier's view, there had been 'serious failures and imprudences on the part of the Executive'.[136] Moreover, the Colonial Office itself was not blameless for it had retained responsibility for the 'general financial policy' of Jamaica.[137]

131 Treasury to Colonial Office, 26 July 1899. 12480. T 7/31.

132 The question of whether Chamberlain was bound by parliamentary pledges to appoint the full number of nominated members is analysed on p. 265.

133 See footnote 111, p. 258.

134 Minute paper 14927. CO 137/607. Minute by J.C., 20 June 1899.

135 Hemming to Chamberlain, Conf., 13 Nov. 1899. 33359. CO 137/605. Minute by S.O., 2 Dec. 1899.

136 Minute paper 14927. CO 137/607. Minute by S.O., 11 Aug. 1899.

137 See p. 56.

It was probably an appreciation of the weakness of the grounds for constitutional change which prompted both Wingfield and Lucas to advise Chamberlain to adopt the *via media* of appointing four additional nominated members under the powers conferred by the constitution. Both would have preferred the establishment of pure crown colony government by, in addition, abolishing the elected members' veto; neither attempted to answer Olivier's cogently argued minute in favour of a more conciliatory course, Lucas simply minuting: 'I think we must do something: it is expected of us . . .'.[138] The lack of a strong case was reflected in Chamberlain's numbered despatch to Hemming of 22 August 1899,[139] informing him of his decision permanently to appoint the full number of nominated members. He made no direct reference to the competency of the elected members, confining himself to the view that the elective system had not been 'fruitful of good results', and that the evidence of recent by-elections indicated that the franchise was not highly valued. He did, however, defend his decision by reference to his parliamentary pledges in connection with Imperial aid. This was misleading in view of the Treasury attitude.[140] Moreover, during the debate in the House of Commons on the Colonial Loans Bill, Chamberlain had declined to pledge himself to appoint the full number of nominated members as a condition for the Colony benefiting under the Colonial Loans Act. In answer to questions he went no further than to state that he would probably appoint them, and that he would not hesitate to do so at once if he thought it necessary.[141] Chamberlain's unwillingness to commit himself in this debate may have reflected his view, expressed two weeks later, that we 'have no excuse' for re-appointing four additional officials 'unless we show a considerable gain to the Colony by

[138] Minute paper 14927. CO 137/607. Minute by C.P.L., 14 Aug. 1899.

[139] Chamberlain to Hemming, No. 313, 22 Aug. 1899. B 14927. CO 137/607.

[140] Chamberlain's implied argument that borrowing under the Colonial Loans Act necessitated a constitutional change seems to have been accepted in Jamaica; yet the Act specifically permitted Barbados to borrow under its terms, a colony which enjoyed full representative government. Local opinion may have been confused by the earlier Colonial Loans Fund Bill, introduced in February 1899 and subsequently abandoned, which included a provision limiting its scope to colonies under the financial control of the secretary of state.

[141] 2 Aug. 1899. *Hansard,* Fourth Series (LXXV), 1158, 1159, 1189, 1190. Chamberlain seems to have had in mind the appointment of officials.

the use of Imperial credit;'[142] Olivier had argued that the financial assistance under consideration did not fulfil this condition.[143] In his reference to parliamentary pledges in his despatch of 22 August, Chamberlain may also have had in mind his more general pledge given in 1898, that a condition for any Imperial grant to a colony would be 'full and absolute control over the taxation and the expenditure'.[144] Yet a steamship subsidy of £5,000 was a small peg on which to hang a constitutional change, and the Treasury on this occasion had not insisted on it as a prior condition for the grant. These considerations probably influenced Olivier, who with Lucas drafted the despatch of 22 August, to put forward as the main justification for appointing the full number of nominated members the broad ground of Barbour's condemnation of the separation of power from responsibility in the Jamaica constitution of 1884:

> It is in fact impossible except where tact and good will and friendly feeling exist in an unusual degree for the government of a country to be carried on when those who are responsible for it are in a permanent minority in the legislature. I decline to allow the Jamaica Government to remain in that position . . .[145]

Chamberlain showed as great caution in the execution of his policy as he had in its formulation. It is true that in a confidential despatch to Hemming, informing him of his decision, he assented to the following passage drafted by Wingfield: 'I do not approve of the present Constitution and I anticipate that it will be necessary at no distant date to reform it . . .';[146] and he himself added to the draft a warning that an irreconcilable attitude on the part of the elected members would leave 'no choice but to revert to Crown Colony Government entirely'. But he also drafted into the despatch the following passage:

[142] Marginal note by J.C., 16 Aug. 1899, on draft of Chamberlain to Hemming, No. 313, 22 Aug. 1899. B 14927. CO 137/607.

[143] See pp. 262–3. The figures quoted are based on a minute by Olivier of 11 Aug. 1899. Minute paper 14927. CO 137/607. In 1899 Jamaica borrowed £130,000 at 2¾ per cent under the Colonial Loans Act, and a further £85,000 in 1900 at 3½ per cent; thus the ultimate gain to Jamaica of borrowing under the Colonial Loans Act was considerably less than Olivier's estimate.

[144] House of Commons, 14 Mar. 1898. *Hansard*, Fourth Series (LIV), 1544.

[145] Chamberlain to Hemming, No. 313, 22 Aug. 1899. B 14927. CO 137/607.

[146] Chamberlain to Hemming, Conf., 22 Aug. 1899. 20413. CO 137/602.

My desire is to use the power now taken as sparingly as possible and only when I consider it absolutely necessary for the benefit of the Colony & the security of its finances.[147]

The differing emphases of the first and third of these passages is unmistakable. Similarly in the numbered despatch informing Hemming of his decision, Chamberlain deleted a condemnation in principle of the constitution, and he agreed to Wingfield's deletion of a reference to the probable necessity at a later date of reducing the size of the Council and abolishing the veto of the elected members. In a final paragraph which he drafted himself, he pledged 'the fullest consideration' for the elected members' views, and his willingness 'to follow their advice in all cases where the responsibility of the Imperial Gov^{t}. does not come in question'.[148] Under pressure from Wingfield, and more especially Lucas who regarded the passage as 'an embarrassing pledge', Chamberlain finally agreed to its being amended to read: '. . . I shall feel it my duty to recognise their position as elected representatives of the community and shall always be ready to give the fullest consideration to any expression of their wishes and views'.[149]

Although Chamberlain was personally convinced of the unsuitability of representative institutions in the West Indies, he had approached their modification in Jamaica with the greatest caution. He did not re-establish complete crown colony government by abolishing the financial veto of the elected members, and it is also significant that, on the evidence of the colonial office minutes, he did not consider raising the franchise qualifications, a course which Hemming and Olivier favoured, and which Barbour had argued might be ultimately necessary. He was more fair-minded than some of his officials and moved more slowly, being conscious of the need for a good case, particularly a parliamentary one; with the exception of Olivier, he was more conciliatory than they were towards local opinion. His policy rested on a firm determination to re-establish crown control, but in a manner which would reduce to a minimum the risk of parliamentary attack, or unrest in Jamaica. This

147 Ibid.

148 See draft of despatch Chamberlain to Hemming, No. 313, 22 Aug. 1899. B 14927. CO 137/607.

149 Ibid.

was a natural course for a politically sensitive secretary of state to follow, but it must also be remembered that the consideration of constitutional change in Jamaica took place against the background of deteriorating Anglo-Boer relations. It is possible that this fact influenced the manner and timing of Chamberlain's policy. By securing crown control in Jamaica when he did, he avoided the danger of a constitutional crisis at a more critical time and in a strategically sensitive colony. By effecting the most moderate change compatible with his purpose and carrying it through in as conciliatory a manner as possible, Chamberlain was protecting himself against parliamentary criticism, and agitation in Jamaica, either of which might have been embarrassing during or immediately preceding a possible Anglo-Boer war.

Chamberlain subsequently held to this firm but conciliatory course. In the autumn of 1899 he declined to accept the advice of Hemming, who now shared Olivier's views regarding the inexpediency of Chamberlain's policy, that the instruction to appoint the four nominated members should be held in abeyance, or alternatively that they should only attend and vote on matters of paramount importance.[150] Nor was he moved by the elected members retiring from the Council in the spring of 1900. They regarded the appointment of the full number of nominated members before a financial programme had been submitted to the Council as a breach of their agreement with Hemming in April 1899,[151] and as a reflection on their good faith and honesty, a view with which Hemming and Olivier sympathized. The elected members were on weaker ground when they contended that Chamberlain's action was also a breach of constitutional convention. They did not define the precise nature of this convention, but in its most convincing form their case rested on the view that while the full number of nominated members might be appointed to carry a matter of paramount importance, it was unconstitutional to do so 'permanently, and in advance, for the general purposes of

[150] Hemming to Chamberlain, Conf., 27 Oct. 1899. 31803. CO 137/605. Hemming to Lucas (personal), 31 Oct. 1899. 31803. CO 137/605. Hemming to Chamberlain, Conf., 28 Oct. 1899. 31804. CO 137/605. Interesting light on Hemming's efforts to reach an accommodation with the elected members is in F. L. Casserly, 'Crown Colony Crisis. The Hemming-Gideon Correspondence', *The Jamaica Historical Review*, vol. 3, 1957–62.

[151] See p. 259.

Government . . .'.[152] There was no ground for this view in Derby's despatch of 28 May 1884 or in the accompanying Order in Council, and it was specifically rejected by Ashley, speaking in the House of Commons on 8 May 1884;[153] it seems, however, to have been shared by colonial office officials in the early 1890s.[154] In January 1900 Olivier, who as an official had strongly opposed the appointment of the full number of nominated members, was appointed colonial secretary in Jamaica. In August, as officer administering the government, he made a further attempt to modify Chamberlain's policy. He proposed that the fifteen *ex-officio* and nominated members should only attend on matters of paramount importance; on other occasions no more than eleven should be present. He also asked for permission to publish Chamberlain's conciliatory but confidential despatch of 2 December 1899, to which reference is made below.[155] Chamberlain declined to make either concession.

But Chamberlain's policy after August 1899 also showed a willingness to conciliate the elected members so long as his central purpose of restoring crown control was not weakened. He informed Hemming confidentially in October 1899 that he might as an experiment 'occasionally absent himself from the Council . . .'.[156] In a further confidential despatch in December, he stated that while no distinction could be made between the four additional nominated members and their nominated colleagues in the Legislative Council, it would 'not be necessary or indeed expedient' to insist at all times on the full attendance of nominated members. It seems that Chamberlain was referring to both official and unofficial nominated members, for he instructed Hemming that heads of departments, in particular, might occasionally absent themselves. He also informed him that not all the additional nominated members need be officials, so long as Hemming could find 'one or more unofficial *gentlemen*' who would accept appointment on condition of supporting

[152] Petition of Jamaica Association (undated). Encl. with Hemming to Chamberlain, No. 624, 26 Oct. 1899. 31723. CO 137/604.

[153] *Hansard*, Third Series (287), 1689.

[154] See pp. 80–1.

[155] For Olivier's proposals see Olivier (O.A.G.) to Chamberlain, Conf., 13 Aug. 1900. 28463. CO 137/612, and Olivier (O.A.G.) to Chamberlain, Conf., 31 Aug. 1900. 30852. CO 137/612.

[156] Chamberlain to Hemming, Conf., 31 Oct. 1899. 27760. CO 137/604.

government measures, and on whose support Hemming could absolutely rely.[157] More generally, Chamberlain wished that the 'course of deliberation and voting' should remain very much the same as before except when it was necessary to use the government majority 'for the public advantage or to prevent breaches of faith by the Govt. . . .'.[158] Chamberlain yielded further ground after the general election of February 1901. In April he informed Hemming in a public despatch that he need not require the presence of all official and nominated members at every meeting of the Council,[159] the instruction he had conveyed confidentially in December 1899. But in an accompanying despatch he stated that 'there must not be the semblance of a suggestion that what has been done will be undone';[160] he therefore proposed that the number absenting themselves should be fewer or more than four, and preferably not the four recently nominated members.

Chamberlain showed a greater willingness to conciliate the elected members than his officials, notably Lucas. This was clearly shown in a personal interview he gave two of the elected members in May 1901.[161] He agreed that if after a fair trial the existing system was shown not to work, he would be prepared to reconsider it in the light of a proposal that four nominated members should be withdrawn, but that the elected members should not vote on matters of paramount importance. It seems that Chamberlain had in mind a trial period of about

[157] Chamberlain to Hemming, Conf., 2 Dec. 1899. 31803. CO 137/605. This conciliatory but confidential despatch was drafted by Olivier. In a numbered despatch of the same date, Chamberlain went no further than saying that with harmonious working of the constitution and reasonable debate and criticism 'it may become unnecessary to insist at all times on the full attendance of all the official members . . .'. Chamberlain to Hemming, No. 502, 2 Dec. 1899. 30236. CO 137/604. The practice of officials absenting themselves from the Council was followed during the session of 1900.

In February 1900 Hemming filled up the nominated seats by appointing three officials and one unofficial. Of the ten members whom he nominated after the election of 1901, six were unofficials. The proposal that some of the additional nominated members should be unofficials was Herbert's; he was temporarily serving in the Colonial Office as permanent under-secretary. His emphasis on '*gentlemen*' was a characteristic distinction which officials made; it excluded most Jamaicans.

[158] Chamberlain to Hemming, Conf., 2 Dec. 1899. 31803. CO 137/605.

[159] Chamberlain to Hemming, No. 165, 11 Apr. 1901. 11128. CO 137/618.

[160] Chamberlain to Hemming, Conf., 11 Apr. 1901. 11128. CO 137/618.

[161] D. S. Gideon and Dr. J. Johnston. For an account of this interview see minute paper 14474. CO 137/618.

a year, but in February 1902 he was of the opinion that a fair trial had not yet been given to the existing arrangements. In the same interview Chamberlain also showed willingness to reconsider the parochial qualification for legislative council membership established by the Order in Council of 1895.[162] He was influenced against this course, however, by the urgent representations of Hemming and the advice of his officials. Hemming argued that if the clause was repealed 'Kingston Lawyers & newspaper editors of a low type'[163] would be elected, and he was particularly apprehensive of the election of Dr. Love, the negro editor of the *Jamaica Advocate*,[164] an able but 'most dangerous' person who would stir up racial feeling.

The resignation of some and the non-attendance of others of the elected members failed to win any further concessions from Chamberlain. Yet even the extent of the concessions which he made is revealing when seen against the background of the harder line often advised by Lucas, the failure of the elected members to act together, and their inability to secure significant support in Jamaica or England. The elected member's lack of unanimity precluded effective collective action such as resignation from the Council. Their stand did not command the sympathy of many of the larger owners of property in Jamaica, and being with one exception white they seem to have been unwilling or unable effectively to agitate the black population, who remained largely indifferent to the constitutional issue. They relied on securing support in the House of Commons, but between 1899 and 1903 only one question was asked on the Jamaica constitution, which Chamberlain was able to answer by reference to the parliamentary papers which he had laid on the table of the House. The views of one member who visited the West Indies in 1899[165] cannot be taken as typical of the House, but it is significant that for Sir C. Quilter,[166] as for Lucas, good government and crown

[162] See pp. 87–8.

[163] Hemming to Ommaney (personal), 4 May 1901. Filed with 14474. CO 137/618.

[164] See p. 64.

[165] Compare also the views of Henry Walker, p. 236 and footnote 55, p. 243.

[166] Member of parliament for Sudbury with business interests in the West Indies. No evidence has been seen to suggest that Quilter's views were especially influential with Chamberlain. There are several of his letters in the Chamberlain papers.

government were synonymous. He informed Chamberlain in January 1899 that one of the essential conditions for 'the progress and prosperity' of the West Indies, and 'the gradual improvement of the coloured race, is that the Government of the Colonies should not be allowed to drift into their hands'. Moreover, Jamaica 'must become in the event of a Panama Canal a highly important strategical base, and the Government should be one that would offer no impediment to Imperial necessities'.[167] Although the strategic importance of Jamaica in the event of the completion of the Panama Canal was stressed by others at this time,[168] it seems probable that this consideration weighed less with the British government than in the early 1880s. The Hay–Pauncefote Treaty of 1902, which conceded the building and control of the Panama Canal to the United States, reflected both better relations with that country and the small value placed by Britain on her interests in the Caribbean,[169] attitudes which were further emphasized by the almost complete withdrawal of the West Indian squadron in 1905 and the running down of the St. Lucia naval base.[170] The strategic importance of Trinidad as a source of oil within the Empire was to be in the future. As late as 1909 the value of exports of crude petroleum from Trinidad was £27; in the same year the first flotilla of ocean-going destroyers wholly dependent on oil was completed.[171]

The inappropriateness of representative institutions for non-white races, and Imperial considerations were the guiding principles of Chamberlain's policy; marked sensitivity to parliamentary and local opinion shaped its implementation. Chamberlain's emphasis on distinctions of race as an impedi-

[167] 'Notes on a Visit to some of the West Indian Islands'. January 1899. Filed with minute paper 9992. CO 318/298.

[168] For example, Sir Nevile Lubbock, *The Present Position of Our West Indian Colonies*. A Paper read before the Liverpool Chamber of Commerce, 10 Dec. 1900 (R.C.S. Lib. pamphlet $\frac{7}{1}$), p. 4.

[169] See A. E. Campbell, *Great Britain and the United States, 1895–1903* (London, 1960).

[170] See, in particular, A. J. Balfour in the House of Commons, 11 May 1905. *Hansard*, Fourth Series (146), 77–78; also 151–2. He stressed the reduced strategic importance of the West Indies, in which he saw no likelihood of a major naval engagement between European powers.

[171] For British policy on the naval use and procurement of oil, see W. S. Churchill, House of Commons, 17 July 1913. *Hansard*, Fifth Series (LV), 1465–82.

ment to constitutional advance was not, on the evidence of the colonial office minutes, shared by his predecessors; as a policy-maker he was more conscious of being 'face to face with Imperial Questions'.

Section 5

The Executive Councils

1880–1903

9

THE DEVELOPMENT OF THE EXECUTIVE COUNCIL

A cautious advance

THE spirit of the 'new departure' led in the early 1880s to a colonial office reconsideration of the membership and function of the executive councils. The main role of the executive council was to advise the governor, and this was clearly established in the latter's instructions.[1] He was bound to consult it on all important matters unless the public interest would suffer or the urgency of the decision prevented it. Although a governor could reject the majority advice of his council, he had to inform the secretary of state of this as soon as possible with the reasons for his decision. In such a case every member had the right to have the grounds of his contrary advice fully recorded in the minutes, copies of which were forwarded to the Colonial Office twice yearly. Thus in theory the Office should have been aware when a governor acted contrary to the advice of the four or five senior officials who normally formed his executive council. In practice, this check was weakened by the degree to which some governors departed from the letter of their instructions regarding consultation.[2]

So long as the main role of the executive council was limited to a formal channel of consultation between governor and senior officials, there was no case for extending its membership to unofficials. Indeed, in view of the confidential matters which might be discussed, there were strong reasons for not so doing. The general trend of colonial policy in the 1870s, to reassert or maintain official control in the West Indian colonies, reinforced these considerations. Thus in 1876 Carnarvon decided that the local executive councils of the Leeward Islands should com-

[1] The executive councils also had other functions such as the hearing of petitions and the suspension of public officers.

[2] See p. 285.

prise only officials; the colonial office view was summarized by Charles Cox, the head of the West India department, who minuted: 'Except under peculiar circumstances I would never have any but officials in the Executive Councils.'[3] Kimberley applied the same policy to the Windward Islands. For example, in 1881 he rejected a proposal by the administrator of Tobago to add an unofficial member to the Executive Council, though he was subsequently forced to concede the principle since the administrator had made a provisional appointment without reference to the Colonial Office. In 1880 St. Vincent and St. Lucia, of the remaining Windwards, had unofficial members in the Executive Council.[4] Knutsford thus summarized the policy of the Colonial Office in July 1882:

> . . . it might be taken as finally decided that, except, perhaps, in some very special case, an Executive Council should be entirely composed of officials with whom the Governor could advise [*sic*] confidentially.[5]

A proposal to reverse the policy of confining the membership of executive councils to officials was made by Sir Henry Norman, the governor of Jamaica, in July 1884. The Jamaica 'Executive Council', known as the Privy Council, comprised, in addition to the governor, the officer commanding the troops, the colonial secretary, the attorney-general, and the director of public works. Norman argued that the appointment of one or more 'non-official gentlemen' 'would add strength to the Government and be a very popular measure'.[6] His proposal to appoint George Stiebel, a wealthy Negro, suggests that he may also have been influenced by the wish to have the advice of a representative of the Negro population, no Negro candidates having come forward to contest the pending general election. Herbert regarded the admission of an unofficial to the confi-

[3] Berkeley to Carnarvon, No. 15, 24 Jan. 1876. 1976. CO 152/125. Minute by C.C., 29 Feb. 1876. This policy was not fully implemented, for in 1880 there were unofficial members in the Executive Councils of Antigua, Montserrat, Nevis, and Dominica.

[4] See Robinson to Kimberley, Conf., 14 Sept. 1880. 16062. CO 321/39. Also the *Colonial Office List* for 1880.

[5] Knutsford, then Sir Henry Holland, was speaking as a private member in a House of Commons debate on the Malta constitution, 28 July 1882. *Hansard*, Third Series (273), 93. He could, however, draw on his experience in the Colonial Office where he had already served as legal adviser and assistant under-secretary.

[6] Norman to Derby, Conf., 30 July 1884. 13941. CO 137/516.

dential discussions of a colonial government as 'very dangerous'; in pressing that Norman be asked to reconsider his proposal, he revealed the importance which he attached to the question, for he had previously shown himself most anxious to strengthen Norman's hand by accepting his advice on all matters. Advised by Herbert, Derby informed Norman that his proposal 'would be virtually an alteration of the principles of the Constitution . . .'. There were, moreover,

> grave objections to admitting into the confidential deliberations of the Government gentlemen who are under no official obligation to support its policy . . .[7]

Norman deferred to this view, but he did not agree with it for it conflicted with his concept of semi-representative government as a partnership between officials and non-officials. With his encouragement the elected members of the Legislative Council unanimously passed a resolution in April 1887, favouring the change which he had recommended in 1884. Norman reported that they felt strongly that one or two unofficial persons who were not elected members should be appointed to the Privy Council. He supported the proposal on the grounds that it 'would be useful as well as popular',[8] that few very confidential matters came before the Privy Council, and that he did not anticipate a breach of confidence on the part of any unofficial whom he might nominate. The appointment should be in the first instance for a maximum of five years. These arguments, together with the fact that Norman had publicly favoured the change, convinced Knutsford and his advisers of the expediency of the proposal. Although the precedents were not mentioned in the minutes, it is also probable that the Colonial Office was influenced by the fact that unofficial members had been admitted to the Grenada and Tobago Executive Councils in 1885 and 1886,[9] in each case to strengthen what were regarded locally and in the Colonial Office as weak Councils.

Knutsford's concession of 1887, by which two unofficials who

[7] Derby to Norman, Conf., 28 Aug. 1884. 13941. CO 137/516.

[8] Norman to Holland, Conf., 5 May 1887. 10425. CO 137/530. Also Norman to Holland, No. 111, 23 Apr. 1887. 9374. CO 137/530.

[9] Stanley to Sendall, Conf., 19 Oct. 1885. 17440. CO 321/87, and Granville to Sendall, Tobago No. 23, 17 Apr. 1886. 4855. CO 321/98.

were not members of the Legislative Council were appointed to the Privy Council,[10] was modified on the advice of Norman's successor, Blake, in 1896. The increase in the number of elected members in the Legislative Council to fourteen necessitated the appointment of four additional nominated members,[11] of whom Blake advised that two should be unofficials, namely Dr. J. Pringle and Lt.-Col. J. C. Ward; they were also at that time the two unofficial members of the Privy Council. Chamberlain's assent to this proposal established the precedent in Jamaica of nominated unofficial members of the Legislative Council sitting in the Privy Council, a precedent which had been already established in the Executive Councils of both the Leeward and Windward Islands.

The final step in the development of the Executive Councils in crown colonies was the introduction of elected members of the Legislative Council, a precedent established in Mauritius in 1887.[12] This change, in relation to Jamaica, was proposed by Olivier in December 1899,[13] shortly before he left for Jamaica as colonial secretary. He argued that the appointment of two of the best of the elected members to the Privy Council would strengthen it; they were better qualified for membership by their public position than the existing unofficials in the Privy Council, who, he claimed, were offered seats in order to induce them to sit as nominated members in the Legislative Council.[14] He further argued that the appointment would conciliate the elected members, and be proof of Chamberlain's

[10] Holland to Norman, No. 146, 29 June 1887. 9374. CO 137/530.

[11] See pp. 86–7.

[12] I am indebted to Dr. Lester Crook for this point.

[13] See minute of 8 Dec. 1899. Filed with minute paper 35760. CO 137/608.

[14] Olivier probably had in mind Chamberlain's instruction to Hemming of December 1899 (see p. 269) that he might appoint to the Legislative Council nominated *unofficial* members so long as he could rely on their loyal support for government measures; they might also be appointed to the Privy Council if this, as Chamberlain supposed, would make it easier to find such men. Acting on these instructions, Hemming appointed Rear-Admiral W. H. Henderson to the Legislative Council and the Privy Council in February 1900. Pringle and Ward, the other two unofficial members of the Privy Council, also supported the government in the legislature; but in their case Olivier's criticism was less apposite since Blake had appointed them to the Privy Council before he had obtained Chamberlain's assent in 1896 to their nomination as unofficial members of the Legislative Council. It does seem, however, that the Jamaica practice of unofficial nominated members of the Legislative Council sitting in the Privy Council was mainly a device for ensuring their support for government policy and measures.

wish to carry them with him, if possible, on all matters; it would be a more satisfactory way of gaining their co-operation than the existing system of *ad hoc* committees, or compacts between governor and elected members on particular questions. Lucas, Herbert, and Chamberlain all regarded the proposal favourably, but the latter wished for a second and more critical opinion based on local experience. Olivier's suggestion was therefore submitted to Norman, who opposed it on two main grounds.[15] Firstly, the change would impair the efficiency of the Privy Council since the elected members might insist, as they were entitled to do, on discussing matters such as the estimates which previously for lack of time had not been brought before the Privy Council. Moreover, if they joined the Privy Council with the idea of opposing the government, there would be 'two more or less unmanageable bodies instead of one'. Secondly, Norman questioned whether the change would conciliate the elected members since it was probable that they would regard their two colleagues on the Privy Council as 'bribed' by the government. Neither Herbert, Selborne, nor Chamberlain were convinced by Norman's arguments, but they deferred to his opinion, while leaving it open for Olivier to raise the matter again after first-hand experience of Jamaica.

It is probable that Olivier influenced Hemming's despatch of 8 February 1901,[16] in which he favoured the addition of a maximum of two elected members to the Privy Council. He argued that the concession would be of advantage in carrying on the administration and in the considering of prospective legislation. Further, by taking such men into the confidence of the government, the feeling of the elected members that they were treated as an opposition would be dispelled and they would be less likely, as a body, to oppose the government. Although his advisers were divided on the merits of this proposal, Chamberlain retained an open mind, Hemming being instructed to consider the matter further in the light of a summary of the views put forward by Olivier and Norman in late 1899. Hemming did so, but his opinion and the reasons for it remained unchanged. The proposal would, in his view, permit the mutual exchange of views between elected members

[15] Minute of Sir Henry Norman, 18 Dec. 1899. Filed with minute paper 35760.

[16] Hemming to Chamberlain, Conf., 8 Feb. 1901. 7498. CO 137/617.

and government before, for example, legislation was introduced into the Legislative Council. By taking the elected members more closely into the confidence of the government, a feeling would be induced among them that they were being treated as its advisers and not its opponents. If the elected members who were appointed consistently opposed the government in the Legislative Council, or voted against measures which they had previously supported in the Privy Council, their appointment could be revoked.[17] These arguments convinced Chamberlain and his advisers, Hemming being authorized to offer a seat in the Privy Council to one elected member of the Legislative Council.[18] This concession was not taken advantage of in the period under review.[19]

In British Guiana there was no formal executive council before the constitutional changes of 1891, the Court of Policy acting in both an administrative and a legislative role. In 1883 Wingfield drew attention to the disadvantages of this situation,[20] and, in particular, to the lack of consultation between governor and officials; as a result the latter were called on to support government measures in the Court of Policy of which they previously knew nothing, the government secretary and attorney-general being in practice the only advisers of the governor. Both he and Herbert agreed that there would be administrative advantages if matters to be submitted to the Court of Policy were first fully and confidentially discussed by the leading officials in an executive council. Irving opposed this change on the grounds that such a derogation of the administrative powers of the Court of Policy would be regarded with hostility by local opinion as a breach of the constitution; it would stimulate demands for representative government, and damage the government's relations with the elected members

[17] Hemming to Chamberlain, Conf., 18 Apr. 1901. 15207. CO 137/618.

[18] Chamberlain to Hemming, Conf., 10 May 1901. 15207. CO 137/618.

[19] The reasons for this are not clear but it seems probable that no elected member was willing to accept the appointment, which would have limited his freedom of action and speech, and, as Norman foresaw, probably lowered his standing in the eyes of his colleagues. It is significant that in April 1887 the elected members of the Jamaica Legislative Council had pressed specifically for an unofficial member in the Privy Council not drawn from their own number. See p. 279.

[20] N. Darnell Davis to Wingfield, 2 July 1883. 11434. CO 111/429. The letter concerned the audit of the British Guiana accounts, Davis having been acting auditor-general. See minute by E.W., 24 July 1883, on this paper.

and with the community at large. Derby and his advisers deferred to this view, and they accepted Irving's suggestion that the official members of the Court of Policy should be treated by the governor as an advisory council. It seems that this informal 'Executive Council' subsequently met and that minutes were kept, but it fell far short of a true executive council; it was not until 1886 that Irving directed that all business coming before the Court of Policy should be previously laid before its official members. This move seems to have been a concession to Charles Bruce, the lieutenant-governor and government secretary, who complained strongly to Granville in 1885 of the engrossment of government business by the attorney-general.[21] The bitter dispute between Bruce and the attorney-general, Haynes Smith, was both personal and political, but one factor underlying it was Irving's failure to consult Bruce and other leading officials on important financial and legislative matters.[22] It was with this in mind that Stanhope specifically instructed Irving, in a confidential despatch of September 1886, to submit all business to the official members of the Court of Policy before its introduction into either Court, and to report to the secretary of state in the event of his acting contrary to the opinions of a majority of them.[23]

The constitutional reforms of 1891 provided Knutsford with an opportunity to place this arrangement on a more formal basis by transferring the executive functions of the Court of Policy to an executive council. Gormanston had proposed this change on the grounds that the Court of Policy was ill-suited to an executive role, its procedure being slow and its rapid change of personnel precluding the discussion of confidential business. He recommended that an executive council 'with the usual powers and functions' should be established; he claimed that there would be opposition in the colony to the change if unofficials were not included.[24] His advice was readily accepted in the Colonial Office, Knutsford informing him that an

[21] Under British Guiana law the attorney-general held a unique position in the constitution, for apart from his normal legal duties he ranked after the governor and before the lieutenant-governor in the legislature, where he had charge of government measures. This anomalous position was ended in 1888.

[22] For this controversy see Irving to Granville, Sep., 23 May 1886. 10267. CO 111/435.

[23] Stanhope to Irving, Conf., 8 Sept. 1886. 15042. CO 111/436.

[24] Gormanston to Knutsford, No. 4, 3 Jan. 1890. 1098. CO 111/455.

executive council 'on the usual model'[25] should be established, comprising the government secretary and the attorney-general, and such other members as the Crown might from time to time appoint,[26] a phrase which permitted the appointment of unofficials. The actual composition finally agreed between Gormanston and the Colonial Office was the governor, the government secretary, and the attorney-general as *ex-officio* members, the auditor-general and the immigration agent general as nominated officials, and three unofficials who would sit for a five-year term subject to re-appointment. In order to strengthen the Council the receiver-general and comptroller of customs were added in December 1895.

None of the constitutional changes effected by Ordinance 1 of 1891 aroused more general dissatisfaction in British Guiana than the transfer of the Court of Policy's administrative functions to an executive council.[27] It was argued in the colony that the change had increased the power of the governor at the expense of the legislature, for not only did he choose the nominated members of the Council but he could also ignore its advice; the change was further criticized on the grounds that the nominated members of the Executive Council need not sit in the Court of Policy, and that the Council's proceedings were secret. The resentment of non-planting opinion was heightened by Gormanston's choice of unofficials who were all directly or indirectly connected with the planting interest; none had seats in the Court of Policy. Their influence was widely believed in the colony to be an important factor in the careful regard for the interests of the planters shown by both Gormanston, and his successor, Sir Charles Lees. When one of these unofficials resigned in 1895, the government secretary informed Wingfield that the public attached 'much importance' to his successor. In spite of this public concern

[25] Knutsford to Gormanston, Conf., 30 Apr. 1890. 1098. CO 111/455.

[26] This provision, which was in the usual form, was included in Additional Instructions to the Governor, 5 Mar. 1891. CO 380/147/3. The lieutenant-governor, if there was one, was also to be a member. See also S. 31, Ord. 1, 1891 (CO 118/8), transferring the executive and administrative functions of the Court of Policy to the Executive Council, and Supplementary Letters Patent, 5 Mar. 1891, establishing an Executive Council. CO 380/147/2.

[27] See, for instance, A. R. F. Webber, *Centenary History and Handbook of British Guiana* (Georgetown, 1931), pp. 309–10. Also James Rodway, *History of British Guiana*, vol. 3 (Georgetown, 1894), p. 275.

and of the adverse reaction of the Colonial Office, Lees chose B. H. Jones, a prominent planter, to fill the vacant seat. This policy was reversed by Hemming, who in 1896 advised the appointment of D. M. Hutson, a coloured barrister with considerable gold mining interests, in place of J. J. Dare, a partner in Booker and Co. His successor, Sendall, further widened the unofficial representation by recommending the appointment in 1901 of J. H. de Jonge, a leading merchant and shipowner with large gold interests, in place of W. A. Wolseley, a plantation owner. Public interest in the composition of the British Guiana Executive Council reflected its more active role compared with that of the Privy Council in Jamaica. The former met regularly, but it seems that Blake seldom consulted his Privy Council.[28] Hemming, who succeeded him in Jamaica, contrasted his experience in British Guiana with that in Jamaica where, he stated, it was the custom to hold Privy Council meetings only when really necessary; nor were the secretary of state's numbered despatches laid before the Privy Council as provided for in colonial regulations. This divergence of local practice, which in the case of Jamaica was corrected after 1898 on Chamberlain's instructions, qualifies any generalization on the significance of changes in the composition of the Executive Councils.

In general, the admission of unofficial members to the Executive Councils was made either to strengthen the Councils in the small islands where there were few officials of ability, or as a means of consulting unofficial opinion before legislation and policy were determined. The arrangement was also used by Jamaica governors to ensure the support of nominated unofficials in the Legislative Council. The more significant concession, whereby elected members of the Legislative Council were appointed to the Executive Council, aimed to draw the elected members closer to the government. It is probable that this aim could only be achieved when relations were already reasonably harmonious. In such cases the presence of elected members in the Executive Council was useful, for they could be consulted prior to, and might assist the passage of, legisla-

[28] See, for instance, para. 59 of Sir David Barbour's Report on the Finances of Jamaica, and Olivier's comment on this on minute paper 14927, CO 137/607. Also Hemming to Chamberlain, Conf., 11 Sept. 1899. 26151. CO 137/603.

tion. But it seems unlikely that the concession, had it been implemented in Jamaica, would have created harmonious relations between government and elected members while there was no basis of mutual trust between them; so long as the elected members, as a body, regarded themselves as an opposition, their privy council colleagues would have had to dissociate themselves from them, or their position on the Privy Council would have been untenable. Norman's governorship had shown that it was possible to win the co-operation of the elected members, but only by closely identifying them with government, by deferring to their views whenever possible, and by treating them with every mark of social respect. The admission of elected members to the Privy Council might have been helpful in this context, but only if part of a larger political and social readjustment on the part of governors which neither Blake nor Hemming seemed able to make.

By 1903 unofficial members sat in the Executive Councils of most of the West Indian colonies, but a notable exception was Trinidad. In part, this reflected the fact that no governor proposed the change until 1897 and like many policy decisions in this period it was normally one which was implemented on the governor's advice. It is true that among the resolutions agreed to by the 'Reform Committee' of 1892[29] was one favouring an executive council of the governor, three officials, and two members nominated by the governor from among the elected members of the Legislative Council. The secretary of the 'Reform Committee', commenting on this proposal, referred to the apparent success of the change in other colonies; Harris, when minuting the reform petition and resolutions, advised the appointment of an unofficial to the Executive Council, the practice, in his view, having worked well in other colonies. But no formal proposal was received from Trinidad until 1897 when Jerningham suggested the appointment of two unofficial members of the Legislative Council to the Executive Council. Besides giving 'general satisfaction', Jerningham argued that the measure would draw the government closer to the Legislative Council and give the Executive Council the benefit of local advice and experience.[30] Although the principle of the

[29] See p. 211.

[30] Jerningham to Chamberlain, No. 229, 23 June 1897. 14812. CO 295/379.

change was not contested in the Colonial Office, Chamberlain was unwilling to implement it before the West India Royal Commission of 1897 had reported. In October 1903 Sir Alfred Moloney recommended the appointment of two unofficials to the Executive Council, one to be elected from their number by the nominated unofficials of the Legislative Council, the other to be nominated by the Trinidad Chamber of Commerce.[31] Moloney was writing in the aftermath of the Port of Spain water riots, and was influenced by the division between government and public which the riots had underlined and on which the commission enquiring into them had adversely commented. His recommended method of selection was a new departure to which colonial office officials objected. More generally, a lack of confidence in the governor, and the fear that a change might be interpreted as a concession to violence, seem to have influenced the decision to postpone a step which on other grounds was generally regarded in the Colonial Office as useful but not of large significance. It is interesting that H. C. Bourne, an official of the West India department who had served in Trinidad as registrar-general and auditor-general, laid more stress on the need to dispel 'the sense of social suppression from which the creoles suffer',[32] by regulating the precedence in the Legislative Council according to seniority of appointment rather than official or unofficial status. Few officials who had spent their working lives in the Colonial Office could have written that.

[31] Moloney to Secretary of State for the Colonies, Conf., 7 Oct. 1903. 38738. CO 295/419.

[32] Ibid. Minute by H.C.B., 26 Oct. 1903. He was using 'creole' in the broader sense of Trinidad-born.

CONCLUSION

THE coincidence of political unrest in the early 1880s in Jamaica, British Guiana, and Trinidad suggests common causes. For these colonies the last three decades of the nineteenth century were years of important economic and social change. The weakening of the economic base on which the political supremacy of the planters rested created conditions in which that supremacy was more easily and naturally questioned by the politically under-represented merchant and professional classes. The same years also witnessed the growth of peasant proprietaries. These parallel economic developments emphasized the problem of the relation of labour to capital which lay at the heart of West Indian politics, the most important aspect of which was the planters' struggle to command the labour market. The development of education and communications permitted this, and other questions, to be debated more widely after 1880; the following decade witnessed the beginnings of a cheaper, more popular press with a rising circulation, and the stirring of political interest among the artisan classes. These years also saw the emergence of a native-born professional class, mainly lawyers educated in England and familiar with its political ideas and methods. They, and others, showed a keen awareness of the importance of press and public meeting, and of the methods of influencing official, parliamentary, and public opinion in Britain. Their trust in the efficacy of such appeals and the sophistication of some of their methods contrasts with the lack of public and parliamentary interest in their cause.

Newspaper editors played a crucial role in expressing and encouraging political discontent, through their editorials, their command of a printing press, and their reporting of constitutional agitation and change in the colony and abroad. Reformers were encouraged by their reading of liberal developments in Britain, Ireland, India and elsewhere in the Empire; reports of agitation in the West Indies helped to foster intercolonial feeling. Newspaper coverage suggests a close interest in the United Kingdom among the reading public, events and influences in the mother country, and elsewhere, contributing to shape their attitudes to political and social problems in the colonies. The effects of such outside influences were conflicting. Not only did some reformers draw encouragement from the policies of Gladstone's second administration. The same apprehension of disruptive social forces, which historians have recently emphasized in England after about 1870,[1] was shared by the propertied classes in the three colonies, and notably in Trinidad, where in the late 1880s it contributed to a withdrawal of support for reform. Increasing emphasis on nationalism and race in England was matched by growing hostility to aliens and rising racial feeling in colonial politics. The liberal social convictions of reformers such as Palache, Rostant, and Goodwille were shaped by influences and events in Britain, Ireland, and the United States.

Specific grievances against crown colony government further stimulated political interest and activity. A central cause of discontent in Jamaica and Trinidad in the early 1880s was rising government expenditure at a time when the buoyancy of public revenue was affected by adverse economic conditions. The restiveness of the propertied and tax-paying classes was directed particularly against the public works departments, which symbolized for many reformers, particularly in Trinidad, the incompetence and extravagance of crown colony government. These departments were also largely staffed from England, and hostility towards expatriate officials, especially on account of their alleged social arrogance, was widespread among reformers. But emphasis on common causes should not disguise the different character of the three movements. The reform movement in British Guiana owed least to the stimulus of outside events or dissatisfaction with incompetent and extravagant administration. In origin, it was the reaction of merchants and professional men against the planters' privileged economic and fiscal position. Reformers united on the need to open up the country and diversify the economy, a condition for which, they argued, was a widening of political representation. The planters skilfully split the opposition by wooing the

[1] See, for instance, Paul Smith, *Disraelian Conservatism and Social Reform* (London, 1967), footnote 2, p. 182.

more substantial merchants. Yet even the demands of the radical reformers were moderate, reflecting their social background and their dependence in many cases on the prosperity of the sugar industry. Little racial feeling seems to have informed the earlier phase of the movement, political divisions and lines of colour only beginning to coincide during the 1890s.

The political influence of the Jamaica planters was weakening in the 1870s, and their agitation for an unofficial nominated majority in the Legislative Council was an attempt to strengthen it. In seeking to play a leading part in the broader movement for more radical reform resulting from the *Florence* affair, they were pursuing the same end by different means. Between 1882 and 1884 a consensus of planting, commercial, and professional opinion, both white and coloured, which has no parallel in this period in British Guiana or Trinidad, favoured the concession of representative government or a modification of it. But the unity of this opinion was fragile, resting as it did on an ill-judged colonial office decision. Subsequently there was a withdrawal of political interest by part of the more substantial propertied class, who seem to have come to regret the change from crown colony government. Few major issues united Jamaica politicians, personal interests and, by the early 1890s, lines of colour often dictating political attitudes. Although the availability and quality of Negro labour was widely discussed in the colony, the central problem of the relation of labour to capital was less urgently debated than in British Guiana or Trinidad. Much remained to be done to improve the economic and social condition of the peasantry, but few elected members took up the task with urgency or conviction.

The Trinidad reform movement shared common characteristics with both the British Guiana and Jamaica movements. Trinidad reformers in the early 1890s showed the same consciousness of their common identity as Trinidadians, as coloured Jamaicans showed in their slogan of 'Jamaica for the Jamaicans'. As in Jamaica, the Trinidad agitation was in origin a broad-based protest against allegedly incompetent and extravagant administration, of which there is much evidence, and as in Jamaica substantial propertied elements withdrew from the agitation though at an earlier stage. The grievance against extravagant and incompetent administration was reinforced in the early 1890s by hostility to the sugar interest and by signs of racial antagonism between coloured and white, though on this last point the evidence is less strong than in Jamaica. In British Guiana political controversy between the planting and non-planting interests centred on the need to open up the country by improved communications and more liberal crown lands regulations. By contrast, in Trinidad Indian immigration was more frequently attacked by reformers hostile to the plantocracy. But the main stimulus for the reform movement in its later stages probably came not from such hostility or from colour antagonism, which not all reformers shared, but from the seeming anomaly of one of the leading British West Indian colonies with an entirely nominated unofficial element in the Legislative Council. The Trinidad reformers appealed primarily to precedent.

The origin of these movements was mainly autochthonous, their methods largely imitative, and their character as various and complex as the societies from which they sprang and the individuals that composed them. But emphasis on the origin and nature of the movements should not obscure the background of widespread political apathy. The evidence suggests that there was little political interest among the mass of the people, and that, with the exception of the Jamaica agitation between 1882 and 1884, the movements for constitutional change described in this study were supported by only a small part of the propertied and educated classes. No generalization can do justice to their complexity, but in the main they were narrowly based, middle-class movements. 'Middle-class' is used in this context primarily to describe merchants, professional men, shopkeepers, and clerks. Its upper and lower limits are indistinct, but in general the group which it represents was one whose interest was not coincident with that of the planters, but whose economic and social position inclined it to only a moderate shift in the balance of political power. Yet even this group embraced a wide range of views. The early leading reformers, particularly in Jamaica and Trinidad, could be regarded as conservative liberals with a considerable stake in property. They charged crown government with incompetence and extravagance; they demanded retrenchment and reform. As the period progresses there is a tendency in all three colonies for a withdrawal of support by the more cautious and substantial propertied elements, and for the movements increasingly to draw their main strength from what has been aptly called in the context of early Victorian England, the 'Middling' or 'Uneasy' class.[2] The latter group, comprising especially small shopkeepers and aspiring but under-employed barristers, had stronger social and economic motives for change. Yet even this analysis should not be pressed too far for prominent in the later stages of the Trinidad and Jamaica reform movements were such eminent and successful barristers as Alcazar, Brown, and Stern. Parallel with the withdrawal of propertied elements, there is a tendency in all three colonies as the period progresses for white to give way to coloured leadership, and for Negroes to begin to achieve political prominence. Here again generalization is difficult for the time-scale varies in each colony. Coloured men came to the fore within this period first in Jamaica; by the early 1890s they were prominent in the political reform movements in each of the colonies, though not to the exclusion of such local-born creoles of European stock as Alcazar. Negroes seem to have emerged earliest in this period in British Guiana where by the middle 1880s Negro barristers were playing an active political role. A few Negroes were also prominent in Trinidad in the second reform movement. In Jamaica they seem to have made little impact in the period between 1880 and 1895, or indeed in the years immediately after, though Dr. Love is a notable exception.

In general, those who played a leading part in the reform movements sought more open societies, but like other middle-class reformers most were determined that their own position should not be eroded from below. They did not as a rule invoke democratic slogans or claim to represent the people. They mostly favoured restrictive franchises and high qualifications for membership of legislatures, and they showed, with few exceptions, small concern for the economic and social condition of the bulk of the population, the safeguarding of whose welfare was the self-imposed responsibility of the Colonial Office. Its

[2] R. S. Neale describes the class as including *petit bourgeois*, lesser professional men, and other educated persons, or literates, who like the professional men were often underemployed. See R. S. Neale, 'Class and class-consciousness in early nineteenth century England: three classes or five?' *Victorian Studies*, vol. XII, 1968, no. 1.

reaction to their political demands therefore throws valuable light on its attitude to crown colony government in the British West Indies in the last decades of the nineteenth century.

Colonial office confidence in crown colony government was barely diminished in the early 1880s, in spite of doubts regarding the availability of good governors and evidence of maladministration. It was the pressure of events which dictated the new departure in Jamaica. The constitutional deadlock following the *Florence* vote illustrated that crown colony government, with a purely nominated unofficial element in the Legislative Council, was unworkable if a large part of educated and propertied opinion withdrew its support. Officials recognized this, and it was primarily on these grounds that they recommended the introduction of elected members. But they also hoped that the change would lead to a more vigorous and efficient legislature, which would be a force for economy. Derby agreed with his officials, but on broader grounds. His liberal opinions were shared by Gladstone, and seem to have influenced Office opinion, which between 1884 and 1886 showed greater receptiveness to proposals for constitutional advance in the crown colonies than at any other time in this period. Officials' acceptance in 1884 of Norman's scheme for semi-representative government in Jamaica illustrated this. It also illustrated how pressing administrative expediency shaped important policy decisions and obscured longer-term considerations. Officials did not foresee the impact elsewhere in the British West Indies of constitutional advance in Jamaica. They also underestimated the difficulties of re-establishing an official majority, because they failed to appreciate the political and social pressures to which the governor of a crown colony was exposed. Herbert had hoped that the elected members would prove a force for economy, but except during the early sessions of the Council they did not do so until after 1897; indeed their attitude to expenditure and taxation in the early 1890s facilitated Blake's imprudent financial policy by enabling him to shield himself behind them. Nor did the Colonial Office foresee that the management of the Council would be made more difficult by the inability of some local officials to hold their own in debate with the elected members, who were often able lawyers.

Derby and his advisers may have conceded more in Jamaica than they intended, but it is also clear that they were manœuvring within a field limited by their conviction of the inappropriateness of responsible government for Jamaica, and of the inexpediency of representative government which did not retain for the Crown a reserve power of legislation. Between 1880 and 1895 the retention of such a power remained a cardinal point of policy; only in 1886, under the influence of Norman's successful governorship, did the Colonial Office contemplate its surrender in Jamaica. It regarded such a power as necessary for the protection of Imperial interests, of which a principal one was almost certainly Britain's strategic interest in Jamaica, and which also included, on the evidence of the Jamaica papers, the fulfilment of international and treaty obligations, the maintenance of law and order, and the safeguarding of Jamaica's public credit from breach of faith by the colonial government. Considerations of foreign policy, and of the safety and control of the Indian immigrant population were, in Herbert's view, additional reasons for securing a more complete power of legislation in British Guiana.

On the evidence of their minutes, officials did not seek to relate their policy of constitutional change in Jamaica to the central purpose of crown colony government, namely the safeguarding of the welfare of the mass of the population. This role had both a positive and a negative aspect. It has been argued[3] that, in general, conditions were not favourable for the Colonial Office to initiate legislation for the benefit of the unrepresented part of the population, and on the evidence of the colonial office papers a reserve power of legislation was not retained for this purpose in Jamaica. But the constitutional changes both in Jamaica and British Guiana afforded an opportunity to make the passage of such measures more likely by widening the representation in the local legislatures. But although formally acknowledging the need in Jamaica for a really popular franchise extending to all who could intelligently exercise it, the Colonial Office did not press this view, and it accepted a high qualification for membership of the Legislative Council. Even so the elected members proved on certain issues responsive to the needs of the peasantry, though it is significant that

[3] See pp. 2–4.

Wingfield noted this fact with surprise. Certainly a greater change was achieved in this direction in Jamaica than in British Guiana, where the initial effect of the reform of 1891 was to reduce the number of registered voters. But the new departure in Jamaica was not incompatible with the responsibility of the Colonial Office in its second, and mainly negative or supervisory, role of carefully scrutinizing and improving colonial legislation, for it left untouched the veto powers of governor and Crown. Yet so long as the elected members were not representative of all classes the Colonial Office shirked its responsibility if, in order to avoid conflict with the elected members, it deferred to their views on issues which concerned the welfare of the population as a whole. There is evidence in this study that it did so in Jamaica. In British Guiana, the Colonial Office could only adequately protect the interests of the mass of the population by establishing crown control over finance, or by widening the class eligible for election to the Combined Court and largely increasing the electorate which chose them. It was deterred from the first course by fear of parliamentary intervention, and from the second by an unwillingness to risk a fight with the planters, as well as by a lack of faith in the outcome of a radical measure of reform. In short, the practical discharge by the Colonial Office of its responsibility to protect the interests of the mass of the population was only compatible with constitutional advance if either the reformed legislatures were representative of all classes, or if the Colonial Office was willing to precipitate a conflict with the elected members in order to protect the interests of the unrepresented classes. Neither condition was fulfilled in Jamaica between 1884 and 1895, or in British Guiana between 1880 and 1895. In the former colony, officials and secretaries of state acted on the principle that the elected members should not be overridden on a major issue except in defence of Imperial interests or in an emergency involving law and order. In British Guiana, the elected members' control in financial matters could only be overcome by a reform of the Combined Court. It is not clear from the colonial office minutes what issues secretaries of state and officials would have regarded as justifying this extreme course, but a study of colonial policy towards British Guiana between 1880 and 1903 suggests that the general welfare of the unrepresented part of the population was not among them.

The new departure was not seen by secretaries of state or officials as part of a long-term progress by Jamaica towards responsible government, and nor did they regard the changes effected as a precedent for other British West Indian colonies. It was only the impact of these changes on Trinidad opinion which caused the Colonial Office to accept as ultimately inevitable the introduction of elected members into the Trinidad Legislative Council; at no time did they contemplate conceding the veto powers and provisional majority extended to the elected members in Jamaica. There was a departmental disposition, which it is not difficult to appreciate, to stave off a change until the weight of local influential opinion in favour was large, for as Herbert minuted in the context of Jamaica, concessions might ultimately lead to there being hardly a crown colony left.

But if precedent in the West Indies seemed to favour constitutional advance, the trend of opinion in England after the middle 1880s was moving against it.[4] A reaction to Gladstonian liberalism and a growing emphasis on strong government was reflected in a tendency to commend direct rule in India and Egypt, and in a reversal of Liberal policy in the former country and Ireland. Froude popularized these ideas in relation to the West Indies, and questioned the suitability in any form of representative institutions for non-white peoples. His work was influential in the Colonial Office and outside, and probably contributed to the reversal of policy in Trinidad in 1889. Similar currents of thought were reflected in Blake's despatches from Jamaica, with their overtones of contemporary theories of racial evolution and their emphasis on the need for strong paternal government in Negro communities; Blake, like others, was influenced by his reading of events in Haiti. A similar trend of thinking is reflected in Lucas's writings in the early 1890s, and in Harris's minutes from the late 1880s. The significance of Chamberlain's despatch of November 1895, refusing

[4] There were contrary liberal currents, notably C. S. Salmon, *The Caribbean Federation* (London, n.d.; published 1888); Charles Wentworth Dilke, *Problems of Greater Britain* (London, 1890), pp. 203–9 for his views on the West Indies; and Sir Robert Hamilton's report on Dominica, C. 7477. P.P. 1894 (LVII).

reform in Trinidad, lies not only in the fact that it embodied Chamberlain's personal decision taken against the unanimous advice of his officials. In describing the grounds for that decision, Chamberlain also gave official expression to the increasingly widely held view that representative institutions were inappropriate for the non-white tropical dependencies. Similarly the note of racialism and nationalism in Chamberlain's minute on which this despatch was based can be detected in the earlier minutes of Harris and Lambert. Nor do the Jamaica papers suggest that Derby and his officials were indifferent to Imperial considerations, though on the evidence of their minutes Chamberlain and Selborne were more conscious of them and gave them more weight. In short, although there was a change of policy under Chamberlain towards constitutional retrogression in the West Indies, the considerations on which it was based can be traced before 1895. They were not, however, sufficiently strong in Wingfield's mind to override the administrative advantages of introducing elected members into the Trinidad Legislative Council; indeed as late as 1895 he still regarded such a concession as ultimately inevitable. The middle 1880s also witnessed increasing concern in Britain regarding her commercial position, and by the late 1880s officials' minutes, influenced probably by Blake's despatches from Jamaica, lay more stress on the need for stable conditions for British capital. But no evidence has been found that this consideration influenced policy towards constitutional change in the colonies under review. Chamberlain's unwillingness to reform the British Guiana constitution, taken with his deep interest in that colony's development and his first-hand knowledge of capitalists' requirements, are grounds for the opposite view.

The evolution of policy has so far been considered as the outcome mainly of the pressure of immediate events and the background of contemporary thought, but the personal dispositions and values of those shaping policy were also significant. There is ample evidence in this study of the influence of governors on policy. Norman's advice led to the grant of semi-representative government to Jamaica. Irving precipitated the decision to reform the British Guiana constitution, and Gormanston in collusion with the planters largely shaped that change. The equivocal attitude of Robinson and Broome probably delayed constitutional change in Trinidad before 1895. Blake's advice was decisive in the timing of the enlargement of the Jamaica Legislative Council. Of the governors mentioned in this study, only Norman seems to have had faith in representative institutions and the capacity to work them. By a happy blend of tact and firmness he won the confidence and co-operation of the elected members. In contrast to crown government, it was an essential condition for the working of semi-representative government that the elected members should both be treated, and regard themselves, not as an opposition but as partners in government. This involved a difficult readjustment of outlook on both sides. For his part Norman found it easier to make than most governors, because he seems to have felt no antipathy towards local politicians whatever their colour or background. In this he was exceptional. Most governors and colonial officials seem to have had little insight into the pride and susceptibilities of the educated classes in the crown colonies, and this intangible but important shortcoming contributed to the ill-working of semi-representative government in Jamaica after 1888, as well as of crown colony government in Trinidad. Colonial office minutes, particularly from the middle 1880s, show increasing hostility towards the politically active class in Jamaica, notably the coloured Jamaica lawyers. Officials' use of the term 'gentleman' reflected the social prejudice which informed their attitude; it was an attitude which strengthened their conviction of the failure of the new departure and caused them to hesitate advising the extension of the elective principle to Trinidad.

The evidence of the minutes suggests that before 1895 the main policy decisions on constitutional reform in the three colonies under review were reached by officials, of whom the most influential was Wingfield. If that policy bears the stamp of administrative expediency it is because Wingfield valued above all trouble-free administration. Lacking strong conviction of the value of constitutional advance, he nevertheless normally advised giving way when the weight of local influential opinion favoured it or when the balance of administrative advantage dictated it. Although the brief minutes of secretaries of state before Chamberlain do not suggest large interest or knowledge, allowance must be made for the different ways in which they conveyed their decisions. Nor did they always follow their officials. Derby favoured constitutional reform in Jamaica for different and well-considered reasons. Knutsford's decision on Trinidad reform in 1887, like Derby's decision on Jamaica, seems to have been guided by principle rather than expediency. Ripon and Buxton kept open the question of Trinidad reform in 1893 against the weight of official advice. There are hints that Knutsford entertained a more liberal attitude towards constitutional change in British Guiana than his officials, until deflected by the planting interest.

On the evidence of the colonial office minutes, the British Guiana reform of 1891 was the only occasion when the pressure of the planting interest, whether exerted locally or through the West India Committee, played an important part in the major policy decisions reviewed in this study. The most important outside influence in this period was parliamentary, in the negative sense that secretaries of state, including Chamberlain, avoided policies of constitutional change involving parliamentary legislation, or the threat of parliamentary intervention. Chamberlain's minutes reflect a greater sensitivity to parliamentary criticism than those of his predecessors, though not a greater unwillingness to meet it. The distinctly liberal attitudes of Derby and Ripon suggest that party convictions may also have been influential, and this view is reinforced by the new departure in policy under Chamberlain.

It is not easy to define the policy of Chamberlain's predecessors between 1880 and 1895; their approach to constitutional change was pragmatic, and as a rule they avoided statements of principle. But, in general, the evidence suggests they favoured cautious constitutional advance.[5] It is true that in 1889 Knutsford reversed his earlier decision of 1887 and declined to introduce elected members into the Trinidad Legislative Council. By 1895, however, officials had come to

[5] This policy was not confined to the colonies under review or to the British West Indies. Representative government was conceded to Cyprus in 1882 and Malta in 1887. Among the non-white dependencies a provisional unofficial elected and nominated majority was granted by Stanley to Mauritius in 1885, and by Ripon to Dominica in 1895. Indirectly elected members were introduced into the Legislative Councils of Hong Kong and the Straits Settlements in 1884 and 1889. A nominated unofficial majority was established in British Honduras in 1892.

favour this change, and on the evidence both of his minutes and his reputation it seems improbable that Ripon would have rejected their advice.

There was a clear change of direction under Chamberlain, both in Trinidad and elsewhere in the British West Indies.[6] In Trinidad it was his personal decision, taken against the unanimous advice of his officials, which led to the retention of a purely nominated council. Chamberlain was probably influenced by the Imperial considerations raised by Selborne, but above all his decision reflected his strong conviction of the inappropriateness of the elective principle in non-British and non-white communities. It was a conviction not shared, on the evidence of their minutes, by any of his predecessors since 1880. But in judging the personal contribution of Chamberlain to the change of policy after 1895, consideration must also be given to the climate of opinion outside the Colonial Office, and to the influence of Lucas who from 1897 was responsible for West Indian affairs. He was a strong advocate of constitutional retrogression in the British West Indies. Indeed he would have moved further and faster than Chamberlain, who acted as a restraining influence. The Jamaica minutes suggest that Chamberlain's caution stemmed from parliamentary considerations and from sensitivity to local opinion. On both grounds he needed 'a good case', but in his search for it he was hindered by his own, and his officials', frank recognition of the failures of the local executive. In Lucas's view, these failures were characteristic of the general weakness of West Indian colonial governments. It is an admission supported by evidence in this study, and no analysis of political unrest in the British West Indies in the late nineteenth century can afford to ignore it.

Chamberlain's minutes are distinguished from those of his predecessors by their length and decisiveness, and by the clear statements of principle which they often embody. His tendency to define and adhere to principles, and rigidly to apply them, sometimes led him to oversimplify problems. But, in general, the colonial office papers suggest an honest, extremely hard-

[6] In addition to the constitutional retrogression in Antigua, Dominica, Trinidad, and Jamaica, an official majority was established in the federal legislature of the Leeward Islands in 1899. Thus by the end of that year crown colony government prevailed throughout the British West Indies except in the Bahamas, Barbados, British Guiana, and British Honduras.

working, and masterful administrator, who on many issues knew his own mind and was less influenced by his officials than any of his predecessors since 1880.

Chamberlain's caution regarding parliamentary criticism was probably excessive for there were strong influences at work during his secretaryship favouring crown colony government in the West Indies. They contributed not only to the shaping of parliamentary opinion but also to the thinking of colonial office officials. It is an argument central to this study, that during the latter part of the nineteenth century the Colonial Office had been inactive in a positive or initiating role in relation to policy in the colonies under review. Such a role required, among other conditions, full control over finance. The unwillingness of the Colonial Office to secure that control in British Guiana, and its partial surrender of it in Jamaica in 1884, indicated that it placed more value on other considerations, such as harmonious relations with the elected members, than on securing or retaining the conditions necessary for initiating measures in the interests of the mass of the population. The case must not be overdrawn. The Colonial Office, particularly under crown colony government, at times originated legislation and even drafted it, and it directly shaped administrative policies by its instructions to governors, both verbal and written, and indirectly in so far as it exercised financial control. But certainly in this period and in the colonies under review, the impulse for progress in such social and economic fields as education, the development of communications, and the establishment of a peasant proprietary had more often come from a few governors like Irving, Robinson, and Blake, than from secretaries of state. Chamberlain was more active than his predecessors in initiating policy, but towards the end of his secretaryship officials, influenced by such writers as Kidd and Livingstone, were considering whether the Colonial Office should not take a more active part in the moral and material improvement of the non-white races of the British West Indies. Their tentative thinking implied increased emphasis on economic and social improvement and less interest in political advance.

BIBLIOGRAPHY

I. MANUSCRIPT SOURCES

A. *Official*

(i) *Colonial Office Records* (Public Record Office)

(a) *General*

CO 537/163, 180, 208, 209, 215, 221, 226, 263, 266, 304. Original Supplementary Correspondence.

CO 380 (selected volumes). Draft Letters Patent, Commissions, Royal Instructions, Warrants, etc.

(b) *West Indies* (general)

CO 384/102–193 (relevant volumes for Jamaica, British Guiana, and Trinidad). Emigration.

CO 318/272–309. Original Correspondence.

CO 537/5. Original Supplementary Correspondence.

(c) *Jamaica*

CO 137/479–638. Original Correspondence.

CO 537/5. Original Supplementary Correspondence.

(d) *British Guiana*

CO 111/371–539. Original Correspondence.

CO 537/2–4. Original Supplementary Correspondence.

(e) *Trinidad*

CO 295/250–421. Original Correspondence.

CO 537/9. Original Supplementary Correspondence.

(ii) *Treasury Records* (Public Record Office)

T7/31. Out Letters, Colonial Affairs.

B. *Private Papers*

Chamberlain Papers (Birmingham University Library)

Salisbury Papers (Christ Church, Oxford, Library)

Gladstone Papers (British Museum)

Carnarvon Papers (Public Record Office)

West India Committee Papers (Norfolk Street, London, W.C.2)
Minutes of the West India Committee, 1880–1901.
Agenda, Jan. 1894–Feb. 1898.

2. PRINTED PRIMARY SOURCES

A. *Official*

(i) *Colonial Office Records* (Public Record Office)

(a) *General*

CO/854 (selected volumes). Circular Despatches.

CO/816 (selected volumes). Original Letters Patent, Warrants, etc.

CO/885 (selected volumes). Confidential Prints, Miscellaneous.

(b) *West Indies* (general)

CO/884 (selected volumes). Confidential Prints, West Indies.

(c) *Jamaica*

CO/139 (selected volumes). Acts.

CO/140 (selected volumes). Sessional Papers.

CO/141 (selected volumes). *Jamaica Gazette.*

CO/142 (selected volumes). Blue Books of Statistics.

(d) *British Guiana*

CO/113 (selected volumes). Acts.

CO/114 (selected volumes). Sessional Papers.

CO/115 (selected volumes). *The Official Gazette.*

CO/116 (selected volumes). Blue Books of Statistics.

(e) *Trinidad*

CO/297 (selected volumes). Acts.

CO/298 (selected volumes). Sessional Papers.

CO/299 (selected volumes). *Government Gazette.*

CO/300 (selected volumes). Blue Books of Statistics.

(ii) *Cabinet Records* (Public Record Office)

Cab. 37/12. Cabinet Papers.

(iii) *Privy Council Office, Registers* (Public Record Office)

PC/2 318, 361.

(iv) *Parliamentary Papers*

1849, F(oreign and) C(ommonwealth) O(ffice) Lib(rary), Colonial Papers Parliamentary, vol. 4, 297. First Report from the Select Committee of the House of Commons on Ceylon and British Guiana; together with the minutes of evidence, and appendix.

1878–79, LI, C.-2437. Correspondence relative to the Financial Arrangements for Indian Coolie Immigration into Jamaica.

1881, LXV, 425. Copy . . . of Correspondence relating to . . . Memorials received from Jamaica setting forth the Grievances which have arisen under the System of Crown Government . . .

1882, XLVI, C.-3453. Correspondence respecting the Case of the Ship 'Florence'.

1883, XLVII, C.-3524. Correspondence on the subject of Alterations in the Constitution of Malta.

1884, XLVI, C.-3840. Report of the Royal Commission appointed in December 1882, to inquire into the public revenues, expenditure, debts, and liabilities of the Islands of Jamaica, Grenada, St. Vincent, Tobago, and St. Lucia, and the Leeward Islands . . .

1884, LV, C.-3854. Petition from the Inhabitants of Jamaica for a change in the constitution . . . together with the reply of Her Majesty's Government thereto . . .

1884, LV, C.-4074. Correspondence relating to the constitution of the Council of Government in Mauritius.

1884, LV, C.-4140. Further correspondence respecting the constitution of the Legislative Council in Jamaica.

1890–91, LVII, C.-6352. Correspondence relating to the Sale of the Jamaica Railway to an American Syndicate.

1893–94, LX, C.-6997. Correspondence respecting change in the constitution of the Legislative Council of Jamaica.

1894, LVII, C.-7477. Report of the Royal Commission to inquire into the Condition and Affairs of the Island of Dominica.

1898, L, C.-8655. Report of the West India Royal Commission.

1898, L, C.-8657. Ibid., Appendix C, vol. II. Proceedings, Evidence, and Documents relating to British Guiana, Barbados, Trinidad, and Tobago.

1899, LIX, C.-9177. Correspondence relating to the Public Finances and Resources of the Island of Jamaica.

1899, LIX, C.-9412. Report on the Finances of Jamaica, by Sir David Barbour.

1899, LIX, C.-9413. Further Correspondence relating to the Finances and Government of the Island of Jamaica.

1900, 55, Cd. 125. Further Correspondence relating to the Finances and Government of the Island of Jamaica.

1901, 37, 94. Statement showing to what Colonies up to the present time sums have been advanced by the Treasury under the Colonial Loans Act, 1899 . . .

(v) *Reports of Local Commissions and other Reports*

Report of the Commissioners of Inquiry upon the condition of the Juvenile Population of Jamaica (Jamaica, 1879). (F.C.O. Lib. folio 7313.)

Trade and Taxes Commission (Trinidad, 1886). (R(oyal) C(ommonwealth) Soc(iety) Lib(rary).)

Report of Commission on the Metairie system (Tobago, 1891.) (F.C.O. Lib. folio 8915.)

Judicial Inquiry Commission (Trinidad, 1892). (F.C.O. Lib. folio 9081.)

Surgeon-Major D. W. D. Comins, Note on Emigration from the East India to Jamaica (Calcutta, 1893).

——, Note on Emigration from India to British Guiana (Calcutta, 1893).

——, Note on Emigration from India to Trinidad (Calcutta, 1893). (R.C. Soc. Lib.)

(vi) Hansard's *Parliamentary Debates*, third, fourth and, fifth series.

B. *Private*

(i) *West India Committee Papers*

Report of the Acting Committee to the Half-Yearly meeting of the Standing Committee of West India Planters and Merchants, to be held on Thursday, 19 December 1878.

Report of the Acting Committee to the Meeting of the Standing Committee of West India planters and merchants, to be held on Thursday, 12 February 1880.

The West India Committee Circular, 1886–1897. Circulated to members of the Committee after 1886, these often give more information of Committee meeting proceedings than the minutes. They were headed confidential until 1891.

(ii) *Memoirs, Autobiographies, and Speeches*

Ed. Boyd, Charles W., *Mr. Chamberlain's Speeches*, 2 vols. (London, 1914).

Broome, Lady, *Colonial Memories* (London, 1904).

Bruce, Sir Charles, *Milestones on my long Journey. Memories of a Colonial Governor* (Glasgow, 1919).

CHAMBERLAIN, JOSEPH, *Foreign & Colonial Speeches* (London, 1897).

DES VOEUX, SIR G. WILLIAM, *My Colonial Service in British Guiana, St. Lucia, Trinidad, Fiji, Australia, Newfoundland and Hong Kong with interludes*, 2 vols. (London, 1903).

KIRKE, HENRY, *Twenty-five years in British Guiana* (London, 1898).

LEE-WARNER, SIR WILLIAM, *Memoirs of Field Marshal Sir Henry Wylie Norman* (London, 1908).

Ed. OLIVIER, MARGARET, *Sydney Olivier. Letters and Selected Writings* (London, 1948).

Selected and edited by T. H. SANDERSON, and E. B. ROSCOE, *Speeches and Addresses of Edward Henry XVth Earl of Derby with a Prefatory Memoir by W. E. H. Lecky* (London, 1894).

TAYLOR, SIR HENRY, *Autobiography of Henry Taylor, 1800–1875*, 2 vols. (London, 1885).

(iii) *Contemporary or Near-Contemporary Books*

BODU, JOSE M., *Trinidadiana; being a chronological review of events which have occurred in the island from the conquest to the present day, with brief notes of the careers of some eminent colonists* (Port-of-Spain, 1890).

BRONKHURST, H. V. P., *Among the Hindus and Creoles of British Guyana* (London, 1888).

——, *The Colony of British Guyana and its Labouring Population* (London, 1883).

CALDECOTT, A., *The Church in the West Indies* (London, 1898).

COLLENS, J. H., *A Guide to Trinidad* (London, 1888).

DE LISSER, H. G., *In Jamaica and Cuba* (Kingston, 1910).

——, *Twentieth Century Jamaica* (Kingston, 1913).

DE VERTEUIL, L. A. A., *Trinidad: Its Geography, Natural Resources, Administration, Present Condition, and Prospects* (London, 1858). Second edition (London, 1884).

DILKE, SIR CHARLES WENTWORTH, *Problems of Greater Britain*, 2 vols. (London, 1890).

Ed. ESCOTT, T. H. S., *Pillars of the Empire* (London, 1879).

Ed. FARRAR, VEN. THOMAS, *Notes of the History of the Church in Guiana* (New Amsterdam, 1892).

FORREST, A. S. and HENDERSON, JOHN, *Jamaica* (London, 1906).

FROUDE, JAMES ANTHONY, *Oceana or England and her Colonies* (London, 1886).

——, *The English in the West Indies or the Bow of Ulysses* (London, 1888).

HENRY, J. D., *Oil Fields of the Empire* (London, 1910).

INNISS, LEWIS OSBORN, *Trinidad and Trinidadians.* A Collection of Papers, Historical, Social and Descriptive about Trinidad and its People (Port-of-Spain, 1910).

IRELAND, W. ALLEYNE, *Demerariana. Essays Historical, Critical and Descriptive* (Georgetown, 1897).

JOHNSTON, SIR HARRY H., *The Negro in the New World* (London, 1910).

KIDD, BENJAMIN, *Social Evolution* (London, 1894).

——, *The Control of the Tropics* (New York, 1898).

LEWIS, SIR GEORGE CORNEWALL, *An Essay on the Government of Dependencies*, with an introduction by C. P. Lucas (Oxford, 1891; originally published 1841).

LIVINGSTONE, W. P., *Black Jamaica. A study in evolution* (London, 1899).

LUCAS, C. P., *A Historical Geography of the British Colonies*, vol. 2, The West Indies (Oxford, 1890). Also edition revised and brought up to date by C. Aitchley (Oxford, 1905).

OLIVIER, SYDNEY, *White Capital and Coloured Labour* (London, 1910).

RODWAY, JAMES, *Hand-book of British Guiana* (Georgetown, 1893).

——, *History of British Guiana from the year 1668 to the present time*, 3 vols. (Georgetown, 1891, 1893, 1894).

SEELEY, J. R., *The Expansion of England* (London, 1883).

STARK, JAMES H., *Stark's Jamaica Guide* (Boston, 1898).

——, *Stark's Guide-Book and History of Trinidad including Tobago, Grenada, and St. Vincent* (Boston, 1897).

TENNANT, R., *British Guiana and its Resources* (London, 1895).

The Handbook of Jamaica (selected years). This is the best source for electoral statistics. It was compiled by two public officers from official and other reliable public records, but in February 1901 Chamberlain directed that the phrase 'Published by authority' be omitted from the title page on the grounds that it was not an official publication.

THOMAS, J. J., *Froudacity. West Indian fables by James Anthony Froude explained by J. J. Thomas* (London, 1889).

WALKER, H. DE R., *The West Indies and the Empire. Study and Travel in the Winter of 1900–1901* (London, 1901).

(iv) *Contemporary or Near-Contemporary Pamphlets*

There are overlapping collections of West Indian pamphlets in the West India Committee Library, the Foreign and Commonwealth Office Library, and the Royal Commonwealth Society Library. The writer has found the last collection the most useful and accessible.

A Contribution to the History of Coolie Missions in British Guiana (Georgetown, 1877). (W(est) I(ndia) C(ommittee) Lib(rary).)

A series of letters on the Labour Question; Proposed Railway to Berbice; Inland Lake; our Free Grown Sugar; and Great Britain's Support of Slave Grown Sugar (Georgetown, 1875). (R.C. Soc. Lib.)

Brief Notices of the Administrative and Judicial Careers of Sir William Robinson, K.C.M.G., Governor, and Sir John Gorrie, Knt., Chief Justice of Trinidad ('Public Opinion' Office, Port-of-Spain, 1888). (R.C. Soc. Lib.)

CLARK, HENRY JAMES, *The Material and Moral Progress of Trinidad During last Fifty Years*. A lecture (Port-of-Spain, 1888). (R.C. Soc. Lib.)

——, *Trinidad. A field for Emigration*. A sketch (Port-of-Spain, 1886). (R.C. Soc. Lib.)

EWEN, WILL, *Labour, Pauperism, Crime. A short view of the present state of things in Jamaica* (Kingston, 1877). (R.C. Soc. Lib.)

LEVY, GEORGE, *A few among many facts, concerning Crown Government in Jamaica and how it is administered* (Kingston, 1881). (R.C. Soc. Lib.)

Attributed to LINDO, A., *A Statement of the causes and object of the present political agitation in Jamaica*. (A copy is filed with minute paper 3048, CO 137/508.)

LUBBOCK, SIR NEVILE, *The Present Position of Our West Indian Colonies*. A Paper read before the Liverpool Chamber of Commerce, 10 December 1900. (R.C. Soc. Lib.)

MUSGRAVE, SIR ANTHONY, *Jamaica: Now, and Fifteen Years Since*. A paper read before the Royal Colonial Institute, 20 Apr. 1880. (F.C.O. Lib. Jamaica Pamphlet No. 24.)

PHILLIPPO, J. C., *Jamaica: Its Government and its People* (Kingston, 1883). (R.C. Soc. Lib.)

ED. PRICE, GEORGE E. *Jamaica. Papers relating to Proposed Change in the Form of Government.* (London, 1884). (R.C. Soc. Lib.)

RUST, RANDOLPH, *Lecture on Trinidad Petroleum and its Products.* Delivered 18 March 1910 at Victoria Institute, Port-of-Spain. (R.C. Soc. Lib.)

——, *Petroleum in Trinidad.* Lecture in West India Committee Rooms, 26 Apr. 1906. (R.C. Soc. Lib.)

SALMON, C. S., *Capital and Labour in the West Indies* (London, 1883).

——, *The Caribbean Confederation* (London, n.d., published 1888).

——, *The Crown Colonies of Great Britain.* An inquiry into their political economy, fiscal systems, and trade (London, n.d., published 1885).

——, *The Crown Colonies of Great Britain.* An inquiry into their social condition and methods of administration . . . (London, n.d., published 1887).

STANLEY, HON. E., *Claims and Resources of the West Indian Colonies* (London, 1850). (British Museum.)

STANLEY, LORD, *Farther facts connected with the West Indies* (London, 1851). (British Museum.)

The First Half Yearly Report of the Jamaica Association, 30 June 1875 (Kingston, 1875). (R.C. Soc. Lib.)

The Labour Question in and the Conditions of Jamaica (Kingston, 1876) (being correspondence between Rev. J. E. Henderson, a Baptist missionary, and W. Bancroft Espeut, a planter). (R.C. Soc. Lib.)

The Rules of 'The Jamaica Association' (Kingston, 1874). Includes a list of members. (R.C. Soc. Lib.)

The Second Half-Yearly Report of the Jamaica Association, 17 December 1875 (Kingston, 1876). (R.C. Soc. Lib.)

WATT, HUGH, *British Guiana; Its Past History, Present Position, & Future Prospects in relation to Venezuela.* A Lecture delivered at Exeter Hall on 25 April 1887. (R.C. Soc. Lib.)

WHITFIELD, RICHARD H., *'Hints' on Villages, Villagers . . . and other matters of vital importance to the colony generally* (Georgetown, 1873). (R.C. Soc. Lib.)

——, *The Present Position & Future Prospects of British Guiana considered . . .* (London and Liverpool, 1872). (R.C. Soc. Lib.)

——, *The Present Position & Future Prospects of British Guiana further considered* . . . (London and Liverpool, 1872). (R.C. Soc. Lib.)

(v) *Contemporary or Near-Contemporary Articles*

BRAMSTON, JOHN, 'The Colonial Office from Within', *The Empire Review*, vol. 1, no. 3, Apr. 1901, pp. 279–87.

CRAIG, E. H. CUNNINGHAM, 'The Oilfields of Trinidad', *Proceedings of the Royal Colonial Institute*, vol. XXXVII, 1905–06, pp. 340–55.

DAVIS, N. DARNELL, 'Mr. Froude's Negrophobia, or Don Quixote as a Cook's Tourist', *Timehri*, vol. 2, new series, 1888, pp. 85–129.

DE THIERRY, MISS C., 'Our Policy in the West Indies', *Proceedings of the Royal Colonial Institute*, vol. XXXVII, 1905–06, pp. 194–206.

——, 'Oil and Strategy', *United Empire*, vol. V, no. 4, Apr. 1914, pp. 332–8.

GRICE, J. WATSON, 'The Oil Resources of the Empire', *United Empire*, vol. IV, no. 9, Sept. 1913, pp. 745–53.

JERNINGHAM, HUBERT E. H., 'Crown Colony Government', *The Empire Review*, vol. 1, no. 1, Feb. 1901, pp. 87–95.

HAMILTON, W. A. BAILLIE, 'Forty-four years at the Colonial Office', *The Nineteenth Century and After*, vols. XIX–XX, Apr. 1909, pp. 599–613.

WALKER, HENRY DE R., 'Impressions of the British West Indies', *Proceedings of the Royal Colonial Institute*, vol. XXXII, 1900–01, pp. 285–314.

(vi) *Newspapers* (British Museum Newspaper Library)

London

Daily Chronicle
The European Mail (West Indies edition)
The Morning Post
The Times

Kingston, Jamaica

The Budget
The Colonial Standard and Jamaica Despatch
The Daily Gleaner

Georgetown, British Guiana

The Demerara Daily Chronicle (from 1 January 1885 the *Daily Chronicle*)

Port of Spain, Trinidad
The Port of Spain Gazette
Public Opinion

St. George's, Grenada
The Grenada People

3. SECONDARY SOURCES

(i) *Later Works*

AMERY, JULIAN, *The Life of Joseph Chamberlain*, vol. iv, 1901–1903 (London, 1951).

Ed. ANDIC, F. M. and MATHEWS, T. G., *The Caribbean in Transition*. Papers on Social, Political, and Economic Development. Second Caribbean Scholars' Conference, Mona, Jamaica. April 1964 (Rio Piedras, Puerto Rico, 1965).

ANDRADE, JACOB A. P. M., *A Record of the Jews in Jamaica from the English Conquest to the Present Time* (Kingston, 1941).

Compiled by F. R. AUGIER and SHIRLEY C. GORDON, *Sources of West Indian History* (London, 1962).

BEACHEY, R. W., *The British West Indies Sugar Industry in the late 19th Century* (Oxford, 1957).

Ed. BENIANS, E. A. and others, *The Cambridge History of the British Empire*, vol. 3 The Empire–Commonwealth 1870–1919 (Cambridge, 1959).

BODELSEN, C. A., *Studies in Mid-Victorian Imperialism* (London, 1960).

BURN, W. L., *The British West Indies* (London, 1951).

BURNS, SIR ALAN, *History of the British West Indies* (London, 1965).

CAMPBELL, A. E., *Great Britain and the United States 1895–1903* (London, 1960).

CARMICHAEL, GERTRUDE, *The History of the West Indian Islands of Trinidad and Tobago 1498–1900* (London, 1961).

CHAPMAN, J. K., *The Career of Arthur Hamilton Gordon, First Lord Stanmore, 1829–1912* (Toronto, 1964).

CLEMENTI, CECIL, *The Chinese in British Guiana* (Georgetown, 1915).

——, *A Constitutional History of British Guiana* (London, 1937).

CURTIN, PHILIP D., *Two Jamaicas. The Role of Ideas in a Tropical Colony 1830–1865* (Cambridge, U.S.A., 1955).

DUNN, WALDO HILARY, *James Anthony Froude. A Biography*, 2 vols. (Oxford, 1961 and 1963).

EISNER, GISELA, *Jamaica, 1830–1930. A Study in Economic Growth* (Manchester 1961).

FIDDES, SIR GEORGE V., *The Dominions and Colonial Offices* (London, 1926).

GARVIN, J. L., *The Life of Joseph Chamberlain*, vol. 3, 1895–1900 (London, 1934).

GOVEIA, ELSA V., *A Study on the Historiography of the British West Indies to the End of the Nineteenth Century* (Instituto Panamericano de Geografia e Historia, Mexico, 1956).

HALL, DOUGLAS, *Free Jamaica, 1838–1865: an economic history* (Yale University, New Haven, 1959).

HALL, H. L., *The Colonial Office: A History* (London, 1937).

KNAPLUND, PAUL, *Gladstone and Britain's Imperial Policy* (London, 1927).

LEWIS, GORDON K., *The Growth of the Modern West Indies* (London, 1968).

MARDER, ARTHUR J., *From the Dreadnought to Scapa Flow. The Royal Navy in the Fisher Era 1904–19*, vol. i, The Road to War, 1904–14 (London, 1961).

MURRAY, D. J., *The West Indies and the Development of Colonial Government, 1801–1834* (Oxford, 1965).

NATH, DWARKA, *A History of Indians in British Guiana* (London, 1950).

OLIVIER, LORD, *Jamaica. The Blessed Island* (London, 1936).

PARKINSON, SIR COSMO, *The Colonial Office from Within 1909–1945* (London, 1947).

PARRY, J. H. and SHERLOCK, P. M., *A Short History of the West Indies* (London, 1963).

REIS, CHARLES, *A History of the Constitution or Government of Trinidad from the earliest times to the present day*, vol. i (Port-of-Spain, 1929).

——, *The Government of Trinidad, being a brief history of its government and laws under Spanish and British rule* (London, 1915).

ROBERTS, W. ADOLPHE, *Six Great Jamaicans*. Biographical sketches (Kingston, 1952).

RUHOMON, PETER, *Centenary History of the East Indians in British Guiana, 1838–1938* (Georgetown, 1947).

SMITH, RAYMOND T., *British Guiana* (Oxford, 1962).

WEBBER, A. R. F., *Centenary History and Handbook of British Guiana* (Georgetown, 1931).

WIGHT, MARTIN, *The Development of the Legislative Council, 1606–1945* (London, 1946).

WILLIAMS, ERIC, *History of the People of Trinidad and Tobago* (London, 1964).

WOOD, DONALD, *Trinidad in Transition: the Years after Slavery* (Oxford, 1968).

WRONG, H. H., *Government of the West Indies* (Oxford, 1923).

YOUNG, ALLAN, *The Approaches to Local Self-Government in British Guiana* (London, 1958).

(ii) *Articles*

AUGIER, F. R., 'The Working of the Jamaica Constitution before Independence: A Commentary', *Caribbean Quarterly*, vol. 8, no. 3 (1962), pp. 173–7.

BURT, ARTHUR E., 'The First Instalment of Representative Government in Jamaica, 1884', *Social and Economic Studies* (published by Institute of Social and Economic Research, University of the West Indies, Jamaica), vol. 11, 1962, pp. 241–59.

CASSERLY, F. L., 'Crown Colony Crisis. The Hemming–Gideon Correspondence', *The Jamaica Historical Review*, vol. 3, 1957–1962.

GOCKING, C. V., 'Early Constitutional History of Jamaica', *Caribbean Quarterly*, vol. 6, nos. 3 and 4, May 1960, pp. 114–33.

HARPER-SMITH, JAMES W., 'The Colonial Stock Acts and the British Guiana Constitution of 1891', *Social and Economic Studies*, vol. 14, no. 3, Sept. 1965, pp. 252–63.

HUGHES, COLIN A., 'Semi Responsible Government in the British West Indies', *Political Science Quarterly*, vol. LXVIII, no. 3, Sept. 1953.

HIGHAM, C. S. S., 'Sir Henry Taylor and the establishment of Crown Colony Government in the West Indies', *Scottish Historical Review*, vol. XXIII, 1926, pp. 92–6.

LEWIS, GORDON K., 'British Colonialism in the West Indies: The Political Legacy', *Caribbean Studies*, vol. 7, no. 1, Apr. 1967, pp. 3–22.

LUCKHOO, J. A., 'The East Indians in British Guiana', *Timehri*, vol. VI, third series, Sept. 1919, pp. 53–65.

MURRAY, R. N., 'The Road Back—Jamaica after 1866', *Caribbean Quarterly*, vol. 6, nos. 3 and 4, May 1960, pp. 134–41.

PENSON, L. M., 'The making of a Crown Colony: British Guiana 1803–33', *Transactions of the Royal Historical Society*, 1926, vol. IX, fourth series, pp. 107–34.

SIRES, RONALD V., 'The Experience of Jamaica with modified Crown Colony Government', *Social and Economic Studies*, vol. 4, no. 2, June 1955, pp. 150–67.

——, 'The Jamaica Constitution of 1884', *Social and Economic Studies*, vol. 3, no. 1, June 1954, pp. 64–81.

WOODING, H. O. B., 'The Constitutional History of Trinidad and Tobago', *Caribbean Quarterly*, vol. 6, nos. 3 and 4, May 1960, pp. 143–59.

Also LEWIS, W. A., The Evolution of the Peasantry in the British West Indies. January 1936. (Typescript) F.C.O. Lib. West Indies and South America Pamphlets, vol. 15, no. 656.

(iii) *Unpublished Theses*

ADAMSON, ALAN HERBERT, *Sugar and the Economy of British Guiana 1838–1904*, London University Ph.D., 1964.

AUGIER, FITZROY, *Crown Colony Government in Jamaica 1865–1885*, St. Andrews University Ph.D., 1954.

GOCKING, C. V., *Constitutional Problems in Jamaica 1850–1866*, Oxford University D.Phil., 1955.

HARPER-SMITH, JAMES W., *The Political Development of British Guiana since 1891*, Oxford University B.Litt., 1964.

INDEX